Dodge & Plymouth Neon Automotive Repair Manual

**by Ed Scott
and John H Haynes**

Member of the Guild of Motoring Writers

Models covered:

All Dodge and Plymouth Neon models
1995 through 1999

(12B3 - 30034)

ABCDE
FGHIJ
KLMN

AUTOMOTIVE
PARTS &
ACCESSORIES
ASSOCIATION
MEMBER

Haynes Publishing Group
Sparkford Nr Yeovil
Somerset BA22 7JJ England

Haynes North America, Inc
861 Lawrence Drive
Newbury Park
California 91320 USA

Acknowledgements

We are grateful to the Chrysler Corporation for providing technical information and certain illustrations. Wiring diagrams originated exclusively for Haynes North America, Inc. by Valley Forge Technical Communications.

A book in the Haynes Automotive Repair Manual Series

Printed in the U.S.A.

ISBN 1 56392 369 6

Library of Congress Catalog Card Number 99-69836

97-288

Contents

Haynes mechanic, author and photographer with 1995 Dodge Neon

About this manual

Its purpose

The purpose of this manual is to help you get the best value from your vehicle. It can do so in several ways. It can help you decide what work must be done, even if you choose to have it done by a dealer service department or a repair shop; it provides information and procedures for routine maintenance and servicing; and it offers diagnostic and repair procedures to follow when trouble occurs.

We hope you use the manual to tackle the work yourself. For many simpler jobs, doing it yourself may be quicker than arranging an appointment to get the vehicle into a shop and making the trips to leave it and pick it up. More importantly, a lot of money can be saved by avoiding the expense the shop must pass on to you to cover its labor and overhead costs. An added benefit is the sense of satisfaction and accomplishment that you feel after doing the job yourself.

Using the manual

The manual is divided into Chapters. Each Chapter is divided into numbered Sections, which are headed in bold type between horizontal lines. Each Section consists of consecutively numbered paragraphs.

At the beginning of each numbered Section you will be referred to any illustrations which apply to the procedures in that Section. The reference numbers used in illustration captions pinpoint the pertinent Section and the Step within that Section. That is, illustration 3.2 means the illustration refers to Section 3 and Step (or paragraph) 2 within that Section.

Procedures, once described in the text, are not normally repeated. When it's necessary to refer to another Chapter, the reference will be given as Chapter and Section number. Cross references given without use of the word "Chapter" apply to Sections and/or paragraphs in the same Chapter. For example, "see Section 8" means in the same Chapter.

References to the left or right side of the vehicle assume you are sitting in the driver's seat, facing forward.

Even though we have prepared this manual with extreme care, neither the publisher nor the author can accept responsibility for any errors in, or omissions from, the information given.

NOTE

A **Note** provides information necessary to properly complete a procedure or information which will make the procedure easier to understand.

CAUTION

A **Caution** provides a special procedure or special steps which must be taken while completing the procedure where the Caution is found. Not heeding a Caution can result in damage to the assembly being worked on.

WARNING

A **Warning** provides a special procedure or special steps which must be taken while completing the procedure where the Warning is found. Not heeding a Warning can result in personal injury.

Introduction to the Dodge and Plymouth Neon

The Dodge/Plymouth Neon is available in four-door sedan and two-door coupe body styles.

The transversely mounted 2.0-liter four-cylinder engine is available in two versions; the standard Single Overhead-Camshaft (SOHC) version is rated at 132 horsepower while the optional Dual Overhead-Camshaft (DOHC) version sports 150 horsepower. Both models are equipped with a sequential multi port electronic fuel injection system.

The engine transmits power to the front wheels through either a five-speed manual transaxle or a three-speed automatic transaxle via independent driveaxles.

The Neon features an all steel uni-body and independent suspension with MacPherson strut/coil spring suspension used on both the front and rear suspensions. The rack and pinion steering unit is mounted behind the engine with power-assist available as optional equipment.

Standard models are equipped with power assisted front disc and rear drum brakes. A power assisted four wheel disc brake system and an Anti-lock Brake System (ABS) are optional.

Vehicle identification numbers

Modifications are a continuing and unpublicized process in vehicle manufacturing. Since spare parts manuals and lists are compiled on a numerical basis, the individual vehicle numbers are essential to correctly identify the component required.

Vehicle Identification Number (VIN)

This very important identification number is located on a plate attached to the dashboard inside the windshield on the driver's side of the vehicle (see illustration). The VIN also appears on the Vehicle Certificate of Title and Registration. It contains information such as where and when the vehicle was manufactured, the model year and the body style.

VIN engine and model year codes

Two particularly important pieces of information found in the VIN are the engine code and the model year code. Counting from the left, the engine code letter designation is the 8th digit and the model year code designation is the 10th digit.

On the models covered by this manual the engine codes are:

C .... 2.0L SOHC
Y .... 2.0L DOHC

On the models covered by this manual the model year codes are:

S 1995
T.. 1996
V 1997
W 1998

Body Code Plate

The Body Code Plate is a stamped metal plate attached to either the radiator support or the right strut tower in the engine compartment (see illustration). It contains more specific information about the manufacturing of the vehicle such as the paint code, trim code and vehicle order number, as well as the VIN.

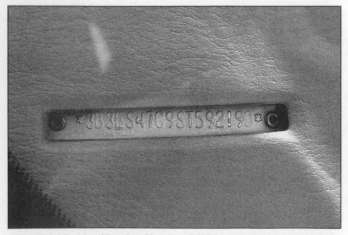

The Vehicle Identification Number (VIN) is stamped into a metal plate fastened to the dashboard on the driver's side - it's visible through the windshield

The Body Code Plate is located on the radiator support

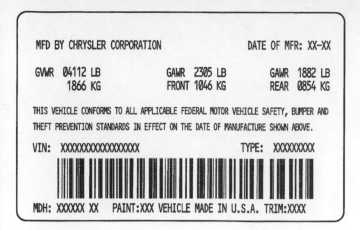

The Vehicle Safety Certification label is affixed to the drivers side door end or post

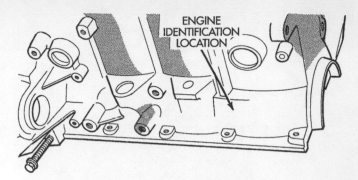

The Engine Identification Number is stamped on the left rear of the engine block (SOHC models)

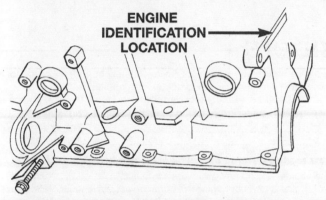

The Engine Identification Number is stamped on the rear of the engine block (DOHC models)

Location of the transaxle bar code label

Vehicle Safety Certification label

The Vehicle Safety Certification label is attached to the driver's side door end or post (see illustration). The label contains the name of the manufacturer, the month and year of production, the Gross Vehicle Weight Rating (GVWR), the Gross Axle Weight Rating (GAWR) and the certification statement.

Engine identification numbers

The engine identification numbers can be found stamped on a pad on either the left rear of the cylinder block, behind the starter (SOHC engine) or on the rear of the cylinder block (DOHC engine) (see illustrations).

Transaxle identification numbers

The transaxle identification information can be found on a bar code label located on the front of the transaxle (see illustration).

Vehicle Emissions Control Information (VECI) label

The emissions control information label is found under the hood, normally on the radiator support or the bottom side of the hood. This label contains information on the emissions control equipment installed on the vehicle, as well as tune-up specifications (see Chapter 6).

Buying parts

Replacement parts are available from many sources, which generally fall into one of two categories - authorized dealer parts departments and independent retail auto parts stores. Our advice concerning these parts is as follows:

Retail auto parts stores: Good auto parts stores will stock frequently needed components which wear out relatively fast, such as clutch components, exhaust systems, brake parts, tune-up parts, etc. These stores often supply new or reconditioned parts on an exchange basis, which can save a considerable amount of money. Discount auto parts stores are often very good places to buy materials and parts needed for general vehicle maintenance such as oil, grease, filters, spark plugs, belts, touch-up paint, bulbs, etc. They also usually sell tools and general accessories, have convenient hours, charge lower prices and can often be found not far from home.

Authorized dealer parts department: This is the best source for parts which are unique to the vehicle and not generally available elsewhere (such as major engine parts, transmission parts, trim pieces, etc.).

Warranty information: If the vehicle is still covered under warranty, be sure that any replacement parts purchased - regardless of the source - do not invalidate the warranty!

To be sure of obtaining the correct parts, have engine and chassis numbers available and, if possible, take the old parts along for positive identification.

Maintenance techniques, tools and working facilities

Maintenance techniques

There are a number of techniques involved in maintenance and repair that will be referred to throughout this manual. Application of these techniques will enable the home mechanic to be more efficient, better organized and capable of performing the various tasks properly, which will ensure that the repair job is thorough and complete.

Fasteners

Fasteners are nuts, bolts, studs and screws used to hold two or more parts together. There are a few things to keep in mind when working with fasteners. Almost all of them use a locking device of some type, either a lockwasher, locknut, locking tab or thread adhesive. All threaded fasteners should be clean and straight, with undamaged threads and undamaged corners on the hex head where the wrench fits. Develop the habit of replacing all damaged nuts and bolts with new ones. Special locknuts with nylon or fiber inserts can only be used once. If they are removed, they lose their locking ability and must be replaced with new ones.

Rusted nuts and bolts should be treated with a penetrating fluid to ease removal and prevent breakage. Some mechanics use turpentine in a spout-type oil can, which works quite well. After applying the rust penetrant, let it work for a few minutes before trying to loosen the nut or bolt. Badly rusted fasteners may have to be chiseled or sawed off or removed with a special nut breaker, available at tool stores.

If a bolt or stud breaks off in an assembly, it can be drilled and removed with a special tool commonly available for this purpose. Most automotive machine shops can perform this task, as well as other repair procedures, such as the repair of threaded holes that have been stripped out.

Flat washers and lockwashers, when removed from an assembly, should always be replaced exactly as removed. Replace any damaged washers with new ones. Never use a lockwasher on any soft metal surface (such as aluminum), thin sheet metal or plastic.

Fastener sizes

For a number of reasons, automobile manufacturers are making wider and wider use of metric fasteners. Therefore, it is important to be able to tell the difference between standard (sometimes called U.S. or SAE) and metric hardware, since they cannot be interchanged.

All bolts, whether standard or metric, are sized according to diameter, thread pitch and length. For example, a standard 1/2 - 13 x 1 bolt is 1/2 inch in diameter, has 13 threads per inch and is 1 inch long. An M12 - 1.75 x 25 metric bolt is 12 mm in diameter, has a thread pitch of 1.75 mm (the distance between threads) and is 25 mm long. The two bolts are nearly identical, and easily confused, but they are not interchangeable.

In addition to the differences in diameter, thread pitch and length, metric and standard bolts can also be distinguished by examining the bolt heads. To begin with, the distance across the flats on a standard bolt head is measured in inches, while the same dimension on a metric bolt is sized in millimeters (the same is true for nuts). As a result, a standard wrench should not be used on a metric bolt and a metric wrench should not be used on a standard bolt. Also, most standard bolts have slashes radiating out from the center of the head to denote the grade or strength of the bolt, which is an indication of the amount of torque that can be applied to it. The greater the number of slashes, the greater the strength of the bolt. Grades 0 through 5 are commonly used on automobiles. Metric bolts have a property class (grade) number, rather than a slash, molded into their heads to indicate bolt strength. In this case, the higher the number, the stronger the bolt. Property class numbers 8.8, 9.8 and 10.9 are commonly used on automobiles.

Strength markings can also be used to distinguish standard hex nuts from metric hex nuts. Many standard nuts have dots stamped into one side, while metric nuts are marked with a number. The greater the number of dots, or the higher the number, the greater the strength of the nut.

Metric studs are also marked on their ends according to property class (grade). Larger studs are numbered (the same as metric bolts), while smaller studs carry a geometric code to denote grade.

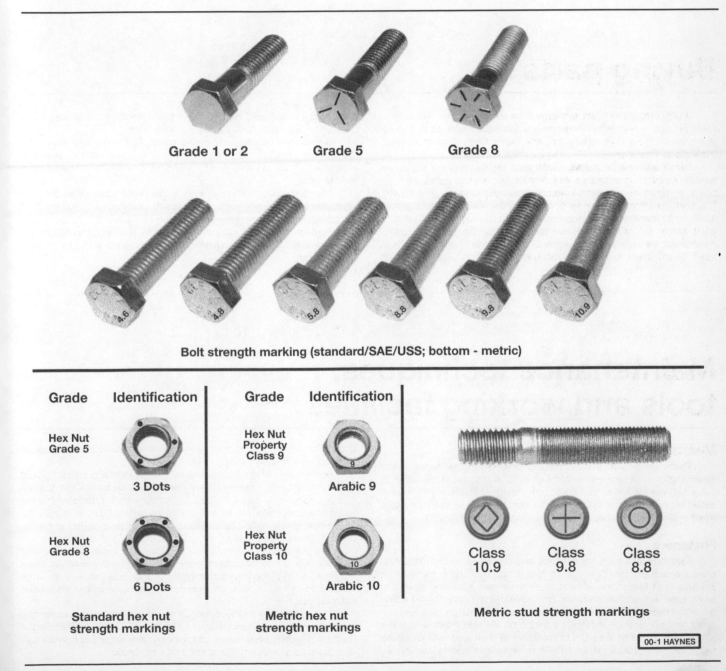

Grade 1 or 2   Grade 5   Grade 8

Bolt strength marking (standard/SAE/USS; bottom - metric)

Grade	Identification
Hex Nut Grade 5	3 Dots
Hex Nut Grade 8	6 Dots

Standard hex nut strength markings

Grade	Identification
Hex Nut Property Class 9	Arabic 9
Hex Nut Property Class 10	Arabic 10

Metric hex nut strength markings

Class 10.9   Class 9.8   Class 8.8

Metric stud strength markings

It should be noted that many fasteners, especially Grades 0 through 2, have no distinguishing marks on them. When such is the case, the only way to determine whether it is standard or metric is to measure the thread pitch or compare it to a known fastener of the same size.

Standard fasteners are often referred to as SAE, as opposed to metric. However, it should be noted that SAE technically refers to a non-metric fine thread fastener only. Coarse thread non-metric fasteners are referred to as USS sizes.

Since fasteners of the same size (both standard and metric) may have different strength ratings, be sure to reinstall any bolts, studs or nuts removed from your vehicle in their original locations. Also, when replacing a fastener with a new one, make sure that the new one has a strength rating equal to or greater than the original.

Tightening sequences and procedures

Most threaded fasteners should be tightened to a specific torque value (torque is the twisting force applied to a threaded component such as a nut or bolt). Overtightening the fastener can weaken it and cause it to break, while undertightening can cause it to eventually come loose. Bolts, screws and studs, depending on the material they are made of and their thread diameters, have specific torque values, many of which are noted in the Specifications at the beginning of each Chapter. Be sure to follow the torque recommendations closely. For fasteners not assigned a specific torque, a general torque value chart is presented here as a guide. These torque values are for dry (unlubricated) fasteners threaded into steel or cast iron (not aluminum). As was previously mentioned, the size and grade of a fastener determine the amount of torque that can safely be applied to it. The figures listed

Metric thread sizes	Ft-lbs	Nm
M-6	6 to 9	9 to 12
M-8	14 to 21	19 to 28
M-10	28 to 40	38 to 54
M-12	50 to 71	68 to 96
M-14	80 to 140	109 to 154
Pipe thread sizes		
1/8	5 to 8	7 to 10
1/4	12 to 18	17 to 24
3/8	22 to 33	30 to 44
1/2	25 to 35	34 to 47
U.S. thread sizes		
1/4 - 20	6 to 9	9 to 12
5/16 - 18	12 to 18	17 to 24
5/16 - 24	14 to 20	19 to 27
3/8 - 16	22 to 32	30 to 43
3/8 - 24	27 to 38	37 to 51
7/16 - 14	40 to 55	55 to 74
7/16 - 20	40 to 60	55 to 81
1/2 - 13	55 to 80	75 to 108

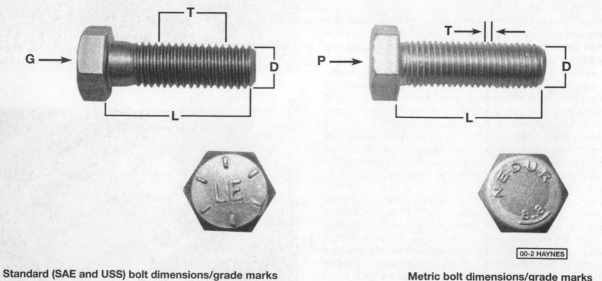

00-2 HAYNES

Standard (SAE and USS) bolt dimensions/grade marks

G   Grade marks (bolt strength)
L   Length (in inches)
T   Thread pitch (number of threads per inch)
D   Nominal diameter (in inches)

Metric bolt dimensions/grade marks

P   Property class (bolt strength)
L   Length (in millimeters)
T   Thread pitch (distance between threads in millimeters)
D   Diameter

here are approximate for Grade 2 and Grade 3 fasteners. Higher grades can tolerate higher torque values.

Fasteners laid out in a pattern, such as cylinder head bolts, oil pan bolts, differential cover bolts, etc., must be loosened or tightened in sequence to avoid warping the component. This sequence will normally be shown in the appropriate Chapter. If a specific pattern is not given, the following procedures can be used to prevent warping.

Initially, the bolts or nuts should be assembled finger-tight only. Next, they should be tightened one full turn each, in a criss-cross or diagonal pattern. After each one has been tightened one full turn, return to the first one and tighten them all one-half turn, following the same pattern. Finally, tighten each of them one-quarter turn at a time until each fastener has been tightened to the proper torque. To loosen and remove the fasteners, the procedure would be reversed.

Component disassembly

Component disassembly should be done with care and purpose to help ensure that the parts go back together properly. Always keep track of the sequence in which parts are removed. Make note of special characteristics or marks on parts that can be installed more than one way, such as a grooved thrust washer on a shaft. It is a good idea to lay the disassembled parts out on a clean surface in the order that they were removed. It may also be helpful to make sketches or take instant photos of components before removal.

When removing fasteners from a component, keep track of their locations. Sometimes threading a bolt back in a part, or putting the washers and nut back on a stud, can prevent mix-ups later. If nuts and bolts cannot be returned to their original locations, they should be kept in a compartmented box or a series of small boxes. A cupcake or muffin tin is ideal for this purpose, since each cavity can hold the bolts and nuts from a particular area (i.e. oil pan bolts, valve cover bolts, engine mount bolts, etc.). A pan of this type is especially helpful when working on assemblies with very small parts, such as the carburetor, alternator, valve train or interior dash and trim pieces. The cavities can be marked with paint or tape to identify the contents.

Whenever wiring looms, harnesses or connectors are separated, it is a good idea to identify the two halves with numbered pieces of masking tape so they can be easily reconnected.

Gasket sealing surfaces

Throughout any vehicle, gaskets are used to seal the mating surfaces between two parts and keep lubricants, fluids, vacuum or pressure contained in an assembly.

Many times these gaskets are coated with a liquid or paste-type gasket sealing compound before assembly. Age, heat and pressure can sometimes cause the two parts to stick together so tightly that they are very difficult to separate. Often, the assembly can be loosened by striking it with a soft-face hammer near the mating surfaces. A regular hammer can be used if a block of wood is placed between the hammer and the part. Do not hammer on cast parts or parts that could be easily damaged. With any particularly stubborn part, always recheck to make sure that every fastener has been removed.

Avoid using a screwdriver or bar to pry apart an assembly, as they can easily mar the gasket sealing surfaces of the parts, which must remain smooth. If prying is absolutely necessary, use an old broom handle, but keep in mind that extra clean up will be necessary if the wood splinters.

After the parts are separated, the old gasket must be carefully scraped off and the gasket surfaces cleaned. Stubborn gasket material can be soaked with rust penetrant or treated with a special chemical to soften it so it can be easily scraped off. A scraper can be fashioned from a piece of copper tubing by flattening and sharpening one end. Copper is recommended because it is usually softer than the surfaces to be scraped, which reduces the chance of gouging the part. Some gaskets can be removed with a wire brush, but regardless of the method used, the mating surfaces must be left clean and smooth. If for some reason the gasket surface is gouged, then a gasket sealer thick enough to fill scratches will have to be used during reassembly of the components. For most applications, a non-drying (or semi-drying) gasket sealer should be used.

Hose removal tips

Warning: *If the vehicle is equipped with air conditioning, do not disconnect any of the A/C hoses without first having the system depressurized by a dealer service department or a service station.*

Hose removal precautions closely parallel gasket removal precautions. Avoid scratching or gouging the surface that the hose mates against or the connection may leak. This is especially true for radiator hoses. Because of various chemical reactions, the rubber in hoses can bond itself to the metal spigot that the hose fits over. To remove a hose, first loosen the hose clamps that secure it to the spigot. Then, with slip-joint pliers, grab the hose at the clamp and rotate it around the spigot. Work it back and forth until it is completely free, then pull it off. Silicone or other lubricants will ease removal if they can be applied between the hose and the outside of the spigot. Apply the same lubricant to the inside of the hose and the outside of the spigot to simplify installation.

As a last resort (and if the hose is to be replaced with a new one anyway), the rubber can be slit with a knife and the hose peeled from the spigot. If this must be done, be careful that the metal connection is not damaged.

If a hose clamp is broken or damaged, do not reuse it. Wire-type clamps usually weaken with age, so it is a good idea to replace them with screw-type clamps whenever a hose is removed.

Tools

A selection of good tools is a basic requirement for anyone who plans to maintain and repair his or her own vehicle. For the owner who has few tools, the initial investment might seem high, but when compared to the spiraling costs of professional auto maintenance and repair, it is a wise one.

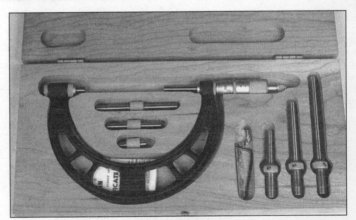

Micrometer set

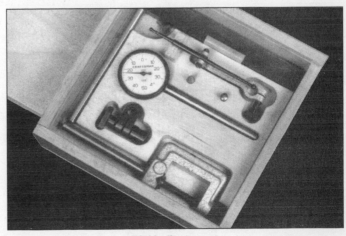

Dial indicator set

Dial caliper

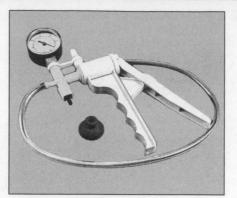
Hand-operated vacuum pump

Timing light

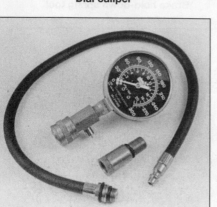
Compression gauge with spark plug hole adapter

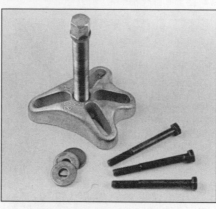
Damper/steering wheel puller

General purpose puller

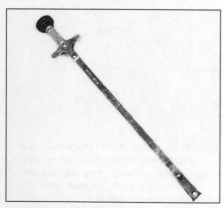
Hydraulic lifter removal tool

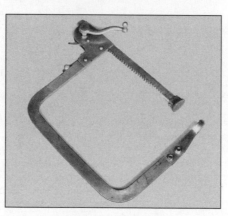
Valve spring compressor

Valve spring compressor

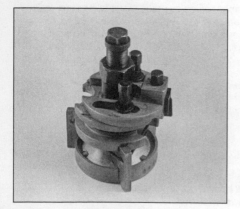
Ridge reamer

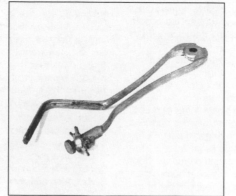
Piston ring groove cleaning tool

Ring removal/installation tool

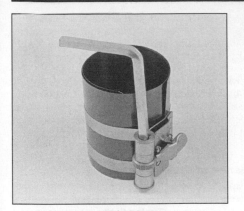

Ring compressor

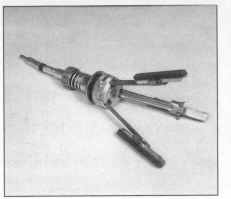

Cylinder hone

Brake hold-down spring tool

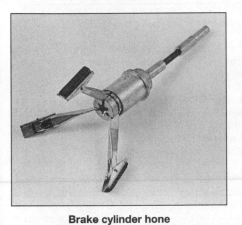

Brake cylinder hone

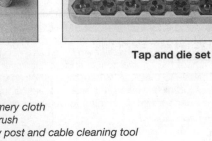

Clutch plate alignment tool

Tap and die set

To help the owner decide which tools are needed to perform the tasks detailed in this manual, the following tool lists are offered: *Maintenance and minor repair, Repair/overhaul* and *Special*.

The newcomer to practical mechanics should start off with the *maintenance and minor repair* tool kit, which is adequate for the simpler jobs performed on a vehicle. Then, as confidence and experience grow, the owner can tackle more difficult tasks, buying additional tools as they are needed. Eventually the basic kit will be expanded into the *repair and overhaul* tool set. Over a period of time, the experienced do-it-yourselfer will assemble a tool set complete enough for most repair and overhaul procedures and will add tools from the special category when it is felt that the expense is justified by the frequency of use.

Maintenance and minor repair tool kit

The tools in this list should be considered the minimum required for performance of routine maintenance, servicing and minor repair work. We recommend the purchase of combination wrenches (box-end and open-end combined in one wrench). While more expensive than open end wrenches, they offer the advantages of both types of wrench.

Combination wrench set (1/4-inch to 1 inch or 6 mm to 19 mm)
Adjustable wrench, 8 inch
Spark plug wrench with rubber insert
Spark plug gap adjusting tool
Feeler gauge set
Brake bleeder wrench
Standard screwdriver (5/16-inch x 6 inch)
Phillips screwdriver (No. 2 x 6 inch)
Combination pliers - 6 inch
Hacksaw and assortment of blades
Tire pressure gauge
Grease gun

Oil can
Fine emery cloth
Wire brush
Battery post and cable cleaning tool
Oil filter wrench
Funnel (medium size)
Safety goggles
Jackstands (2)
Drain pan

Note: *If basic tune-ups are going to be part of routine maintenance, it will be necessary to purchase a good quality stroboscopic timing light and combination tachometer/dwell meter. Although they are included in the list of special tools, it is mentioned here because they are absolutely necessary for tuning most vehicles properly.*

Repair and overhaul tool set

These tools are essential for anyone who plans to perform major repairs and are in addition to those in the maintenance and minor repair tool kit. Included is a comprehensive set of sockets which, though expensive, are invaluable because of their versatility, especially when various extensions and drives are available. We recommend the 1/2-inch drive over the 3/8-inch drive. Although the larger drive is bulky and more expensive, it has the capacity of accepting a very wide range of large sockets. Ideally, however, the mechanic should have a 3/8-inch drive set and a 1/2-inch drive set.

Socket set(s)
Reversible ratchet
Extension - 10 inch
Universal joint
Torque wrench (same size drive as sockets)
Ball peen hammer - 8 ounce
Soft-face hammer (plastic/rubber)
Standard screwdriver (1/4-inch x 6 inch)

Standard screwdriver (stubby - 5/16-inch)
Phillips screwdriver (No. 3 x 8 inch)
Phillips screwdriver (stubby - No. 2)
Pliers - vise grip
Pliers - lineman's
Pliers - needle nose
Pliers - snap-ring (internal and external)
Cold chisel - 1/2-inch
Scribe
Scraper (made from flattened copper tubing)
Centerpunch
Pin punches (1/16, 1/8, 3/16-inch)
Steel rule/straightedge - 12 inch
Allen wrench set (1/8 to 3/8-inch or 4 mm to 10 mm)
A selection of files
Wire brush (large)
Jackstands (second set)
Jack (scissor or hydraulic type)

Note: *Another tool which is often useful is an electric drill with a chuck capacity of 3/8-inch and a set of good quality drill bits.*

Special tools

The tools in this list include those which are not used regularly, are expensive to buy, or which need to be used in accordance with their manufacturer's instructions. Unless these tools will be used frequently, it is not very economical to purchase many of them. A consideration would be to split the cost and use between yourself and a friend or friends. In addition, most of these tools can be obtained from a tool rental shop on a temporary basis.

This list primarily contains only those tools and instruments widely available to the public, and not those special tools produced by the vehicle manufacturer for distribution to dealer service departments. Occasionally, references to the manufacturer's special tools are included in the text of this manual. Generally, an alternative method of doing the job without the special tool is offered. However, sometimes there is no alternative to their use. Where this is the case, and the tool cannot be purchased or borrowed, the work should be turned over to the dealer service department or an automotive repair shop.

Valve spring compressor
Piston ring groove cleaning tool
Piston ring compressor
Piston ring installation tool
Cylinder compression gauge
Cylinder ridge reamer
Cylinder surfacing hone
Cylinder bore gauge
Micrometers and/or dial calipers
Hydraulic lifter removal tool
Balljoint separator
Universal-type puller
Impact screwdriver
Dial indicator set
Stroboscopic timing light (inductive pick-up)
Hand operated vacuum/pressure pump
Tachometer/dwell meter
Universal electrical multimeter
Cable hoist
Brake spring removal and installation tools
Floor jack

Buying tools

For the do-it-yourselfer who is just starting to get involved in vehicle maintenance and repair, there are a number of options available when purchasing tools. If maintenance and minor repair is the extent of the work to be done, the purchase of individual tools is satisfactory. If, on the other hand, extensive work is planned, it would be a good idea to purchase a modest tool set from one of the large retail chain stores. A set can usually be bought at a substantial savings over the individual tool prices, and they often come with a tool box. As additional tools are needed, add-on sets, individual tools and a larger tool box can be purchased to expand the tool selection. Building a tool set gradually allows the cost of the tools to be spread over a longer period of time and gives the mechanic the freedom to choose only those tools that will actually be used.

Tool stores will often be the only source of some of the special tools that are needed, but regardless of where tools are bought, try to avoid cheap ones, especially when buying screwdrivers and sockets, because they won't last very long. The expense involved in replacing cheap tools will eventually be greater than the initial cost of quality tools.

Care and maintenance of tools

Good tools are expensive, so it makes sense to treat them with respect. Keep them clean and in usable condition and store them properly when not in use. Always wipe off any dirt, grease or metal chips before putting them away. Never leave tools lying around in the work area. Upon completion of a job, always check closely under the hood for tools that may have been left there so they won't get lost during a test drive.

Some tools, such as screwdrivers, pliers, wrenches and sockets, can be hung on a panel mounted on the garage or workshop wall, while others should be kept in a tool box or tray. Measuring instruments, gauges, meters, etc. must be carefully stored where they cannot be damaged by weather or impact from other tools.

When tools are used with care and stored properly, they will last a very long time. Even with the best of care, though, tools will wear out if used frequently. When a tool is damaged or worn out, replace it. Subsequent jobs will be safer and more enjoyable if you do.

How to repair damaged threads

Sometimes, the internal threads of a nut or bolt hole can become stripped, usually from overtightening. Stripping threads is an all-too-common occurrence, especially when working with aluminum parts, because aluminum is so soft that it easily strips out.

Usually, external or internal threads are only partially stripped. After they've been cleaned up with a tap or die, they'll still work. Sometimes, however, threads are badly damaged. When this happens, you've got three choices:

1) *Drill and tap the hole to the next suitable oversize and install a larger diameter bolt, screw or stud.*
2) *Drill and tap the hole to accept a threaded plug, then drill and tap the plug to the original screw size. You can also buy a plug already threaded to the original size. Then you simply drill a hole to the specified size, then run the threaded plug into the hole with a bolt and jam nut. Once the plug is fully seated, remove the jam nut and bolt.*
3) *The third method uses a patented thread repair kit like Heli-Coil or Slimsert. These easy-to-use kits are designed to repair damaged threads in straight-through holes and blind holes. Both are available as kits which can handle a variety of sizes and thread patterns. Drill the hole, then tap it with the special included tap. Install the Heli-Coil and the hole is back to its original diameter and thread pitch.*

Regardless of which method you use, be sure to proceed calmly and carefully. A little impatience or carelessness during one of these relatively simple procedures can ruin your whole day's work and cost you a bundle if you wreck an expensive part.

Working facilities

Not to be overlooked when discussing tools is the workshop. If anything more than routine maintenance is to be carried out, some sort of suitable work area is essential.

It is understood, and appreciated, that many home mechanics do not have a good workshop or garage available, and end up removing an engine or doing major repairs outside. It is recommended, however, that the overhaul or repair be completed under the cover of a roof.

A clean, flat workbench or table of comfortable working height is an absolute necessity. The workbench should be equipped with a vise that has a jaw opening of at least four inches.

As mentioned previously, some clean, dry storage space is also required for tools, as well as the lubricants, fluids, cleaning solvents, etc. which soon become necessary.

Sometimes waste oil and fluids, drained from the engine or cooling system during normal maintenance or repairs, present a disposal problem. To avoid pouring them on the ground or into a sewage system, pour the used fluids into large containers, seal them with caps and take them to an authorized disposal site or recycling center. Plastic jugs, such as old antifreeze containers, are ideal for this purpose.

Always keep a supply of old newspapers and clean rags available. Old towels are excellent for mopping up spills. Many mechanics use rolls of paper towels for most work because they are readily available and disposable. To help keep the area under the vehicle clean, a large cardboard box can be cut open and flattened to protect the garage or shop floor.

Whenever working over a painted surface, such as when leaning over a fender to service something under the hood, always cover it with an old blanket or bedspread to protect the finish. Vinyl covered pads, made especially for this purpose, are available at auto parts stores.

Booster battery (jump) starting

Observe these precautions when using a booster battery to start a vehicle:

a) *Before connecting the booster battery, make sure the ignition switch is in the Off position.*

b) *Turn off the lights, heater and other electrical loads.*

c) *Your eyes should be shielded. Safety goggles are a good idea.*

d) *Make sure the booster battery is the same voltage as the dead one in the vehicle.*

e) *The two vehicles MUST NOT TOUCH each other!*

f) *Make sure the transaxle is in Neutral (manual) or Park (automatic).*

g) *If the booster battery is not a maintenance-free type, remove the vent caps and lay a cloth over the vent holes.*

Connect the red jumper cable to the positive (+) terminals of each battery **(see illustration).**

Connect one end of the black jumper cable to the negative (-) terminal of the booster battery. The other end of this cable should be connected to a good ground on the vehicle to be started, such as a bolt or bracket on the body.

Start the engine using the booster battery, then, with the engine running at idle speed, disconnect the jumper cables in the reverse order of connection.

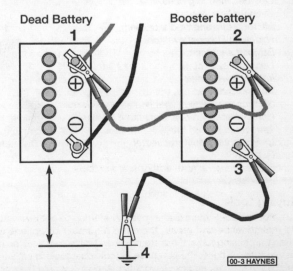

Make the booster battery cable connections in the numerical order shown (note that the negative cable of the booster battery is NOT attached to the negative terminal of the dead battery)

Jacking and towing

Jacking

Warning: *The jack supplied with the vehicle should only be used for changing a tire or placing jackstands under the frame. Never work under the vehicle or start the engine while this jack is being used as the only means of support.*

The vehicle should be on level ground. Place the shift lever in Park, if you have an automatic, or Reverse if you have a manual transaxle. Block the wheel diagonally opposite the wheel being changed. Set the parking brake.

Remove the spare tire and jack from stowage. Remove the wheel cover and trim ring (if so equipped) with the tapered end of the lug nut wrench by inserting and twisting the handle and then prying against the back of the wheel cover. Loosen the wheel lug nuts about 1/4-to-1/2 turn each.

Place the scissors-type jack under the side of the vehicle and adjust the jack height until it fits in the notch in the vertical rocker panel flange nearest the wheel to be changed. There is a front and rear jacking point on each side of the vehicle **(see illustration)**.

Turn the jack handle clockwise until the tire clears the ground. Remove the lug nuts and pull the wheel off. Replace it with the spare.

Install the lug nuts with the beveled edges facing in. Tighten them snugly. Don't attempt to tighten them completely until the vehicle is lowered or it could slip off the jack. Turn the jack handle counterclockwise to lower the vehicle. Remove the jack and tighten the lug nuts in a diagonal pattern.

Install the cover (and trim ring, if used) and be sure it's snapped into place all the way around.

Stow the tire, jack and wrench. Unblock the wheels.

Towing

As a general rule, the vehicle should be towed with the front (drive) wheels off the ground. If they can't be raised, place them on a dolly. The ignition key must be in the ACC position, since the steering lock mechanism isn't strong enough to hold the front wheels straight while towing.

Vehicles equipped with an automatic transaxle can be towed from the front only with all four wheels on the ground, provided that speeds don't exceed 30 mph and the distance is not over 40 miles. Before towing, check the transmission fluid level (see Chapter 1). If the level is below the HOT line on the dipstick, add fluid or use a towing dolly.

Caution: *Never tow a vehicle with an automatic transaxle from the rear with the front wheels on the ground.*

When towing a vehicle equipped with a manual transaxle with all four wheels on the ground, be sure to place the shift lever in neutral and release the parking brake.

Equipment specifically designed for towing should be used. It should be attached to the main structural members of the vehicle, not the bumpers or brackets.

Safety is a major consideration when towing and all applicable state and local laws must be obeyed. A safety chain system must be used at all times.

The jack fits over the rocker panel flange (there are two jacking points on each side of the vehicle, indicated by a notch in the rocker panel flange)

Automotive chemicals and lubricants

A number of automotive chemicals and lubricants are available for use during vehicle maintenance and repair. They include a wide variety of products ranging from cleaning solvents and degreasers to lubricants and protective sprays for rubber, plastic and vinyl.

Cleaners

Carburetor cleaner and choke cleaner is a strong solvent for gum, varnish and carbon. Most carburetor cleaners leave a dry-type lubricant film which will not harden or gum up. Because of this film it is not recommended for use on electrical components.

Brake system cleaner is used to remove grease and brake fluid from the brake system, where clean surfaces are absolutely necessary. It leaves no residue and often eliminates brake squeal caused by contaminants.

Electrical cleaner removes oxidation, corrosion and carbon deposits from electrical contacts, restoring full current flow. It can also be used to clean spark plugs, carburetor jets, voltage regulators and other parts where an oil-free surface is desired.

Demoisturants remove water and moisture from electrical components such as alternators, voltage regulators, electrical connectors and fuse blocks. They are non-conductive, non-corrosive and non-flammable.

Degreasers are heavy-duty solvents used to remove grease from the outside of the engine and from chassis components. They can be sprayed or brushed on and, depending on the type, are rinsed off either with water or solvent.

Lubricants

Motor oil is the lubricant formulated for use in engines. It normally contains a wide variety of additives to prevent corrosion and reduce foaming and wear. Motor oil comes in various weights (viscosity ratings) from 5 to 80. The recommended weight of the oil depends on the season, temperature and the demands on the engine. Light oil is used in cold climates and under light load conditions. Heavy oil is used in hot climates and where high loads are encountered. Multi-viscosity oils are designed to have characteristics of both light and heavy oils and are available in a number of weights from 5W-20 to 20W-50.

Gear oil is designed to be used in differentials, manual transmissions and other areas where high-temperature lubrication is required.

Chassis and wheel bearing grease is a heavy grease used where increased loads and friction are encountered, such as for wheel bearings, balljoints, tie-rod ends and universal joints.

High-temperature wheel bearing grease is designed to withstand the extreme temperatures encountered by wheel bearings in disc brake equipped vehicles. It usually contains molybdenum disulfide (moly), which is a dry-type lubricant.

White grease is a heavy grease for metal-to-metal applications where water is a problem. White grease stays soft under both low and high temperatures (usually from -100 to +190-degrees F), and will not wash off or dilute in the presence of water.

Assembly lube is a special extreme pressure lubricant, usually containing moly, used to lubricate high-load parts (such as main and rod bearings and cam lobes) for initial start-up of a new engine. The assembly lube lubricates the parts without being squeezed out or washed away until the engine oiling system begins to function.

Silicone lubricants are used to protect rubber, plastic, vinyl and nylon parts.

Graphite lubricants are used where oils cannot be used due to contamination problems, such as in locks. The dry graphite will lubricate metal parts while remaining uncontaminated by dirt, water, oil or acids. It is electrically conductive and will not foul electrical contacts in locks such as the ignition switch.

Moly penetrants loosen and lubricate frozen, rusted and corroded fasteners and prevent future rusting or freezing.

Heat-sink grease is a special electrically non-conductive grease that is used for mounting electronic ignition modules where it is essential that heat is transferred away from the module.

Sealants

RTV sealant is one of the most widely used gasket compounds. Made from silicone, RTV is air curing, it seals, bonds, waterproofs, fills surface irregularities, remains flexible, doesn't shrink, is relatively easy to remove, and is used as a supplementary sealer with almost all low and medium temperature gaskets.

Anaerobic sealant is much like RTV in that it can be used either to seal gaskets or to form gaskets by itself. It remains flexible, is solvent resistant and fills surface imperfections. The difference between an anaerobic sealant and an RTV-type sealant is in the curing. RTV cures when exposed to air, while an anaerobic sealant cures only in the absence of air. This means that an anaerobic sealant cures only after the assembly of parts, sealing them together.

Thread and pipe sealant is used for sealing hydraulic and pneumatic fittings and vacuum lines. It is usually made from a Teflon compound, and comes in a spray, a paint-on liquid and as a wrap-around tape.

Chemicals

Anti-seize compound prevents seizing, galling, cold welding, rust and corrosion in fasteners. High-temperature ant-seize, usually made with copper and graphite lubricants, is used for exhaust system and exhaust manifold bolts.

Anaerobic locking compounds are used to keep fasteners from vibrating or working loose and cure only after installation, in the absence of air. Medium strength locking compound is used for small nuts, bolts and screws that may be removed later. High-strength locking compound is for large nuts, bolts and studs which aren't removed on a regular basis.

Oil additives range from viscosity index improvers to chemical treatments that claim to reduce internal engine friction. It should be noted that most oil manufacturers caution against using additives with their oils.

Gas additives perform several functions, depending on their chemical makeup. They usually contain solvents that help dissolve gum and varnish that build up on carburetor, fuel injection and intake parts. They also serve to break down carbon deposits that form on the inside surfaces of the combustion chambers. Some additives contain upper cylinder lubricants for valves and piston rings, and others contain chemicals to remove condensation from the gas tank.

Miscellaneous

Brake fluid is specially formulated hydraulic fluid that can withstand the heat and pressure encountered in brake systems. Care must be taken so this fluid does not come in contact with painted surfaces or plastics. An opened container should always be resealed to prevent contamination by water or dirt.

Weatherstrip adhesive is used to bond weatherstripping around doors, windows and trunk lids. It is sometimes used to attach trim pieces.

Undercoating is a petroleum-based, tar-like substance that is designed to protect metal surfaces on the underside of the vehicle from corrosion. It also acts as a sound-deadening agent by insulating the bottom of the vehicle.

Waxes and polishes are used to help protect painted and plated surfaces from the weather. Different types of paint may require the use of different types of wax and polish. Some polishes utilize a chemical or abrasive cleaner to help remove the top layer of oxidized (dull) paint on older vehicles. In recent years many non-wax polishes that contain a wide variety of chemicals such as polymers and silicones have been introduced. These non-wax polishes are usually easier to apply and last longer than conventional waxes and polishes.

Conversion factors

Length (distance)
Inches (in)	X	25.4	= Millimetres (mm)	X 0.0394	= Inches (in)
Feet (ft)	X	0.305	= Metres (m)	X 3.281	= Feet (ft)
Miles	X	1.609	= Kilometres (km)	X 0.621	= Miles

Volume (capacity)
Cubic inches (cu in; in^3)	X	16.387	= Cubic centimetres (cc; cm^3)	X 0.061	= Cubic inches (cu in; in^3)
Imperial pints (Imp pt)	X	0.568	= Litres (l)	X 1.76	= Imperial pints (Imp pt)
Imperial quarts (Imp qt)	X	1.137	= Litres (l)	X 0.88	= Imperial quarts (Imp qt)
Imperial quarts (Imp qt)	X	1.201	= US quarts (US qt)	X 0.833	= Imperial quarts (Imp qt)
US quarts (US qt)	X	0.946	= Litres (l)	X 1.057	= US quarts (US qt)
Imperial gallons (Imp gal)	X	4.546	= Litres (l)	X 0.22	= Imperial gallons (Imp gal)
Imperial gallons (Imp gal)	X	1.201	= US gallons (US gal)	X 0.833	= Imperial gallons (Imp gal)
US gallons (US gal)	X	3.785	= Litres (l)	X 0.264	= US gallons (US gal)

Mass (weight)
Ounces (oz)	X	28.35	= Grams (g)	X 0.035	Ounces (oz)
Pounds (lb)	X	0.454	= Kilograms (kg)	X 2.205	= Pounds (lb)

Force
Ounces-force (ozf; oz)	X	0.278	= Newtons (N)	X 3.6	= Ounces-force (ozf; oz)
Pounds-force (lbf; lb)	X	4.448	= Newtons (N)	X 0.225	= Pounds-force (lbf; lb)
Newtons (N)	X	0.1	= Kilograms-force (kgf; kg)	X 9.81	= Newtons (N)

Pressure
Pounds-force per square inch (psi; lbf/in^2; lb/in^2)	X	0.070	= Kilograms-force per square centimetre (kgf/cm^2; kg/cm^2)	X 14.223	= Pounds-force per square inch (psi; lbf/in^2; lb/in^2)
Pounds-force per square inch (psi; lbf/in^2; lb/in^2)	X	0.068	= Atmospheres (atm)	X 14.696	= Pounds-force per square inch (psi; lbf/in^2; lb/in^2)
Pounds-force per square inch (psi; lbf/in^2; lb/in^2)	X	0.069	= Bars	X 14.5	= Pounds-force per square inch (psi; lbf/in^2; lb/in^2)
Pounds-force per square inch (psi; lbf/in^2; lb/in^2)	X	6.895	= Kilopascals (kPa)	X 0.145	= Pounds-force per square inch (psi; lbf/in^2; lb/in^2)
Kilopascals (kPa)	X	0.01	= Kilograms-force per square centimetre (kgf/cm^2; kg/cm^2)	X 98.1	= Kilopascals (kPa)

Torque (moment of force)
Pounds-force inches (lbf in; lb in)	X	1.152	= Kilograms-force centimetre (kgf cm; kg cm)	X 0.868	= Pounds-force inches (lbf in; lb in)
Pounds-force inches (lbf in; lb in)	X	0.113	= Newton metres (Nm)	X 8.85	= Pounds-force inches (lbf in; lb in)
Pounds-force inches (lbf in; lb in)	X	0.083	= Pounds-force feet (lbf ft; lb ft)	X 12	= Pounds-force inches (lbf in; lb in)
Pounds-force feet (lbf ft; lb ft)	X	0.138	= Kilograms-force metres (kgf m; kg m)	X 7.233	= Pounds-force feet (lbf ft; lb ft)
Pounds-force feet (lbf ft; lb ft)	X	1.356	= Newton metres (Nm)	X 0.738	= Pounds-force feet (lbf ft; lb ft)
Newton metres (Nm)	X	0.102	= Kilograms-force metres (kgf m; kg m)	X 9.804	= Newton metres (Nm)

Power
Horsepower (hp)	X	745.7	= Watts (W)	X 0.0013	= Horsepower (hp)

Velocity (speed)
Miles per hour (miles/hr; mph)	X	1.609	= Kilometres per hour (km/hr; kph)	X 0.621	= Miles per hour (miles/hr; mph)

Fuel consumption*
Miles per gallon, Imperial (mpg)	X	0.354	= Kilometres per litre (km/l)	X 2.825	= Miles per gallon, Imperial (mpg)
Miles per gallon, US (mpg)	X	0.425	= Kilometres per litre (km/l)	X 2.352	= Miles per gallon, US (mpg)

Temperature
Degrees Fahrenheit = (°C x 1.8) + 32   Degrees Celsius (Degrees Centigrade; °C) = (°F - 32) x 0.56

*It is common practice to convert from miles per gallon (mpg) to litres/100 kilometres (l/100km), where mpg (Imperial) x l/100 km = 282 and mpg (US) x l/100 km = 235

Safety first!

Regardless of how enthusiastic you may be about getting on with the job at hand, take the time to ensure that your safety is not jeopardized. A moment's lack of attention can result in an accident, as can failure to observe certain simple safety precautions. The possibility of an accident will always exist, and the following points should not be considered a comprehensive list of all dangers. Rather, they are intended to make you aware of the risks and to encourage a safety conscious approach to all work you carry out on your vehicle.

Essential DOs and DON'Ts

DON'T rely on a jack when working under the vehicle. Always use approved jackstands to support the weight of the vehicle and place them under the recommended lift or support points.

DON'T attempt to loosen extremely tight fasteners (i.e. wheel lug nuts) while the vehicle is on a jack - it may fall.

DON'T start the engine without first making sure that the transmission is in Neutral (or Park where applicable) and the parking brake is set.

DON'T remove the radiator cap from a hot cooling system - let it cool or cover it with a cloth and release the pressure gradually.

DON'T attempt to drain the engine oil until you are sure it has cooled to the point that it will not burn you.

DON'T touch any part of the engine or exhaust system until it has cooled sufficiently to avoid burns.

DON'T siphon toxic liquids such as gasoline, antifreeze and brake fluid by mouth, or allow them to remain on your skin.

DON'T inhale brake lining dust - it is potentially hazardous (see *Asbestos* below).

DON'T allow spilled oil or grease to remain on the floor - wipe it up before someone slips on it.

DON'T use loose fitting wrenches or other tools which may slip and cause injury.

DON'T push on wrenches when loosening or tightening nuts or bolts. Always try to pull the wrench toward you. If the situation calls for pushing the wrench away, push with an open hand to avoid scraped knuckles if the wrench should slip.

DON'T attempt to lift a heavy component alone - get someone to help you.

DON'T rush or take unsafe shortcuts to finish a job.

DON'T allow children or animals in or around the vehicle while you are working on it.

DO wear eye protection when using power tools such as a drill, sander, bench grinder, etc. and when working under a vehicle.

DO keep loose clothing and long hair well out of the way of moving parts.

DO make sure that any hoist used has a safe working load rating adequate for the job.

DO get someone to check on you periodically when working alone on a vehicle.

DO carry out work in a logical sequence and make sure that everything is correctly assembled and tightened.

DO keep chemicals and fluids tightly capped and out of the reach of children and pets.

DO remember that your vehicle's safety affects that of yourself and others. If in doubt on any point, get professional advice.

Asbestos

Certain friction, insulating, sealing, and other products - such as brake linings, brake bands, clutch linings, torque converters, gaskets, etc. - may contain asbestos. Extreme care must be taken to avoid inhalation of dust from such products, since it is hazardous to health. If in doubt, assume that they do contain asbestos.

Fire

Remember at all times that gasoline is highly flammable. Never smoke or have any kind of open flame around when working on a vehicle. But the risk does not end there. A spark caused by an electrical short circuit, by two metal surfaces contacting each other, or even by static electricity built up in your body under certain conditions, can ignite gasoline vapors, which in a confined space are highly explosive. Do not, under any circumstances, use gasoline for cleaning parts. Use an approved safety solvent.

Always disconnect the battery ground (-) cable at the battery before working on any part of the fuel system or electrical system. Never risk spilling fuel on a hot engine or exhaust component. It is strongly recommended that a fire extinguisher suitable for use on fuel and electrical fires be kept handy in the garage or workshop at all times. Never try to extinguish a fuel or electrical fire with water.

Fumes

Certain fumes are highly toxic and can quickly cause unconsciousness and even death if inhaled to any extent. Gasoline vapor falls into this category, as do the vapors from some cleaning solvents. Any draining or pouring of such volatile fluids should be done in a well ventilated area.

When using cleaning fluids and solvents, read the instructions on the container carefully. Never use materials from unmarked containers.

Never run the engine in an enclosed space, such as a garage. Exhaust fumes contain carbon monoxide, which is extremely poisonous. If you need to run the engine, always do so in the open air, or at least have the rear of the vehicle outside the work area.

If you are fortunate enough to have the use of an inspection pit, never drain or pour gasoline and never run the engine while the vehicle is over the pit. The fumes, being heavier than air, will concentrate in the pit with possibly lethal results.

The battery

Never create a spark or allow a bare light bulb near a battery. They normally give off a certain amount of hydrogen gas, which is highly explosive.

Always disconnect the battery ground (-) cable at the battery before working on the fuel or electrical systems.

If possible, loosen the filler caps or cover when charging the battery from an external source (this does not apply to sealed or maintenance-free batteries). Do not charge at an excessive rate or the battery may burst.

Take care when adding water to a non maintenance-free battery and when carrying a battery. The electrolyte, even when diluted, is very corrosive and should not be allowed to contact clothing or skin.

Always wear eye protection when cleaning the battery to prevent the caustic deposits from entering your eyes.

Household current

When using an electric power tool, inspection light, etc., which operates on household current, always make sure that the tool is correctly connected to its plug and that, where necessary, it is properly grounded. Do not use such items in damp conditions and, again, do not create a spark or apply excessive heat in the vicinity of fuel or fuel vapor.

Secondary ignition system voltage

A severe electric shock can result from touching certain parts of the ignition system (such as the spark plug wires) when the engine is running or being cranked, particularly if components are damp or the insulation is defective. In the case of an electronic ignition system, the secondary system voltage is much higher and could prove fatal.

Troubleshooting

Contents

This section provides an easy reference guide to the more common problems which may occur during the operation of your vehicle. These problems and their possible causes are grouped under headings denoting various components or systems, such as Engine, Cooling system, etc. They also refer you to the chapter and/or section which deals with the problem.

Remember that successful troubleshooting is not a mysterious black art practiced only by professional mechanics. It is simply the result of the right knowledge combined with an intelligent, systematic approach to the problem. Always work by a process of elimination, starting with the simplest solution and working through to the most complex - and never overlook the obvious. Anyone can run the gas tank dry or leave the lights on overnight, so don't assume that you are exempt from such oversights.

Finally, always establish a clear idea of why a problem has occurred and take steps to ensure that it doesn't happen again. If the electrical system fails because of a poor connection, check the other connections in the system to make sure that they don't fail as well. If a particular fuse continues to blow, find out why - don't just replace one fuse after another. Remember, failure of a small component can often be indicative of potential failure or incorrect functioning of a more important component or system.

Engine

1 Engine will not rotate when attempting to start

1 Battery terminal connections loose or corroded (Chapter 1).
2 Battery discharged or faulty (Chapter 1).
3 Automatic transaxle not completely engaged in Park (Chapter 7) or clutch pedal not completely depressed (Chapter 8).
4 Broken, loose or disconnected wiring in the starting circuit (Chapters 5 and 12).
5 Starter motor pinion jammed in flywheel ring gear (Chapter 5).
6 Starter solenoid faulty (Chapter 5).
7 Starter motor faulty (Chapter 5).
8 Ignition switch faulty (Chapter 12).
9 Starter pinion or flywheel teeth worn or broken (Chapter 5).
10 Defective fusible link (see Chapter 12)

2 Engine rotates but will not start

1 Fuel tank empty.
2 Battery discharged (engine rotates slowly) (Chapter 5).
3 Battery terminal connections loose or corroded (Chapter 1).
4 Leaking fuel injector(s), faulty fuel pump, pressure regulator, etc. (Chapter 4).
5 Broken or stripped timing belt Chapter 2).
6 Ignition components damp or damaged (Chapter 5).
7 Worn, faulty or incorrectly gapped spark plugs (Chapter 1).
8 Broken, loose or disconnected wiring in the starting circuit (Chapter 5).
9 Broken, loose or disconnected wires at the ignition coils or faulty coils (Chapter 5).
10 Defective crankshaft sensor or PCM (see Chapter 6).

3 Engine hard to start when cold

1 Battery discharged or low (Chapter 1).
2 Malfunctioning fuel system (Chapter 4).
3 Faulty coolant temperature sensor or intake air temperature sensor (Chapter 6).
4 Fuel injector(s) leaking (Chapter 4).
5 Faulty ignition system (Chapter 5).
6 Defective MAP sensor (see Chapter 6).

4 Engine hard to start when hot

1 Air filter clogged (Chapter 1).
2 Fuel not reaching the fuel injection system (Chapter 4).
3 Corroded battery connections, especially ground (Chapter 1).
4 Faulty coolant temperature sensor or intake air temperature sensor (Chapter 6).

5 Starter motor noisy or excessively rough in engagement

1 Pinion or flywheel gear teeth worn or broken (Chapter 5).
2 Starter motor mounting bolts loose or missing (Chapter 5).

6 Engine starts but stops immediately

1 Loose or faulty electrical connections at ignition coil (Chapter 5).
2 Insufficient fuel reaching the fuel injector(s) (Chapters 4).
3 Vacuum leak at the gasket between the intake manifold/plenum and throttle body (Chapter 4).
4 Fault in the engine control system (Chapter 6).
5 Intake air leaks, broken vacuum lines (see Chapter 4)

7 Oil puddle under engine

1 Oil pan gasket and/or oil pan drain bolt washer leaking (Chapter 2).
2 Oil pressure sending unit leaking (Chapter 2).
3 Valve covers leaking (Chapter 2).
4 Engine oil seals leaking (Chapter 2).

8 Engine lopes while idling or idles erratically

1 Vacuum leakage (Chapters 2 and 4).
2 Leaking EGR valve (Chapter 6).
3 Air filter clogged (Chapter 1).
4 Fuel pump not delivering sufficient fuel to the fuel injection system (Chapter 4).
5 Leaking head gasket (Chapter 2).
6 Timing belt and/or pulleys worn (Chapter 2).
7 Camshaft lobes worn (Chapter 2).

9 Engine misses at idle speed

1 Spark plugs worn or not gapped properly (Chapter 1).
2 Faulty spark plug wires (Chapter 1).
3 Vacuum leaks (Chapters 2 and 4).
4 Faulty ignition coil(s) (Chapter 5).
5 Uneven or low compression (Chapter 2).
6 Faulty fuel injector(s) (Chapter 4).

10 Engine misses throughout driving speed range

1 Fuel filter clogged and/or impurities in the fuel system (Chapter 1).
2 Low fuel output at the fuel injector(s) (Chapter 4).
3 Faulty or incorrectly gapped spark plugs (Chapter 1).
4 Leaking spark plug wires (Chapters 1 or 5).
5 Faulty emission system components (Chapter 6).
6 Low or uneven cylinder compression pressures (Chapter 2).
7 Burned valves (Chapter 2).
8 Weak or faulty ignition system (Chapter 5).
9 Vacuum leak in fuel injection system, throttle body, intake manifold or vacuum hoses (Chapter 4).

11 Engine stumbles on acceleration

1 Spark plugs fouled (Chapter 1).
2 Problem with fuel injection system (Chapter 4).
3 Fuel filter clogged (Chapters 1 and 4).

4   Fault in the engine control system (Chapter 6).
5   Intake manifold air leak (Chapters 2 and 4).
6   EGR system malfunction (Chapter 6).

12   Engine surges while holding accelerator steady

1   Intake air leak (Chapter 4).
2   Fuel pump or fuel pressure regulator faulty (Chapter 4).
3   Problem with fuel injection system (Chapter 4).
4   Problem with the emissions control system (Chapter 6).

13   Engine stalls

1   Idle speed incorrect (Chapter 1).
2   Fuel filter clogged and/or water and impurities in the fuel system (Chapters 1 and 4).
3   Ignition components damp or damaged (Chapter 5).
4   Faulty emissions system components (Chapter 6).
5   Faulty or incorrectly gapped spark plugs (Chapter 1).
6   Faulty spark plug wires (Chapter 1).
7   Vacuum leak in the fuel injection system, intake manifold or vacuum hoses (Chapters 2 and 4).

14   Engine lacks power

1   Worn camshaft lobes (Chapter 2).
2   Burned valves or incorrect valve timing (Chapter 2).
3   Faulty spark plug wires or faulty coil (Chapters 1 and 5).
4   Faulty or incorrectly gapped spark plugs (Chapter 1).
5   Problem with the fuel injection system (Chapter 4).
6   Plugged air filter (Chapter 1).
7   Brakes binding (Chapter 9).
8   Automatic transaxle fluid level incorrect (Chapter 1).
9   Clutch slipping (Chapter 8).
10   Fuel filter clogged and/or impurities in the fuel system (Chapters 1 and 4).
11   Emission control system not functioning properly (Chapter 6).
12   Low or uneven cylinder compression pressures (Chapter 2).
13   Restricted exhaust system (Chapters 4).

15   Engine backfires

1   Emission control system not functioning properly (Chapter 6).
2   Faulty spark plug wires or coil(s) (Chapter 5).
3   Problem with the fuel injection system (Chapter 4).
4   Vacuum leak at fuel injector(s), intake manifold or vacuum hoses (Chapters 2 and 4).
5   Burned valves or incorrect valve timing (Chapter 2).

16   Pinging or knocking engine sounds during acceleration or uphill

1   Incorrect grade of fuel.
2   Problem with the engine control system (Chapter 6).
3   Fuel injection system faulty (Chapter 4).
4   Improper or damaged spark plugs or wires (Chapter 1).
5   EGR valve not functioning (Chapter 6).
6   Vacuum leak (Chapters 2 and 4).

17   Engine runs with oil pressure light on

1   Low oil level (Chapter 1).
2   Idle rpm below specification (Chapter 1).

3   Short in wiring circuit (Chapter 12).
4   Faulty oil pressure sender (Chapter 2).
5   Worn engine bearings and/or oil pump (Chapter 2).

18   Engine diesels (continues to run) after switching off

1   Idle speed too high (Chapter 1).
2   Excessive engine operating temperature (Chapter 3).
3   Excessive carbon deposits on valves and pistons (see Chapter 2).

Engine electrical system

19   Battery will not hold a charge

1   Alternator drivebelt defective or not adjusted properly (Chapter 1).
2   Battery electrolyte level low (Chapter 1).
3   Battery terminals loose or corroded (Chapter 1).
4   Alternator not charging properly (Chapter 5).
5   Loose, broken or faulty wiring in the charging circuit (Chapter 5).
6   Short in vehicle wiring (Chapter 12).
7   Internally defective battery (Chapters 1 and 5).

20   Alternator light fails to go out

1   Faulty alternator or charging circuit (Chapter 5).
2   Alternator drivebelt defective or out of adjustment (Chapter 1).
3   Alternator voltage regulator inoperative (Chapter 5).

21   Alternator light fails to come on when key is turned on

1   Warning light bulb defective (Chapter 12).
2   Fault in the printed circuit, dash wiring or bulb holder (Chapter 12).

Fuel system

22   Excessive fuel consumption

1   Dirty or clogged air filter element (Chapter 1).
2   Emissions system not functioning properly (Chapter 6).
3   Fuel injection system not functioning properly (Chapter 4).
4   Low tire pressure or incorrect tire size (Chapter 1).

23   Fuel leakage and/or fuel odor

1   Leaking fuel feed or return line (Chapters 1 and 4).
2   Tank overfilled.
3   Evaporative canister filter clogged (Chapters 1 and 6).
4   Problem with fuel injection system (Chapter 4).

Cooling system

24   Overheating

1   Insufficient coolant in system (Chapter 1).
2   Water pump defective (Chapter 3).
3   Radiator core blocked or grille restricted (Chapter 3).
4   Thermostat faulty (Chapter 3).
5   Electric coolant fan inoperative or blades broken (Chapter 3).
6   Radiator cap not maintaining proper pressure (Chapter 3).

25 Overcooling

1 Faulty thermostat (Chapter 3).
2 Inaccurate temperature gauge sending unit (Chapter 3)

26 External coolant leakage

1 Deteriorated/damaged hoses; loose clamps (Chapters 1 and 3).
2 Water pump defective (Chapter 3).
3 Leakage from radiator core or coolant reservoir bottle (Chapter 3).
4 Engine drain or water jacket core plugs leaking (Chapter 2).

27 Internal coolant leakage

1 Leaking cylinder head gasket (Chapter 2).
2 Cracked cylinder bore or cylinder head (Chapter 2).

28 Coolant loss

1 Too much coolant in system (Chapter 1).
2 Coolant boiling away because of overheating (Chapter 3).
3 Internal or external leakage (Chapter 3).
4 Faulty pressure cap (Chapter 3).

29 Poor coolant circulation

1 Inoperative water pump (Chapter 3).
2 Restriction in cooling system (Chapters 1 and 3).
3 Thermostat sticking (Chapter 3).

Clutch

30 Pedal travels to floor - no pressure or very little resistance

1 Broken or disconnected clutch cable (Chapter 8).
2 Broken release bearing or fork (Chapter 8).

31 Unable to select gears

1 Faulty transaxle (Chapter 7).
2 Faulty clutch disc or pressure plate (Chapter 8).
3 Faulty release lever or release bearing (Chapter 8).
4 Faulty shift lever assembly or rods (Chapter 8).

32 Clutch slips (engine speed increases with no increase in vehicle speed)

1 Clutch plate worn (Chapter 8).
2 Clutch plate is oil soaked by leaking rear main seal (Chapter 8).
3 Clutch plate not seated (Chapter 8).
4 Warped pressure plate or flywheel (Chapter 8).
5 Weak diaphragm springs (Chapter 8).
6 Clutch plate overheated. Allow to cool.
7 Faulty clutch self-adjusting mechanism (Chapter 8).

33 Grabbing (chattering) as clutch is engaged

1 Oil on clutch plate lining, burned or glazed facings (Chapter 8).
2 Worn or loose engine or transaxle mounts (Chapters 2 and 7).
3 Worn splines on clutch plate hub (Chapter 8).
4 Warped pressure plate or flywheel (Chapter 8).
5 Burned or smeared resin on flywheel or pressure plate (Chapter 8).

34 Transaxle rattling (clicking)

1 Release fork loose (Chapter 8).
2 Low engine idle speed (Chapter 1).

35 Noise in clutch area

Faulty bearing (Chapter 8).

36 Clutch pedal stays on floor

1 Broken release bearing or fork (Chapter 8).
2 Broken or disconnected clutch cable (Chapter 8).

37 High pedal effort

1 Binding clutch cable (Chapter 8).
2 Pressure plate faulty (Chapter 8).

Manual transaxle

38 Knocking noise at low speeds

1 Worn driveaxle constant velocity (CV) joints (Chapter 8).
2 Worn side gear shaft counterbore in differential case (Chapter 7A).*

39 Noise most pronounced when turning

Differential gear noise (Chapter 7A).*

40 Clunk on acceleration or deceleration

1 Loose engine or transaxle mounts (Chapters 2 and 7A).
2 Worn differential pinion shaft in case.*
3 Worn side gear shaft counterbore in differential case (Chapter 7A).*
4 Worn or damaged driveaxle inboard CV joints (Chapter 8).

41 Clicking noise in turns

Worn or damaged outboard CV joint (Chapter 8).

42 Vibration

1 Rough wheel bearing (Chapters 1 and 10).
2 Damaged driveaxle (Chapter 8).
3 Out of round tires (Chapter 1).

4   Tire out of balance (Chapters 1 and 10).
5   Worn CV joint (Chapter 8).

43   Noisy in neutral with engine running

1   Damaged input gear bearing (Chapter 7A).*
2   Damaged clutch release bearing (Chapter 8).

44   Noisy in one particular gear

1   Damaged or worn constant mesh gears (Chapter 7A).*
2   Damaged or worn synchronizers (Chapter 7A).*
3   Bent reverse fork (Chapter 7A).*
4   Damaged fourth speed gear or output gear (Chapter 7A).*
5   Worn or damaged reverse idler gear or idler bushing (Chapter 7A).*

45   Noisy in all gears

1   Insufficient lubricant (Chapter 7A).
2   Damaged or worn bearings (Chapter 7A).*
3   Worn or damaged input gear shaft and/or output gear shaft (Chapter 7A).*

46   Slips out of gear

1   Worn or improperly adjusted linkage (Chapter 7A).
2   Transaxle loose on engine (Chapter 7A).
3   Shift linkage does not work freely, binds (Chapter 7A).
4   Input gear bearing retainer broken or loose (Chapter 7A).*
5   Dirt between clutch cover and engine housing (Chapter 7A).
6   Worn shift fork (Chapter 7A).*

47   Leaks lubricant

1   Driveshaft seals worn (Chapter 7A).
2   Excessive amount of lubricant in transaxle (Chapters 1 and 7A).
3   Loose or broken input gear shaft bearing retainer (Chapter 7A).*
4   Input gear bearing retainer O-ring and/or lip seal damaged (Chapter 7A).*
5   Vehicle speed sensor O-ring leaking (Chapter 7A).

48   Hard to shift

Shift linkage loose or worn (Chapter 7A).

Although the corrective action necessary to remedy the symptoms described is beyond the scope of this manual, the above information should be helpful in isolating the cause of the condition so that the owner can communicate clearly with a professional mechanic.

Automatic transaxle

Note: *Due to the complexity of the automatic transaxle, it is difficult for the home mechanic to properly diagnose and service this component. For problems other than the following, the vehicle should be taken to a dealer or transaxle shop.*

49   Fluid leakage

1   Automatic transaxle fluid is a deep red color. Fluid leaks should not be confused with engine oil, which can easily be blown onto the transaxle by air flow.
2   To pinpoint a leak, first remove all built-up dirt and grime from the transaxle housing with degreasing agents and/or steam cleaning. Then drive the vehicle at low speeds so air flow will not blow the leak far from its source. Raise the vehicle and determine where the leak is coming from. Common areas of leakage are:
    a) *Pan (Chapters 1 and 7)*
    b) *Dipstick tube (Chapters 1 and 7)*
    c) *Transaxle oil lines (Chapter 7)*
    d) *Speed sensor (Chapter 7)*
    e) *Driveaxle oil seals (Chapter 7).*

50   Transaxle fluid brown or has a burned smell

Transaxle fluid overheated (Chapter 1).

51   General shift mechanism problems

1   Chapter 7, Part B, deals with checking and adjusting the shift linkage on automatic transaxles. Common problems which may be attributed to poorly adjusted linkage are:
    a) *Engine starting in gears other than Park or Neutral.*
    b) *Indicator on shifter pointing to a gear other than the one actually being used.*
    c) *Vehicle moves when in Park.*
2   Refer to Chapter 7B for the shift linkage adjustment procedure.

52   Transaxle will not downshift with accelerator pedal pressed to the floor

The transaxle is electronically controlled. This type of problem - which is caused by a malfunction in the control unit, a sensor or solenoid, or the circuit itself - is beyond the scope of this book. Take the vehicle to a dealer service department or a competent automatic transmission shop.

53   Engine will start in gears other than Park or Neutral

Neutral start switch out of adjustment or malfunctioning (Chapter 7B).

54   Transaxle slips, shifts roughly, is noisy or has no drive in forward or reverse gears

There are many probable causes for the above problems, but the home mechanic should be concerned with only one possibility - fluid level. Before taking the vehicle to a repair shop, check the level and condition of the fluid as described in Chapter 1. Correct the fluid level as necessary or change the fluid and filter if needed. If the problem persists, have a professional diagnose the cause.

Driveaxles

55   Clicking noise in turns

Worn or damaged outboard CV joint (Chapter 8).

56   Shudder or vibration during acceleration

1   Excessive toe-in (Chapter 10).

2   Incorrect spring heights (Chapter 10).
3   Worn or damaged inboard or outboard CV joints (Chapter 8).
4   Sticking inboard CV joint assembly (Chapter 8).

57 Vibration at highway speeds

1   Out of balance front wheels and/or tires (Chapters 1 and 10).
2   Out of round front tires (Chapters 1 and 10).
3   Worn CV joint(s) (Chapter 8).

Brakes

Note: *Before assuming that a brake problem exists, make sure that:*
   a) *The tires are in good condition and properly inflated (Chapter 1).*
   b) *The front end alignment is correct (Chapter 10).*
   c) *The vehicle is not loaded with weight in an unequal manner.*

58 Vehicle pulls to one side during braking

1   Incorrect tire pressures (Chapter 1).
2   Front end out of alignment (have the front end aligned).
3   Front, or rear, tire sizes not matched to one another.
4   Restricted brake lines or hoses (Chapter 9).
5   Malfunctioning drum brake or caliper assembly (Chapter 9).
6   Loose suspension parts (Chapter 10).
7   Loose calipers (Chapter 9).
8   Excessive wear of brake shoe or pad material or disc/drum on one side.

59 Noise (high-pitched squeal when the brakes are applied)

Front and/or rear disc brake pads worn out. The noise comes from the wear sensor rubbing against the disc (does not apply to all vehicles). Replace pads with new ones immediately (Chapter 9).

60 Brake roughness or chatter (pedal pulsates)

1   Excessive lateral runout (Chapter 9).
2   Uneven pad wear (Chapter 9).
3   Defective disc (Chapter 9).

61 Excessive brake pedal effort required to stop vehicle

1   Malfunctioning power brake booster (Chapter 9).
2   Partial system failure (Chapter 9).
3   Excessively worn pads or shoes (Chapter 9).
4   Piston in caliper or wheel cylinder stuck or sluggish (Chapter 9).
5   Brake pads or shoes contaminated with oil or grease (Chapter 9).
6   Brake disc grooved and/or glazed (Chapter 1).
7   New pads or shoes installed and not yet seated. It will take a while for the new material to seat against the disc or drum.

62 Excessive brake pedal travel

1   Partial brake system failure (Chapter 9).
2   Insufficient fluid in master cylinder (Chapters 1 and 9).
3   Air trapped in system (Chapters 1 and 9).

63 Dragging brakes

1   Incorrect adjustment of brake light switch (Chapter 9).
2   Master cylinder pistons not returning correctly (Chapter 9).
3   Restricted brakes lines or hoses (Chapters 1 and 9).
4   Incorrect parking brake adjustment (Chapter 9).

64 Grabbing or uneven braking action

1   Malfunction of proportioning valve (Chapter 9).
2   Malfunction of power brake booster unit (Chapter 9).
3   Binding brake pedal mechanism (Chapter 9).

65 Brake pedal feels spongy when depressed

1   Air in hydraulic lines (Chapter 9).
2   Master cylinder mounting bolts loose (Chapter 9).
3   Master cylinder defective (Chapter 9).

66 Brake pedal travels to the floor with little resistance

1   Little or no fluid in the master cylinder reservoir caused by leaking caliper piston(s) (Chapter 9).
2   Loose, damaged or disconnected brake lines (Chapter 9).

67 Parking brake does not hold

Parking brake linkage improperly adjusted (Chapters 1 and 9).

Suspension and steering systems

Note: *Before attempting to diagnose the suspension and steering systems, perform the following preliminary checks:*
   a) *Tires for wrong pressure and uneven wear.*
   b) *Steering universal joints from the column to the rack and pinion for loose connectors or wear.*
   c) *Front and rear suspension and the rack and pinion assembly for loose or damaged parts.*
   d) *Out-of-round or out-of-balance tires, bent rims and loose and/or rough wheel bearings.*

68 Vehicle pulls to one side

1   Mismatched or uneven tires (Chapter 10).
2   Broken or sagging springs (Chapter 10).
3   Wheel alignment out-of-specifications (Chapter 10).
4   Front brake dragging (Chapter 9).

69 Abnormal or excessive tire wear

1   Wheel alignment out-of-specifications (Chapter 10).
2   Sagging or broken springs (Chapter 10).
3   Tire out-of-balance (Chapter 10).
4   Worn strut damper (Chapter 10).
5   Overloaded vehicle.
6   Tires not rotated regularly.

70   Wheel makes a thumping noise

1   Blister or bump on tire (Chapter 10).
2   Improper strut damper action (Chapter 10).

71   Shimmy, shake or vibration

1   Tire or wheel out-of-balance or out-of-round (Chapter 10).
2   Loose or worn wheel bearings (Chapters 1, 8 and 10).
3   Worn tie-rod ends (Chapter 10).
4   Worn lower balljoints (Chapters 1 and 10).
5   Excessive wheel runout (Chapter 10).
6   Blister or bump on tire (Chapter 10).

72   Hard steering

1   Lack of lubrication at balljoints, tie-rod ends and rack and pinion assembly (Chapter 10).
2   Front wheel alignment out-of-specifications (Chapter 10).
3   Low tire pressure(s) (Chapters 1 and 10).

73   Poor returnability of steering to center

1   Lack of lubrication at balljoints and tie-rod ends (Chapter 10).
2   Binding in balljoints (Chapter 10).
3   Binding in steering column (Chapter 10).
4   Lack of lubricant in steering gear assembly (Chapter 10).
5   Front wheel alignment out-of-specifications (Chapter 10).

74   Abnormal noise at the front end

1   Lack of lubrication at balljoints and tie-rod ends (Chapters 1 and 10).
2   Damaged strut mounting (Chapter 10).
3   Worn control arm bushings or tie-rod ends (Chapter 10).
4   Loose stabilizer bar (Chapter 10).
5   Loose wheel nuts (Chapters 1 and 10).
6   Loose suspension bolts (Chapter 10)

75   Wander or poor steering stability

1   Mismatched or uneven tires (Chapter 10).
2   Lack of lubrication at balljoints and tie-rod ends (Chapters 1 and 10).
3   Worn strut assemblies (Chapter 10).
4   Loose stabilizer bar (Chapter 10).
5   Broken or sagging springs (Chapter 10).
6   Wheels out of alignment (Chapter 10).

76   Erratic steering when braking

1   Wheel bearings worn (Chapter 10).
2   Broken or sagging springs (Chapter 10).
3   Leaking wheel cylinder or caliper (Chapter 10).
4   Warped rotors or drums (Chapter 10).

77   Excessive pitching and/or rolling around corners or during braking

1   Loose stabilizer bar (Chapter 10).
2   Worn strut dampers or mountings (Chapter 10).
3   Broken or sagging springs (Chapter 10).
4   Overloaded vehicle.

78   Suspension bottoms

1   Overloaded vehicle.
2   Worn strut dampers (Chapter 10).
3   Incorrect, broken or sagging springs (Chapter 10).

79   Cupped tires

1   Front wheel or rear wheel alignment out-of-specifications (Chapter 10).
2   Worn strut dampers (Chapter 10).
3   Wheel bearings worn (Chapter 10).
4   Excessive tire or wheel runout (Chapter 10).
5   Worn balljoints (Chapter 10).

80   Excessive tire wear on outside edge

1   Inflation pressures incorrect (Chapter 1).
2   Excessive speed in turns.
3   Front end alignment incorrect (excessive toe-in). Have professionally aligned.
4   Suspension arm bent or twisted (Chapter 10).

81   Excessive tire wear on inside edge

1   Inflation pressures incorrect (Chapter 1).
2   Front end alignment incorrect (toe-out). Have professionally aligned.
3   Loose or damaged steering components (Chapter 10).

82   Tire tread worn in one place

1   Tires out-of-balance.
2   Damaged or buckled wheel. Inspect and replace if necessary.
3   Defective tire (Chapter 1).

83   Excessive play or looseness in steering system

1   Wheel bearing(s) worn (Chapter 10).
2   Tie-rod end loose (Chapter 10).
3   Steering gear loose (Chapter 10).
4   Worn or loose steering intermediate shaft (Chapter 10).

84   Rattling or clicking noise in steering gear

1   Steering gear loose (Chapter 10).
2   Steering gear defective.

Chapter 1
Tune-up and routine maintenance

Contents

Specifications

Recommended lubricants and fluids

Note: *Listed here are manufacturer recommendations at the time this manual was written. Manufacturers occasionally upgrade their fluid and lubricant specifications, so check with your local auto parts store for current recommendations.*

Engine oil
Type .... API Certified, SH, SG, SH/CD, or SG/CD multigrade and fuel efficient oil
Viscosity .... See accompanying chart

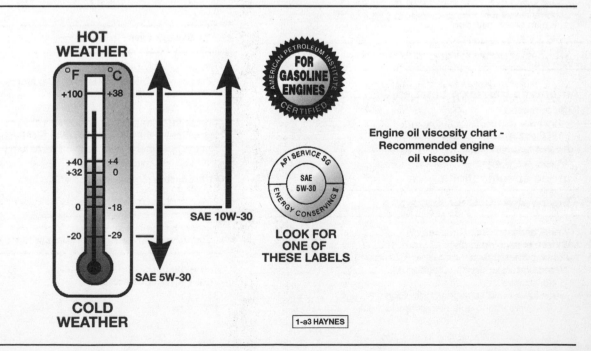

Engine oil viscosity chart -
Recommended engine
oil viscosity

1-a3 HAYNES

Recommended lubricants and fluids (continued)

Manual transaxle lubricant	Mopar manual transaxle fluid or equivalent
Automatic transaxle fluid	Mopar automatic transaxle fluid ATF+3, Type 7176 or equivalent
Pokwer steering fluid	Mopar power steering fluid or equivalent
Brake fluid	DOT 3 brake fluid
Engine coolant	50/50 mixture of ethylene glycol-based antifreeze and water
Parking brake mechanism grease	White lithium-based grease NLGI no. 2
Chassis lubrication grease	NLGI no. 2 EP grease
Hood, door and trunk hinge lubricant	Engine oil
Door hinge and check spring grease	NLGI no. 2 multi-purpose grease
Key lock cylinder lubricant	Graphite spray
Hood latch assembly lubricant	Mopar Lubriplate or equivalent
Door latch striker lubricant	Mopar Door Ease no. 3744859 or equivalent

Capacities*

Engine oil (including filter)	4.5 quarts
Automatic transaxle	
Dry fill (including torque converter - when overhauling transaxle)	8.9 quarts
Drain and refill (when following procedure in this Chapter)	4 quarts
Manual transaxle	2.3 quarts
Cooling system	
1995	7.4 quarts
1996 and later	6.5 quarts

*All capacities approximate. Add as necessary to bring to appropriate level.

Brakes

Disc brake pad wear limit (including metal shoe)	
Front	5/16 inch
Rear	9/32 inch
Drum brake shoe wear limit	1/16 inch

Ignition system

Spark plug type	
1995	Champion RC9YC, or equivalent
1996 and later	
SOHC	Champion RC9YC, or equivalent
DOHC	Champion RC9YC5, or equivalent
Spark plug gap	
1995	0.035 inch
1996 and later	
SOHC	0.035 inch
DOHC	0.050 inch
Spark plug wire resistance	
No. 1 and 4	3050 to 4250 ohms
No. 2 and 3	2300 to 3300 ohms
Firing order	1-3-4-2

Cylinder numbering and coil terminal location

Automatic transaxle band adjustment

Kickdown band	
1995	Tighten to 72 in-lbs, then back off 2 1/2 turns
1996 and later	Tighten to 72 in-lbs, then back off 2 1/4 turns
Low-reverse band	Tighten to 41 in-lbs, then back off 3 1/2 turns

Torque specifications

Ft-lbs (unless otherwise indicated)

Spark plugs	20
Wheel lug nuts	
1995	95
1996 and later	100
Manual transaxle drain plug	22
Automatic transaxle	
Pan bolts	165 in-lbs
Filter screws	40 in-lbs
Kickdown band adjusting screw locknut	35
Low-reverse band adjusting screw locknut	120 in-lbs

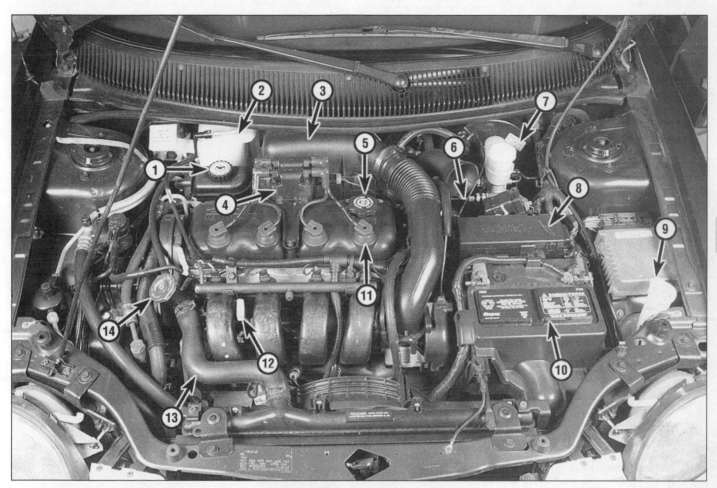

Typical engine compartment layout

1	Power steering fluid reservoir	6	Automatic transmission dipstick	11	Spark plug boot
2	Engine coolant reservoir	7	Brake master cylinder reservoir	12	Engine oil dipstick
3	Air filter housing	8	Power distribution center	13	Upper radiator hose
4	Ignition coil pack	9	Windshield washer fluid reservoir	14	Coolant pressure cap
5	Engine oil filler cap	10	Battery		

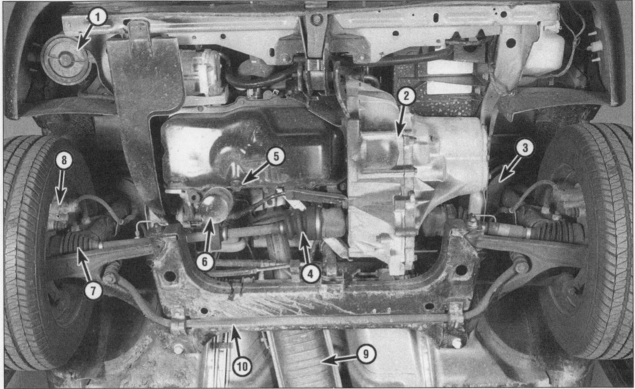

Typical engine compartment underside components

1	Evaporative system canister	5	Engine oil drain plug	8	Front brake caliper
2	Transaxle	6	Engine oil filter	9	Catalytic converter
3	Spring and shock absorber strut	7	Driveaxle outer CV joint boot	10	Front stabilizer bar
4	Driveaxle inner boot				

Typical rear underside components

1	Lateral arm	3	Shock and spring assembly	5	Strut rod
2	Muffler	4	Fuel filler hose	6	Fuel tank

1 Dodge and Plymouth Neon Maintenance schedule

The following maintenance intervals are based on the assumption that the vehicle owner will be doing the maintenance or service work, as opposed to having a dealer service department do the work. Although the time/mileage intervals are loosely based on factory recommendations, most have been shortened to ensure, for example, that such items as lubricants and fluids are checked/changed at intervals that promote maximum engine/driveline service life. Also, subject to the preference of the individual owner interested in keeping his or her vehicle in peak condition at all times, and with the vehicle's ultimate resale in mind, many of the maintenance procedures may be performed more often than recommended in the following schedule. We encourage such owner initiative.

When the vehicle is new it should be serviced initially by a factory authorized dealer service department to protect the factory warranty. In many cases the initial maintenance check is done at no cost to the owner (check with your dealer service department for more information).

Every 250 miles or weekly, whichever comes first

Check the engine oil level; add oil as necessary (see Section 4)
Check the engine coolant level; add coolant as necessary (see Section 4)
Check the windshield washer fluid level (see Section 4)
Check the battery electrolyte level (see Section 4)
Check the brake fluid level (see Section 4)
Check the tires and tire pressures (see Section 5)
Check the automatic transaxle fluid level (see Section 6)
Check the power steering fluid level (see Section 7)
Check the operation of all lights
Check the horn operation

Every 3000 miles or 3 months, whichever comes first

Change the engine oil and filter (see Section 8)*

Every 7,500 miles or 6 months, whichever comes first

Check and clean the battery (see Section 9)
Check the manual transaxle fluid level (see Section 16)
Check the cooling system hoses and connections for leaks and damage (see Section 10)
Check the condition of all vacuum hoses and connections (see Section 11)
Check the wiper blade condition (see Section 12)
Rotate the tires (see Section 13)
Check for freeplay in the steering linkage and balljoints (see Section 14)
Check the CV joints and front suspension components (see Section 14)
Check the exhaust pipes and hangers (see Section 15)

Every 15,000 miles or 12 months, whichever comes first

Lubricate the front suspension steering balljoints (see Section 17)*
Check the brakes (see Section 18)*

Check the fuel system hoses and connections for leaks and damage (see Section 19)
Check the drivebelts and adjust if necessary (see Section 20)

Every 30,000 miles or 24 months, whichever comes first

Replace the air filter element (see Section 21)*
Change the automatic transaxle fluid and filter (see Section 22)*
Check the driveaxle boots (see Section 23)*
Change the manual transaxle lubricant (see Section 24)*
Drain and replace the engine coolant (see Section 26)
Replace fuel filter (1995 models only) (see Section 27)
Check and replace, if necessary, the PCV valve (see Section 28)
Check the fuel evaporative emission system hoses (see Section 29)
Replace the spark plugs (see Section 30)
Check the condition of the primary ignition wires and spark plug wires (see Section 31)
Check the operation of the seat belts (see Section 32)

Every 60,000 miles or 48 months, whichever comes first

Replace drive belts (see Section 20)

Every 105,000 miles or 48 months, whichever comes first

Replace the timing belt (see Chapter 2B)

*This item is affected by "severe" operating conditions as described below. If the vehicle in question is operated under "severe" conditions, perform all maintenance procedures marked with an asterisk (*) at the intervals specified by the mileage headngs below.

Consider the conditions "severe" if most driving is done . . .
In dusty areas
Towing a trailer
Idling for extended periods and/or low-speed operation
When outside temperatures remain below freezing and most trips are less than four miles
In heavy city traffic where outside temperatures regularly reach 90-degrees F or higher

Every 2,000 miles

Change the engine oil and filter

Every 9,000 miles

Check the driveaxle, suspension and steering boots
Check the brakes
Lubricate the tie-rod ends

Every 15,000 miles

Replace the air filter element
Change the automatic transaxle fluid and filter
Adjust the automatic transaxle bands

2   Introduction

This Chapter is designed to help the home mechanic maintain the Dodge and Plymouth Neon models with the goals of maximum performance, economy, safety and reliability in mind.

Included is a master maintenance schedule, followed by procedures dealing specifically with each item on the schedule. Visual checks, adjustments, component replacement and other helpful items are included. Refer to the accompanying illustrations of the engine compartment and the underside of the vehicle for the locations of various components.

Adhering to the mileage/time maintenance schedule and following the step-by-step procedures, which is simply a preventive maintenance program, will result in maximum reliability and vehicle service life. Keep in mind that it's a comprehensive program - maintaining some items but not others at the specified intervals will not produce the same results.

As you service the vehicle, you'll discover that many of the procedures can - and should - be grouped together because of the nature of the particular procedure you're performing or because of the close proximity of two otherwise unrelated components to one another.

For example, if the vehicle is raised, you should inspect the exhaust, suspension, steering and fuel systems while you're under the vehicle. When you're rotating the tires, it makes good sense to check the brakes, since the wheels are already removed. Finally, let's suppose you have to borrow or rent a torque wrench. Even if you only need it to tighten the spark plugs, you might as well check the torque of as many critical fasteners as time allows.

The first step in this maintenance program is to prepare yourself before the actual work begins. Read through all the procedures you're planning to do, then gather up all the parts and tools needed. If it looks like you might run into problems during a particular job, seek advice from a mechanic or an experienced do-it-yourselfer.

3   Tune-up general information

The term "tune-up" is used in this manual to represent a combination of individual operations rather than one specific procedure.

If, from the time the vehicle is new, the routine maintenance schedule is followed closely and frequent checks are made of fluid levels and high wear items, as suggested throughout this manual, the engine will be kept in relatively good running condition and the need for additional work will be minimized.

More likely than not, however, there will be times when the engine is running poorly due to lack of regular maintenance. This is even more likely if a used vehicle, which hasn't received regular and frequent maintenance checks, is purchased. In such cases, an engine tune-up will be needed outside of the regular routine maintenance intervals.

The first step in any tune-up or diagnostic procedure to help correct a poor running engine is a cylinder compression check. A compression check (see Chapter 2, Part B) will help determine the condition of internal engine components and should be used as a guide for tune-up and repair procedures. For instance, if a compression check indicates serious internal engine wear, a conventional tune-up will not improve the performance of the engine and would be a waste of time and money. Because of its importance, the compression check should be done by someone with the right equipment and the knowledge to use it properly.

The following procedures are those most often needed to bring a generally poor running engine back into a proper state of tune:

Minor tune-up

Check all engine related fluids (see Section 4)
Clean, inspect and test the battery (see Section 9)
Replace the spark plugs (see Section 30)
Inspect the spark plug wires (see Section 31)
Check and adjust the drivebelts (see Section 20)

Check the air filter (see Section 21)
Check the PCV valve (see Section 28)
Check all underhood hoses (see Section 11)
Service the cooling system (see Section 26)

Major tune-up

All items listed under Minor tune-up plus . . .
Replace the air filter (see Section 21)
Check the fuel system (see Section 19)
Replace the fuel filter (see Section 27)
Check the charging system (see Chapter 5)

4   Fluid level checks (every 250 miles or weekly)

Note: *The following are fluid level checks to be done on a 250 mile or weekly basis. Additional fluid level checks can be found in specific maintenance procedures which follow. Regardless of the intervals, develop the habit of checking under the vehicle periodically for evidence of fluid leaks.*

1   Fluids are an essential part of the lubrication, cooling, brake and window washer systems. Because the fluids gradually become depleted and/or contaminated during normal operation of the vehicle, they must be replenished periodically. See Recommended lubricants and fluids at the beginning of this Chapter before adding fluid to any of the following components. **Note:** *The vehicle must be on level ground when fluid levels are checked.*

Engine oil

Refer to illustrations 4.2, 4.4 and 4.5

2   The engine oil level is checked with a dipstick which is located at the front right (passenger's) side of the engine **(see illustration)**. The dipstick extends through a tube and into the oil pan at the bottom of the engine.

3   The oil level should be checked before the vehicle has been driven, or about 15 minutes after the engine has been shut off. If the oil is checked immediately after driving the vehicle, some of the oil will remain in the upper engine components, resulting in an inaccurate reading on the dipstick.

4   Pull the dipstick out of the tube and wipe all the oil off the end with a clean rag or paper towel. Insert the clean dipstick all the way back into the tube, then pull it out again. Note the oil level at the end of the dipstick. Add oil as necessary to keep the level at the MAX or SAFE mark **(see illustration)**.

5   Oil is added to the engine after removing a cap located on the top right (passenger's) side of the valve cover **(see illustration)**. The cap will be marked "Engine oil" or something similar. A funnel may help

4.2 The engine oil dipstick is located at the front left (passenger's side) of the engine

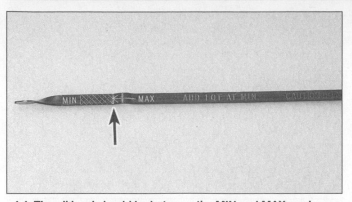

4.4 The oil level should be between the MIN and MAX marks on the dipstick - if it isn't, add enough oil to bring the level up to or near the MAX mark (it takes one quart to raise the level from the MIN to MAX mark)

4.5 Turn the oil filler cap counterclockwise to remove it

reduce spills as the oil is poured in.

6   Don't allow the level to drop below the ADD mark or engine damage may occur. On the other hand, don't overfill the engine by adding too much oil - it may result in oil aeration and loss of oil pressure and also could result in oil fouled spark plugs, oil leaks or seal failures.

7   Checking the oil level is an important preventive maintenance step. A consistently low oil level indicates oil leakage through damaged seals, defective gaskets or past worn rings or valve guides. If the oil looks milky in color or has water droplets in it, the block or head may be cracked and leaking coolant. The engine should be checked immediately. The condition of the oil should also be checked. Each time you check the oil level, slide your thumb and index finger up the dipstick before wiping off the oil. If you see small dirt or metal particles clinging to the dipstick, the oil should be changed (see Section 8).

Engine coolant

Refer to illustrations 4.9 and 4.11

Warning: *Do not allow coolant (antifreeze) to come in contact with your skin or painted surfaces of the vehicle. Flush contaminated areas immediately with plenty of water. Don't store new coolant or leave old coolant lying around where it's accessible to children or pets - they're attracted by its sweet smell. Ingestion of even a small amount of coolant can be fatal! Wipe up garage floor and drip pan spills immediately. Keep antifreeze containers covered and repair cooling system leaks as soon as they're noticed. Check with local authorities about disposing of used antifreeze. Many communities have collection centers which will see that antifreeze is disposed of properly.*

8   All vehicles covered by this manual are equipped with a pressur-

ized coolant recovery system, which makes coolant level checks very easy. A coolant reservoir attached to the engine compartment firewall on the right (passenger's) side is connected by a hose to the radiator filler neck. As the engine warms up, some coolant escapes through a valve in the radiator cap and travels through the hose into the reservoir. As the engine cools, the coolant is automatically drawn back into the cooling system to maintain the correct level.

9   The coolant level should be checked when the engine is at normal operating temperature. Simply note the fluid level in the reservoir - it should be between the MAX and MIN marks when the engine is at normal operating temperature **(see illustration)**.

10   If only a small amount of coolant is required to bring the system up to the proper level, regular water can be used. However, to maintain the proper antifreeze/water mixture in the system, both should be mixed together to replenish a low level. High-quality antifreeze/coolant should be mixed with water in the proportion specified on the antifreeze container.

11   Coolant should be added to the reservoir after removing the cap **(see illustration)**. **Warning:** *Never remove the pressure cap on the filler neck to add coolant while the engine is warm!*

12   As the coolant level is checked, note the condition of the coolant as well. It should be relatively clean and the color of new antifreeze. If it's brown or rust colored, the system should be drained, flushed and refilled (see Section 26).

13   If the coolant level drops consistently, there may be a leak in the system. Check the radiator, hoses, filler cap, drain plugs and water pump (see Section 26). If no leaks are noted, have the filler cap pressure tested by a service station.

1

4.9 Make sure the coolant level in the reservoir is at or near the MAX mark - if it's below the MIN mark, add more coolant mixture or water

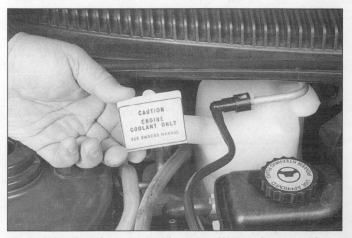

4.11 Remove the cap to add more coolant to the reservoir

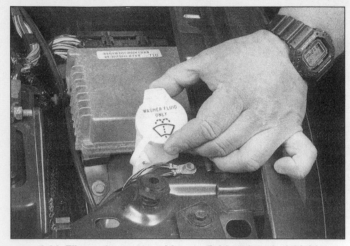

4.14 Flip up the cap to add more fluid to the windshield washer reservoir

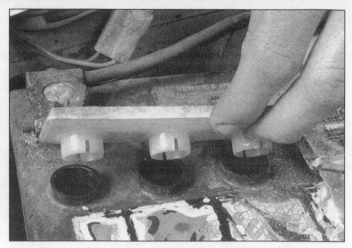

4.18 Remove the cell caps to check the water level in the battery - if the level is low add distilled water only

Windshield washer fluid

Refer to illustration 4.14

14   The fluid for the windshield washer system is stored in a plastic reservoir. The level inside each reservoir should be maintained about one inch below the filler cap. The reservoir is accessible after opening the hood and is located on the left (driver's) side of the engine compartment **(see illustration)**.

15   In milder climates, plain water can be used in the reservoir, but it should be kept no more than two-thirds full to allow for expansion if the water freezes. In colder climates, use windshield washer system antifreeze, available at any auto parts store, to lower the freezing point of the fluid. Mix the antifreeze with water in accordance with the manufacturer's directions on the container. **Caution:** *Don't use cooling system antifreeze - it'll damage the vehicle's paint. To help prevent icing in cold weather, warm the windshield with the defroster before using the washer.*

Battery electrolyte

Refer to illustration 4.18

Warning: *Certain precautions must be followed when checking or servicing a battery. Hydrogen gas, which is highly flammable, is produced in the cells, so keep lighted tobacco, open flames, bare light bulbs and sparks away from the battery. The electrolyte inside the battery is dilute sulfuric acid, which can burn skin and cause serious injury if splashed in your eyes (wear safety glasses). It'll also ruin clothes and painted surfaces. Remove all metal jewelry which could contact the positive battery terminal and a grounded metal source, causing a direct short.*

16   Vehicles equipped with a maintenance-free battery require no maintenance - the battery case is sealed and has no removable caps for adding water.

17   If a maintenance-type battery is installed, the caps on top of the battery should be removed periodically to check for a low electrolyte level. This check is more critical during warm summer months.

18   Remove each of the caps and add distilled water to bring the level in each cell to the split ring in the filler opening **(see illustration)**.

19   At the same time the battery water level is checked, the overall condition of the battery and related components should be noted. See Section 9 for complete battery check and maintenance procedures.

Brake fluid

Refer to illustration 4.21

20   The brake master cylinder is located on the driver's side of the engine compartment firewall.

21   The level should be maintained at the FULL mark on the reservoir **(see illustration)**.

22   If additional fluid is necessary to bring the level up, use a rag to clean all dirt off the top of the reservoir. If any foreign matter enters the master cylinder when the cap is removed, blockage in the brake system lines can occur. Also, make sure all painted surfaces around the master cylinder are covered, since brake fluid will ruin paint. Carefully pour new, clean brake fluid into the master cylinder. Be careful not to spill the fluid on painted surfaces. Be sure the specified fluid is used; mixing different types of brake fluid can cause damage to the system. See *Recommended lubricants and fluids* at the beginning of this Chapter or your owner's manual.

23   At this time the fluid and the master cylinder can be inspected for contamination. Normally the brake hydraulic system won't need periodic draining and refilling, but if rust deposits, dirt particles or water droplets are seen in the fluid, the system should be dismantled, cleaned and refilled with fresh fluid.

24   Reinstall the master cylinder cap.

25   The brake fluid in the master cylinder will drop slightly as the brake shoes or pads at each wheel wear down during normal operation. If the master cylinder requires repeated replenishing to keep the level up, it's an indication of leaks in the brake system which should be corrected immediately. Check all brake lines and connections, along with the wheel cylinders and booster (see Chapter 9 for more information).

26   If you discover that the reservoir is empty or nearly empty, the brake system should be thoroughly inspected and then bled (see Chapter 9).

4.21 The brake fluid level, indicated on the translucent white plastic brake fluid reservoir, should be kept at the FULL mark (arrow)

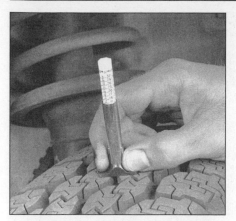

CUPPING

Cupping may be caused by:

- Underinflation and/or mechanical irregularities such as out-of-balance condition of wheel and/or tire, and bent or damaged wheel.
- Loose or worn steering tie-rod or steering idler arm.
- Loose, damaged or worn front suspension parts.

5.2 Use a tire tread depth indicator to monitor tire wear - they are available at auto parts stores and service stations and cost very little

UNDERINFLATION

INCORRECT TOE-IN OR EXTREME CAMBER

OVERINFLATION

FEATHERING DUE TO MISALIGNMENT

5.4a If a tire loses air on a steady basis, check the valve core first to make sure it's snug (special inexpensive wrenches are commonly available at auto parts stores)

5.3 This chart will help you determine the condition of the tires, the probable cause(s) of abnormal wear and the corrective action necessary

5 Tire and tire pressure checks (every 250 miles or weekly)

Refer to illustrations 5.2, 5.3, 5.4a, 5.4b and 5.8

1   Periodic inspection of the tires may spare you the inconvenience of being stranded with a flat tire. It can also provide you with vital information regarding possible problems in the steering and suspension systems before major damage occurs.

2   The original tires on this vehicle are equipped with 1/2-inch wide bands that will appear when tread depth reaches 1/16-inch, but they don't appear until the tires are worn out. Tread wear can be monitored with a simple, inexpensive device known as a tread depth indicator **(see illustration)**.

3   Note any abnormal tread wear **(see illustration)**. Tread pattern irregularities such as cupping, flat spots and more wear on one side than the other are indications of front end alignment and/or balance problems. If any of these conditions are noted, take the vehicle to a tire shop or service station to correct the problem.

4   Look closely for cuts, punctures and embedded nails or tacks. Sometimes a tire will hold air pressure for a short time or leak down very slowly after a nail has embedded itself in the tread. If a slow leak persists, check the valve stem core to make sure it's tight **(see illustration)**. Examine the tread for an object that may have embedded itself in the tire or for a "plug" that may have begun to leak (radial tire punctures are repaired with a plug that's installed in a puncture). If a puncture is suspected, it can be easily verified by spraying a solution

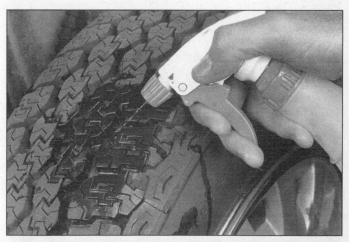

5.4b If the valve core is tight, raise the corner of the vehicle with the low tire and spray a soapy water solution onto the tread as the tire is turned slowly - leaks will cause small bubbles to appear

of soapy water onto the puncture area **(see illustration)**. The soapy solution will bubble if there's a leak. Unless the puncture is unusually large, a tire shop or service station can usually repair the tire.

5   Carefully inspect the inner sidewall of each tire for evidence of

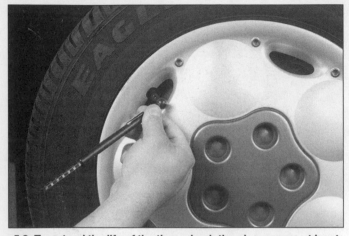

5.8 **To extend the life of the tires, check the air pressure at least once a week with an accurate gauge (don't forget the spare!)**

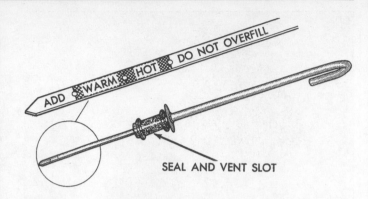

SEAL AND VENT SLOT

6.4 **Check the fluid with the transaxle at normal operating temperature - the level should be kept in the HOT range (between the two upper holes or marks)**

brake fluid leakage. If you see any, inspect the brakes immediately.

6   Correct air pressure adds miles to the life span of the tires, improves mileage and enhances overall ride quality. Tire pressure cannot be accurately estimated by looking at a tire, especially if it's a radial. A tire pressure gauge is essential. Keep an accurate gauge in the vehicle. The pressure gauges attached to the nozzles of air hoses at gas stations are often inaccurate.

7   Always check tire pressure when the tires are cold. Cold, in this case, means the vehicle has not been driven over a mile in the three hours preceding a tire pressure check. A pressure rise of four to eight pounds is not uncommon once the tires are warm.

8   Unscrew the valve cap protruding from the wheel or hubcap and push the gauge firmly onto the valve stem **(see illustration)**. Note the reading on the gauge and compare the figure to the recommended tire pressure shown on the placard on the driver's side door pillar. Be sure to reinstall the valve cap to keep dirt and moisture out of the valve stem mechanism. Check all four tires and, if necessary, add enough air to bring them up to the recommended pressure.

9   Don't forget to keep the spare tire inflated to the specified pressure (refer to your owner's manual or the tire sidewall). Note that the pressure recommended for the compact spare is higher than for the tires on the vehicle.

6   Automatic transaxle fluid level check (every 250 miles or weekly)

Refer to illustration 6.4

1   The fluid inside the transaxle should be at normal operating temperature to get an accurate reading on the dipstick. This is done by driving the vehicle for several miles, making frequent starts and stops to allow the transaxle to shift through all gears.

2   Park the vehicle on a level surface, apply the parking brake, place the gear selector lever in Park and leave the engine running.

3   Remove the transaxle dipstick, located behind the power distribution panel and wipe all the fluid from the end with a clean rag.

4   Push the dipstick back into the transaxle until the cap seats completely. Remove the dipstick again and note the fluid on the end. The level should be in the area marked Hot (between the two upper holes in the dipstick) **(see illustration)**. If the fluid isn't hot (temperature about 100-degrees F), the level should be in the area marked Warm (between the two lower holes).

5   If the fluid level is at or below the ADD mark on the dipstick, add enough fluid to raise the level to within the marks indicated for the appropriate temperature. Fluid should be added directly into the dipstick hole, using a funnel to prevent spills.

6   Do not overfill the transaxle. Never allow the fluid level to go

above the upper hole on the dipstick - it could cause internal transaxle damage. The best way to prevent overfilling is to add fluid a little at a time, driving the vehicle and checking the level between additions.

7   Use only the transaxle fluid specified by the manufacturer. This information can be found in the *Recommended lubricants and fluids* Section at the beginning of this Chapter.

8   The condition of the fluid should also be checked along with the level. If it's a dark reddish-brown color, or if it smells burned, it should be changed. If you're in doubt about the condition of the fluid, purchase some new fluid and compare the two for color and smell.

7   Power steering fluid level check (every 250 miles or weekly)

Refer to illustrations 7.2 and 7.5

1   Unlike manual steering, the power steering system relies on fluid which may, over a period of time, require replenishing.

2   The reservoir for the power steering pump is located at the rear of the engine on the right (passenger's) side of the engine compartment **(see illustration)**.

3   The power steering fluid level can be checked with the engine either hot or cold.

4   With the engine off, use a rag to clean the reservoir cap and the area around the cap. This will help prevent foreign material from falling into the reservoir when the cap is removed.

5   Turn and pull out the reservoir cap, which has a dipstick attached to it. Remove the fluid at the bottom of the dipstick with a clean rag.

7.2 **The power steering reservoir dipstick is located at the right (passenger's side) rear of the engine compartment**

7.5 The power steering fluid dipstick on most models is marked on both sides for checking the fluid cold (as shown) or hot

Reinstall the cap to get a fluid level reading. Remove the cap again and note the fluid level. It should be at the FULL COLD mark on the dipstick **(see illustration)**. If the engine is warm, the level can be checked on the other side of the dipstick.

6   If additional fluid is required, pour the specified type directly into the reservoir using a funnel to prevent spills.

7   If the reservoir requires frequent fluid additions, all power steering hoses, hose connections, the power steering pump and the steering box should be carefully checked for leaks.

8   Engine oil and filter change (every 3000 miles or 3 months)

Refer to illustrations 8.3, 8.9, 8.14 and 8.19

1   Frequent oil changes are the most important preventive maintenance procedures that can be done by the home mechanic. When engine oil ages, it gets diluted and contaminated, which ultimately leads to premature engine wear.

2   Although some sources recommend oil filter changes every other oil change, a new filter should be installed every time the oil is changed.

3   Gather together all necessary tools and materials before beginning this procedure **(see illustration)**. **Note:** *To avoid rounding off the corners of the drain plug, use a six-point wrench or socket.*

4   In addition, you should have plenty of clean rags and newspapers handy to mop up any spills. Access to the underside of the vehicle is greatly improved if it can be lifted on a hoist, driven onto ramps or supported by jackstands. **Warning:** *Don't work under a vehicle that is supported only by a jack!*

5   If this is your first oil change on the vehicle, crawl underneath it and familiarize yourself with the locations of the oil drain plug and the oil filter. Since the engine and exhaust components will be warm during the actual work, it's a good idea to figure out any potential problems beforehand.

6   Allow the engine to warm up to normal operating temperature. If oil or tools are needed, use the warm-up time to gather everything necessary for the job. The correct type of oil to buy for your application can be found in the *Recommended lubricants and fluids* Section at the beginning of this Chapter.

7   With the engine oil warm (warm oil will drain better and more built-up sludge will be removed with it), raise the vehicle and support it securely on jackstands. They should be placed under the portions of the body designated as hoisting and jacking points (see *Jacking and towing* at the front of this manual).

8   Move all necessary tools, rags and newspapers under the vehicle. Place the drain pan under the drain plug. Keep in mind that the oil will initially flow from the engine with some force, so position the pan accordingly.

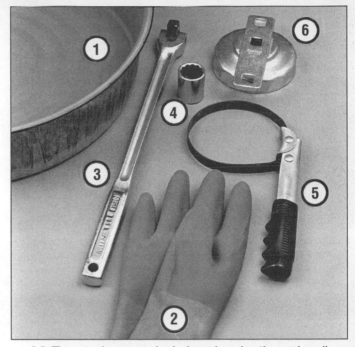

8.3 These tools are required when changing the engine oil and filter

1   **Drain pan** - It should be fairly shallow in depth, but wide to prevent spills

2   **Rubber gloves** - When removing the drain plug and filter, you will get oil on your hands (the gloves will prevent burns)

3   **Breaker bar** - Sometimes the oil drain plug is tight, and a long breaker bar is needed to loosen it

4   **Socket** - To be used with the breaker bar or a ratchet (must be the correct size to fit the drain plug - six-point preferred)

5   **Filter wrench** - This is a metal band-type wrench, which requires clearance around the filter to be effective

6   **Filter wrench** - This type fits on the bottom of the filter and can be turned with a ratchet or breaker bar (different-size wrenches are available for different types of filters)

9   Being careful not to touch any of the hot exhaust components, use the breaker bar and socket to remove the drain plug near the bottom of the oil pan **(see illustration)**. Depending on how hot the oil is, you may want to wear gloves while unscrewing the plug the final few turns.

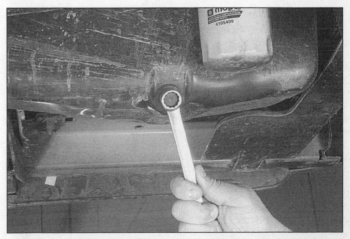

8.9 To avoid rounding off the corners, use the correct size box-end wrench or a socket to remove the engine oil drain plug

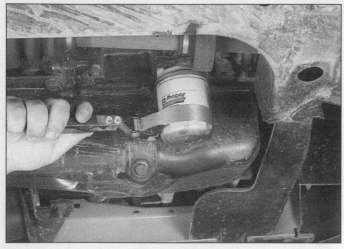

8.14 The oil filter is usually on very tight and normally will require a special wrench for removal - DO NOT use the wrench to tighten the filter!

8.19 Lubricate the oil filter gasket with clean engine oil before installing the filter on the engine

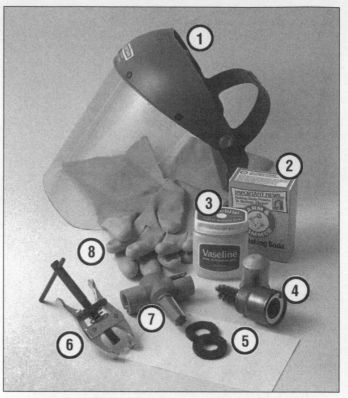

9.1 Tools and materials required for battery maintenance

1 **Face shield/safety goggles** - *When removing corrosion with a brush, the acidic particles can easily fly up into your eyes*
2 **Baking soda** - *A solution of baking soda and water can be used to neutralize corrosion*
3 **Petroleum jelly** - *A layer of this on the battery posts will help prevent corrosion*
4 **Battery post/cable cleaner** - *This wire brush cleaning tool will remove all traces of corrosion from the battery posts and cable clamps*
5 **Treated felt washers** - *Placing one of these on each post, directly under the cable clamps, will help prevent corrosion*
6 **Puller** - *Sometimes the cable clamps are very difficult to pull off the posts, even after the nut/bolt has been completely loosened. This tool pulls the clamp straight up and off the post without damage*
7 **Battery post/cable cleaner** - *Here is another cleaning tool which is a slightly different version of Number 4 above, but it does the same thing*
8 **Rubber gloves** - *Another safety item to consider when servicing the battery; remember that's acid inside the battery!*

10   Allow the oil to drain into the pan. It may be necessary to move the pan further under the engine as the oil flow reduces to a trickle.

11   After all the oil has drained, clean the plug thoroughly with a rag. Small metal particles may cling to it and would immediately contaminate the new oil.

12   Clean the area around the oil pan opening and reinstall the plug. Tighten it securely.

13   Move the drain pan into position under the oil filter.

14   Now use the filter wrench to loosen the oil filter **(see illustration)**.

15   Sometimes the oil filter is on so tight it cannot be loosened, or it's positioned in an area inaccessible with a conventional filter wrench. Other type of tools, which fit over the end of the filter and turned with a ratchet/breaker bar, are available and may be better suited for removing the filter. If the filter is extremely tight, position the filter wrench near the threaded end of the filter, close to the engine.

16   Completely unscrew the old filter. Be careful, it's full of oil. Empty the old oil inside the filter into the drain pan.

17   Compare the old filter with the new one to make sure they're identical.

18   Use a clean rag to remove all oil, dirt and sludge from the area where the oil filter mounts on the engine. Check the old filter to make sure the rubber gasket isn't stuck to the engine mounting surface.

19   Apply a light coat of oil to the rubber gasket on the new oil filter **(see illustration)**.

20   Attach the new filter to the engine following the tightening directions printed on the filter canister or packing box. Most filter manufacturers recommend against using a filter wrench due to the possibility of overtightening and damaging the canister.

21   Remove all tools and materials from under the vehicle, being careful not to spill the oil in the drain pan. Lower the vehicle off the jackstands.

22   Move to the engine compartment and locate the oil filler cap on the engine **(see illustration 4.5)**.

23   If the filler opening is obstructed, use a funnel when adding oil.

24   Pour the specified amount of new oil into the engine. Wait a few minutes to allow the oil to drain to the pan, then check the level on the dipstick (see Section 4 if necessary). If the oil level is at or above the Add mark, start the engine and allow the new oil to circulate.

9.5 On these models the battery is secured by a clamp at the base - make sure the nut is tight (arrow)

9.6a Battery terminal corrosion usually appears as light, fluffy powder

25   Run the engine for only about a minute, then shut it off. Immediately look under the vehicle and check for leaks at the oil pan drain plug and around the oil filter. If either one is leaking, tighten with a bit more force.

26   With the new oil circulated and the filter now completely full, recheck the level on the dipstick. If necessary, add enough oil to bring the level to the Full mark on the dipstick.

27   During the first few trips after an oil change, make it a point to check for leaks and keep a close watch on the oil level.

28   The old oil drained from the engine cannot be reused in its present state and should be disposed of. Oil reclamation centers, auto repair shops and gas stations will normally accept the oil. After the oil has cooled, it should be drained into containers (plastic bottles with screw-on tops are preferred) for transport to a disposal site.

9   Battery check, maintenance and charging (every 7,500 miles or 6 months)

Refer to illustrations 9.1, 9.5, 9.6a, 9.6b, 9.6c, 9.7a and 9.7b

1   A routine preventive maintenance program for the battery in your vehicle is the only way to ensure quick and reliable starts. But before performing any battery maintenance, make sure that you have the proper equipment necessary to work safely around the battery **(see illustration)**.

2   There are also several precautions that should be taken whenever battery maintenance is performed. Before servicing the battery, always turn the engine and all accessories off and disconnect the cable from the negative terminal of the battery.

3   The battery produces hydrogen gas, which is both flammable and explosive. Never create a spark, smoke or light a match around the battery. Always charge the battery in a ventilated area.

4   Electrolyte contains poisonous and corrosive sulfuric acid. Do not allow it to get in your eyes, on your skin on your clothes. Never ingest it. Wear protective safety glasses when working near the battery. Keep children away from the battery.

5   Note the external condition of the battery. If the positive terminal and cable clamp on your vehicle's battery is equipped with a rubber protector, make sure that it's not torn or damaged. It should completely cover the terminal. Look for any corroded or loose connections, cracks in the case or cover or loose hold-down clamp nut **(see illustration)**. Also check the entire length of each cable for cracks and frayed conductors.

6   If corrosion, which looks like white, fluffy deposits **(see illustration)** is evident, particularly around the terminals, the battery should be removed for cleaning. Loosen the cable clamp nuts with a wrench, being careful to remove the negative cable first, and slide them off the terminals **(see illustrations)**. If necessary, remove the thermoguard and disconnect the hold-down clamp nut, remove the clamp and lift the battery from the engine compartment.

9.6b Loosen the cable clamp with a wrench - sometimes special battery pliers are required for this procedure if corrosion has caused deterioration of the nut hex (always remove the ground cable first and hook it up last!)

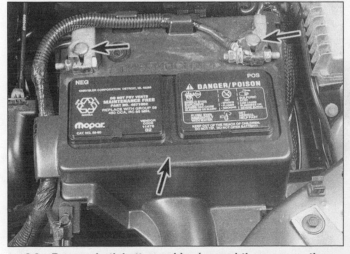

9.6c Remove both battery cables (arrows) then remove the thermoguard (arrow)

9.7a When cleaning the cable clamps, all corrosion must be removed (the inside of the clamp is tapered to match the taper on the post, so don't remove too much material)

9.7b Regardless of the type of tool used on the battery posts, a clean, shiny surface should be the result

7   Clean the cable clamps thoroughly with a battery brush or a terminal cleaner and a solution of warm water and baking soda **(see illustration)**. Wash the terminals and the top of the battery case with the same solution but make sure that the solution doesn't get into the battery. When cleaning the cables, terminals and battery top, wear safety goggles and rubber gloves to prevent any solution from coming in contact with your eyes or hands. Wear old clothes too - even diluted, sulfuric acid splashed onto clothes will burn holes in them. If the terminals have been extensively corroded, clean them up with a terminal cleaner **(see illustration)**. Thoroughly wash all cleaned areas with plain water.

8   Before reinstalling the battery in the engine compartment, inspect the plastic battery carrier. If it's dirty or covered with corrosion, remove it and clean it in the same solution of warm water and baking soda.

9   If removed, reinstall the battery carrier back into the engine compartment. Position the battery with the positive (+) terminal toward the left (driver's) side and reinstall the battery back into the battery carrier. Make sure that no parts or wires are laying on the carrier during installation of the battery.

10   Install the thermoguard, then install a pair of specially treated felt washers around the terminals (available at auto parts stores), then coat the terminals and the cable clamps with petroleum jelly or grease to prevent further corrosion. Install the cable clamps and tighten the nuts, being careful to install the negative cable last.

11   Install the hold-down clamp and nut. Tighten the nut only enough to hold the battery firmly in place. Overtightening this nut can crack the battery case.

Charging

12   Remove all of the cell caps (if equipped) and cover the holes with a clean cloth to prevent spattering electrolyte. Disconnect the negative battery cable and hook the battery charger leads to the battery posts (positive to positive, negative to negative), then plug in the charger. Make sure it is set at 12 volts if it has a selector switch.

13   If you're using a charger with a rate higher than two amps, check the battery regularly during charging to make sure it doesn't overheat. If you're using a trickle charger, you can safely let the battery charge overnight after you've checked it regularly for the first couple of hours.

14   If the battery has removable cell caps, measure the specific gravity with a hydrometer every hour during the last few hours of the charging cycle. Hydrometers are available inexpensively from auto parts stores - follow the instructions that come with the hydrometer. Consider the battery charged when there's no change in the specific gravity reading for two hours and the electrolyte in the cells is gassing (bubbling) freely. The specific gravity reading from each cell should be very close to the others. If not, the battery probably has a bad cell(s).

15   Some batteries with sealed tops have built-in hydrometers on the top that indicate the state of charge by the color displayed in the hydrometer window. Normally, a bright-colored hydrometer indicates a full charge and a dark hydrometer indicates the battery still needs charging. Check the battery manufacturer's instructions to be sure you know what the colors mean. **Note:** *If may be necessary to jiggle the battery or vehicle to bring the test indicator into view.*

16   If the battery has a sealed top and no built-in hydrometer, you can hook up a digital voltmeter across the battery terminals to check the charge. A fully charged battery should read 12.6 volts or higher.

17   Further information on the battery and jump starting can be found in Chapter 5 and at the front of this manual.

10 Cooling system check (every 7,500 miles or 6 months)

Refer to illustrations 10.4a, 104b and 10.5
Warning: *The electric cooling fan(s) on these models can activate at any time the ignition switch is in the On position. Make sure the ignition is Off when working in the vicinity of the fan(s).*

1   Many major engine failures can be attributed to a faulty cooling system. If the vehicle is equipped with an automatic transaxle, the cooling system is also used to cool the transaxle fluid.

2   The cooling system should be checked with the engine cold. Do this before the vehicle is driven for the day or after it has been shut off for three or four hours.

3   Remove the radiator cap and thoroughly clean the cap (inside and out) with water. Also clean the filler neck on the radiator. All traces of corrosion should be removed.

4   Carefully check the upper and lower radiator hoses along with the smaller diameter heater hoses. Inspect the entire length of each hose, replacing any that are cracked, swollen or deteriorated **(see illustration)**. Cracks may become more apparent when a hose is squeezed **(see illustration)**.

5   Also check that all hose connections are tight **(see illustration)**. A leak in the cooling system will usually show up as white or rust-colored deposits on the areas adjoining the leak.

6   Use compressed air or a soft brush to remove bugs, leaves, and other debris from the front of the radiator or air conditioning condenser. Be careful not to damage the delicate cooling fins, or cut yourself on them.

7   Finally, have the cap and system pressure tested. If you do not have a pressure tester, most gas stations and repair shops will do this for a minimal charge.

Check for a chafed area that could fail prematurely.

Check for a soft area indicating the hose has deteriorated inside.

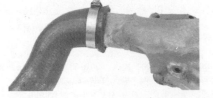

Overtightening the clamp on a hardened hose will damage the hose and cause a leak.

Check each hose for swelling and oil-soaked ends. Cracks and breaks can be located by squeezing the hose.

10.4a Hoses, like drivebelts, have a habit of failing at the worst possible time - to prevent the inconvenience of a blown radiator or heater hose, inspect them carefully as shown here

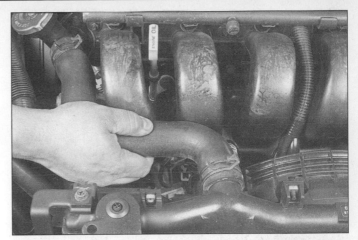

10.4b Squeeze the hose to locate cracks or breaks that cause leaks

10.5 Make sure the hose clamps are tight at all connections

11 Underhood hose check and replacement (every 7,500 miles or 6 months)

Warning: *Replacement of air conditioning hoses must be left to a dealer service department or air conditioning shop equipped to depressurize the system safely. Never remove air conditioning components or hoses until the system has been depressurized.*

General

1 High temperatures under the hood can cause the deterioration of the rubber and plastic hoses used for engine, accessory and emission systems operation. Periodic inspection should be made for cracks, loose clamps, material hardening and leaks.

2 Information specific to the cooling system hoses can be found in Section 26.

3 Some hoses use clamps to secure the hoses to fittings. Where clamps are used, check to be sure they haven't lost their tension, allowing the hose to leak. Where clamps are not used, make sure the hose hasn't expanded and/or hardened where it slips over the fitting, allowing it to leak.

Vacuum hoses

4 It's quite common for vacuum hoses, especially those in the emissions system, to be color coded or identified by colored stripes molded into the hose. Various systems require hoses with different wall thickness, collapse resistance and temperature resistance. When replacing hoses, make sure the new ones are made of the same material.

5 Often the only effective way to check a hose is to remove it completely from the vehicle. Where more than one hose is removed, be sure to label the hoses and their attaching points to insure proper reattachment.

6 When checking vacuum hoses, be sure to include any plastic T-fittings in the check. Check the fittings for cracks and the hose where it fits over the fitting for enlargement, which could cause leakage.

7 A small piece of vacuum hose (1/4-inch inside diameter) can be used as a stethoscope to detect vacuum leaks. Hold one end of the hose to your ear and probe around vacuum hoses and fittings, listening for the "hissing" sound characteristic of a vacuum leak. **Warning:** *When probing with the vacuum hose stethoscope, be careful not to allow your body or the hose to come into contact with moving engine components such as the drivebelt, cooling fan, etc.*

Fuel hose

Warning: *Gasoline is extremely flammable, so take extra precautions when you work on any part of the fuel system. Don't smoke or allow open flames or bare light bulbs near the work area, and don't work in a garage where a natural gas-type appliance (such as a water heater or clothes dryer) with a pilot light is present. If you spill any fuel on your skin, rinse it off immediately with soap and water. When you perform any kind of work on the fuel system, wear safety glasses and have a Class B type fire extinguisher on hand. Before working on any part of the fuel system, relieve the fuel system pressure (see Chapter 4).*

12.3 Remove the cap and check the mounting nut for tightness

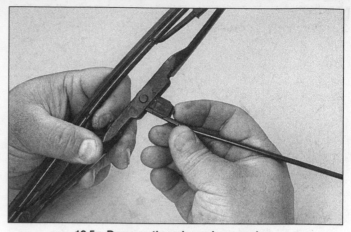

12.5a Depress the release lever and . . .

8   Check all rubber fuel hoses for damage and deterioration. Check especially for cracks in areas where the hose bends and just before clamping points, such as where a hose attaches to the fuel injection system.

9   High quality fuel line, specifically designed for fuel injection systems, should be used for fuel line replacement. **Warning:** *Never use vacuum line, clear plastic tubing or water hose for fuel lines.*

Metal lines

10   Sections of metal line are often used for fuel line between the fuel tank and fuel injection system. Check carefully to be sure the line has not been bent and crimped and that cracks have not started in the line.

11   If a section of metal fuel line must be replaced, only seamless steel tubing should be used, since copper and aluminum tubing do not have the strength necessary to withstand normal engine operating vibration.

12   Check the metal brake lines where they enter the master cylinder and brake proportioning or ABS unit (if used) for cracks in the lines or loose fittings. Any sign of brake fluid leakage calls for an immediate thorough inspection of the brake system.

12   Wiper blade inspection and replacement (every 7,500 miles or 6 months)

Refer to illustrations 12.3, 12.5a and 12.5b

1   The windshield wiper blade elements should be checked periodically for cracks and deterioration.

2   Road film can build up on the wiper blades and affect their effi-

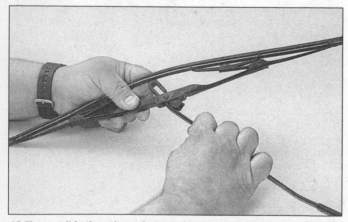

12.5b . . . slide the wiper element down out of the hook in the end of the arm

ciency, so they should be washed regularly with a mild detergent solution.

3   The action of the wiping mechanism can loosen bolts, nuts and fasteners, so they should be checked and tightened, as necessary **(see illustration)**, at the same time the wiper blades are checked.

4   Lift the wiper blade assembly away from the glass.

5   Press the release lever and slide the blade assembly out of the hook in the end of the wiper arm **(see illustrations)**.

6   Use needle-nose pliers to extract the two metal rods, then slide the element out of the frame.

7   Slide the new element into the frame and insert the two metal rods to lock it in place.

8   Installation is the reverse of removal.

13   Tire rotation (every 7,500 miles or 6 months)

Refer to illustration 13.2

1   The tires should be rotated at the specified intervals and whenever uneven wear is noticed. Since the vehicle will be raised and the tires removed anyway, this is a good time to check the brakes (see Section 18).

2   Radial tires must be rotated in a specific pattern **(see illustration)**.

3   See the information in *Jacking and towing* at the front of this manual for the proper procedures to follow when raising the vehicle and changing a tire; however, if the brakes are to be checked, don't apply the parking brake as stated. Make sure the tires are blocked to prevent the vehicle from rolling. **Note:** *Prior to raising the vehicle, slightly loosen all lug nuts.*

4   Preferably, the entire vehicle should be raised at the same time.

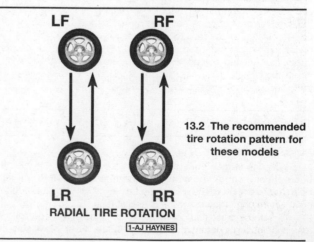

13.2 The recommended tire rotation pattern for these models

RADIAL TIRE ROTATION

1-AJ HAYNES

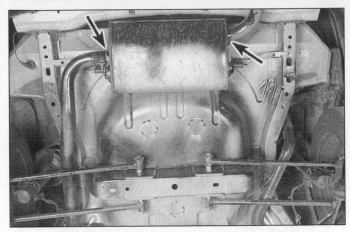

15.2a Check all exhaust connections for leaks or damage (arrows)

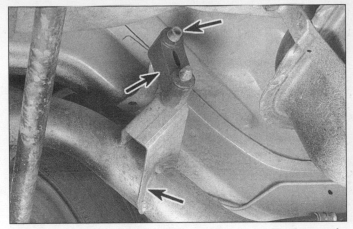

15.2b Check the exhaust system mounting bolts, brackets and hangers for damage (arrows)

This can be done on a hoist or by jacking up each corner of the vehicle and lowering it onto jackstands. Always use four jackstands and make sure the vehicle is safely supported.

5   After the tire rotation, check and adjust the tire pressures as necessary and tighten the wheel lug nuts to the torque listed in this Chapter's specifications.

14   Steering and suspension check (every 7,500 miles or 6 months)

1   Whenever the front of the vehicle is raised for service it is a good idea to visually check the suspension and steering components for wear and damage.
2   Indications of wear and damage include excessive play in the steering wheel before the front wheels react, excessive lean around corners, body movement over rough roads or binding at some point as the steering wheel is turned.
3   Before the vehicle is raised for inspection, test the shock absorbers by pushing down to rock the vehicle at each corner. If it does not come back to a level position within one or two bounces, the shocks are worn and should be replaced. As this is done, check for squeaks and unusual noises from the suspension components. Check the shock absorbers for fluid leakage. Information on shock absorbers and suspension components can be found in Chapter 10.
4   Now raise the front end of the vehicle and support it securely with jackstands placed under the jacking and hoisting points (see *Jacking and towing* at the front of this manual). Because of the work to be done, the vehicle must be stable and safely supported.
5   Crawl under the vehicle and check for loose bolts, broken or disconnected parts and deteriorated rubber bushings on all suspension and steering components. Look for grease or fluid leaking from around the steering gear boots. Check the power steering hoses and connections for leaks. Check the steering joints for wear.
6   Have an assistant turn the steering wheel from side-to-side and check the steering components for free movement, chafing and binding. If the wheels don't respond the movement of the steering wheel, try to determine where the slack is located.

15   Exhaust system check (every 7,500 or 6 months)

Refer to illustrations 15.2a and 15.2b
1   With the engine cold (at least three hours after the vehicle has been driven), check the complete exhaust system from its starting point at the engine to the end of the tailpipe. This should be done on a hoist where unrestricted access is available.
2   Check the pipes and connections for signs of leakage and/or corrosion indicating a potential failure **(see illustration)**. Make sure that all

brackets and hangers are in good condition and tight **(see illustration)**.
3   At the same time, inspect the underside of the body for holes, corrosion and open seams which may allow exhaust gases to enter the passenger compartment. Seal all body openings with silicone sealant or body putty.
4   Rattles and other noises can often be traced to the exhaust system, especially the mounts and hangers. Try to move the pipes, muffler and catalytic converter. If the components can come into contact with the body, secure the exhaust system with new mounts.
5   This is also an ideal time to check the running condition of the engine by inspecting the very end of the tailpipe. The exhaust deposits here are an indication of engine state-of-tune. If the pipe is black and sooty or coated with white deposits, the engine may be in need of a tune-up (including a thorough fuel injection system inspection).

16   Manual transaxle lubricant level check (every 7500 miles or 6 months)

Refer to illustration 16.3
1   Manual transaxles do not have a dipstick. The lubricant level is checked by removing a rubber plug from the side of the transaxle case. Check the lubricant level with the engine cold.
2   Locate the plug and use a rag to clean it and the surrounding area. It may be necessary to remove the left inner fenderwell cover for access to the plug.
3   Pry the plug out with a large screwdriver **(see illustration)**. If

16.3 Pry the rubber plug from the oil fill hole on the side of the transaxle housing

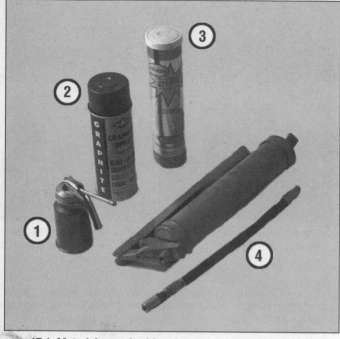

17.1 Materials required for chassis and body lubrication

1 **Engine oil** - Light engine oil in a can like this can be used for door and hood hinges
2 **Graphite spray** - Used to lubricate lock cylinders
3 **Grease** - Grease, in a variety of types and weights, is available for use in a grease gun. Check the Specifications for your requirements
4 **Grease gun** - A common grease gun, shown here with a detachable hose and nozzle, is needed for chassis lubrication. After use, clean it thoroughly

lubricant immediately starts leaking out, insert the plug back into the transaxle - the lubricant level is all right. If lubricant doesn't leak out, completely remove the plug and use a finger to feel the lubricant level. The lubricant level should be even with the bottom of the plug hole.
4   If the transaxle requires additional lubricant, use a funnel with a rubber tube or a syringe to pour or squeeze the recommended lubricant into the plug hole to restore the level. **Caution:** *Use only the specified transaxle lubricant - see* Recommended lubricants and fluids *at the beginning of this Chapter.*
5   Push the plug securely back into the transaxle. Drive the vehicle and check for leaks around the plug.

17 Chassis lubrication (every 15,000 miles or 12 months)

Refer to illustration 17.1
1   A grease gun and a cartridge filled with the proper grease (see *Recommended lubricants and fluids*), graphite spray and an oil can filled with engine oil will be required to lubricate the chassis components **(see illustration)**.
2   For easier access under the vehicle, raise it with a jack and place jackstands under the portions of the body designated as hoisting and jacking points front and rear (see *Jacking and towing* at the front of this manual). Make sure it's securely supported by the stands.
3   Before beginning, force a little grease out of the nozzle to remove any dirt from the end of the gun. Wipe the nozzle clean with a rag.
4   With the grease gun and plenty of clean rags, crawl under the vehicle and begin lubricating the components.
5   Wipe the grease fitting clean and push the nozzle firmly over it. Operate the lever on the grease gun to force grease into the fitting until

it oozes out of the joint between the two components. If grease escapes around the grease gun nozzle, the fitting is clogged or the nozzle is not completely seated on the fitting. Resecure the gun nozzle to the fitting and try again. If necessary, replace the fitting with a new one.
6   Lubricate the sliding contact and pivot points of the parking brake cable along with the cable guides and levers. This can be done by smearing some of the chassis grease onto the cable and related parts with your fingers.
7   Lower the vehicle to the ground.
8   Open the hood and smear a little chassis grease on the hood latch mechanism. Have an assistant pull the hood release lever from inside the vehicle as you lubricate the cable at the latch.
9   Lubricate all the hinges (door, hood, trunk, etc.) with the recommended lubricant to keep them in proper working order.
10   The key lock cylinders can be lubricated with spray-on graphite or silicone lubricant which is available at auto parts stores.
11   Lubricate the door weather-stripping with silicone spray. This will reduce chafing and retard wear.
12   Some components should not be lubricated for the following reasons. Some are permanently lubricated, some lubricants will cause component failure or the lubricants will be detrimental to the components operating characteristics. Do not lubricate the following: air pump, generator bearings, drive belts, idler arm assembly, front wheel bearings, rubber bushings, starter bearings, suspension strut bearings, throttle control cable, throttle linkage ball bearings and water pump bearings.

18 Brake system check (every 15,000 miles or 12 months)

Refer to illustrations 18.6, 18.14 and 18.16
Warning: *Dust created by the brake system may contain asbestos, which is harmful to your health. Never blow it out with compressed air and don't inhale any of it. An approved filtering mask should be worn when working on brakes. Do not, under any circumstances, use petroleum-based solvents to clean brake parts. Use brake system cleaner only!*
1   The brakes should be inspected every time the wheels are removed or whenever a defect is suspected. Indications of a potential brake system problem include the vehicle pulling to one side when the brake pedal is depressed, noises coming from the brakes when they are applied, excessive brake pedal travel, pulsating pedal and leakage of fluid, usually seen on the inside of the tire or wheel.

Disc brakes

2   Disc brakes can be visually checked without removing any parts except the wheels.
3   Raise the vehicle and place it securely on jackstands. Remove the wheels (see *Jacking and towing* at the front of this manual if necessary).
4   Now visible is the disc brake caliper which contains the pads. There is an outer brake pad and an inner pad. Both should be checked for wear.
5   Note the pad thickness by looking at each end of the caliper **(see illustration)** and through the inspection hole in the caliper body. If the combined thickness of the pad lining and metal shoe is 5/16-inch or less, the pads should be replaced.
6   Since it'll be difficult, if not impossible, to measure the exact thickness of the pad, if you're in doubt as to the pad quality, remove them for further inspection or replacement. See Chapter 9 for disc brake pad replacement.
7   Before installing the wheels, check for leakage around the brake hose connections leading to the caliper and for damaged brake hoses (cracks, leaks, chafed areas, etc.). Replace the hoses or fittings as necessary (see Chapter 9).
8   Also check the disc for score marks, wear and burned spots. If these conditions exist, the hub/disc assembly should be removed for servicing (see Chapter 9).

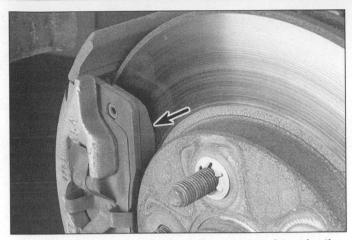

18.5 By looking at the end of the caliper, you can determine the thickness of the remaining friction material on both the inner and outer pads

18.14 If the lining is bonded to the brake shoe, measure the lining thickness from the outer surface to the metal shoe, as shown here; if the lining is riveted to the shoe, measure from the lining outer surface to the rivet head

Drum brakes

9 Raise the vehicle and support it securely on jackstands. Block the front tires to prevent the vehicle from rolling; however, don't apply the parking brake or it will lock the drums in place.

10 Remove the rear wheels, referring to *Jacking and towing* at the front of this manual if necessary.

11 Mark the hub so it can be reinstalled in the same position. Use a scribe, chalk, etc. on the drum, hub and backing plate.

12 Remove the brake drum as described in Chapter 9.

13 With the drum removed, carefully clean off any accumulations of dirt and dust using brake system cleaner. **Warning:** *Don't blow the dust out with compressed air and don't inhale any of it (it may contain asbestos, which is harmful to your health).*

14 Note the thickness of the lining material on both front and rear brake shoes. If the material has worn away to within 9/32-inch of the recessed rivets or metal backing, the shoes should be replaced **(see illustration)**. The shoes should also be replaced if they're cracked, glazed (shiny areas), or covered with brake fluid.

15 Make sure all the brake assembly springs are connected and in good condition.

16 Check the brake components for signs of fluid leakage. Carefully pry back the rubber cups on the wheel cylinder located at the top of the brake shoes **(see illustration)**. Any leakage here is an indication that the wheel cylinders should be overhauled immediately (see Chapter 9). Also, check all hoses and connections for signs of leakage.

17 Wipe the inside of the drum with a clean rag and denatured alco-

hol or brake cleaner. Again, be careful not to breathe the dangerous asbestos dust.

18 Check the inside of the drum for cracks, score marks, deep scratches and "hard spots" which will appear as small discolored areas. If imperfections cannot be removed with fine emery cloth, the drum must be taken to an automotive machine shop for resurfacing.

19 Repeat the procedure for the remaining wheel. If the inspection reveals that all parts are in good condition, reinstall the brake drums. Install the wheels and lower the vehicle to the ground.

Parking brake

20 The parking brake is operated by a foot pedal and locks the rear brake system. The easiest, and perhaps most obvious, method of periodically checking the operation of the parking brake assembly is to park the vehicle on a steep hill with the parking brake set and the transmission in Neutral. If the parking brake cannot prevent the vehicle from rolling, it needs service (see Chapter 9).

19 Fuel system check (every 15,000 miles or 12 months)

Refer to illustration 19.6

Warning: *Gasoline is extremely flammable, so take extra precautions when you work on any part of the fuel system. Don't smoke or allow open flames or bare light bulbs near the work area, and don't work in a garage where a natural gas-type appliance (such as a water heater or clothes dryer) with a pilot light is present. If you spill any fuel on your skin, rinse it off immediately with soap and water. When you perform any kind of work on the fuel system, wear safety glasses and have a Class B type fire extinguisher on hand.*

1 The fuel system on fuel injected models is under pressure even when the engine is off. Consequently, the fuel system must be depressurized (see Chapter 4) before servicing the system. Even after depressurization, if any fuel lines are disconnected for servicing, be prepared to catch some fuel as it spurts out. Plug all disconnected fuel lines immediately to prevent the tank from emptying itself.

2 The fuel system is most easily checked with the vehicle raised on a hoist where the components on the underside are readily visible and accessible.

3 If the smell of gasoline is noticed while driving, or after the vehicle has been parked in the sun, the fuel system should be thoroughly inspected immediately.

4 Remove the gas tank cap and check for damage, corrosion and a proper sealing imprint on the gasket. Replace the cap with a new one if necessary.

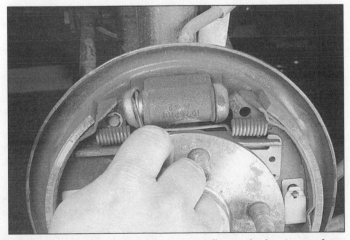

18.16 Use a small screwdriver to carefully pry the boot away from the cylinder and check for fluid leakage

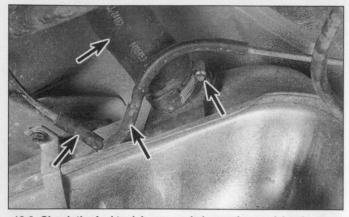

19.6 Check the fuel tank hoses and clamps (arrows) for damage and deterioration

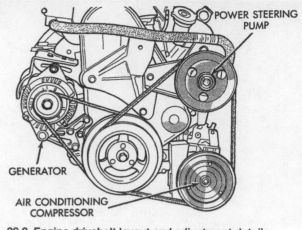

20.2 Engine drivebelt layout and adjustment details

5   Inspect the gas tank and filler neck for punctures, cracks and other damage. The connection between the filler neck and the tank is especially critical. Sometimes a rubber filler neck will leak due to loose clamps or deteriorated rubber; problems a home mechanic can usually rectify. **Warning:** *Do not, under any circumstances, try to repair a fuel tank yourself (except to replace rubber components). A welding torch*

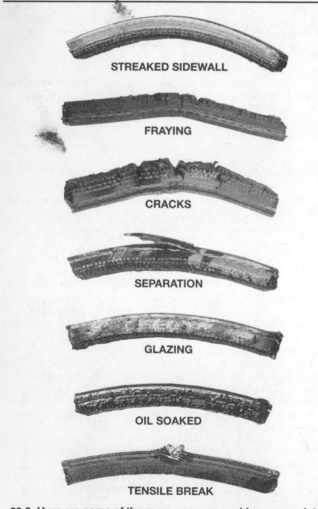

STREAKED SIDEWALL

FRAYING

CRACKS

SEPARATION

GLAZING

OIL SOAKED

TENSILE BREAK

20.3 Here are some of the more common problems associated with V-belts (check the belts very carefully to prevent an untimely breakdown)

or any open flame can easily cause the fuel vapors to explode if the proper precautions are not taken.
6   Carefully check all rubber hoses and metal lines leading away from the fuel tank. Check for loose connections, deteriorated hoses, crimped lines and damage of any kind **(see illustration)**. Follow the lines up to the front of the vehicle, carefully inspecting them all the way. Repair or replace damaged sections as necessary (see Chapter 4).

20   Drivebelt check, adjustment and replacement (every 15,000 miles or 12 months)

Refer to illustrations 20.2, 20.3, 20.4, 20.5a, 20.5b and 20.5c
Warning: *The electric cooling fan(s) on these models can activate at any time the ignition switch is in the On position. Make sure the ignition is Off when working in the vicinity of the fan(s).*
1   The drivebelts, or V-belts as they are sometimes called, at the front of the engine, play an important role in the overall operation of the vehicle and its components. Due to their function and material makeup, the belts are prone to failure after a period of time and should be inspected and adjusted periodically to prevent major damage.
2   The number of belts used depends on the engine accessories. All engines equipped with power steering and/or air conditioning are equipped with two drivebelts **(see illustration)**. One drive belt drives the alternator while the other belt drives the air conditioning compressor and/or the power steering pump.
3   With the engine off, open the hood and locate the drivebelts at the front of the engine. With a flashlight, check each belt: On V-belts, check for cracks and separation of the belt plies **(see illustration)**. On V-ribbed belts, check for separation of the adhesive rubber on both sides of the core, core separation from the belt side, a severed core, separation of the ribs from the adhesive rubber, cracking or separation of the ribs, and torn or worn ribs or cracks in the inner ridges of the ribs. On both belt types, check for fraying and glazing, which gives the belt a shiny appearance. Both sides of the belt should be inspected, which means you will have to twist the belt to check the underside. Use your fingers to feel the belt where you can't see it. If any of the above conditions are evident, replace the belt.
4   The tension of each belt is checked by pushing on it at a distance halfway between the pulleys. Apply about 10 pounds of force with your thumb and see how much the belt moves down (deflects). Measure the deflection with a ruler **(see illustration)**. The belt should deflect about 1/4-inch if the distance between pulleys is between 7 and 11 inches and around 1/2-inch if the distance is between 12 and 16 inches.

Adjustment

5   If adjustment is necessary, it's done by moving the belt-driven accessory on the bracket **(see illustrations)**. For each component,

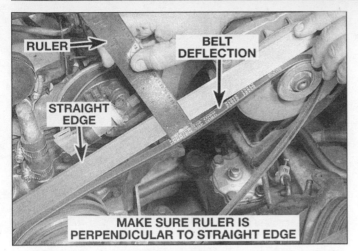

20.4 Measuring drivebelt deflection with a straightedge and ruler

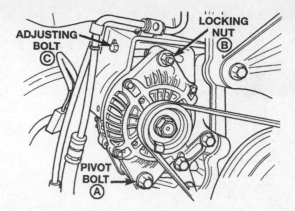

20.5a Loosen the alternator pivot bolt (A) and locking nut (B) and turn the adjusting bolt (C) to achieve the proper belt tension

20.5b Loosen the power steering pump locking bolts (A) and (B) . . .

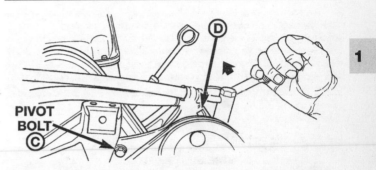

20.5c . . . and the pivot bolt (C), then, using a 1/2-inch breaker bar inserted in the square hole (D) on the power steering pump bracket, adjust the belt to the correct tension

there's a locking bolt or nut and pivot bolt. Both must be loosened slightly to move the component.

6   After the bolts and/or nut have loosened, move the component away from the engine (to tighten the belt) or toward the engine (to loosen the belt). The power steering pump is equipped with a square hole designed to accept a 1/2-inch square drive breaker bar. The bar can be used to lever the component and tension the drivebelt. Hold the accessory in position and check belt tension. If it's correct, tighten the bolts and/or nut until snug, then recheck the tension. If it's all right, tighten the bolts and/or nut completely.

Replacement

7   To replace a belt, follow the above procedures for drivebelt adjustment but slip the belt off the crankshaft pulley and remove it. If you are replacing the generator belt, you have to remove power steering or air conditioning belt first because of the way they are arranged on the crankshaft pulley. Because of this and because belts tend to wear out more or less together, it is a good idea to replace both belts at the same time. Mark each belt and its appropriate pulley groove so the replacement belts can be installed in their proper positions.

8   Take the old belt(s) to the parts store in order to make a direct comparison for length, width and design.

9   Adjust the belt(s) in accordance with the procedure previously outlined.

21   Air filter replacement (every 30,000 miles or 24 months)

Refer to illustrations 21.3a, 21.3b, 21.4a, 21.4b and 21.6

1   At the specified intervals, the air filter element should be replaced.

2   The air filter element is located in a housing in the center rear portion of the engine compartment.

3   On 1996 and later models, remove the wing nut and lift off the outer and inner air inlet ducts **(see illustrations)**.

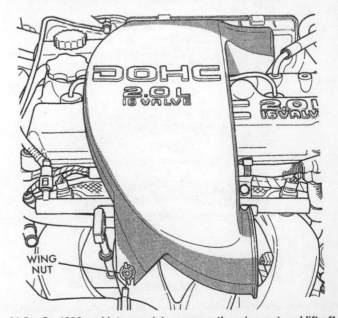

21.3a On 1996 and later models, remove the wing nut and lift off the outer air inlet duct . . .

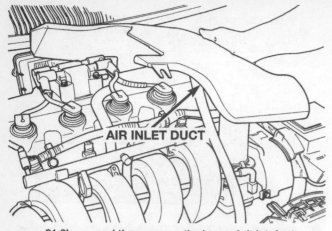

21.3b . . . and then remove the inner air inlet duct

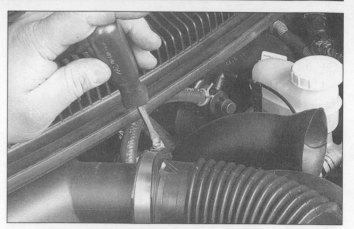

21.4a On 1995 models, using a screwdriver, loosen the clamp screw . . .

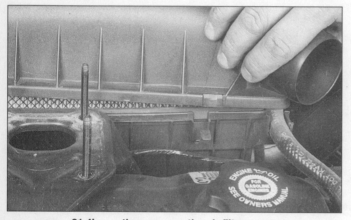

21.4b . . . then remove the air filter cover

21.6 Remove the air filter element from the case

4   On 1995 models, loosen the clamp screw and remove the air inlet tube from the air filter cover. Remove the cover (**see illustrations**).
5   On 1995 models, lift the element out.
6   On 1996 and later models, unfasten the clasps. On all models, lift the element out (**see illustration**).
7   Be careful not to drop anything down into the air cleaner assembly. Clean the inside of the housing with a rag.
8   Place the new filter element in position and install the cover(s). Be sure to tighten any hose clamps which were loosened or removed.

22 Automatic transaxle fluid and filter change (every 30,000 miles or 24 months)

Refer to illustrations 22.3, 22.4, 22.5 and 22.7
1   The automatic transaxle fluid and filter should be changed and the magnet cleaned at the recommended intervals.
2   Raise the front of the vehicle and support it securely on jackstands. Apply the parking brake.

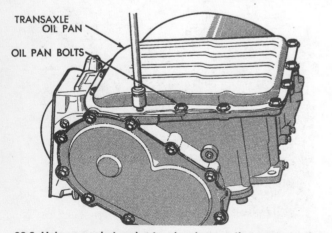

22.3 Using a socket and extension, loosen, then remove, the transaxle pan bolts

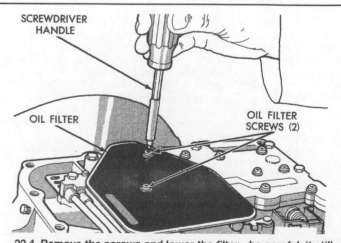

22.4 Remove the screws and lower the filter - be careful, it still contains residual fluid

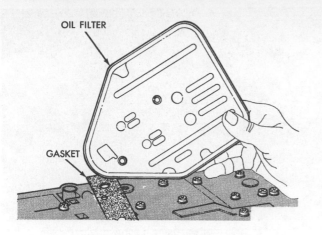

22.5 Install the new gasket and filter

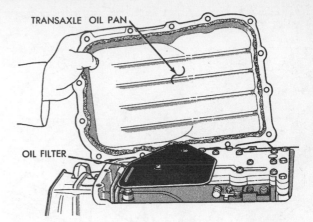

22.7 Apply a 1/8-inch bead of RTV sealant to the pan sealing surface, position the pan on the transaxle and install the bolts

3   Position a container under the transaxle fluid pan. Loosen the pan bolts **(see illustration)**. Completely remove the bolts along the rear of the pan. Tap the corner of the pan to break the seal and allow the fluid to drain into the container (the remaining bolts will prevent the pan from separating from the transaxle). Remove the remaining bolts and detach the pan.
4   Remove the screws and remove the filter **(see illustration)**.
5   Install the new gasket and filter **(see illustration)**. Tighten the filter screws securely.
6   Carefully remove all traces of old sealant from the pan and transaxle body (don't nick or gouge the sealing surfaces). Clean the magnet in the pan with a clean, lint-free cloth.
7   Apply a 1/8-inch bead of RTV sealant to the pan sealing surface **(see illustration)** and to the underside of the pan bolt flanges, then position the pan on the transaxle. Install the bolts and tighten them to the torque listed in this Chapter's Specifications following a criss-cross pattern. Work up to the final torque in three or four steps.
8   Lower the vehicle and add four quarts of the specified fluid (see *Recommended lubricants and fluids* at the beginning of this Chapter) to the transaxle. Start the engine and allow it to idle for at least two minutes, then move the shift lever through each of the gear positions, ending in Park or Neutral. Check for fluid leakage around the pan.
9   If necessary, add more fluid (a little at a time) until the level is between the Add and Full marks (be careful not to overfill it).
10   Make sure the dipstick is seated completely or dirt could get into the transaxle.

23   Automatic transaxle band adjustment (every 30,000 miles or 24 months)

Refer to illustrations 23.3, 23.8 and 23.9
1   The transaxle bands should be adjusted when specified in the maintenance schedule or at the time of a fluid and filter change.

Kickdown band

2   The kickdown band adjustment screw and locknut is located at the top left side of the transaxle case. To access the adjustment screw, remove the battery and the battery tray. Detach the fuse box and position it aside.
3   Loosen the locknut approximately five turns and make sure the adjusting screw turns freely **(see illustration)**.
4   Tighten the adjusting screw to the torque listed in this Chapter's Specifications.
5   Back the adjusting screw off the specified number of turns (see the Specifications section at the beginning of this Chapter).
6   Hold the screw in position and tighten the locknut to the torque listed in this Chapter's Specifications.

Low-Reverse band

7   To gain access to the Low-Reverse band, the transaxle pan must be removed (see Section 22).
8   Pry off the parking rod E-clip and remove the parking rod **(see illustration)**.

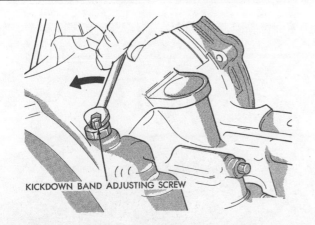

23.3 Loosen the locknut approximately five turns, then make sure the adjusting screw turns freely

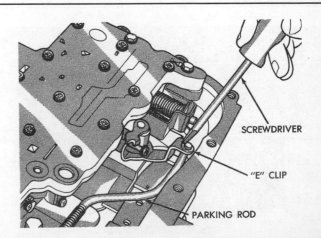

23.8 Pry off the parking rod E-clip and remove the parking rod

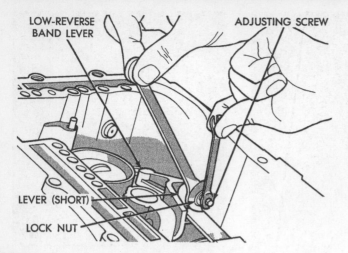

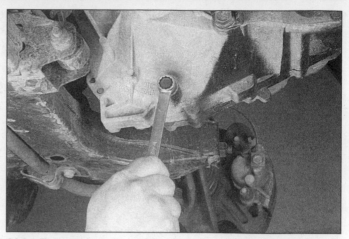

24.2a To avoid rounding off the corners, use the correct size box-end wrench or a socket to remove the transaxle oil drain plug . . .

23.9 Loosen the locknut approximately five turns, then tighten the adjusting screw to the specified torque

9   Loosen the locknut approximately five turns. Use an inch-pound torque wrench to tighten the adjusting screw to the torque listed in this Chapter's Specifications **(see illustration)**.
10   Back the screw off the specified number of turns (see the Specifications section at the beginning of this Chapter).
11   Hold the adjusting screw in position and tighten the locknut securely.
12   Push the shift pawl in the transaxle case to the rear and reinstall the parking rod.
13   Install the pan and refill the transaxle (see Section 22).

24   Manual transaxle lubricant change (every 30,000 or 24 months)

Refer to illustrations 24.2a and 24.2b
1   Raise the front of the vehicle and support it securely on jack-stands. Apply the parking brake.
2   Remove the drain plug and drain the fluid into a suitable container **(see illustrations)**.
3   Install the drain plug and tighten it securely.
4   Fill the transaxle with the recommended lubricant (see *Recommended lubricants and fluids* at the beginning of this Chapter), adding the fluid through the fill hole **(see illustration 16.3)**, until the level is at the bottom edge of the hole.

25   Driveaxle boot check (every 30,000 miles or 24 months)

Refer to illustration 25.3
1   If the driveaxle boots are damaged or deteriorated, serious and costly damage can occur to the CV joints the boots are designed to protect. The boots should be inspected very carefully at the recommended intervals.
2   Raise the front of the vehicle and support it securely on jack-stands (see *Jacking and towing* at the front of this manual if necessary).
3   Crawl under the vehicle and check the four driveaxle boots (two on each driveaxle) very carefully for cracks, tears, holes, deteriorated rubber and loose or missing clamps **(see illustration)**. If the boots are dirty, wipe them clean before beginning the inspection.
4   If damage or deterioration is evident, replace the boots with new ones and check the CV joints for damage (see Chapter 8).

26   Cooling system servicing (draining, flushing and refilling) (every 30,000 miles or 24 months)

Refer to illustration 26.5
Warning 1: *Do not allow coolant (antifreeze) to come in contact with your skin or painted surfaces of the vehicle. Flush contaminated areas immediately with plenty of water. Don't store new coolant or leave old*

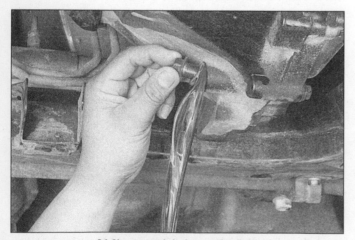

24.2b . . . and drain out the fluid

25.3 Check the driveaxle boot for cracks and/or leaking grease

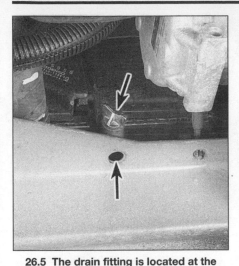

26.5 The drain fitting is located at the bottom of the radiator and the coolant will drain through the opening in the drain hole in the facia panel

27.4a Remove the retaining bolts from the front . . .

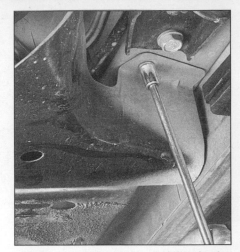

27.4b . . . and rear of the fuel filter/tank module protective cover, then remove the cover

coolant lying around where it's accessible to children or pets - they're attracted by its sweet smell. Ingestion of even a small amount of coolant can be fatal! Wipe up garage floor and drip pan spills immediately. Keep antifreeze containers covered and repair cooling system leaks as soon as they're noticed. Check with local authorities about disposing of used antifreeze. Many communities have collection centers which will see that antifreeze is disposed of properly.

Warning 2: *The electric cooling fan(s) on these models can activate at any time, even when the ignition switch is in the Off position. Disconnect the fan motor(s) or the negative battery cable when working in the vicinity of the fan(s).*

1   Periodically, the cooling system should be drained, flushed and refilled to replenish the coolant (antifreeze) mixture and prevent formation of rust and corrosion, which can impair the performance of the cooling system and cause engine damage. When the cooling system is serviced, all hoses and the radiator cap should be checked and replaced, if necessary.

Draining

2   At the same time the cooling system is serviced, all hoses and the radiator cap should be inspected and replaced if faulty (see Section 10).

3   With the engine cold, remove the pressure cap and set the heater control to maximum heat.

4   Move a large container under the radiator drain fitting to catch the coolant mixture as it's drained.

5   Open the drain fitting at the bottom of the radiator **(see illustration)**. The coolant will drain out through the drain hole in the front facia panel.

6   Remove the thermostat housing and the thermostat (see Chapter 3).

Flushing

7   Place a hose (common garden hose is okay) in the upper radiator hose and then the thermostat opening in the engine block and flush the system until the water runs clear at all drain outlets.

8   In severe cases of contamination or clogging of the radiator, remove it (see Chapter 3) and reverse flush it. This involves inserting the hose in the bottom radiator outlet to allow the clean water to run against the normal flow, draining out through the top. A radiator repair shop should be consulted if further cleaning or repair is necessary.

9   When the coolant is regularly drained and the system refilled with the correct coolant mixture there should be no need to employ chemical cleaners or descalers.

10   Disconnect the coolant reservoir hose, remove the reservoir and flush it with clean water.

Refilling

11   Install the thermostat and the thermostat housing (see Chapter 3).

12   Install the reservoir, reconnect the hose and close the radiator drain fitting.

13   Add the correct mixture of coolant through the filler neck until it reaches the pressure cap seat.

14   Add the same coolant mixture to the reservoir until it the level is between the FULL and ADD marks.

15   Run the engine until normal operating temperature is reached and, with the engine idling, add coolant up to the correct level. Install the pressure cap.

16   Always refill the system with a mixture of coolant and water in the proportion called for on the coolant container or in your owner's manual. Chapter 3 also contains information on coolant mixtures.

17   Keep a close watch on the coolant level and the various cooling system hoses during the first few miles of driving and check for any coolant leaks Tighten the hose clamps and add more coolant mixture as necessary.

27 Fuel filter replacement (1995 models only) (every 30,000 miles or 24 months)

Refer to illustrations 27.4a, 27.4b, 27.6a and 27.6b

Warning: *Gasoline is extremely flammable, so take extra precautions when you work on any part of the fuel system. Don't smoke or allow open flames or bare light bulbs near the work area, and don't work in a garage where a natural gas-type appliance (such as a water heater or clothes dryer) with a pilot light is present. If you spill any fuel on your skin, rinse it off immediately with soap and water. When you perform any kind of work on the fuel system, wear safety glasses and have a Class B type fire extinguisher on hand.*

Note: *Only 1995 models use a replaceable inline fuel filter. The manufacturer does not suggest periodic fuel filter replacement on 1996 and later models. See Chapter 4 Section 14 if the fuel filter requires replacement due to fuel contamination on a 1996 and later model.*

1   Relief the fuel system pressure (see Chapter 4).

2   Raise the rear of the vehicle and support it securely on jackstands.

3   The fuel filter is a disposable type and is mounted on the frame rail next to the fuel pump module on the right (passenger's) side of the fuel tank.

4   Remove the mounting bolts and the splash pan protecting the fuel filter and fuel pump module **(see illustrations)**.

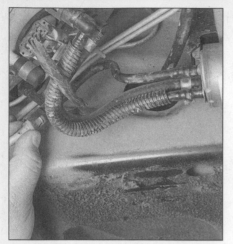

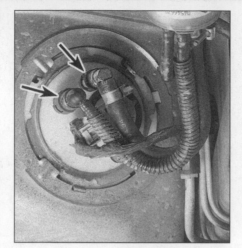

27.6a Squeeze the retainer tabs to detach the fuel line quick-disconnect fittings

27.6b Disconnect the two fittings from the fuel tank module

28.2a Remove the clamp with pliers and pull the PCV valve hose off the fitting (SOHC model shown)

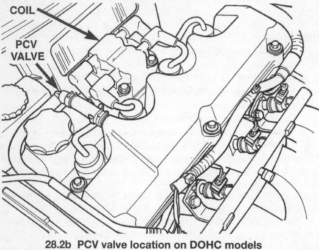

28.2b PCV valve location on DOHC models

28.4 Disconnect the valve from the valve cover hose (SOHC model shown)

5   Wrap a cloth around the fuel lines to catch the residual fuel (which may still be under slight pressure).

6   Squeeze the retainer tabs together and disconnect the fuel lines from the fuel filter hose and the fuel tank module fittings **(see illustrations)**.

7   Remove the mounting bolts and detach the filter and bracket from the frame.

8   Place the new filter into position, install the mounting bolts and tighten securely.

9   Lubricate the fittings with clean engine oil and insert the quick disconnect fittings into place until they lock together.

10   Start the engine and check carefully for leaks at the hose connections.

11   Reinstall the splash pan.

28 Positive Crankcase Ventilation (PCV) valve check and replacement (every 30,000 miles or 24 months)

Refer to illustrations 28.2a, 28.2b and 28.4

1   The PCV valve is located in the rubber hose connected to the intake manifold plenum and the valve cover.

2   With the engine idling at normal operating temperature, remove the clamp and detach the hose from the valve fitting on the intake manifold hose **(see illustrations)**.

3   A hissing sound should be heard. Place your finger over the valve opening. If there's no vacuum at the valve, check for a plugged hose, plenum port or valve. Replace any plugged or deteriorated hoses.

4   To replace the valve, disconnect the valve from the valve cover hose **(see illustration)**.

5   When purchasing a replacement PCV valve, make sure it's for your particular vehicle and engine size. Compare the old valve with the new one to make sure they're the same.

6   Insert the valve into the valve cover hose, then push the valve into the intake manifold hose and install the clamp.

29 Evaporative emissions control system check (every 30,000 miles or 24 months)

Refer to illustration 29.2

1   The function of the evaporative emissions control system is to draw fuel vapors from the gas tank and fuel system, store them in a charcoal canister and route them to the intake manifold during normal engine operation.

2   The most common symptom of a fault in the evaporative emissions system is a strong fuel odor in the engine compartment. If a fuel odor is detected, inspect the charcoal canister, located in the engine compartment on the passenger's side, behind the front lower facia.

29.2 Inspect the charcoal canister hoses for cracks and make sure the hose clamps are tight

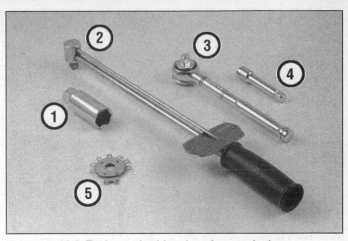

30.2 Tools required for changing spark plugs

1 *Spark plug socket* - This will have special padding inside to protect the spark plug's porcelain insulator
2 *Torque wrench* - Although not mandatory, using this tool is the best way to ensure the plugs are tightened properly
3 *Ratchet* - Standard hand tool to fit the spark plug socket
4 *Extension* - Depending on model and accessories, you may need special extensions and universal joints to reach one or more of the plugs
5 *Spark plug gap gauge* - This gauge for checking the gap comes in a variety of styles. Make sure the gap for your engine is included

Check the canister and all hoses for damage and deterioration **(see illustration)**.
3   The evaporative emissions control system is explained in more detail in Chapter 6.

30   Spark plug check and replacement (every 30,000 miles or 24 months)

Refer to illustrations 30.2, 30.5a, 30.5b, 30.8a, 30.8b, 30.10, 30.12 and 30.13

1   The spark plugs are located on the top of the engine.
2   In most cases the tools necessary for spark plug replacement include a spark plug socket which fits onto a ratchet (this special socket will be padded inside to protect the porcelain Insulators on the new plugs), various extensions and a feeler gauge to check and adjust the spark plug gap **(see illustration)**. A special plug wire removal tool is available for separating the wire boot from the spark plug, but it isn't absolutely necessary. Since these engines are equipped with an aluminum cylinder head, a torque wrench should be used for tightening the spark plugs.
3   The best approach when replacing the spark plugs is to purchase the new spark plugs beforehand, adjust them to the proper gap and then replace each plug one at a time. When buying the new spark plugs, be sure to obtain the correct plug for your specific engine. This

information can be found in the Specifications at the front of this Chapter, in the owner's manual or on the Vehicle Emissions Control Information label located under the hood. If differences exist between the sources, purchase the spark plug type specified on the VECI label as it was printed for your specific engine.
4   Allow the engine to cool completely before attempting to remove any of the plugs. During this cooling off time, each of the new spark plugs can be inspected for defects and the gaps can be checked.
5   The gap is checked by inserting the proper thickness gauge between the electrodes at the tip of the plug **(see illustration)**. The gap between the electrodes should be as specified on the VECI label in the engine compartment or as listed in this Chapter's Specifications. The wire should touch each of the electrodes. If the gap is incorrect, use the adjuster on the thickness gauge body to bend the curved side electrode slightly until the proper gap is obtained **(see illustration)**.

30.5a Spark plug manufacturers recommend using a wire-type gauge when checking the gap - if the wire does not slide between the electrodes with a slight drag, adjustment is required

30.5b To change the gap, bend the side electrode only, as indicated by the arrows, and be very careful not to crack or chip the porcelain insulator surrounding the center electrode

30.8a Pull on the spark plug wire boot and twist it back-and-forth while pulling it from the ignition coil pack . . .

30.8b . . . then use a twisting motion to free the boot and wire from the spark plug

Also, at this time check for cracks in the spark plug body (if any are found, the plug should not be used). If the side electrode is not exactly over the center one, use the adjuster to align the two.

6   Cover the fender to prevent damage to the paint.

7   On 1996 and later models, remove the screw and lift off the air inlet duct (see illustration 21.3a).

8   **Note:** *Due to the short length of the spark plug wire, always dis-connect the spark plug wire from the ignition coil pack first.* With the engine cool, first disconnect one of the spark plug wires from the igni-tion coil pack (see illustration). Pull only on the boot at the end of the wire; don't pull on the wire. Use a twisting motion to free the boot and wire from the valve cover (see illustration). Disconnect the same spark plug wire from the spark plug, using the same method used when disconnecting the wire from the ignition coil. Disconnect the spark plug wire from any retaining clips.

9   If compressed air is available, use it to blow any dirt or foreign material away from the spark plug area. A common bicycle pump will also work. The idea here is to eliminate the possibility of material falling into the cylinder through the plug hole as the spark plug is removed.

10   Place the spark plug socket over the plug and remove it from the engine by turning it in a counterclockwise direction (see illustration).

11   Compare the spark plug with the chart on the inside back cover of this manual to get an indication of the overall running condition of the engine.

12   It's a good idea to lightly coat the threads of the spark plugs with anti-seize compound (see illustration) to insure that the spark plugs

30.10 Use a ratchet and extension to remove the spark plugs

do not seize in the aluminum cylinder head.

13   It's often difficult to insert spark plugs into their holes without cross-threading them. To avoid this possibility, fit a piece of 3/8-inch ID rubber hose over the end of the spark plug (see illustration). The flexible hose acts as a universal joint to help align the plug with the plug hole. Should the plug begin to cross-thread, the hose will slip on the spark plug, preventing thread damage. Tighten the spark plug to the torque listed in this Chapter's Specifications.

30.12 Apply a thin coat of anti-seize compound to the spark plug threads

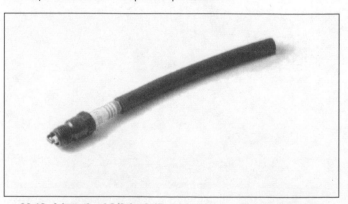

30.13 A length of 3/8-inch ID rubber hose will save time and prevent damaged threads when installing the spark plugs

14   Attach the plug wire to the new spark plug, again using a twisting motion on the boot until it is firmly seated on the end of the spark plug. Attach the other end to the ignition coil pack, then attach the spark plug wire to any retaining clips to keep the wires in their proper location on the valve cover.

15   Follow the above procedure for the remaining spark plugs, replacing them one at a time to prevent mixing up the spark plug wires.

31 Spark plug wire check and replacement (every 30,000 miles or 24 months)

1   The spark plug wires should be checked at the recommended intervals or whenever new spark plugs are installed.

2   The wires should be inspected one at a time to prevent mixing up the order which is essential for proper engine operation.

3   With the engine cool, first disconnect one of the spark plug wires from the ignition coil. **Note:** *Due to the short length of the spark plug wire, always disconnect the spark plug wire from the ignition coil first.* Pull only on the boot at the end of the wire; don't pull on the wire. Use a twisting motion to free the boot and wire from the coil. Disconnect the same spark plug wire from the spark plug, using the same method used when disconnecting the wire from the ignition coil (see Section 30). Disconnect the spark plug wire from any retaining clips.

4   Check inside the boot for corrosion, which will look like a white, crusty powder (don't mistake the white dielectric grease used on some plug wire boots for corrosion protection).

5   Now push the wire and boot back onto the end of the spark plug. It should be a tight fit on the plug end. If not, remove the wire and use a pair of pliers to carefully crimp the metal connector inside the wire boot until the fit is snug.

6   Now push the wire and boot back into the end of the ignition coil terminal. It should be a tight fit in the terminal. If not, remove the wire and use a pair of pliers to carefully crimp the metal connector inside the wire boot until the fit is snug.

7   Now, using a cloth, clean each wire along its entire length. Remove all built-up dirt and grease. As this is done, inspect for burned areas, cracks and any other form of damage. Bend the wires in several places to ensure that the conductive material inside hasn't hardened. Repeat the procedure for the remaining wires.

8   If new spark plug wires are needed, purchase a complete set for your particular engine. The terminals and rubber boots should already be installed on the wires. Replace the wires one at a time to avoid mixing up the firing order and make sure the terminals are securely seated in the coil pack and on the spark plugs.

9   Attach the plug wire to the new spark plug and to the ignition coil pack using a twisting motion on the boot until it is firmly seated on the end of the spark plug and to the ignition coil pack. Attach the spark plug wire to any retaining clips to keep the wires in their proper location on the valve cover.

32 Seat belt check (every 30,000 miles or 24 months)

1   Check the seat belts, buckles, latch plates and guide loops for obvious damage and signs of wear.

2   See if the seat belt reminder light comes on when the key is turned to the Run or Start positions. A chime should also sound.

3   The seat belts are designed to lock up during a sudden stop or impact, yet allow free movement during normal driving. Make sure the retractors return the belt against your chest while driving and rewind the belt fully when the buckle is unlatched.

4   If any of the above checks reveal problems with the seat belt system, replace parts as necessary.

1

Notes

Chapter 2 Part A Engines

Contents

2A

Specifications

General

Bore	3.445 inches
Stroke	3.267 inches
Displacement	122 cubic inches (2.0 liters)
Firing order	1-3-4-2

Camshaft

Bearing journal diameter
SOHC
No. 1	1.619 to 1.6199 inches
No. 2	1.634 to 1.635 inches
No. 3	1.650 to 1.651 inches
No. 4	1.666 to 1.667 inches
No. 5	1.682 to 1.6829 inches
DOHC	1.021 to 1.022 inches

Bearing bore diameter
SOHC
No. 1	1.622 to 1.6228 inches
No. 2	1.637 to 1.638 inches
No. 3	1.653 to 1.654 inches
No. 4	1.669 to 1.670 inches
No. 5	1.685 to 1.6858 inches
DOHC	1.024 to 1.025 inches

End play
SOHC	0.0059 inch
DOHC	0.002 to 0.006 inch
Bearing clearance	0.0027 to 0.003 inch

Lobe lift
SOHC
Intake	0.307 inch
Exhaust	0.277 inch

DOHC
Intake	0.344 inch
Exhaust	0.314 inch

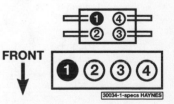

Cylinder numbering and coil terminal location

Camshaft (continued)

Cylinder head warpage
    Head gasket surface .... 0.004 inch maximum
    Exhaust manifold mounting surfaces .... 0.006 inch maximum

Intake and exhaust manifolds

Warpage limit .... 0.006 inch maximum

Rocker arm shaft assemblies (SOHC engine only)

Rocker arm shaft diameter .... 0.786 to 0.7867 inch
Rocker arm inside diameter .... 0.787 to 0.788 inch
Rocker arm-to-shaft clearance .... 0.0006 to 0.0021 inch
Rocker arm shaft retainer width
    Intake .... 1.12 inches
    Exhaust
        No. 1 and No. 5 .... 1.14 inches
        No. 2, No. 3 and No. 4 .... 1.59 inches

Oil pump

Cover warpage limit .... 0.003 inch
Inner rotor thickness (minimum) .... 0.301 inch
Outer rotor thickness (minimum) .... 0.301 inch
Outer rotor diameter (minimum) .... 3.148 inch
Rotor-to-pump cover clearance .... 0.004 inch
Outer rotor-to-housing clearance .... 0.015 inch
Inner rotor-to-outer rotor lobe clearance .... 0.008 inch
Pressure relief spring free length .... 2.39 inches (approximate)

Torque specifications   **Ft-lbs (unless otherwise indicated)**

Camshaft bearing cap bolts (DOHC)
    Caps 2 through 5 .... 105 inch-lbs
    Caps 1 and 6 18
Camshaft position sensor bolt .... 85 inch-lbs
Camshaft sprocket bolt 85
Crankshaft damper bolt 105
Cylinder head bolts
    SOHC
        Step 1 25
        Step 2 50
        Step 3 50
        Step 4 .... Tighten an additional 90-degrees (1/4 turn)
    DOHC **(see illustration 14.14b for bolt numbers)**
        Step 1
            Bolts 1 through 6 25
            Bolts 7 through 10 20
        Step 2
            Bolts 1 through 6 50
            Bolts 7 through 10 20
        Step 3
            Bolts 1 through 6 50
            Bolts 7 through 10 20
        Step 4 .... Tighten an additional 90-degrees (1/4 turn)
Cylinder head cover bolts .... 105 inch-lbs
Engine mounting bracket bolts 30
Exhaust manifold-to-cylinder head bolts 16
Exhaust manifold-to-exhaust pipe bolts 20
Exhaust manifold heat shield bolts
    SOHC .... 105 inch-lbs
    DOHC .... 130 inch-lbs
Flywheel/driveplate-to-crankshaft bolts 70
Intake manifold bolts
    SOHC .... 105 inch-lbs
    DOHC 21
Oil filter adapter fastener 60
Oil pan bolts .... 105 inch-lbs
Oil pump
    Attaching bolts 21
    Cover screws .... 105 inch-lbs
    Pick-up tube bolt 21
    Relief valve cap 40

Rocker arm shaft bolts (SOHC)	21
Structural collar	
Step 1 (collar-to-oil pan bolts)...	30 in-lbs
Step 2 (collar-to-transaxle bolts)...	80
Step 3 (collar-to-oil pan bolts)...	40
Thermostat housing bolts..	16
Timing belt	
Cover bolts..	105 inch-lbs
Tensioner bolt	
SOHC...	23
DOHC...	21
Tensioner pulley assembly plate bolts	30
Tensioner pulley bolt	50
Valve cover bolts..	105 inch-lbs
Water pump mounting bolt..	105 inch-lbs

Refer to Part B for additional torque specifications

1 General information

This Part of Chapter 2 is devoted to in-vehicle engine repair procedures. Information concerning engine removal and installation and engine block and cylinder head overhaul can be found in Part B of this Chapter.

The following repair procedures are based on the assumption that the engine is installed in the vehicle. If the engine has been removed from the vehicle and mounted on a stand, many of the steps outlined in this Part of Chapter 2 will not apply.

The Specifications included in this Part of Chapter 2 apply only to the procedures contained in this Part. Part B of Chapter 2 contains the Specifications necessary for cylinder head and engine block rebuilding.

There are two types of four-cylinder engines installed in the models covered in this book: The standard 2.0L Single Overhead Camshaft (SOHC) engine and the optional 2.0L Double Overhead Camshaft (DOHC) engine.

2 Repair operations possible with the engine in the vehicle

Many major repair operations can be accomplished without removing the engine from the vehicle.

Clean the engine compartment and the exterior of the engine with some type of degreaser before any work is done. It will make the job easier and help keep dirt out of the internal areas of the engine.

Depending on the components involved, it may be helpful to remove the hood to improve access to the engine as repairs are performed (refer to Chapter 11 if necessary). Cover the fenders to prevent damage to the paint. Special pads are available, but an old bedspread or blanket will also work.

If vacuum, exhaust, oil or coolant leaks develop, indicating a need for gasket or seal replacement, the repairs can generally be made with the engine in the vehicle. The intake and exhaust manifold gaskets, oil pan gasket, camshaft and crankshaft oil seals and cylinder head gasket are all accessible with the engine in place.

Exterior engine components, such as the intake and exhaust manifolds, the oil pan, the oil pump, the water pump, the starter motor, the alternator, the distributor and the fuel system components can be removed for repair with the engine in place.

Since the camshaft(s) and cylinder head can be removed without pulling the engine, valve component servicing can also be accomplished with the engine in the vehicle. Replacement of the timing belt and sprockets is also possible with the engine in the vehicle.

In extreme cases caused by a lack of necessary equipment, repair or replacement of piston rings, pistons, connecting rods and rod bearings is possible with the engine in the vehicle. However, this practice is not recommended because of the cleaning and preparation work that must be done to the components involved.

3 Top Dead Center (TDC) for number one piston - locating

Refer to illustration 3.9

Note: *The crankshaft timing marks on both engines aren't visible until after the timing belt cover has been removed. The number one cylinder can be positioned at TDC by using this procedure without removing the timing belt cover.*

1   Top Dead Center (TDC) is the highest point in the cylinder that each piston reaches as it travels up-and-down when the crankshaft turns. Each piston reaches TDC on the compression stroke and again on the exhaust stroke, but TDC generally refers to piston position on the compression stroke. The cast-in timing mark arrow on the crankshaft timing belt pulley installed on the front of the crankshaft is referenced to the number one piston at TDC when the arrow is straight up, or at "12 o'clock", and aligned with the cast-in timing mark arrow on the oil pump housing (see Section 7).

2   Positioning a specific piston at TDC is an essential part of many procedures such as camshaft(s) removal, rocker arm removal (SOHC) timing belt and sprocket replacement.

3   In order to bring any piston to TDC, the crankshaft must be turned using one of the methods outlined below. When looking at the front of the engine, normal crankshaft rotation is clockwise. **Warning:** *Before beginning this procedure, be sure to set the emergency brake, place the transmission in Park or Neutral and disable the ignition system by disconnecting the primary electrical connector from the ignition coil pack.*

a) *The preferred method is to turn the crankshaft with a large socket and breaker bar attached to the crankshaft balancer hub bolt that is threaded into the front of the crankshaft.*

b) *A remote starter switch, which may save some time, can also be used. Attach the switch leads to the S (switch) and B (battery) terminals on the starter solenoid. Once the piston is close to TDC, discontinue with the remote switch and use a socket and breaker bar as described in the previous paragraph.*

c) *If an assistant is available to turn the ignition switch to the Start position in short bursts, you can get the piston close to TDC without out a remote starter switch. Use a socket and breaker bar as described in Paragraph a) to complete the procedure.*

4   Remove all spark plugs as this will make it easier to rotate the engine by hand.

5   Insert a compression gauge (screw-in type with a hose) in the number 1 spark plug hole. Place the gauge dial where you can see it while turning the crankshaft balancer hub bolt. **Note:** *The number one cylinder is located at the front (timing belt end) of the engine.*

6   Turn the crankshaft clockwise until you see compression building up on the gauge - you are on the compression stroke for that cylinder. If you did not see compression build up, continue with one more complete revolution to achieve TDC for the number one cylinder.

2A

3.9 Check the alignment of the camshaft timing marks (SOHC model shown)

4.5a Remove the valve cover perimeter mounting bolts . . .

7   Remove the compression gauge. Through the number one cylinder spark plug hole insert a section of wooden dowel or plastic rod and slowly push it down until it reaches the top surface of the piston crown. **Caution:** *Don't insert a metal or sharp object into the spark plug hole as the piston crown may be damaged.*

8   With the dowel or rod in place on top of the piston crown, slowly rotate the crankshaft clockwise until the dowel or rod is pushed upward, stops, and then starts to move back down. At this point, rotate the crankshaft slightly counterclockwise until the dowel or rod has reached it upper most travel. At this point the number one piston is at the TDC position.

9   Remove the timing access plug on the timing belt cover and check the alignment of the camshaft timing marks **(see the accompanying illustration or illustration 7.10b)**. At this point the camshaft(s) timing marks should be aligned. If not repeat this procedure until alignment is correct.

10   After the number one piston has been positioned at TDC on the compression stroke, TDC for any of the remaining cylinders can be located by turning the crankshaft 180-degrees (1/2-turn) at a time and following the firing order (refer to the Specifications).

4   Valve cover - removal and installation

Removal

Refer to illustrations 4.5a, 4.5b, 4.7 and 4.8

1   Disconnect the battery cable from the negative battery terminal.
2   Remove the air filter air inlet duct (see Chapter 1).
3   Remove the ignition coil pack from the valve cover (see Chapter 5).
4   Clearly label and then disconnect any emission hoses and electrical cables which connect to or cross over the valve cover.
5   Remove the valve cover bolts and lift the cover off **(see illustrations)**. If the cover sticks to the cylinder head, tap on it with a soft-face hammer or place a wood block against the cover and tap on the wood with a hammer. **Caution:** *If you have to pry between the valve cover and the cylinder head, be extremely careful not to gouge or nick the gasket surfaces of either part. A leak could develop after reassembly.*
6   Remove the valve cover perimeter rubber seal. Thoroughly clean the valve cover and remove all traces of old gasket material. Gasket removal solvents are available from auto parts stores and may prove helpful. After cleaning the surfaces, degrease them with a rag soaked in lacquer thinner or acetone.

Installation

7   Inspect the spark plug tube seal for deterioration and hardness, replace if necessary **(see illustration)**.
8   Install a new gasket on the cover, using RTV sealant to hold it in place **(see illustration)**.

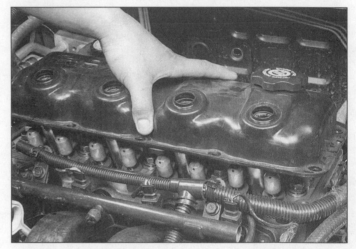

4.5b . . . and lift the cover and gasket off the cylinder head

On DOHC models, apply RTV to the camshaft cap corners and at the top edges of the half-round seal. Place the cover on the engine and install the cover bolts.

9   Tighten the bolts to the torque listed in this Chapter's Specifications. The remaining steps are the reverse of removal. When finished, run the engine and check for oil leaks.

4.7 Remove and inspect each spark plug tube seal for deterioration and hardness; install new seals as a set and make sure they are properly seated in the cover

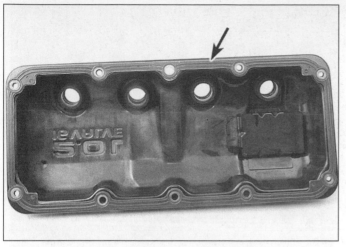

4.8 Apply a light coat of RTV onto the cover sealing surface and install the new gasket

4.12 After applying a small amount of red Loctite No. 271, or equivalent, to the lower end of the tube, install it and carefully tap the tube into place until it seats on the cylinder head

2A

5.4a Remove the bolts and all brackets mounted on the cylinder head

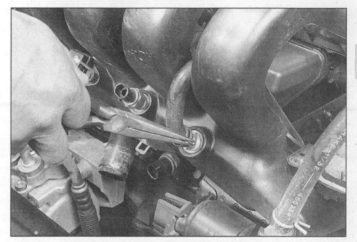

5.4b Disconnect the PCV valve hose from the intake manifold fitting

Spark plug tube replacement (SOHC engine only)

Refer to illustration 4.12

10   Grasp spark plug tube with locking pliers, carefully twist back and forth and remove the tube from cylinder head.
11   Clean locking agent from tube receptacle in cylinder head with

5.4c Disconnect all hoses from the intake manifold and cylinder head

solvent and dry.
12   Apply a small amount of red Loctite No. 271, or equivalent, around the lower end of the tube and install the tube into the cylinder head. Carefully tap the tube into the receptacle with a wood block and mallet. Tap the tube in until it seat against the cylinder head **(see illustration)**.

5   Intake manifold - removal and installation

Removal

Refer to illustrations 5.4a, 5.4b, 5.4c, 5.10, 5.12a and 5.12b

1   Relieve the fuel system pressure (see Chapter 4), then disconnect the cable from the negative battery terminal.
2   Drain the cooling system (see Chapter 1).
3   Remove the air filter air inlet duct (see Chapter 1).
4   Clearly label and disconnect all hoses, wires, brackets and emission lines which run to the fuel injection system and intake manifold **(see illustrations)**.
5   Remove the fuel rail assembly (see Chapter 4).
6   Disconnect the accelerator cables (see Chapter 4).
7   Disconnect the starter motor electrical connectors (see Chapter 5).
8   On SOHC models, remove the transmission to throttle body support bracket fasteners. Be sure to disconnect any electrical connections that are fastened to the support bracket before trying to move the parts out of the way.

5.10 Remove the mounting bolts and the EGR tube from the intake manifold, then remove the EGR valve (arrow)

5.12a Remove the intake manifold mounting bolts in a criss-cross pattern . . .

5.12b . . . then remove the intake manifold from the cylinder head

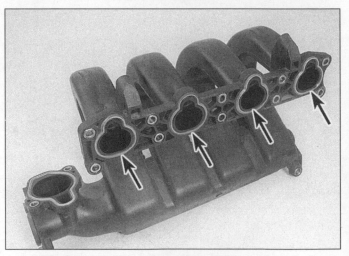

5.14 On SOHC models, inspect the condition of each O-ring seal gasket on the intake ports; replace as a set if any require replacement

9   Remove the throttle body (see Chapter 4).
10   Remove mounting bolts and remove EGR tube from intake manifold and EGR valve **(see illustration)**.
11   On SOHC models, remove the water inlet-to-intake manifold tube fastener.
12   Unbolt the intake manifold and remove it from the engine **(see illustrations)**. If it sticks, tap the manifold with a soft-face hammer or carefully pry it from the head. **Caution:** *Do not pry between gasket sealing surfaces or tap on the fuel injectors.*

Installation

Refer to illustration 5.14

13   On DOHC models, remove intake manifold gasket by carefully scraping all traces of gasket material from both the cylinder head and the intake manifold. **Caution:** *The cylinder head and intake manifold are made of aluminum and are easily nicked or gouged. Don't damage the gasket surfaces or a leak may result after the work is complete. Gasket removal solvents are available from auto parts stores and may prove helpful.*
14   On SOHC models, inspect the O-ring seal gaskets on each intake port **(see illustration)**. **Caution:** *The intake manifold is made of plastic and can be easily damaged, don't scrape hard when removing any dirt or residue. Replace the O-rings as a set if any are damaged or deteriorated.*
15   Using a straightedge and feeler gauge, check the intake manifold mating surface for warpage. Check the intake manifold surface on the cylinder head also. If the warpage on any surface exceeds the limits

listed in this Chapter's Specifications, the intake manifold and/or cylinder head must be replaced or resurfaced at an automotive machine shop.
16   Install the manifold, using a new gasket. Tighten the nuts in several stages, working from the center out, to the torque listed in this Chapter's Specifications.
17   Reinstall the remaining parts in the reverse order of removal.
18   Adjust the accelerator cable (see Chapter 4).
19   Add coolant, run the engine and check for leaks and proper operation.

6   Exhaust manifold - removal and installation

Warning: *Allow the engine to cool completely before beginning this procedure.*

Removal

Refer to illustrations 6.4, 6.5, 6.6, 6.7a, 6.7b and 6.8

1   Disconnect the battery cable from the negative terminal of the battery.
2   Remove the air filter assembly and bracket (see Chapter 4).
3   Set the parking brake and block the rear wheels. Raise the vehicle and support it securely on jackstands.

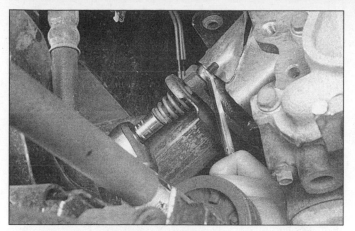

6.4 Using a box wrench on the nuts and a socket on the bolt, remove the shoulder bolts, springs and nuts securing the exhaust pipe to the exhaust manifold

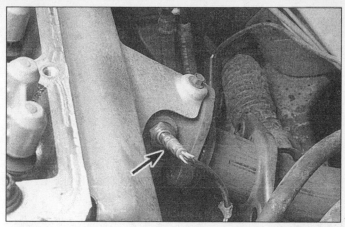

6.5 Follow the harness from the upstream oxygen sensor (arrow) and disconnect the connector

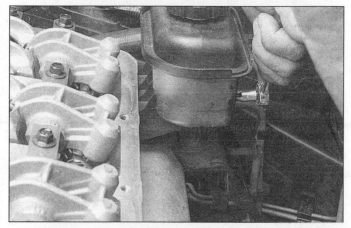

6.6 Remove the power steering reservoir mounting bolts, keep the reservoir upright and move it out of the way

6.7a Remove the heat shield perimeter mounting bolts . . .

4   Working from under the vehicle, remove the shoulder bolts, springs and nuts that secure the exhaust pipe to the exhaust manifold **(see illustration).** Apply penetrating oil to the threads to make removal easier.

5   Disconnect the wiring harness from the upstream oxygen sensor **(see illustration).**

6   Remove the mounting bolts and move the power steering reservoir out of the way **(see illustration).**

7   Remove the bolts that secure the heat shield to the exhaust

manifold and remove the heat shield **(see illustrations).**

8   Remove the exhaust manifold mounting bolts and remove the exhaust manifold **(see illustration).**

Installation

9   Using a wire brush, clean the locking agent from the exhaust manifold bolts, replacing any that show thread damage.

10   Using a scraper, remove all traces of gasket material from the mating surfaces and inspect them for wear and cracks. **Caution:** *When*

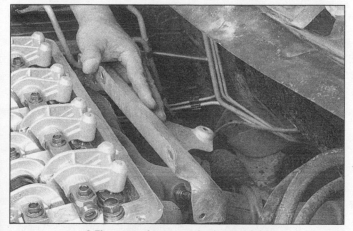

6.7b . . . and remove the heat shield

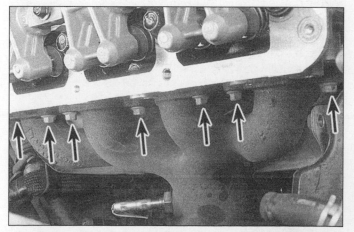

6.8 Remove the exhaust manifold mounting bolts (arrows) and separate the exhaust manifold from the cylinder head

2A

7.6 Insert a large screwdriver or bar through the opening in the pulley and wedge it against the engine block, then loosen the bolt with a socket and breaker bar

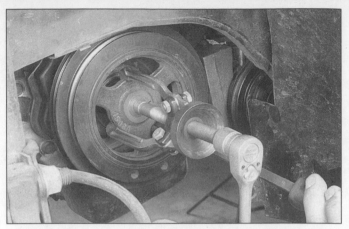

7.7 Install a 3-jaw puller onto the damper pulley, position the center post of the puller on the crankshaft end (use the proper insert to keep from damaging the crankshaft threads), tighten the puller and remove the pulley from the crankshaft

removing gasket material from any surface, especially aluminum, be very careful not to scratch or gouge the gasket surface. Any damage to the surface may a leak after reassembly. Gasket removal solvents are available from auto parts stores and may prove helpful.

11   Using a straightedge and feeler gauge, check the exhaust manifold mating surface for warpage. Check the exhaust manifold surface on the cylinder head also. If the warpage on any surface exceeds the limits listed in this Chapter's Specifications, the exhaust manifold and/or cylinder head must be replaced or resurfaced at an automotive machine shop.

12   Apply red Loctite No. 271 to the mounting bolt threads prior to installation.

13   Install a new gasket, the manifold and bolts. Tighten the bolts in several stages, working from the center out, to the torque listed in this Chapter's Specifications.

14   Reinstall the remaining parts in the reverse order of removal. Install a new gasket between the exhaust manifold and exhaust pipe.

15   Run the engine and check for exhaust leaks.

7   Timing belt - removal, inspection and installation

Caution: *If the timing belt failed with the engine operating, damage to the valves may have occurred. Perform an engine compression check to confirm damage.*

Removal

Refer to illustrations 7.6, 7.7, 7.9a, 7.9b, 7.10a, 7.10b and 7.11

Caution: *Do not turn the crankshaft or camshaft(s) after the timing belt has been removed, as this will damage the valves from contact with the pistons. Do not try to turn the crankshaft with the camshaft sprocket bolt(s) and do not rotate the crankshaft counterclockwise.*

1   Position the number one piston at Top Dead Center (see Section 3).

2   Disconnect the battery cable from the negative battery terminal.

3   Remove the drivebelts (see Chapter 1).

4   Set the parking brake and block the rear wheels. Raise the front of the vehicle and support it securely on jackstands.

5   Remove the right (passenger) side fender inner splash shield.

6   Loosen the large bolt in the center of the crankshaft damper pulley. It might be very tight, to break it loose insert a large screwdriver or bar through the opening in the pulley to keep the pulley stationary and loosen the bolt with a socket and breaker bar **(see illustration)**.

7   Install a 3-jaw puller onto the damper pulley and remove the pulley from the crankshaft **(see illustration)**. Use the proper insert to keep the puller from damaging the crankshaft bolt threads. If the pulley is difficult to remove, tap the center bolt of the puller with a brass mallet to break it loose. Reinstall the bolt with a spacer so you can rotate the crankshaft later.

8   Remove the mounting bolts and the right (passenger) engine

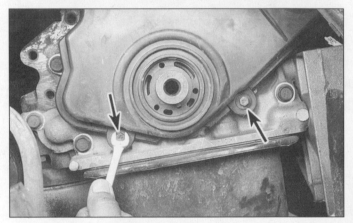

7.9a Remove the two lower bolts (arrows) that attach the timing belt outer cover to the engine

mounting bracket (see Section 19). **Note:** *Make sure the engine is supported with a floor jack placed under the oil pan. Place a wood block on the jack head to prevent the floor jack from denting or damaging the oil pan.*

9   Remove the lower bolts and upper clips that secure the timing belt outer cover and lift off the cover **(see illustrations)**.

10   Make sure the camshaft sprocket timing marks align before removing the timing belt **(see illustrations)**. **Note:** *If you plan to reuse the timing belt, paint an arrow on it to indicate the direction of rotation (clockwise).*

7.9b Carefully remove the timing belt outer cover

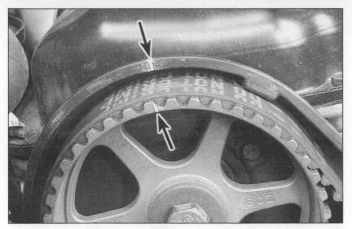

7.10a Note the locations of the camshaft sprocket timing mark and the mark on the timing belt rear cover (arrows) (SOHC models) - If you'll be reusing the timing belt, mark an arrow on the belt in the direction of rotation (clockwise) so it may be reinstalled in the same direction

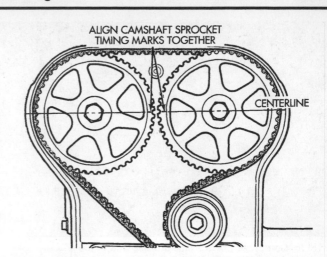

7.10b Camshaft timing mark details (DOHC models) - to check the marks while the timing belt cover is still installed, remove the bolt and lift off the upper center cover

2A

7.11 Loosen, then remove the timing belt tensioner mounting bolts (arrows) and remove the tensioner

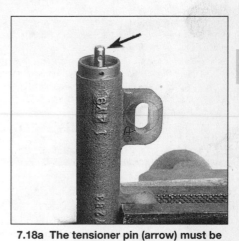

7.16 Carefully inspect the timing belt - bending it backwards will often make wear or damage more apparent

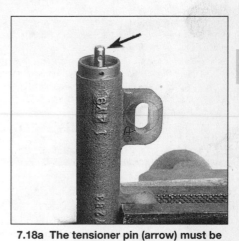

7.18a The tensioner pin (arrow) must be compressed into the tensioner housing prior to installation

11   Loosen, then remove the timing belt tensioner mounting bolts (see illustration) and remove the tensioner. Note: The tensioner plunger will extend when the assembly is removed.

12   Carefully slip the timing belt off the sprockets and set it aside. If you plan to reuse the timing belt, place it in a plastic bag - do not allow the belt to come in contact with any type of oil or water at this will greatly shorten belt life.

7.18b Place the tensioner in the vise so the hole (arrow) faces up

13   If it's necessary to remove the camshaft sprocket(s), belt tensioner pulley and/or rear cover (for camshaft seal replacement, see Section 9).

14   Inspect the oil pump seal for leaks and replace it if necessary (see Section 16).

Inspection

Refer to illustration 7.16

15   Rotate the tensioner pulley and idler pulley by hand and move them side-to-side to detect roughness and excess play. Visually inspect the sprockets for any signs of damage and wear. Replace parts as necessary.

16   Inspect the timing belt for cracks, separation, wear, missing teeth and oil contamination. Replace the belt if it's in questionable condition (see illustration).

17   Check the automatic tensioner for leaks or any obvious damage to the body.

Installation

Refer to illustrations 7.18a, 7.18b, 7.18c, 7.20a, 7.20b, 7.20c and 7.24

18   The tensioner pin must be compressed into the tensioner housing prior to installation. Place the tensioner in the vise so the surface with the hole faces up. Slowly compress the tensioner, then install a 5/64-inch Allen wrench or similar tool through the body to retain the plunger in this position until it is installed (see illustrations). Remove the tensioner from the vise.

7.18c Compress the pin with the vise and place a small Allen wrench (arrow), or something similar, through the hole to keep the pin retracted for reassembly on the engine

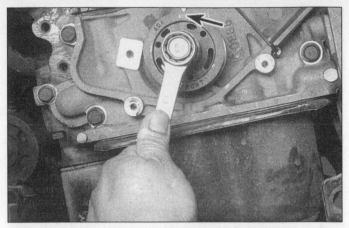

7.20a Using a box wrench, rotate the crankshaft timing sprocket until the TDC mark on the sprocket is aligned with the arrow on the oil pump housing (arrow) . . .

7.20b . . . then back it off counterclockwise 3 notches BTDC (arrows)

7.20c Rotate the crankshaft timing sprocket clockwise to 1/2-notch BTDC (arrows)

19   Confirm that the camshaft sprocket timing marks are aligned **(see illustration 7.10a and 7.10b)**.

20   Position the crankshaft timing sprocket as follows **(see illustrations)**:

a) *Initially align the TDC mark on the sprocket with the arrow on the oil pump housing.*

b) *Back it off counterclockwise 3 notches BTDC.*

c) *Rotate the crankshaft timing sprocket clockwise to 1/2-notch BTDC.*

21   Install the timing belt as follows; first place the belt onto the crankshaft sprocket, maintaining tension on the belt, wrap it around the water pump sprocket, idler pulley (DOHC models) and camshaft sprocket, then slip the belt onto the tensioner pulley.

22   To take the slack out of the timing belt, rotate the crankshaft timing sprocket clockwise to align the marks (TDC), make sure the camshaft sprocket timing marks remain aligned.

23   Install the tensioner assembly- don't tighten the bolts at this time.

24   Place a torque wrench on the center bolt of the tensioner pulley and apply 250 inch-lbs of torque. With the torque applied to the tensioner pulley, move the tensioner up against the tensioner pulley bracket and tighten the tensioner bolts to the torque listed in this Chapter's Specifications **(see illustration)**. Remove the torque wrench.

25   Release the Allen wrench or pin from the tensioner. The timing belt tension is correct when the pin can be withdrawn and reinserted easily. Double check that the timing marks on both the camshaft sprocket(s) and crankshaft sprocket are still aligned at TDC.

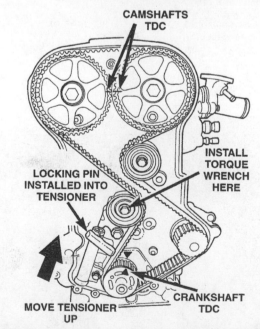

7.24 Using a torque wrench on the tensioner pulley, apply 250 inch-lbs of torque, move the tensioner up against the tensioner pulley bracket and tighten the tensioner mounting bolts

8.2 Attach a bolt-type gear puller to the crankshaft sprocket and remove the sprocket from the crankshaft

26   Using the bolt in the center of the crankshaft sprocket, turn the crankshaft clockwise through two complete revolutions. **Caution:** *If you feel resistance while turning the crankshaft - STOP, the valves may be hitting the pistons from incorrect valve timing. Stop and re-check the valve timing.* **Note:** *The camshaft and crankshaft sprocket marks will align every two revolutions of the crankshaft.* Recheck the alignment of the timing marks. If the marks do not align properly, loosen the tensioner, slip the belt off the camshaft sprocket, realign the marks, reinstall the belt, and check the alignment again.
27   Reinstall the remaining parts in the reverse order of removal.
28   Start the engine and road test the vehicle.

8   Crankshaft front oil seal - replacement

Refer to illustrations 8.2, 8.3, 8.5 and 8.6
Caution: *Do not rotate the camshaft(s) or crankshaft when the timing belt is removed or damage to the engine may occur.*
1   Remove the timing belt (see Section 7).
2   Pull the crankshaft sprocket from the crankshaft with a bolt-type gear puller **(see illustration)**. Remove the Woodruff key.
3   Wrap the tip of a small screwdriver with tape. Working from below the right inner fender, use the screwdriver to pry the seal out of its bore **(see illustration)**. Take care to prevent damaging the oil pump assembly, the crankshaft and the seal bore.

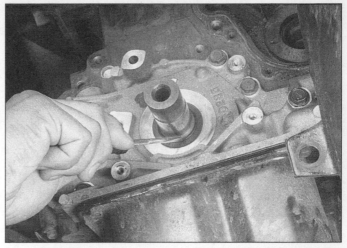

8.3 Working from below the right inner fender, use the screwdriver to pry the seal out of its bore

4   Thoroughly clean and inspect the seal bore and sealing surface on the crankshaft. Minor imperfections can be removed with emery cloth. If there is a groove worn in the crankshaft sealing surface (from contact with the seal), installing a new seal will probably not stop the leak.
5   Lubricate the new seal with engine oil and drive the seal into place with a hammer and a appropriate size socket **(see illustration)**.
6   The remaining steps are the reverse of removal. **Note:** *Position the crankshaft sprocket with the word FRONT facing out* **(see illustration)**.
7   Reinstall the timing belt and related components as described in Section 7.
8   Run the engine and check for oil leaks.

9   Camshaft oil seal - replacement

Refer to illustrations 9.4a, 9.4b, 9.5, 9.6, 9.8 and 9.10
Caution: *Do not rotate the camshaft(s) or crankshaft when the timing belt is removed or damage to the engine may occur.*
1   Remove the timing belt (see Section 7).
2   Rotate the crankshaft counterclockwise until the crankshaft sprocket is three notches BTDC **(see illustration 7.20b)**. This will prevent engine damage if the camshaft sprocket is inadvertently rotated during removal.

8.5 Lubricate the new seal with engine oil and drive the seal into place with a hammer and socket

8.6 Position the crankshaft sprocket with the word FRONT facing out and install it onto the crankshaft

2A

9.4a Remove the tensioner pulley mounting bracket bolts (arrows) . . .

9.4b . . . and remove the pulley and bracket assembly

3   Remove the camshaft sprocket bolt(s) and using two large screw-drivers, lever the sprocket(s) off the camshaft. **Note:** *It will be necessary to use an appropriate tool to hold the camshaft sprocket(s) while loosening the bolt(s). A strap-type damper/pulley holder tool is available at most auto parts stores and is recommended for this procedure.*
4   Remove the bolts securing the tensioner pulley bracket to the engine block and remove the pulley and bracket assembly **(see illustrations)**. Do not attempt to loosen the center bolt on the pulley or the pulley pivot bolt, remove the pulley and bracket together. Remove the idler pulley on DOHC models.
5   Remove the bolts securing the rear cover to the engine block and remove the rear cover **(see illustration).**
6   Note how far the seal is seated in the bore, then carefully pry it out with a small screwdriver **(see illustration)**. Don't scratch the bore or damage the camshaft in the process (if the camshaft is damaged, the new seal will end up leaking).
7   Clean the bore and coat the outer edge of the new seal with engine oil or multi-purpose grease. Also lubricate the seal lip.
8   Using a socket with an outside diameter slightly smaller than the outside diameter of the seal **(see illustration)**, carefully drive the new seal into place with a hammer. Make sure it's installed squarely and driven in to the same depth as the original. If a socket isn't available, a short section of pipe will also work.
9   Install the rear timing belt cover, tensioner pulley/bracket and idler pulley (DOHC models).
10   Install the camshaft sprocket, aligning the pin in the camshaft with

9.5 Remove the rear timing belt cover

the hole in the sprocket **(see illustration)**. Use an appropriate tool to hold the camshaft sprocket(s) while tightening the bolt(s) to the torque listed in this Chapter's Specifications.
11   Reinstall the timing belt (see Section 7).
12   Run the engine and check for oil leaks at the camshaft seal.

9.6 Carefully pry the camshaft seal out of the bore - DO NOT nick or scratch the camshaft or seal bore

9.8 Gently tap the new seal into place with the spring side toward the engine

9.10 When installing a camshaft sprocket, make sure the pin in the camshaft is aligned with the hole in the sprocket (arrows)

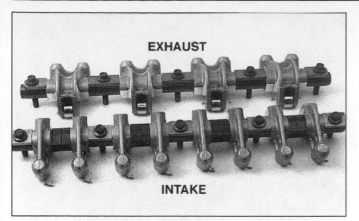

10.6 Intake and exhaust rocker arms and shaft assemblies are unique - don't intermix any of the parts

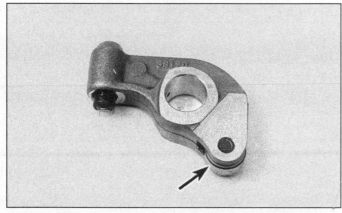

10.11 On SOHC models, visually check the rocker-arm-shaft bore and roller (arrow) for score marks, pitting and evidence of overheating (blue, discolored areas)

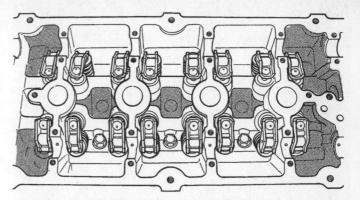

10.9 On DOHC models, once the camshafts have been removed, the rocker arms can be lifted off. If necessary, the lash adjuster below the rocker arm can also be removed - be sure to keep the rocker arms and lash adjusters in order so they can be returned to their original locations!

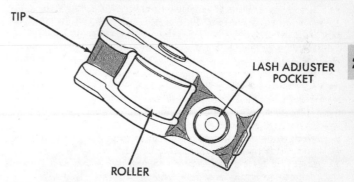

10.12 On DOHC models, check the roller, tip and lash-adjuster contact area for score marks and pitting

10 Rocker arm assembly - removal, inspection and installation

Removal

SOHC engine

Refer to illustration 10.6

1   Position the number one piston at Top Dead Center (see Section 3).
2   Disconnect the negative cable from the battery.
3   Remove the valve cover (see Section 4).
4   Prior to removing the rocker arm shafts, mark the front shaft as the intake rocker arm shaft and the rear shaft as the exhaust. **Caution:** *Do not interchange the rocker arms onto a different shaft as this could lead to premature wear.*
5   Loosen the rocker arm shaft bolts 1/4-turn at a time each, until the spring pressure is relieved, in the reverse of the TIGHTENING sequence **(see illustration 10.18)**. Completely loosen the bolts, but do not remove them, since leaving them in place will prevent the assembly from falling apart when it is lifted off the cylinder head.
6   Lift the rocker arms and shaft assemblies from the cylinder head and set them on the workbench **(see illustration)**.
7   Inspect the rocker arm assemblies.

DOHC engine

Refer to illustration 10.9

8   Remove both camshafts (see Section 11).
9   Once the camshafts have been removed, the rocker arms can be lifted off **(see illustration)**. **Caution:** *Each rocker arm must be placed back in the same location it was removed from, so mark each rocker*

arm or place them in a container (such as an egg carton) so they won't get mixed up. The lash adjusters can remain in the head at this time, unless they are being replaced (see Section 12).

Inspection

Refer to illustrations 10.11 and 10.12

10   On SOHC models, disassemble the rocker arm shaft components **(see illustration 10.6)**. **Caution:** *Before disassembly, mark the rocker arm shafts, rocker arms, shaft retainers and plastic shaft spacers (intake only) so all the parts are reassembled in the same locations they were removed from. To keep the rocker arms and related parts in order, it's a good idea to remove them and put them onto two lengths of wire (such as unbent coat hangers) in the same order as they're removed, marking each wire (which simulates the rocker shaft) as to which end would be the front of the engine.*
11   On SOHC models, visually check the rocker arms for wear **(see illustration)**. Replace them if evidence of wear or damage is found.
12   On DOHC models, visually check the rocker arm tip, roller and lash adjuster pocket for wear **(see illustration)**. Replace them if evidence of wear or damage is found.
13   On SOHC models, check all the rocker shaft components. Look for worn or scored shafts, etc. and replace any of the parts found to be damaged.

Installation

Refer to illustrations 10.16, 10.17 and 10.18

14   On SOHC models, prior to installation, make sure each lash adjuster is at least partially full of oil (see Section 12).
15   When reassembling the parts, be sure they all go back on in the same locations they were removed from.

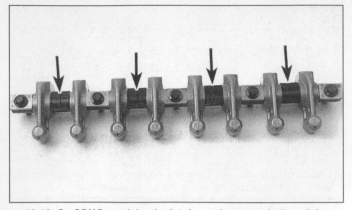

10.16 On SOHC models, the intake rocker arm shaft and the plastic spacers (arrows) must be installed in the correct location

10.17 Both rocker arm shafts must be positioned with the notch facing UP (arrows)

16   On SOHC models, on the intake rocker arm shaft, make sure the plastic spacers are installed on the shaft in the correct location **(see illustration)**.

17   On SOHC models, prior to installing the rocker arm shaft, to prevent internal damage, rotate the crankshaft to position the crankshaft timing sprocket at the 3 notches BTDC **(see illustration 7.20b)**. Install the rocker arm assemblies with the notch in each rocker arm shaft located at the timing belt end of the engine and facing UP **(see illustration)**.

18   On SOHC models, tighten the rocker arm bolts in sequence **(see illustration)** to the torque listed in this Chapter's Specifications.

19   The remainder of the reassembly is in the reverse order of disassembly. Run the engine and check for oil leaks and proper operation.

11   Camshaft - removal, inspection and installation

Removal
SOHC engine

Note: *The camshaft can't be removed with the cylinder head installed in the vehicle.*

1   Remove the cylinder head (see Section 14).
2   Remove the camshaft position sensor (see Chapter 6).
3   Carefully withdraw the camshaft from the opening in the rear of the cylinder head. **Caution:** *Don't damage the camshaft lobes or bearing journals during removal and installation through the opening in the cylinder head..*

DOHC engine

Refer to illustrations 11.5 and 11.6

4   Remove the timing belt (see Section 7). Remove the camshaft sprockets and the rear timing belt cover (see section 8).
5   The camshaft bearing caps are identified with their numbered location in the cylinder head **(see illustration)**.
6   Remove the outside bearing caps at each end of the camshafts first. Remove the remaining camshaft bearing caps, loosening the bolts a little at a time to prevent distorting the camshaft(s) by loosening the caps in the sequence shown **(see illustration)**. Once the bearing caps have all been loosened enough for removal, they may still be difficult to remove. Using the bearing cap bolts for extra leverage, move the cap back and forth to loosen the cap from the cylinder head. If they are still difficult to remove you can tap them gently with a soft face mallet so they can be lifted off. **Caution:** *Store them in order so they can be returned to their original locations, with the same side facing forward.*
7   Carefully lift the camshafts out of the cylinder head. Mark the camshafts INTAKE and EXHAUST, they cannot be mixed-up.

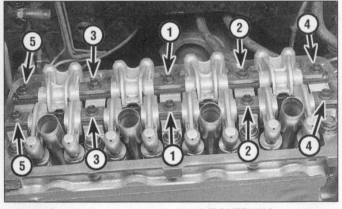

10.18 Camshaft rocker arm shaft bolt TIGHTENING sequence (SOHC models)

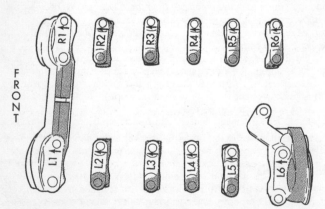

11.5 Note the camshaft bearing cap location numbers - they must be reinstalled in the same location in the cylinder head

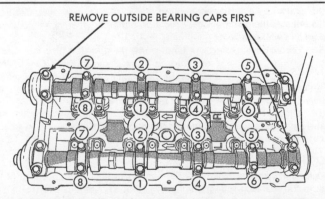

11.6 First, remove the outside bearing caps, then remove the remaining camshaft bearing caps in the sequence shown

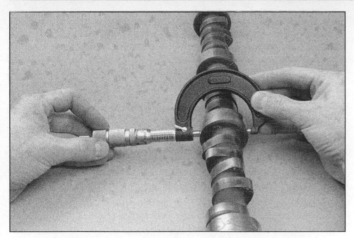

11.9 Measure the camshaft bearing journal diameters
with a micrometer

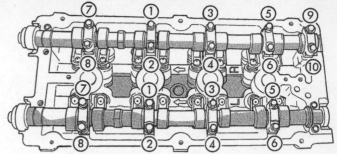

11.20 Except for the No. 1 and No. 6 end caps, install the bearing
caps and tighten in the sequence shown

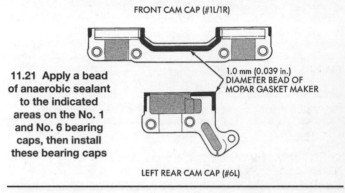

FRONT CAM CAP (#1L/1R)

11.21 Apply a bead of anaerobic sealant to the indicated areas on the No. 1 and No. 6 bearing caps, then install these bearing caps

1.0 mm (0.039 in.)
DIAMETER BEAD OF
MOPAR GASKET MAKER

LEFT REAR CAM CAP (#6L)

Inspection

Refer to illustration 11.9

8   Remove the seal(s) from the camshaft(s) and thoroughly clean the camshaft(s) and the gasket surface. Visually inspect the camshaft for wear and/or damage to the lobe surfaces, bearing journals and seal contact surfaces. Visually inspect the camshaft bearing surfaces in the cylinder head and bearing caps (DOHC) for scoring and other damage.

9   Measure the camshaft bearing journal diameters **(see illustration)**. Measure the inside diameter of the camshaft bearing surfaces in the cylinder head, using a telescoping gauge (on DOHC models, temporarily install the bearing caps). Subtract the journal measurement from the bearing measurement to obtain the camshaft bearing oil clearance. Compare this clearance with this Chapter's Specifications. Lubricate the camshaft journals with clean engine oil and install the camshaft(s) into the cylinder head. On SOHC models, install the camshaft sensor. On DOHC models, install the rear camshaft bearing cap. Set up a dial indicator and measure the camshaft endplay. Compare your measurement with the value listed in this Chapter's Specifications.

10   Replace the camshaft if it fails any of the above inspections. **Note:** *If the lobes are worn, replace the rocker arms along with the camshaft.* Cylinder head replacement may be necessary if the camshaft bearing surfaces in the head are damaged or excessively worn or if the endplay is excessive.

Installation

SOHC engine

11   Very carefully clean the camshaft and bearing journals. Liberally coat the journals, lobes and thrust portions of the camshaft with assembly lube or engine oil.

12   Carefully install the camshaft in the cylinder head.

13   Install a new camshaft oil seal (see Section 9).

14   Install the camshaft position sensor (see Chapter 6).

15   Install the cylinder head (see Section 14).

16   Install the rocker arm shaft assembly (see Section 10).

DOHC engine

Refer to illustrations 11.20 and 11.21

17   If removed, install the valve lash adjusters and rocker arms.

18   Clean the camshaft and bearing journals and caps. Liberally coat the journals, lobes and thrust portions of the camshaft with assembly lube or engine oil.

19   Carefully install the camshaft in the cylinder head in their correct location. Temporarily install the camshaft sprockets and rotate the camshafts so their timing marks align **(see illustration 7.10b)**. Make sure the crankshaft is positioned with the crankshaft sprocket timing mark at three notches BTDC **(see illustration 7.20b)**. **Caution:** *If the pistons are at TDC when tightening the camshaft bearing caps, damage to the engine may occur.*

20   Except for the No. 1 and No. 6 end caps, install the bearing caps **(see illustration 11.5)** and tighten them in the sequence shown **(see illustration)** to the torque listed in this Chapter's Specifications.

21   Apply a bead of anaerobic sealant to the No. 1 and No. 6 bearing caps **(see illustration)**. Install the bearing caps and tighten the bolts to the torque listed in this Chapter's Specifications.

22   Install new camshaft oil seals (see Section 9).

23   Install the timing belt and covers (see Section 7).

24   Run the engine while checking for oil leaks.

12 Valve lash adjusters - removal, inspection and installation

SOHC engine

Note: *The valve lash adjuster is an integral part of each rocker arm and can't be replaced separately.*

1   Remove the rocker arm shafts (see Section 10). Don't remove the rocker arms from the shafts.

2   Turn the rocker arm assembly upside down on the workbench. Inspect each lash adjuster carefully for signs of wear and damage, particularly on the surface that contacts the valve tip. Since the lash adjusters frequently become clogged, we recommend replacing the rocker arm/lash adjuster assembly if you're concerned about their condition or if the engine is exhibiting valve "tapping" noises.

3   If any are removed, assemble the rocker arms onto their shaft(s) (see Section 10).

4   The lash adjusters must be partially full of engine oil - indicated by little or no plunger action when the adjuster is depressed. If there's excessive plunger travel, place the rocker arm assembly into clean engine oil and pump the plunger until the plunger travel is eliminated. **Note:** *If the plunger still travels within the rocker arm when full of oil it's defective and the rocker arm assembly must be replaced.*

5   When re-starting the engine after replacing the rocker arm/lash adjusters, the adjusters will normally make "tapping" noises. After warm-up, raise the speed of the engine from idle to 3,000 rpm for one minute. If the adjuster(s) do not become silent, replace the defective rocker arm/lash adjuster assembly(ies).

2A

DOHC engine

6   Remove the camshafts (see Section 11).

7   Remove the rocker arms (see Section 10).

8   If the lash adjusters aren't already removed from the head, lift them out now. **Caution:** *Be sure to keep the adjusters in order so they can be placed back in the same location in the cylinder head it was removed from.*

9   Inspect each adjuster carefully for signs of wear and damage, particularly on the ball tip that contacts the rocker arm. Since the lash adjusters frequently become clogged, we recommend replacing them if you're concerned about their condition or if the engine is exhibiting valve "tapping" noises.

10   The lash adjusters must be partially full of engine oil - indicated by little or no plunger action when the adjuster is depressed. If there's excessive plunger travel, place the lash adjuster into clean engine oil and pump the plunger until the plunger travel is eliminated. **Note:** *If the plunger still travels within the lash adjuster when full of oil it's defective and the lash adjuster must be replaced.*

11   When re-starting the engine after replacing the adjusters, the adjusters will normally make "tapping" noises. After warm-up, raise the speed of the engine from idle to 3,000 rpm for one minute. If the adjuster(s) do not become silent, replace the defective ones.

13   Valve springs, retainers and seals - replacement

Refer to illustrations 13.4, 13.7, 13.8, 13.13 and 13.15

Note: *Broken valve springs and defective valve stem seals can be replaced without removing the cylinder heads. Two special tools and a compressed air source are normally required to perform this operation, so read through this Section carefully and rent or buy the tools before beginning the job.*

1   Remove the valve cover (see Section 4).

2   Remove the spark plug from the cylinder which has the defective component. If all of the valve stem seals are being replaced, all of the spark plugs should be removed.

3   Turn the crankshaft until the piston in the affected cylinder is at top dead center on the compression stroke (refer to Section 3). If you're replacing all of the valve stem seals, begin with cylinder number one and work on the valves for one cylinder at a time. Move from cylinder-to-cylinder following the firing order sequence (see this Chapter's Specifications).

4   Thread an adapter into the spark plug hole **(see illustration)** and connect an air hose from a compressed air source to it. Most auto parts stores can supply the air hose adapter. **Note:** *Many cylinder compression gauges utilize a screw-in fitting that may work with your air hose quick-disconnect fitting.*

5   Remove the camshaft(s) and rocker arm assembly (SOHC model)

13.4 This is what the air hose adapter that threads into the spark plug hole looks like - they're easily available from auto parts stores

(see Sections 10 and 11).

6   Apply compressed air to the cylinder. **Warning:** *The piston may be forced down by compressed air, causing the crankshaft to turn suddenly. If the wrench used when positioning the number one piston at TDC is still attached to the bolt in the crankshaft nose, remove it as it could cause damage or injury when the crankshaft moves.*

7   Stuff clean shop rags into the cylinder head holes above and below the valves to prevent parts and tools from falling into the engine, then use a valve spring compressor to compress the spring. Remove the keepers with small needle-nose pliers or a magnet **(see illustration)**.

8   Remove the spring retainer and valve spring, then remove the valve guide seal/spring seat assembly **(see illustration)**. **Caution:** *If air pressure fails to hold the valve in the closed position during this operation, the valve face and/or seat is probably damaged. If so, the cylinder head will have to be removed for additional repair operations.*

9   Wrap a rubber band or tape around the top of the valve stem so the valve won't fall into the combustion chamber, then release the air pressure.

10   Inspect the valve stem for damage. Rotate the valve in the guide and check the end for eccentric movement, which would indicate that the valve is bent.

11   Move the valve up-and-down in the guide and make sure it doesn't bind. If the valve stem binds, either the valve is bent or the guide is damaged. In either case, the head will have to be removed for repair.

12   Pull up on the valve stem to close the valve, reapply air pressure to the cylinder to retain the valve in the closed position, then remove the tape or rubber band from the valve stem.

13   Lubricate the valve stem with engine oil and install a new valve guide seal/spring seat assembly. Tap into place with deep socket **(see illustration)**.

13.7 Use needle-nose pliers (shown) or a small magnet to remove the valve spring keepers - be careful not to drop them down into the engine!

13.8 Remove the valve guide seal with a pair of pliers

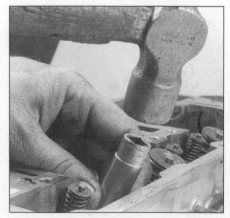

13.13 Gently tap the new seal into place with a hammer and a deep socket

13.15 Apply a small dab of grease to each keeper before installation to hold it in place on the valve stem until the spring is released

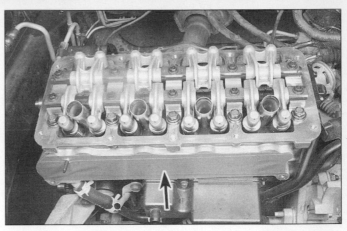

14.4 Cover the intake ports with duct tape (arrow) to keep out debris before removing the cylinder head

14   Install the spring in position over the valve.

15   Install the valve spring retainer. Compress the valve spring and carefully position the keepers in the groove. Apply a small dab of grease to the inside of each keeper to hold it in place if necessary **(see illustration)**.

16   Remove the pressure from the spring tool and make sure the keepers are seated.

14.10a Carefully lift the cylinder head straight up and place the head on wood blocks to prevent damage to the sealing surfaces

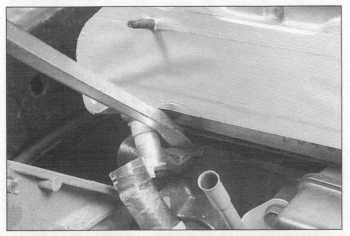

14.10b If the head sticks to the engine block, dislodge it by placing a wood block against the head casting and tapping the wood with a hammer or by prying the head with a prybar placed carefully on a casting protrusion

17   Disconnect the air hose and remove the adapter from the spark plug hole.

18   Install the camshaft(s) and rocker arm assembly (SOHC model) (see Sections 10 and 11).

19   Install the spark plug(s) and connect the wire(s).

20   Refer to Section 4 and install the valve cover.

21   Start and run the engine, then check for oil leaks and unusual sounds coming from the valve cover area.

2A

14   Cylinder head - removal and installation

Caution: *Allow the engine to cool completely before beginning this procedure.*

Removal

Refer to illustrations 14.4, 14.10a and 14.10b

1   Position the number one piston at Top Dead Center (see Section 3).

2   Disconnect the battery cable from the negative battery terminal.

3   Drain the cooling system and remove the spark plugs (see Chapter 1).

4   Remove the intake manifold (see Section 5). Cover the intake ports with duct tape to keep out debris **(see illustration)**.

5   If necessary, remove the exhaust manifold (see Section 6). **Note:** *The exhaust manifold is easier to remove after the cylinder head is removed.*

6   Remove the ignition system components (see Chapter 5).

7   Remove the timing belt (see Section 7).

8   Remove the valve cover (see Section 4).

9   Loosen the cylinder head bolts, 1/4-turn at a time, in the reverse of the tightening sequence **(see illustrations 14.14a or 14.14b)** until they can be removed by hand. **Note:** *Write down the location of the different length bolts so they will be reinstalled in the correct location.*

10   Carefully lift the cylinder head **(see illustration)** straight up and place the head on wood blocks to prevent damage to the sealing surfaces. If the head sticks to the engine block, dislodge it by placing a wood block against the head casting and tapping the wood with a hammer or by prying the head with a prybar placed carefully on a casting protrusion **(see illustration)**. **Note:** *Cylinder head disassembly and inspection procedures are covered in Chapter 2, Part B.* It's a good idea to have the head checked for warpage, even if you're just replacing the gasket.

11   **Caution:** *The cylinder head is aluminum, be very careful not to gouge the sealing surfaces.* Special gasket removal solvents that soften gaskets and make removal much easier are available at auto parts stores. Remove all traces of old gasket material from the block and head. Do not allow anything to fall into the engine. Clean and inspect all threaded fasteners and be sure the threaded holes in the block are clean and dry.

14.14a Tighten the cylinder head bolts in the sequence shown
(SOHC model)

Installation

Refer to illustrations 14.14a and 14.14b

12   Place a new gasket and the cylinder head in position on the engine block.

13   Apply clean engine oil to the cylinder head bolt threads prior to installation. The four short bolts (4.330 inch long) are to be installed in each corner of the cylinder head.

14   Tighten the cylinder head bolts in several stages in the recommended sequence **(see illustrations)** to the torque listed in this Chap-

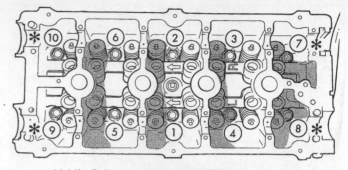

14.14b Cylinder head bolt TIGHTENING sequence
for the DOHC engine

ter's Specifications. **Note:** *The final step in the tightening procedure requires you to tighten the bolts a specific number of degrees. An angle-torque gauge, that fits on your torque wrench, is available at most auto parts stores and is highly recommended for this procedure. If the tool is not available, paint marks on the bolt heads and tighten then in sequence until the mark is the specified number of degrees from the starting point.*

15   Reinstall the timing belt (see Section 7).

16   Reinstall the remaining parts in the reverse order of removal.

17   Be sure to refill the cooling system and check all fluid levels. Rotate the crankshaft clockwise slowly by hand through six complete revolutions. Recheck the camshaft timing marks (see Section 7).

18   Start the engine and run it until normal operating temperature is reached. Check for leaks and proper operation.

15   Oil pan - removal and installation

Removal

Refer to illustrations 15.8a, 15.8b, 15.8c, 15.9a, 15.9b and 15.10

1   Disconnect the cable from the negative battery terminal.

2   Raise the vehicle and support it securely on jackstands.

3   Drain the engine oil (see Chapter 1).

4   Remove the transmission support bracket and structural collar (models so equipped).

5   Remove the front engine mount and bracket (see Section 19).

6   Remove the transaxle inspection cover.

7   If equipped with air conditioning, remove the oil filter and adapter.

8   Remove the mounting bolts and lower the oil pan from the vehicle **(see illustrations)**. If the pan is stuck, tap it with a soft-face hammer **(see illustration)** or place a wood block against the pan and tap the wood block with a hammer. **Caution:** *If you're wedging something between the oil pan and the engine block to separate the two, be extremely careful not to gouge or nick the gasket surface of either part;*

15.8a Using a criss-cross pattern, loosen and remove
the oil pan bolts . . .

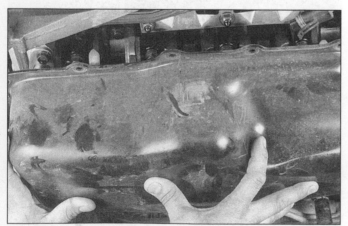

15.8b . . . and lower the pan carefully as there may still be some
residual oil in the pan

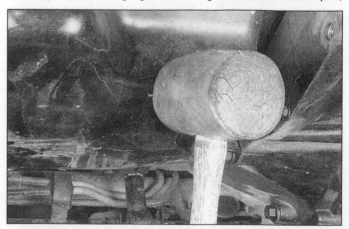

15.8c If the pan is stuck, tap it with a soft-face hammer or place a
wood block against the pan and tap the wood block with a hammer

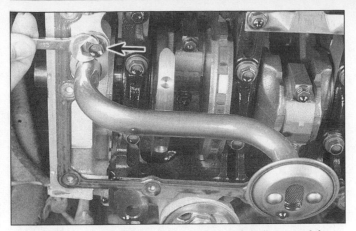

15.9a Remove the bolt (arrow) and remove the oil pump pick-up tube and screen assembly - clean both the tube and screen thoroughly before reassembly

an oil leak could result.

9   Remove the oil pump pickup tube and screen assembly **(see illustration)** and clean both the tube and screen thoroughly. Install the pick-up tube and screen with a new seal **(see illustration)**.
10   Thoroughly clean the oil pan and sealing surfaces on the block and pan **(see illustration)**. Use a scraper to remove all traces of old gasket material. Gasket removal solvents are available at auto parts stores and may prove helpful. Check the oil pan sealing surface for distortion. Straighten or replace as necessary. After cleaning and straightening (if necessary), wipe the gasket surfaces of the pan and block clean with a rag soaked in lacquer thinner or acetone.

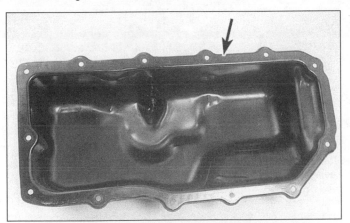

15.10 Thoroughly clean the oil pan and sealing surfaces on the engine block and oil pan (arrow) with a scraper to remove all traces of old gasket material

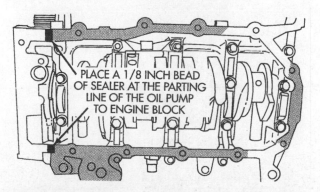

15.11 Apply a 1/8-inch bead of RTV sealant to the cylinder block-to-oil pump assembly joint at the oil pan flange

PLACE A 1/8 INCH BEAD OF SEALER AT THE PARTING LINE OF THE OIL PUMP TO ENGINE BLOCK

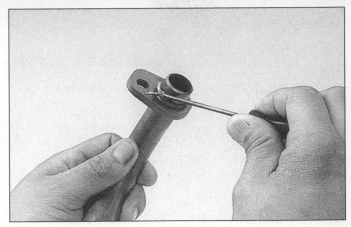

15.9b Install a new seal on the mounting plate

Installation

Refer to illustration 15.11

11   Apply a 1/8-inch bead of RTV sealant at the cylinder block-to-oil pump assembly joint at the oil pan flange **(see illustration)**. Install a new oil pan gasket.
12   Place the oil pan into position and install the bolts finger tight. Working side-to-side from the center out, tighten the bolts to the torque listed in this Chapter's Specifications.
13   On models so equipped, install the structural collar and tighten the oil pan bolts to the first stage. Tighten the transaxle bolts, then tighten the oil pan bolts to the second stage.
14   Reinstall the remaining parts in the reverse order of removal.
15   Refill the crankcase with the proper quantity and grade of oil and run the engine, checking for leaks. Road test the vehicle and check for leaks again.

16   Oil pump - removal, inspection and installation

Removal

Refer to illustrations 16.4, 16.5a, 16.5b, 16.6a, 16.6b and 16.6c

1   Disconnect the cable from the negative battery terminal.
2   Remove the oil pan and pick-up tube/strainer assembly (see Section 15).
3   Remove the timing belt and crankshaft sprocket (see Section 7).
4   Remove the two bolts securing the air conditioning compressor bracket to the side of the oil pump **(see illustration)**. Don't remove this bracket.

16.4 Remove the two air conditioning compressor bracket bolts (arrows) to the side of the oil pump - it is not necessary to remove this bracket or the remaining bolts

5   Remove the bolts and detach the oil pump assembly from the engine **(see illustration)**. **Caution:** *If the pump doesn't come off by hand, tap it gently with a soft-faced hammer or pry on a casting boss* **(see illustration)**.

6   Remove the mounting screws and remove the cover **(see illustration)**. Remove the inner and outer rotor from the body **(see illustrations)**. **Caution:** *Be very careful with these parts. Close tolerances are critical in creating the correct oil pressure. Any nicks or other damage will require replacement of the complete pump assembly.*

7   If necessary, replace the crankshaft front seal within the oil pump body (see Section 8).

Inspection

Refer to illustrations 16.9a, 16.9b, 16.10a, 16.10b, 1610c, 16.10d and 16.10e

8   Clean all components including the block surfaces, with solvent, then inspect all surfaces for excessive wear and/or damage.

9   Disassemble the relief valve, unscrew the cap bolt and remove the bolt, washer, spring and relief valve **(see illustrations)**. Check the oil pressure relief valve piston sliding surface and valve spring. If either the spring or the valve is damaged, they must be replaced as a set. If no damage is found reassemble the relief valve parts. Make sure to install the relief valve into the pump body with the grooved end going in first. Coating the parts with oil, and reinstall them in the oil pump body. Tighten the cap bolt securely.

10   Check the clearance of the oil pump components with a micrometer and a feeler gauge **(see illustrations)** and compare the results to this Chapter's Specifications.

16.5a Remove the oil pump assembly mounting bolts (arrows) and remove the assembly

Installation

Refer to illustrations 16.12a, 16.12b

11   Lubricate the housing and the inner and outer rotors with clean engine oil and install both rotors in the body. Install the cover and tighten the cover screws securely. Prime the oil pump with clean engine oil.

16.5b If the pump doesn't come off by hand, tap it gently with a soft-faced hammer or pry gently on a casting protrusion

16.6a Remove the cover mounting screws (arrows) . . .

16.6b . . . and the cover

16.6c Arrangement of oil pump components

A Cover	C Inner rotor
B Outer rotor	D Oil pump body

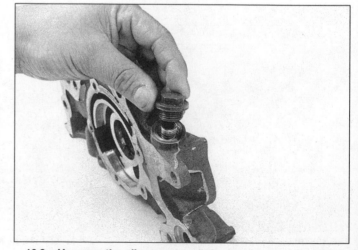

16.9a Unscrew the oil pressure relief valve cap from the body

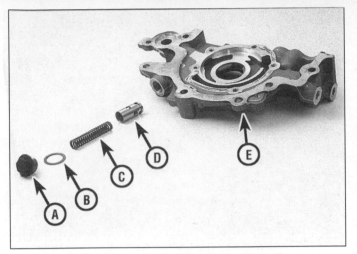

16.9b Oil pressure relief valve components

A Cap	D Relief valve
B Gasket	E Oil pump body
C Spring	

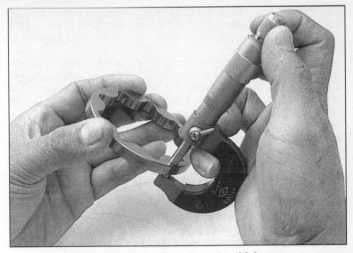

16.10a Measure the outer rotor thickness

12   Install a new O-ring in the oil discharge passage **(see illustration)**. Apply sealant to the oil pump body **(see illustration)**, and attach the pump assembly to the block. Tighten the bolts to the torque listed in this Chapter's Specifications.

13   Install the crankshaft sprocket and timing belt (see Section 7).
14   Install the pick-up tube/strainer assembly and oil pan (see Section 15).
15   Install a new oil filter and engine oil (see Chapter 1).
16   Start the engine and check for oil pressure and leaks.
17   Recheck the engine oil level.

2A

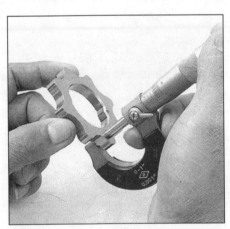

16.10b Measure the inner rotor thickness

16.10c Use a dial caliper and measure the outer diameter of the outer rotor

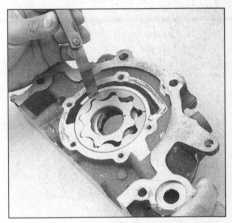

16.10d Use a flat feeler gauge and measure the outer rotor-to-case clearance

16.10e Place a precision straightedge over the rotors and measure the clearance between the rotors and the cover

16.12a Install a new O-ring seal in the oil pump body - apply clean engine oil to the seal

16.12b Apply a bead of anaerobic sealant to the housing sealing surface as shown

17.4 Mark the relative position of the flywheel or driveplate to the crankshaft and, using an appropriate tool to hold the flywheel, remove the bolts

17   Flywheel/driveplate - removal and installation

Refer to illustrations 17.4 and 17.5

Removal

1   Raise the vehicle and support it securely on jackstands, then refer to Chapter 7 and remove the transaxle assembly.

2   Remove the pressure plate and clutch disc (manual transaxle equipped vehicles) (see Chapter 8). Now is a good time to check/replace the clutch components and the pilot bearing.

3   To ensure correct alignment during reinstallation, mark the position of the flywheel/driveplate to the crankshaft before removal.

4   Remove the bolts that secure the flywheel/driveplate to the crankshaft **(see illustration)**. A tool is available a most auto parts stores to hold the flywheel/driveplate while loosening the bolts, if the tool is not available wedge a screwdriver in the ring gear teeth to jam the flywheel.

5   Remove the flywheel/driveplate from the crankshaft **(see illustration)**. Since the flywheel is fairly heavy, be sure to support it while removing the last bolt.

6   Clean the flywheel to remove grease and oil. To inspect the flywheel, see Chapter 8.

7   Clean and inspect the mating surfaces of the flywheel/driveplate and the crankshaft. If the crankshaft rear main seal is leaking, replace it before reinstalling the flywheel/driveplate (see Section 18).

Installation

8   Position the flywheel/driveplate against the crankshaft. Align the previously applied match marks. Before installing the bolts, apply thread locking compound to the threads.

9   Hold the flywheel/driveplate with the holding tool, or wedge a screwdriver in the ring gear teeth to keep the flywheel/driveplate from turning as you tighten the bolts to the torque listed in this Chapter's Specifications.

10   The remainder of installation is the reverse of the removal procedure.

18   Rear main oil seal - replacement

Refer to illustrations 18.2 and 18.4

1   The one-piece rear main oil seal is pressed into a bore machined into the rear main bearing cap and engine block. Remove the transaxle, clutch components (if equipped) and flywheel or driveplate (see Section 17).

2   **Note:** *Observe that the oil seal is installed flush with the outer surface of the block.* Pry out the old seal with a 3/16-inch flat blade screw-

17.5 Remove the flywheel/driveplate from the crankshaft

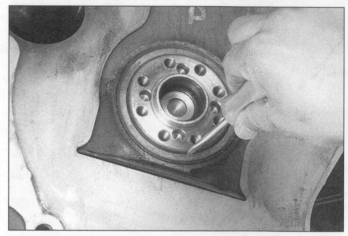

18.2 Carefully pry the crankshaft seal out of the bore - DO NOT nick or scratch the crankshaft or seal bore

driver **(see illustration)**. **Caution:** *To prevent an oil leak after the new seal is installed, be very careful not to scratch or otherwise damage the crankshaft sealing surface or the bore in the engine block.*

3   Clean the crankshaft and seal bore in the block thoroughly and

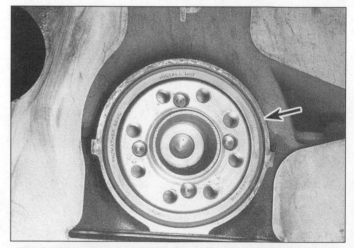

18.4 Position the new seal with the words THIS SIDE OUT facing out, toward the rear of the engine. Gently drive the seal into the cylinder block until it is flush with the outer surface of the block. Do not drive it past flush or there will be an oil leak - the seal must be flush

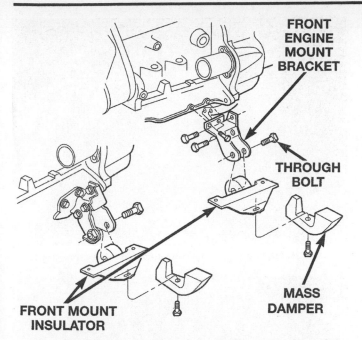

19.9a Installation details of the front engine mount and brackets

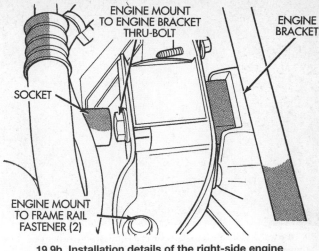

19.9b Installation details of the right-side engine mount and brackets

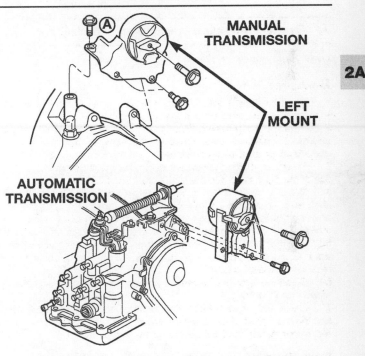

19.9c Installation details of the left-side engine mount

de-grease these areas by wiping them with a rag soaked in lacquer thinner or acetone. Do not lubricate the lip or outer diameter of the new seal - it must be installed as it comes from the manufacturer.

4   Position the new seal onto the crankshaft. **Note:** *When installing the new seal, If so marked, the words THIS SIDE OUT on the seal must face out, toward the rear of the engine.* Using an appropriate size driver and pilot tool, drive the seal into the cylinder block until it is flush with the outer surface of the block. If the seal is driven in past flush, there will be a oil leak. Check that the seal is flush **(see illustration)**.

5   The remainder of installation is the reverse of removal.

19 Engine mounts - check and replacement

1   Engine mounts seldom require attention, but broken or deteriorated mounts should be replaced immediately or the added strain placed on the driveline components may cause damage or wear.

Check

2   During the check, the engine must be raised slightly to remove the weight from the mounts.

3   Raise the vehicle and support it securely on jackstands, then position a jack under the engine oil pan. Place a large wood block between the jack head and the oil pan to prevent oil pan damage, then carefully raise the engine just enough to take the weight off the mounts. **Warning:** *DO NOT place any part of your body under the engine when it's supported only by a jack!*

4   Check the mounts to see if the rubber is cracked, hardened or separated from the metal backing. Sometimes the rubber will split right down the center.

5   Check for relative movement between the mount plates and the engine or frame (use a large screwdriver or pry bar to attempt to move the mounts). If movement is noted, lower the engine and tighten the mount fasteners.

6   Rubber preservative may be applied to the mounts to slow deterioration.

Replacement

Refer to illustrations 19.9a, 19.9b and 19.9c

7   Disconnect the battery cable from the negative battery terminal, then raise the vehicle and support it securely on jackstands (if not already done).

8   Place a floor jack under the engine (with a wood block between the jack head and oil pan) and raise the engine slightly to relieve the weight from the mounts.

9   Remove the fasteners and detach the mount from the frame and engine **(see illustrations). Caution:** *Do not disconnect more than one mount at a time, except during engine removal.*

10   Installation is the reverse of removal. Use thread locking compound on the mount bolts and be sure to tighten them securely.

2A

Notes

Chapter 2 Part B
General engine overhaul procedures

Contents

Specifications

General

Cylinder compression pressure
- Standard ... 170 to 225 psi
- Service limit ... 100 psi
- Difference between cylinders ... 25%

Oil pressure
- Minimum (at idle) ... 4 psi
- Maximum (at 3,000 rpm) ... 25 to 80 psi

Cylinder head warpage
- Head gasket surface ... 0.004 inch maximum
- Intake/exhaust manifold mounting surfaces ... 0.006 inch maximum

Valves and related components

Face angle ... 45 to 45-1/2 degrees
Seat angle ... 45 degrees
Valve length
- SOHC
  - Intake ... 4.515 to 4.535 inches
  - Exhaust ... 4.603 to 4.623 inches
- DOHC
  - Intake ... 4.389 to 4.409 inches
  - Exhaust ... 4.314 to 4.334 inches
Valve margin width
- Intake ... 0.0452 to 0.0582 inch
- Exhaust ... 0.058 to 0.071 inch

Valves and related components (continued)

Valve stem diameter
Intake	0.234 to 0.235 inch
Exhaust	0.233 to 0.234 inch

Valve stem-to-guide clearance
SOHC engine	
Intake	0.0018 to 0.0025 inch
Exhaust	0.0029 to 0.0037 inch
DOHC	
Intake	0.0009 to 0.0025 inch
Exhaust	0.0029 to 0.0037 inch

Valve spring
Out of square limit	1/16 inch
Free length (approximate)	
SOHC	1.747 inches
DOHC	1.811 inches
Installed height	
SOHC	1.580 inches
DOHC	1.525 inches

Crankshaft and connecting rods

Connecting rod journal
Diameter	1.8894 to 1.8900 inches
Out-of-round	0.0001 inch (maximum)
Taper limit	0.0001 inch (maximum)
Connecting rod bearing oil clearance	0.001 to 0.0023 inch
Connecting rod endplay (side clearance)	0.005 to 0.015 inch
Large end bore	2.0075 to 2.0081 inches
Crankshaft main bearing journal	
Diameter	2.0469 to 2.0475 inches
Out-of-round limits	0.0001 inch
Taper limit	0.0001 inch
Crankshaft end play	0.0035 to 0.0094 inch
Crankshaft main bearing oil clearance	0.008 to 0.0024 inch

Engine block

Cylinder bore diameter	3.4446 to 3.4452 inches
Out-of-round and cylinder taper limits	0.002 inch

Pistons and piston rings

Piston diameter (nominal)*
Low emission vehicle (LEV)	3.4432 to 3.4439 inches
All other vehicles	3.4434 to 3.4441 inches

Piston-to-bore clearance
SOHC	
1995	0.0002 to 0.0015 inch
1996 on	0.0004 to 0.0017 inch
DOHC	
1996	0.0002 to 0.0015 inch
1997 on	0.0007 to 0.0020 inch

Piston-to-ring clearance
Both compression rings	0.0010 to 0.0026 inch
Oil ring (pack)	0.0002 to 0.0070 inch

Piston ring end gap
Number 1 (top) compression ring	0.009 to 0.020 inch
Number 2 compression ring	0.019 to 0.031 inch
Oil ring (steel rails)	0.009 to 0.026 inch

Measured 11/16-inch up from the bottom of the piston skirt.

Torque specifications

Ft-lbs (unless otherwise indicated)

Main bearing cap bolts (11 mm)	60
Main bearing bedplate bolts (8 mm)	
SOHC	
1995	25
1996 on	22
DOHC	22
Connecting rod cap bolts	
Step 1	20
Step 2	Tighten an additional 90-degrees

1 General information

Included in this portion of Chapter 2 are the general overhaul procedures for the cylinder head and internal engine components. The information ranges from advice concerning preparation for an overhaul and the purchase of replacement parts to detailed, step-by-step procedures covering removal and installation of internal engine components and the inspection of parts.

The following Sections have been written based on the assumption that the engine has been removed from the vehicle. For information concerning in-vehicle engine repair, as well as removal and installation of the external components necessary for the overhaul, see Part A of this Chapter. For information on determining models and engine numbers, refer to the Vehicle Identification Numbers at the front of this manual.

The Specifications included in this Part are only those necessary for the inspection and overhaul procedures which follow. Refer to Part A for additional Specifications.

There are two types of four-cylinder engines installed in the models covered in this book: The standard 2.0L Single Overhead Camshaft (SOHC) engine and the optional 2.0L Double Overhead Camshaft (DOHC) engine.

2 Engine overhaul - general information

It's not always easy to determine when, or if, an engine should be completely overhauled, as a number of factors must be considered.

High mileage is not necessarily an indication that an overhaul is needed, while low mileage doesn't preclude the need for an overhaul. Frequency of servicing is probably the most important consideration. An engine that's had regular and frequent oil and filter changes, as well as other required maintenance, will most likely give many thousands of miles of reliable service. Conversely, a neglected engine may require an overhaul very early in its life.

Excessive oil consumption is an indication that piston rings, valve seals and/or valve guides are in need of attention. Make sure that oil leaks aren't responsible before deciding that the rings and/or guides are bad. Perform a compression check to determine the extent of the work required (see Section 3).

Check the oil pressure with a gauge installed in place of the oil pressure sending unit, located under the exhaust manifold in front of the transaxle bell housing, and compare it to the Specifications in this Chapter. If it's extremely low, the bearings and/or oil pump are probably worn out.

Loss of power, rough running, knocking or metallic engine noises, excessive valve train noise and high fuel consumption rates may also point to the need for an overhaul, especially if they're all present at the same time. If a complete tune-up doesn't remedy the situation, major mechanical work is the only solution.

An engine overhaul involves restoring the internal parts to the specifications of a new engine. During an overhaul, the piston rings are replaced and the cylinder walls are reconditioned (rebored and/or honed). If a re-bore is done by an automotive machine shop, new oversize pistons will also be installed. The main bearings, connecting rod bearings and camshaft bearings are generally replaced with new ones and, if necessary, the crankshaft may be reground to restore the journals. Generally, the valves are serviced as well, since they're usually in less-than-perfect condition at this point. While the engine is being overhauled, other components, such as the distributor, starter and alternator, can be rebuilt as well. The end result should be a like-new engine that will give many trouble free miles. **Note:** *Critical cooling system components such as the hoses, drivebelts, thermostat and water pump MUST be replaced with new parts when an engine is overhauled. The radiator should be checked carefully to ensure that it isn't clogged or leaking (see Chapter 3). Also, we don't recommend overhauling the oil pump - always install a new one when an engine is rebuilt.*

Before beginning the engine overhaul, read through the entire procedure to familiarize yourself with the scope and requirements of the job. Overhauling an engine isn't difficult, but it is time consuming. Plan on the vehicle being tied up for a minimum of two weeks, especially if parts must be taken to an automotive machine shop for repair or reconditioning. Check on availability of parts and make sure that any necessary special tools and equipment are obtained in advance. Most work can be done with typical hand tools, although a number of precision measuring tools are required for inspecting parts to determine if they must be replaced. Often an automotive machine shop will handle the inspection of parts and offer advice concerning reconditioning and replacement. **Note:** *Always wait until the engine has been completely disassembled and all components, especially the engine block, have been inspected before deciding what service and repair operations must be performed by an automotive machine shop. Since the block's condition will be the major factor to consider when determining whether to overhaul the original engine or buy a rebuilt one, never purchase parts or have machine work done on other components until the block has been thoroughly inspected. As a general rule, time is the primary cost of an overhaul, so it doesn't pay to install worn or substandard parts.*

As a final note, to ensure maximum life and minimum trouble from a rebuilt engine, everything must be assembled with care in a spotlessly clean environment.

3 Cylinder compression check

1 A compression check will tell you what mechanical condition the upper end (pistons, rings, valves, head gasket) of your engine is in. Specifically, it can tell you if the compression is down due to leakage caused by worn piston rings, defective valves and seats or a blown head gasket. **Note:** *The engine must be at normal operating temperature and the battery must be fully charged for this check.*

2 Begin by cleaning the area around the spark plugs before you remove them (compressed air should be used, if available, otherwise a small brush or even a bicycle tire pump will work). The idea is to prevent dirt from getting into the cylinders as the compression check is being done.

3 Remove all of the spark plugs from the engine (Chapter 1).

4 Block the throttle wide open.

5 Disconnect the primary (low voltage) wire electrical connector from the ignition coil pack (see Chapter 5).

6 Install the compression gauge in the number one spark plug hole.

7 Crank the engine over at least seven compression strokes and watch the gauge. The compression should build up quickly in a healthy engine. Low compression on the first stroke, followed by gradually increasing pressure on successive strokes, indicates worn piston rings. A low compression reading on the first stroke, which doesn't build up during successive strokes, indicates leaking valves or a blown head gasket (a cracked head could also be the cause). Deposits on the undersides of the valve heads can also cause low compression. Record the highest gauge reading obtained.

8 Repeat the procedure for the remaining cylinders and compare the results to the Specifications in this Chapter.

9 Add some engine oil (about three squirts from a plunger-type oil can) to each cylinder, through the spark plug hole, and repeat the test.

10 If the compression increases after the oil is added, the piston rings are definitely worn. If the compression doesn't increase significantly, the leakage is occurring at the valves or head gasket. Leakage past the valves may be caused by burned valve seat(s), and/or faces or warped, cracked or bent valve(s).

11 If two adjacent cylinders have equally low compression, there's a strong possibility that the head gasket between them is blown. The appearance of coolant in the combustion chambers or the crankcase would verify this condition.

12 If one cylinder is 20 percent lower than the others, and the engine has a slightly rough idle, a worn exhaust lobe on the camshaft could be the cause.

13 If the compression is unusually high, the combustion chambers

2B

are probably coated with carbon deposits. If that's the case, the cylinder head should be removed and de-carbonized.

14   If compression is way down or varies greatly between cylinders, it would be a good idea to have a leak-down test performed by an automotive repair shop. This test will pinpoint exactly where the leakage is occurring and how severe it is.

4   Vacuum gauge diagnostic checks

A vacuum gauge provides valuable information about what is going on in the engine at a low-cost. You can check for worn rings or cylinder walls, leaking head or intake manifold gaskets, restricted exhaust, stuck or burned valves, weak valve springs, improper ignition or valve timing and ignition problems.

Unfortunately, vacuum gauge readings are easy to misinterpret, so they should be used in conjunction with other tests to confirm the diagnosis.

Both the absolute readings and the rate of needle movement are important for accurate interpretation. Most gauges measure vacuum in inches of mercury (in-Hg). The following references to vacuum assume the diagnosis is being performed at sea level. As elevation increases (or atmospheric pressure decreases), the reading will decrease. For every 1,000 foot increase in elevation above approximately 2000 feet, the gauge readings will decrease about one inch of mercury.

Connect the vacuum gauge directly to intake manifold vacuum, not to ported (throttle-body) vacuum. Be sure no hoses are left disconnected during the test or false readings will result.

Before you begin the test, allow the engine to warm up completely. Block the wheels and set the parking brake. With the transmission in neutral (or Park, on automatics), start the engine and allow it to run at normal idle speed. **Warning:** *Carefully inspect the fan blades for cracks or damage before starting the engine. Keep your hands and the vacuum tester clear of the fan and do not stand in front of the vehicle or in line with the fan when the engine is running.*

Read the vacuum gauge; an average, healthy engine should normally produce about 17 to 22 inches of vacuum with a fairly steady needle. Refer to the following vacuum gauge readings and what they indicate about the engines condition.

1   A low steady reading usually indicates a leaking gasket between the intake manifold and throttle body, a leaky vacuum hose, late ignition timing or incorrect camshaft timing. Check ignition timing with a timing light and eliminate all other possible causes, utilizing the tests provided in this Chapter before you remove the timing belt cover to check the timing marks.

2   If the reading is three to eight inches below normal and it fluctuates at that low reading, suspect an intake manifold gasket leak at an intake port or a faulty injector.

3   If the needle has regular drops of about two to four inches at a steady rate the valves are probably leaking. Perform a compression or leak-down test to confirm this.

4   An irregular drop or down-flick of the needle can be caused by a sticking valve or an ignition misfire. Perform a compression or leak-down test and read the spark plugs.

5   A rapid vibration of about four in-Hg vibration at idle combined with exhaust smoke indicates worn valve guides. Perform a leak-down test to confirm this. If the rapid vibration occurs with an increase in engine speed, check for a leaking intake manifold gasket or head gasket, weak valve springs, burned valves or ignition misfire.

6   A slight fluctuation, say one inch up and down, may mean ignition problems. Check all the usual tune-up items and, if necessary, run the engine on an ignition analyzer.

7   If there is a large fluctuation, perform a compression or leak-down test to look for a weak or dead cylinder or a blown head gasket.

8   If the needle moves slowly through a wide range, check for a clogged PCV system, incorrect idle fuel mixture, throttle body or intake manifold gasket leaks.

9   Check for a slow return after revving the engine by quickly snapping the throttle open until the engine reaches about 2,500 rpm and let it shut. Normally the reading should drop to near zero, rise above normal idle reading (about 5 in-Hg over) and then return to the previous idle reading. If the vacuum returns slowly and doesn't peak when the throttle is snapped shut, the rings may be worn. If there is a long delay, look for a restricted exhaust system (often the muffler or catalytic converter). An easy way to check this is to temporarily disconnect the exhaust ahead of the suspected part and repeat the test.

5   Engine removal - methods and precautions

If you've decided that an engine must be removed for overhaul or major repair work, several preliminary steps should be taken.

Locating a suitable place to work is extremely important. Adequate work space, along with storage space for the vehicle, will be needed. If a shop or garage isn't available, at the very least a flat, level, clean work surface made of concrete or asphalt is required.

Cleaning the engine compartment and engine before beginning the removal procedure will help keep tools clean and organized.

An engine hoist or A-frame will also be necessary. Make sure the equipment is rated in excess of the combined weight of the engine and accessories. Safety is of primary importance, considering the potential hazards involved in lifting the engine out of the vehicle.

If the engine is being removed by a novice, a helper should be available. Advice and aid from someone more experienced would also be helpful. There are many instances when one person cannot simultaneously perform all of the operations required when lifting the engine out of the vehicle.

Plan the operation ahead of time. Arrange for or obtain all of the tools and equipment you'll need prior to beginning the job. Some of the equipment necessary to perform engine removal and installation safely and with relative ease are (in addition to an engine hoist) a heavy duty floor jack, complete sets of wrenches and sockets as described in the front of this manual, wooden blocks and plenty of rags and cleaning solvent for mopping up spilled oil, coolant and gasoline. If the hoist must be rented, make sure that you arrange for it in advance and perform all of the operations possible without it beforehand. This will save you money and time.

Plan for the vehicle to be out of use for quite a while. A machine shop will be required to perform some of the work which the do-it-yourselfer can't accomplish without special equipment. These shops often have a busy schedule, so it would be a good idea to consult them before removing the engine in order to accurately estimate the amount of time required to rebuild or repair components that may need work.

Always be extremely careful when removing and installing the engine. Serious injury can result from careless actions. Plan ahead, take your time and a job of this nature, although major, can be accomplished successfully.

6   Engine - removal and installation

Refer to illustration 6.8

Note 1: *Read through the entire Section before beginning this procedure. The engine and transaxle are removed as a unit and then separated outside the vehicle.*

Note 2: *The engine and transaxle are removed from the vehicle as an assembly and separated once out of the vehicle.*

Removal

1   If the vehicle is equipped with air conditioning, have the system discharged by a dealer service department or a service station.

2   Place protective covers on the front fenders.

3   Remove the hood (see Chapter 11). Relieve the fuel system pressure (see Chapter 4).

4   Disconnect and remove the battery and battery tray (see Chapter 5).

5   Set the Powertrain Control Module aside out of the way (see Chapter 6).

6   Remove the air cleaner assembly (see Chapter 4).

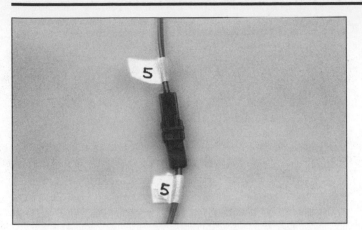

6.8 Label both ends of each wire or vacuum connection before disconnecting them

7   Drain and remove the radiator and all hoses (see Chapter 3). **Note:** *On vehicles equipped with an automatic transaxle, remove the cooler hoses from the radiator (see Chapter 3). Plug the ends to prevent the entry of foreign matter.*

8   Carefully label, then disconnect all vacuum lines, coolant and emissions hoses and wire harness connectors. Masking tape and felt-tip pens work well for marking items **(see illustration)**. If necessary, take instant photos or sketch the locations to ensure correct reinstallation.

9   Disconnect the fuel lines from the fuel injection system (see Chapter 4) and cap them to prevent leakage and contamination.

10   Detach the throttle cables (see Chapter 4).

11   On manual transaxle-equipped models, refer to Chapter 7 and detach the shift cables and the clutch release cable (see Chapter 8).

12   On automatic transaxle-equipped vehicles, detach the shift control cable from the transaxle (see Chapter 7).

13   Raise the vehicle and support it securely on jackstands.

14   Remove the right side splash shield (if not already done) located at the drivebelt end of the engine. Remove all drive belts (see Chapter 3).

15   Drain the engine oil and transaxle fluid and remove the oil filter (see Chapter 1).

16   Remove the driveaxles from the transaxle (see Chapter 8). Stuff clean rags into the transaxle openings to prevent the entry of foreign material.

17   Disconnect the exhaust pipe from the exhaust manifold.

18   Detach the vehicle speed sensor electrical connector from the transaxle.

19   Remove the front engine mount (see Chapter 2A).

20   On 1997 and later manual transaxle-equipped models, remove the torque damper from the transaxle.

21   Lower the vehicle.

22   If equipped, remove the air conditioning compressor (see Chapter 3).

23   If equipped, remove the power steering pump and reservoir from the brackets without disconnecting the hoses and set them aside.

24   Disconnect the ground straps to the body.

25   Attach a chain or an engine lifting fixture to the engine lifting brackets (or to bolts which are securely mounted in the cast iron block or accessory mounting bracket) and hook up the hoist. **Warning:** *Attaching the engine lifting chain to a bolt or stud located in an aluminum component (such as the cylinder head) may not provide the necessary strength to support the weight of the engine/transaxle assembly during removal. Take up the slack until there is tension on the chain to support the engine/transaxle assembly.*

26   Support the transaxle with a floor jack. Place a block of wood on the jack pad to protect the transaxle. **Warning:** *Do not place any part of your body under the engine/transaxle when it's supported only by a hoist or other lifting device.*

27   Remove the mount through-bolts on all of the engine or transaxle mounts (see Chapter 2A).

28   Confirm that all of the cables, hoses, wires and other items are disconnected from the engine/transaxle.

29   Carefully push the transaxle down, or adjust the chain to position the engine slightly higher than the transaxle, while lifting the engine up to clear obstructions.

30   Lift the engine and transaxle high enough to clear the front of the vehicle and slowly move the hoist away.

31   Lower the hoist and set the transaxle on blocks - leave the hoist hooked to the engine.

32   With the transaxle securely supported, remove the driveplate-to-torque converter bolts (automatic transaxle only) and transaxle-to-engine bolts and separate the engine from the transaxle. Refer to Chapter 7 if necessary.

33   Remove the clutch components, if equipped (see Chapter 8) and flywheel (or driveplate) (see Chapter 2, Part A) and the engine rear plate. Mount the engine on a stand.

Installation

34   Check the engine/transaxle mounts. If they're worn or damaged, replace them.

35   On manual transaxle equipped models, inspect the clutch components (see Chapter 8) and apply a very small amount of high temperature grease to the transaxle input shaft splines.

36   On automatic transaxle equipped vehicles, inspect the converter seal and bushing.

37   Carefully rejoin the transaxle and engine following the procedure outlined in Chapter 7. **Caution:** *Do not use the bolts to force the engine and transaxle into alignment. It may crack or damage major components.*

38   Install the transaxle-to-engine bolts and tighten them securely.

39   Attach the hoist to the engine and carefully lower the engine/transaxle assembly into the vehicle.

40   Install the mount bolts and tighten them securely.

41   Reinstall the remaining components and fasteners in the reverse order of removal.

42   Add coolant, oil, power steering and transmission fluid/lubricant as needed (see Chapter 1).

43   Run the engine and check for proper operation and leaks. Shut off the engine and recheck the fluid levels.

7   Engine rebuilding alternatives

The do-it-yourselfer is faced with a number of options when performing an engine overhaul. The decision to replace the engine block, piston/connecting rod assemblies and crankshaft depends on a number of factors, with the number one consideration being the condition of the block. Other considerations are cost, access to machine shop facilities, parts availability, time required to complete the project and the extent of prior mechanical experience on the part of the do-it-yourselfer.

Some of the rebuilding alternatives include:

Individual parts - If the inspection procedures reveal that the engine block and most engine components are in reusable condition, purchasing individual parts may be the most economical alternative. The block, crankshaft and piston/connecting rod assemblies should all be inspected carefully. Even if the block shows little wear, the cylinder bores should be surface honed.

Short block - A short block consists of an engine block with a crankshaft and piston/connecting rod assemblies already installed. All new bearings are incorporated and all clearances will be correct. The existing camshaft, valve train components, cylinder head(s) and external parts can be bolted to the short block with little or no machine shop work necessary.

Long block - A long block consists of a short block plus an oil pump, oil pan, cylinder head, rocker arm cover, camshaft(s) and valve train components, timing sprockets and timing covers. All components

2B

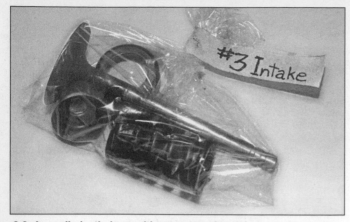

9.2 A small plastic bag, with an appropriate label, can be used to store the valvetrain components so they can be kept together and reinstalled in the correct guide location

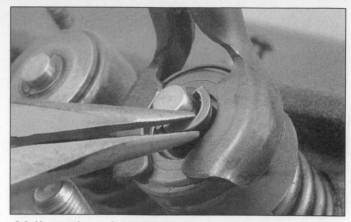

9.3 Use a valve spring compressor to compress the spring, then remove the keepers from the valve stem

are installed with new bearings, seals and gaskets incorporated throughout. The installation of manifolds and external parts is all that's necessary.

Give careful thought to which alternative is best for you and discuss the situation with local automotive machine shops, auto parts dealers and experienced rebuilders before ordering or purchasing replacement parts.

8   Engine overhaul - disassembly sequence

1   It's much easier to disassemble and work on the engine if it's mounted on a portable engine stand. A stand can often be rented quite cheaply from an equipment rental yard. Before the engine is mounted on a stand, the flywheel/driveplate should be removed from the engine.
2   If a stand isn't available, it's possible to disassemble the engine with it blocked up on the floor. Be extra careful not to tip or drop the engine when working without a stand.
3   If you're going to obtain a rebuilt engine, all external components must come off the old engine first, to be transferred to the replacement engine, just as they will if you're doing a complete engine overhaul yourself. These include:

Alternator and brackets
Emissions control components
Coil pack, spark plug wires and spark plugs
Thermostat cover, thermostat and housing
Water pump
Fuel injection components
Intake and exhaust manifolds
Oil filter
Engine mounts
Clutch and flywheel/driveplate

Note: *When removing the external components from the engine, pay close attention to details that may be helpful or important during installation. Note the installed position of gaskets, seals, spacers, pins, brackets, washers, bolts and other small items.*
4   If you're obtaining a short block, which consists of the engine block, crankshaft, pistons and connecting rods all assembled, then the cylinder head, oil pan and oil pump will have to be removed as well. See *Engine rebuilding alternatives* for additional information regarding the different possibilities to be considered.
5   If you're planning a complete overhaul, the engine must be disassembled and the internal components removed in the general following order:

Valve cover
Intake and exhaust manifolds
Rocker arms and shafts (SOHC engine)
Timing belt covers
Timing belt and sprockets

Camshaft(s)
Cam followers and hydraulic lash adjusters (DOHC engine)
Cylinder head
Oil pan and oil pickup
Oil pump
Piston/connecting rod assemblies
Crankshaft and main bearing cap/bed plate assembly

6   Before beginning the disassembly and overhaul procedures, make sure the following items are available. Also, refer to *Engine overhaul - reassembly sequence* for a list of tools and materials needed for engine reassembly.

Common hand tools
Small cardboard boxes or plastic bags for storing parts
Gasket scraper
Ridge reamer
Micrometers
Telescoping gauges
Dial indicator set
Valve spring compressor
Cylinder surfacing hone
Piston ring groove cleaning tool
Electric drill motor
Tap and die set
Wire brushes
Oil gallery brushes
Cleaning solvent

9   Cylinder head - disassembly

Refer to illustrations 9.2, 9.3 and 9.4
Note: *New and rebuilt cylinder heads are commonly available for most engines at dealerships and auto parts stores. Due to the fact that some specialized tools are necessary for the disassembly and inspection procedures, and replacement parts may not be readily available, it may be more practical and economical for the home mechanic to purchase a replacement head rather than taking the time to disassemble, inspect and recondition the original.*
1   Cylinder head disassembly involves removal of the intake and exhaust valves and related components. If they're still in place, remove the rocker arm shafts and camshaft, on the SOHC engine (see Chapter 2A) or the bearing caps, camshafts, cam followers and lash adjusters, on the DOHC engine (see Chapter 2A). Label the parts or store them separately so they can be reinstalled in their original locations.
2   Before the valves are removed, arrange to label and store them, along with their related components, so they can be kept separate and reinstalled in the same valve guides they are removed from **(see illustration)**.

9.4 If the valve won't pull through the guide, deburr the edge of the stem end and the area around the top of the keeper groove with a file or whetstone

3   Compress the springs on the first valve with a spring compressor and remove the keepers **(see illustration)**. Carefully release the valve spring compressor and remove the retainer and the spring.

4   Pull the valve out of the head, then remove the oil seal/spring seat assembly from the guide. If the valve binds in the guide (won't pull through), push it back into the head and deburr the area around the keeper groove with a fine file or whetstone **(see illustration)**.

5   Repeat the procedure for the remaining valves. Remember to keep all the parts for each valve together so they can be reinstalled in the same locations.

6   Pull off the valve stem seals with pliers and discard them.

7   Once the valves and related components have been removed and stored in an organized manner, the head should be thoroughly cleaned and inspected. If a complete engine overhaul is being done, finish the engine disassembly procedures before beginning the cylinder head cleaning and inspection process.

10 Cylinder head - cleaning and inspection

Refer to illustrations 10.10, 10.11, 10.14, 10.15, 10.16 and 10.17

1   Thorough cleaning of the cylinder head and related valvetrain components, followed by a detailed inspection, will enable you to decide how much valve service work must be done during the engine overhaul. **Note:** *If the engine was severely overheated, the cylinder head is probably warped (see Step 12).*

Cleaning

2   Scrape all traces of old gasket material and sealing compound off the head gasket, intake manifold and exhaust manifold sealing surfaces. **Caution:** *The cylinder head is aluminum, be very careful not to gouge the sealing surfaces.* Special gasket removal solvents that soften gaskets and make removal much easier are available at auto parts stores.

3   Remove all built-up scale from the coolant passages.

4   Run a stiff wire brush through the various holes to remove deposits that may have formed in them.

5   Run an appropriate size tap into each of the threaded holes to remove corrosion and thread sealant that may be present. If compressed air is available, use it to clear the holes of debris produced by this operation. **Warning:** *Wear eye protection when using compressed air!*

6   Clean the cylinder head with solvent and dry it thoroughly. Compressed air will speed the drying process and ensure that all holes and recessed areas are clean. **Note:** *Decarbonizing chemicals are available and may prove very useful when cleaning cylinder heads and valve train components. They are very caustic and should be used with caution. Be sure to follow the instructions on the container.*

10.10 Thoroughly inspect the head for cracks, evidence of coolant leakage and other damage

7   On SOHC engines, clean the rocker arm/hydraulic lash adjusters, spacers and shafts with solvent. On DOHC engines, clean the cam followers and hydraulic lash adjusters with solvent. Dry all parts thoroughly (don't mix them up during the cleaning process). Compressed air will speed the drying process and can be used to clean out the oil passages.

8   Clean all the valve springs, spring seats, keepers and retainers with solvent and dry them thoroughly. Do the components from one valve at a time to avoid mixing up the parts.

9   Scrape off any heavy deposits that may have formed on the valves, then use a motorized wire brush to remove deposits from the valve heads and stems. **Warning:** *Wear eye protection! Again, make sure the valves don't get mixed up.*

Inspection

Note: *Be sure to perform all of the following inspection procedures before concluding that machine shop work is required. Make a list of the items that need attention.*

Cylinder head

10   Inspect the head very carefully for cracks, evidence of coolant leakage and other damage **(see illustration)**. If cracks are found, check with an automotive machine shop concerning repair. If repair isn't possible, a new cylinder head should be obtained.

11   Using a straightedge and feeler gauge, check the head gasket mating surface **(see illustration)**. Check the intake and exhaust manifold surfaces on the cylinder head also. If the warpage on any of the surfaces exceeds the limits listed in this Chapter's Specifications, they can be resurfaced at an automotive machine shop.

10.11 Check the cylinder head gasket surfaces for warpage by trying to slip a feeler gauge under a precision straightedge (see this Chapter's Specifications for the maximum warpage allowed and use a feeler gauge of that thickness)

2B

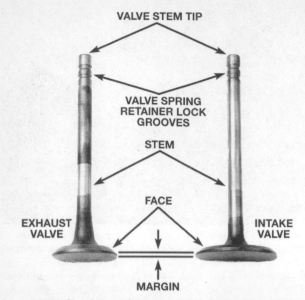

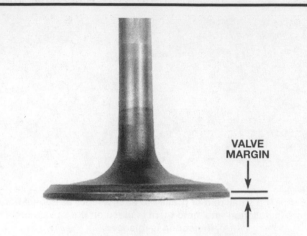

10.15 The margin width on each valve must be as specified (if no margin exists, the valve cannot be reused)

10.14 Check for valve wear at the points shown here

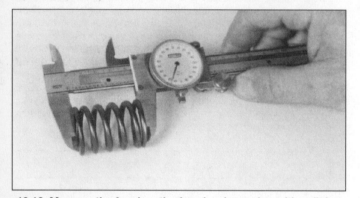

10.16 Measure the free length of each valve spring with a dial or vernier caliper

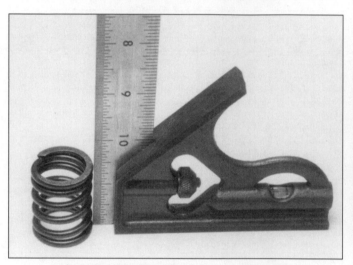

10.17 Check each valve spring for squareness

12   Examine the valve seats in each of the combustion chambers. If they're pitted, cracked or burned, the head will require valve service that's beyond the scope of the home mechanic.

13   Check the valve stem-to-guide clearance, using a clamping dial indicator base attached securely to the head, by measuring the lateral movement of the valve stem inside the valve guide. **Note:** *If you only have a magnetic dial indicator base and a steel bench or vise, you can clamp or bolt the head down to the bench and mount the indicator next to the head and extend the dial indicator to the valve stem and measure the side play. The valve must be in the guide and approximately 1/16-inch off the seat. The total valve stem movement indicated by the gauge needle must be divided by two to obtain the actual clearance. After this is done, if there's still some doubt regarding the condition of the valve guides they should be checked by an automotive machine shop (the cost should be minimal).*

Valves

14   Carefully inspect each valve face for uneven wear, deformation, cracks, pits and burned areas **(see illustration)**. Check the valve stem for scuffing and galling and the neck for cracks. Rotate the valve and check for any obvious indication that it's bent. Look for pits and excessive wear on the end of the stem. The presence of any of these conditions indicates the need for valve service by an automotive machine shop.

15   Measure the margin width on each valve **(see illustration)**. Any valve with a margin narrower than listed in this Chapter's Specifications will have to be replaced with a new one.

Valve components

16   Check each valve spring for wear (on the ends) and pits. Measure the free length **(see illustration)** and compare it to the Specifications listed in this Chapter. Any springs that are shorter than specified have sagged and should not be reused. The tension of all springs should be checked with a special fixture before deciding that they're suitable for use in a rebuilt engine (take the springs to an automotive machine shop for this check).

17   Stand each spring on a flat surface and check it for squareness **(see illustration)**. If any of the springs are distorted or sagged, replace all of them with new parts.

18   Check the spring retainers and keepers for obvious wear and cracks. Any questionable parts should be replaced with new ones, as extensive damage will occur if they fail during engine operation.

Rocker arm (SOHC engine), cam followers (DOHC) components

19   Refer to Chapter 2, Part A, for the rocker arm/hydraulic lash adjusters and shaft (SOHC) or the cam followers and hydraulic lash adjusters (DOHC) for inspection procedures.

20   Any damaged or excessively worn parts must be replaced with new ones.

21   If the inspection process indicates that the valve components are in generally poor condition and worn beyond the limits specified, which is usually the case in an engine that's being overhauled, reassemble the valves in the cylinder head and refer to Section 11 for valve servicing recommendations.

12.6 Apply a small dab of grease to each keeper as shown here before installation - it'll hold them in place on the valve stem as the spring is released

12.8 Be sure to check the valve spring installed height (the distance from the top of the seat/shim to the top of the spring)

11 Valves - servicing

1   Because of the complex nature of the job and the special tools and equipment needed, servicing of the valves, the valve seats and the valve guides, commonly known as a valve job, should be done by a professional.

2   The home mechanic can remove and disassemble the head, do the initial cleaning and inspection, then reassemble and deliver it to a dealer service department or an automotive machine shop for the actual service work. Doing the inspection will enable you to see what condition the head and valvetrain components are in and will ensure that you know what work and new parts are required when dealing with an automotive machine shop.

3   The dealer service department, or automotive machine shop, will remove the valves and springs, recondition or replace the valves and valve seats, recondition the valve guides, check and replace the valve springs, spring retainers and keepers (as necessary), replace the valve seals with new ones, reassemble the valve components and make sure the installed spring height is correct. The cylinder head gasket surface will also be resurfaced if it's warped.

4   After the valve job has been performed by a professional, the head will be in like-new condition. When the head is returned, be sure to clean it again before installation on the engine to remove any metal particles and abrasive grit that may still be present from the valve service or head resurfacing operations. Use compressed air, if available, to blow out all the oil holes and passages.

12 Cylinder head - reassembly

Refer to illustrations 12.6 and 12.8

1   Regardless of whether or not the head was sent to an automotive repair shop for valve servicing, make sure it's clean before beginning reassembly.

2   If the head was sent out for valve servicing, the valves and related components will already be in place. Begin the reassembly procedure with Step 8.

3   Install new oil seal/spring seat assemblies on each of the valve guides. Using a hammer and a deep socket or seal installation tool, gently tap each oil seal/spring seat assembly into place until it's completely seated on the guide. Don't twist or cock the seals during installation or they won't seal properly on the valve stems.

4   Beginning at one end of the head, lubricate and install the first valve. Apply moly-based grease or clean engine oil to the valve stem.

5   Install spring over the valve guide and set the spring and retainer in place.

6   Compress the spring with a valve spring compressor and carefully install the keepers in the upper groove, then slowly release the compressor and make sure the keepers seat properly. Apply a small dab of grease to each keeper to hold it in place if necessary **(see illustration)**.

7   Repeat the procedure for the remaining valves. Be sure to return the components to their original locations - don't mix them up!

8   Check the installed valve spring height with a vernier or dial caliper. If the head was sent out for service work, the installed height should be correct (but don't automatically assume that it is). The measurement is taken from the spring seat to the top of the valve stem **(see illustration)**. If the height is greater than listed in this Chapter's Specifications, shims can be added under the springs to correct it. **Caution:** *Do not shim the springs to the point where the installed height is less than specified.*

9   Apply moly-base grease to the rocker arm faces, the camshaft and the rocker shafts, then install the camshaft and rocker arm shafts, on the SOHC engine or the, cam followers, lash adjusters, camshafts and bearing caps on the DOHC engine (see Chapter 2A).

13 Pistons and connecting rods - removal

Refer to illustrations 13.1, 13.3 and 13.4
Note: *Prior to removing the piston/connecting rod assemblies, remove the cylinder head and the oil pan by referring to the appropriate Sections in Chapter 2, Part A.*

1   Use your fingernail to feel if a ridge has formed at the upper limit of ring travel (about 1/4-inch down from the top of each cylinder). If carbon deposits or cylinder wear have produced ridges, they must be completely removed with a special tool **(see illustration)**. Follow the manufacturer's instructions provided with the tool. Failure to remove the ridges before attempting to remove the piston/connecting rod

13.1 A ridge reamer is required to remove the ridge from the top of each cylinder - do this BEFORE removing the pistons!

13.3 Check the connecting rod side clearance (endplay) with a flat feeler gauge

13.4 The connecting rods and caps should be marked to indicate which cylinder they're installed in - if they aren't, mark them with a center-punch to avoid confusion during reassembly

assemblies may result in piston breakage.

2   After the cylinder ridges have been removed, turn the engine upside-down so the crankshaft is facing up.

3   Before the main bearing cap/bed plate and connecting rods are removed, check the endplay with feeler gauges. Slide them between the first connecting rod and the crankshaft throw until the play is removed **(see illustration)**. The endplay is equal to the thickness of the feeler gauge(s). If the endplay exceeds the service limit, new connecting rods will be required. If new rods (or a new crankshaft) are installed, the endplay may fall under the minimum listed in this Chapter's Specifications (if it does, the rods will have to be machined to restore it - consult an automotive machine shop for advice if necessary). Repeat the procedure for the remaining connecting rods.

4   Check the connecting rods and caps for identification marks **(see illustration)**. If they aren't plainly marked, use a small center-punch to make the appropriate number of indentations on each rod and cap (1, 2, 3, etc., depending on the cylinder they're associated with).

5   Loosen each of the connecting rod cap bolts 1/2-turn at a time until they can be removed by hand. Remove the number one connecting rod cap and bearing insert. Don't drop the bearing insert out of the cap.

6   Remove the bearing insert and push the connecting rod/piston assembly out through the top of the engine. Use a wooden or plastic hammer handle to push on the upper bearing surface in the connecting rod. If resistance is felt, double-check to make sure that all of the ridge was removed from the cylinder.

7   Repeat the procedure for the remaining cylinders.

8   After removal, reassemble the connecting rod caps and bearing inserts in their respective connecting rods and install the cap bolts finger tight. Leaving the old bearing inserts in place until reassembly will help prevent the connecting rod bearing surfaces from being accidentally nicked or gouged.

9   Don't separate the pistons from the connecting rods (see Section 18 for additional information).

14 Crankshaft - removal

Refer to illustration 14.1
Note: *The crankshaft can be removed only after the engine has been removed from the vehicle. It's assumed that the flywheel or driveplate, crankshaft pulley, timing belt, oil pan, oil pump body, oil filter and piston/connecting rod assemblies have already been removed. The rear main oil seal housing must be unbolted and separated from the block before proceeding with crankshaft removal.*

1   Before the crankshaft is removed, check the endplay. Mount a dial indicator with the stem in line with the crankshaft and just touching

14.1 Checking crankshaft endplay with a dial indicator

one of the crank throws **(see illustration)**.

2   Push the crankshaft all the way to the rear and zero the dial indicator. Next, pry the crankshaft to the front as far as possible and check the reading on the dial indicator. The distance that it moves is the endplay. If it's greater than listed in this Chapter's Specifications, check the crankshaft thrust surfaces for wear. If no wear is evident, new main bearings should correct the endplay.

3   If a dial indicator isn't available, feeler gauges can be used. Gently pry or push the crankshaft all the way to the front of the engine. Slip feeler gauges between the crankshaft and the front face of the thrust main bearing to determine the clearance.

4   Loosen the main bearing cap/bed plate assembly bolts 1/4-turn at a time each, until they can be removed by hand.

5   Gently tap the main bearing cap/bed plate assembly with a soft-face hammer around the perimeter of the assembly. Pull the assembly straight up and off the cylinder block and the three locating dowels. Remove the oil passage O-ring seal and the three locating dowels. Try not to drop the bearing inserts if they come out with the assembly.

6   Carefully lift the crankshaft out of the engine. It may be a good idea to have an assistant available, since the crankshaft is quite heavy. With the bearing inserts in place in the engine block and main bearing caps, reinstall the main bearing cap/bed plate assembly on the engine block and tighten the bolts finger tight.

15.1a Use a hammer and a large punch to knock the core plugs sideways in their bores

15.1b Pull the core plugs from the block with pliers

15.8 All bolt holes in the block - particularly the main bearing cap and head bolt holes - should be cleaned and restored with a tap (be sure to remove debris from the holes after this is done)

15.10 A large socket on an extension can be used to drive the new core plugs into the bores

2B

15 Engine block - cleaning

Refer to illustrations 15.1a, 15.1b, 15.8 and 15.10

1 Remove the core plugs from the engine block. To do this, knock one side of the plugs into the block with a hammer and a punch, then grasp them with large pliers and pull them out **(see illustrations)**.

2 Using a gasket scraper, remove all traces of gasket material from the engine block. Be very careful not to nick or gouge the gasket sealing surfaces.

3 Remove the main bearing cap/bed plate assembly and separate the bearing inserts from the caps and the engine block. **Note:** *The upper bearings are equipped with the oil groove and hole, the thrust bearing is in the No. 3 (center) location.* Tag the bearings, indicating which cylinder they were removed from, then set them aside.

4 Remove all of the threaded oil gallery plugs from the block. The plugs are usually very tight - they may have to be drilled out and the holes retapped. Use new plugs when the engine is reassembled.

5 If the engine is extremely dirty it should be taken to an automotive machine shop for cleaning.

6 After the block is returned, clean all oil holes and oil galleries one more time. Brushes specifically designed for this purpose are available at most auto parts stores. Flush the passages with warm water until the water runs clear, dry the block thoroughly and wipe all machined surfaces with a light, rust preventive oil. If you have access to compressed air, use it to speed the drying process and to blow out all the oil holes and galleries. **Warning:** *Wear eye protection when using compressed air!*

7 If the block isn't extremely dirty or slugged up, you can do an adequate cleaning job with hot soapy water and a stiff brush. Take plenty of time and do a thorough job. Regardless of the cleaning method used, be sure to clean all oil holes and galleries very thoroughly, dry the block completely and coat all machined surfaces with light oil.

8 The threaded holes in the block must be clean to ensure accurate torque readings during reassembly. Run the proper size tap into each of the holes to remove rust, corrosion, thread sealant or sludge and restore damaged threads **(see illustration)**. If possible, use compressed air to clear the holes of debris produced by this operation. Now is a good time to clean the threads on the head bolts and the main bearing cap bolts as well.

9 Reinstall the main bearing cap/bed plate assembly and the bearing inserts in the correct location. Tighten the bolts finger tight.

10 After coating the sealing surfaces of the new core plugs with Permatex no. 2 sealant (or equivalent), install them in the engine block **(see illustration)**. Make sure they're driven in straight and seated properly or leakage could result. Special tools are available for this purpose, but a large socket, with an outside diameter that will just slip into the core plug, a 1/2-inch drive extension and a hammer will work just as well.

11 Apply non-hardening sealant (such as Permatex No. 2 or Teflon pipe sealant) to the new oil gallery plugs and thread them into the holes in the block. Make sure they're tightened securely.

12 If the engine isn't going to be reassembled right away, cover it with a large plastic trash bag to keep it clean.

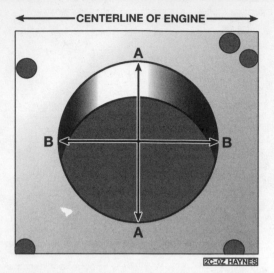

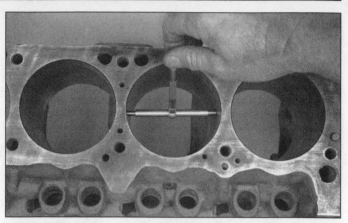

16.4b The ability to "feel" when the telescoping gauge is at the correct point will be developed over time, so work slowly and repeat the check until you're satisfied that the bore measurement is accurate

16.4a Measure the diameter of each cylinder at a right angle to the engine centerline (A) and parallel to the engine centerline (B) - out-of-round is the difference between A and B; taper is the difference between A and B at the top of the cylinder and A and B at the bottom of the cylinder

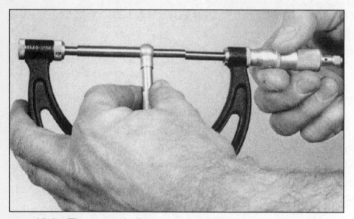

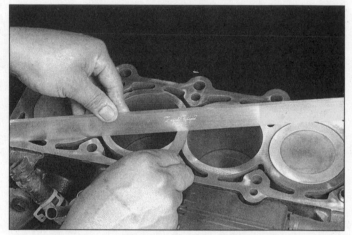

16.8 Check the cylinder block gasket surface for warpage by trying to slip a feeler gauge under a precision straightedge in the different directions shown (see the Specifications for the maximum warpage allowed and use a feeler gauge of that thickness)

16.4c The gauge is then measured with a micrometer to determine the bore size

16   Engine block - inspection

Refer to illustrations 16.4a, 16.4b. 16.4c and 16.8

1   Before the block is inspected, it should be cleaned as described in Section 15.

2   Visually check the block for cracks, rust and corrosion. Look for stripped threads in the threaded holes. It's also a good idea to have the block checked for hidden cracks by an automotive machine shop that has the special equipment to do this type of work. If defects are found, have the block repaired, if possible, or replaced.

3   Check the cylinder bores for scuffing and scoring.

4   Check the cylinders for taper and out-of-round conditions as follows **(see illustrations)**:

a) *Measure the diameter of each cylinder at the top (just under the ridge area), center and bottom of the cylinder bore, parallel to the crankshaft axis.*

b) *Next, measure each cylinder's diameter at the same three locations perpendicular to the crankshaft axis.*

c) *The taper of each cylinder is the difference between the bore diameter at the top of the cylinder and the diameter at the bottom. The out-of-round specification is the difference between the parallel and perpendicular measurements. Compare the results to this Chapter's Specifications.*

5   Repeat the procedure for the remaining pistons and cylinders.

6   If the cylinder walls are badly scuffed or scored, or if they're out-of-round or tapered beyond the limits given in this Chapter's Specifications, have the engine block rebored and honed at an automotive machine shop. If a rebore is done, oversize pistons and rings will be required.

7   If the cylinders are in reasonably good condition and not worn to the outside of the limits, and if the piston-to-cylinder clearances can be maintained properly, then they don't have to be rebored. Honing is all that's necessary (see Section 17).

8   Using a precision straightedge and a feeler gauge, check the block deck (the surface that mates with the cylinder head) for distortion **(see illustration)**. If it's distorted beyond the specified limit, it can be resurfaced by an automotive machine shop.

17   Cylinder honing

Refer to illustrations 17.3a and 17.3b

1   Prior to engine reassembly, the cylinder bores must be honed so the new piston rings will seat correctly and provide the best possible combustion chamber seal. **Note:** *If you don't have the tools or don't want to tackle the honing operation, most automotive machine shops will do it for a reasonable fee.*

17.3a A "bottle brush" hone will produce better results if you have never honed cylinders before

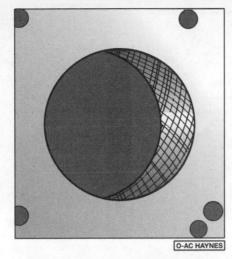

17.3b The cylinder hone should leave a smooth, crosshatch pattern with the lines intersecting at approximately a 60-degree angle

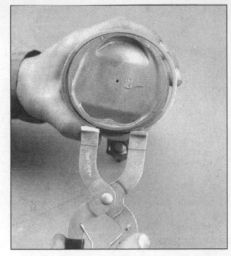

18.2 Use a special tool to remove the piston rings from the piston

2   Before honing the cylinders, install the main bearing cap/bed plate assembly and tighten the bolts to the torque listed in this Chapter's Specifications.

3   Two types of cylinder hones are commonly available - the flex hone or "bottle brush" type and the more traditional surfacing hone with spring-loaded stones. Both will do the job, but for the less experienced mechanic the "bottle brush" hone will probably be easier to use. You'll also need some kerosene or honing oil, rags and an electric drill motor. Proceed as follows:

a) *Mount the hone in the drill motor, compress the stones and slip it into the first cylinder* **(see illustration)**. *Be sure to wear safety goggles or a face shield!*

b) *Lubricate the cylinder with plenty of honing oil, turn on the drill and move the hone up-and-down in the cylinder at a pace that will produce a fine crosshatch pattern on the cylinder walls* **(see illustration)**. *Ideally, the crosshatch lines should intersect at approximately a 60-degree angle. Be sure to use plenty of lubricant and don't take off any more material than is absolutely necessary to produce the desired finish.* **Note:** *Piston ring manufacturers may specify a smaller crosshatch angle than the traditional 60-degrees - read and follow any instructions included with the new rings.*

c) *Don't withdraw the hone from the cylinder while it's running. Instead, shut off the drill and continue moving the hone up-and-down in the cylinder until it comes to a complete stop, then compress the stones and withdraw the hone. If you're using a "bottle brush" type hone, stop the drill motor, then turn the chuck in the normal direction of rotation while withdrawing the hone from the cylinder.*

d) *Wipe the oil out of the cylinder and repeat the procedure for the remaining cylinders.*

4   After the honing job is complete, chamfer the top edges of the cylinder bores with a small file so the rings won't catch when the pistons are installed. Be very careful not to nick the cylinder walls with the end of the file.

5   The entire engine block must be washed again very thoroughly with warm, soapy water to remove all traces of the abrasive grit produced during the honing operation. **Note:** *The bores can be considered clean when a lint-free white cloth - dampened with clean engine oil - used to wipe them out doesn't pick up any more honing residue, which will show up as gray areas on the cloth. Be sure to run a brush through all oil holes and galleries and flush them with running water.*

6   After rinsing, dry the block and apply a coat of light rust preventive oil to all machined surfaces. Wrap the block in a plastic trash bag to keep it clean and set it aside until reassembly.

18 Pistons and connecting rods - inspection

Refer to illustrations 18.2, 18.4a, 18.4b, 18.10 and 18.11

1   Before the inspection process can be carried out, the piston/connecting rod assemblies must be cleaned and the original piston rings removed from the pistons. **Note:** *Always use new piston rings when the engine is reassembled.*

2   Using a piston ring removal tool **(see illustration)**, carefully remove the rings from the pistons. Be careful not to nick or gouge the pistons in the process.

3   Scrape all traces of carbon from the top of the piston. A hand-held wire brush or a piece of fine emery cloth can be used once the majority of the deposits have been scraped away. Do not, under any circumstances, use a wire brush mounted in a drill motor to remove deposits from the pistons. The piston material is soft and may be eroded away by the wire brush.

4   Use a piston ring groove cleaning tool to remove carbon deposits from the ring grooves. If a tool isn't available, a piece broken off the old ring will do the job. Be very careful to remove only the carbon deposits - don't remove any metal and do not nick or scratch the sides of the ring grooves **(see illustrations)**.

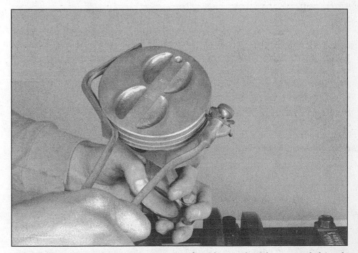

18.4a The piston ring grooves can be cleaned with a special tool like this one . . .

2B

18.4b . . . or a section of a broken ring

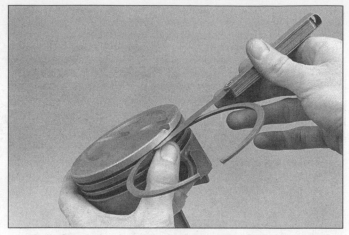

18.10 Check the ring side clearance with a feeler gauge at several points around the groove

5   Once the deposits have been removed, clean the piston/rod assemblies with solvent and dry them with compressed air (if available). Make sure the oil return holes in the back sides of the ring grooves are clear.

6   If the pistons and cylinder walls aren't damaged or worn excessively, and if the engine block is not rebored, new pistons won't be necessary. Normal piston wear appears as even, vertical wear on the piston thrust surfaces and slight looseness of the top ring in its groove. New piston rings, however, should always be used when an engine is rebuilt.

7   Carefully inspect each piston for cracks around the skirt, at the pin bosses and at the ring lands.

8   Look for scoring and scuffing on the thrust faces of the skirt, holes in the piston crown and burned areas at the edge of the crown. If the skirt is scored or scuffed, the engine may have been suffering from overheating and/or abnormal combustion, which caused excessively high operating temperatures. The cooling and lubrication systems should be checked thoroughly. A hole in the piston crown is an indication that abnormal combustion (preignition) was occurring. Burned areas at the edge of the piston crown are usually evidence of spark knock (detonation). If any of the above problems exist, the causes must be corrected or the damage will occur again. The causes may include intake air leaks, incorrect fuel/air mixture, incorrect ignition timing and EGR system malfunctions.

9   Corrosion of the piston, in the form of small pits, indicates that coolant is leaking into the combustion chamber and/or the crankcase. Again, the cause must be corrected or the problem may persist in the rebuilt engine.

10   Measure the piston ring side clearance by laying a new piston ring in each ring groove and slipping a feeler gauge in beside it **(see illustration)**. Check the clearance at three or four locations around each groove. Be sure to use the correct ring for each groove - they are different. If the side clearance is greater than specified, new pistons will have to be installed. If new pistons are installed, repeat this step with the new pistons and rings.

11   Check the piston-to-bore clearance by measuring the bore (see Section 16) and the piston diameter. Make sure the pistons and bores are correctly matched. Measure the piston across the skirt 11/16-inch above the bottom of the piston, at a 90-degree angle to and in line with the piston pin **(see illustration)**. Subtract the piston diameter from the bore diameter to obtain the clearance. If it's greater than specified, the block will have to be rebored and new pistons and rings installed.

12   Check the piston-to-rod clearance by twisting the piston and rod in opposite directions. Any noticeable play indicates excessive wear, which must be corrected. The piston/connecting rod assemblies should be taken to an automotive machine shop to have the pistons and rods resized and new pins installed.

13   If the pistons must be removed from the connecting rods for any reason, they should be taken to an automotive machine shop. While

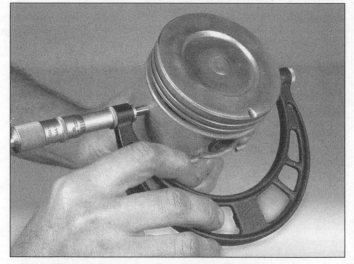

18.11 Measure the piston diameter at a 90-degree angle to the piston pin and in line with it. Check for evidence of seizure such as scratches or dark streaks in the piston or cracks in the piston - replace it if any of these indications are found

they are there have the connecting rods checked for bend and twist, since automotive machine shops have special equipment for this purpose. **Note:** *Unless new pistons and/or connecting rods must be installed, do not disassemble the pistons and connecting rods.*

14   Check the connecting rods for cracks and other damage. Temporarily remove the rod caps, lift out the old bearing inserts, wipe the rod and cap bearing surfaces clean and inspect them for nicks, gouges and scratches. After checking the rods, replace the old bearings, slip the caps into place and tighten the nuts finger tight. **Note:** *If the engine is being rebuilt because of a connecting rod knock, be sure to install new rods.*

19 Crankshaft - inspection

Refer to illustration 19.1, 19.2, 19.4 and 19.7

1   Remove all burrs from the crankshaft oil holes with a stone, file or scraper **(see illustration)**.

2   Clean the crankshaft with solvent and dry it with compressed air (if available). Be sure to clean the oil holes with a stiff brush and flush them with solvent **(see illustration)**. **Warning:** *If compressed air is used always wear eye protection to prevent solvents or debris from*

19.1 The oil holes should be chamfered so sharp edges don't gouge or scratch the new bearings

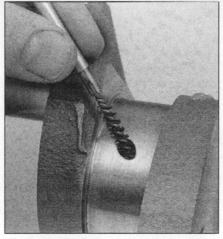

19.2 Use a wire or stiff bristle brush to clean the oil passages in the crankshaft

19.4 Rubbing a penny lengthwise on each journal will reveal its condition - if copper rubs off and is embedded in the crankshaft, the journals should be reground

2B

19.7 Measure the diameter of each crankshaft journal at several points to detect taper and out-of-round conditions

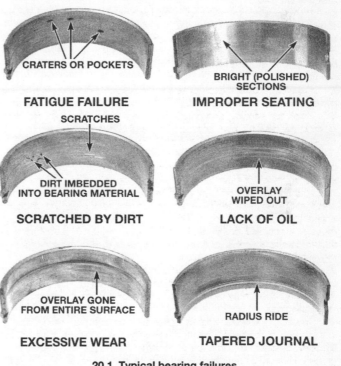

CRATERS OR POCKETS

FATIGUE FAILURE

BRIGHT (POLISHED) SECTIONS

IMPROPER SEATING

SCRATCHES

DIRT IMBEDDED INTO BEARING MATERIAL

SCRATCHED BY DIRT

OVERLAY WIPED OUT

LACK OF OIL

OVERLAY GONE FROM ENTIRE SURFACE

EXCESSIVE WEAR

RADIUS RIDE

TAPERED JOURNAL

20.1 Typical bearing failures

causing and injury to your eyes.

3   Check the main and connecting rod bearing journals for uneven wear, scoring, pits and cracks.

4   Rub a penny across each journal several times. If a journal picks up copper from the penny, it's too rough and must be reground **(see illustration)**.

5   Remove all burrs from the crankshaft oil holes with a stone, file or scraper.

6   Check the rest of the crankshaft for cracks and other damage. It should be magnafluxed to reveal hidden cracks - an automotive machine shop will handle the procedure.

7   Using a micrometer, measure the diameter of the main and connecting rod journals and compare the results to the Specifications **(see illustration)** listed in this Chapter. By measuring the diameter at a number of points around each journal's circumference, you'll be able to determine whether or not the journal is out-of-round. Take the measurement at each end of the journal, near the crank throws, to determine if the journal is tapered.

8   If the crankshaft journals are damaged, tapered, out-of-round or worn beyond the limits given in the Specifications, have the crankshaft reground by an automotive machine shop. Be sure to use the correct size bearing inserts if the crankshaft is reconditioned.

9   Check the oil seal journals at each end of the crankshaft for wear and damage. If the seal has worn a groove in the journal, or if it's nicked or scratched, the new seal may leak when the engine is reassembled. In some cases, an automotive machine shop may be able to repair the journal by pressing on a thin sleeve. If repair isn't fea-

sible, a new or different crankshaft should be installed.

10   Refer to Section 20 and examine the main and rod bearing inserts.

20   Main and connecting rod bearings - inspection

Refer to illustrations 20.1 and 20.3

1   Even though the main and connecting rod bearings should be replaced with new ones during the engine overhaul, the old bearings should be retained for close examination, as they may reveal valuable information about the condition of the engine **(see illustration)**.

2   Bearing failure occurs because of lack of lubrication, the presence of dirt or other foreign particles, overloading the engine and cor-

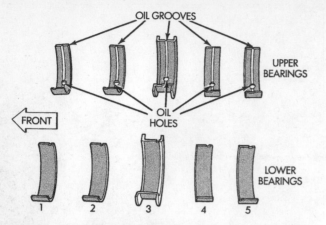

20.3 Remove the bearings from the engine block, the main bearing caps, the connecting rods and the rod caps and keep them in the order of removal in the same general position as their location in the engine

rosion. Regardless of the cause of bearing failure, it must be corrected before the engine is reassembled to prevent it from happening again.

3   When examining the bearings, remove them from the engine block, the main bearing caps, the connecting rods and the rod caps and lay them out on a clean surface in the same general position as their location in the engine **(see illustration)**. This will enable you to match any bearing problems with the corresponding crankshaft journal.

4   Dirt and other foreign particles get into the engine in a variety of ways. It may be left in the engine during assembly, or it may pass through filters or the PCV system. It may get into the oil, and from there into the bearings. Metal chips from machining operations and normal engine wear are often present. Abrasives are sometimes left in engine components after reconditioning, especially when parts are not thoroughly cleaned using the proper cleaning methods. Whatever the source, these foreign objects often end up embedded in the soft bearing material and are easily recognized. Large particles will not embed in the bearing and will score or gouge the bearing and journal. The best prevention for this cause of bearing failure is to clean all parts thoroughly and keep everything spotlessly clean during engine assembly. Frequent and regular engine oil and filter changes are also recommended.

5   Lack of lubrication (or lubrication breakdown) has a number of interrelated causes. Excessive heat (which thins the oil), overloading (which squeezes the oil from the bearing face) and oil leakage or throw off (from excessive bearing clearances, worn oil pump or high engine speeds) all contribute to lubrication breakdown. Blocked oil passages, which usually are the result of misaligned oil holes in a bearing shell, will also oil starve a bearing and destroy it. When lack of lubrication is the cause of bearing failure, the bearing material is wiped or extruded from the steel backing of the bearing. Temperatures may increase to the point where the steel backing turns blue from overheating.

6   Driving habits can have a definite effect on bearing life. Full throttle, low speed operation (lugging the engine) puts very high loads on bearings, which tends to squeeze out the oil film. These loads cause the bearings to flex, which produces fine cracks in the bearing face (fatigue failure). Eventually the bearing material will loosen in pieces and tear away from the steel backing. Short trip driving leads to corrosion of bearings because insufficient engine heat is produced to drive off the condensed water and corrosive gases. These products collect in the engine oil, forming acid and sludge. As the oil is carried to the engine bearings, the acid attacks and corrodes the bearing material.

7   Incorrect bearing installation during engine assembly will lead to bearing failure as well. Tight fitting bearings leave insufficient bearing oil clearance and will result in oil starvation. Dirt or foreign particles trapped behind a bearing insert result in high spots on the bearing which lead to failure.

21   Engine overhaul - reassembly sequence

1   Before beginning engine reassembly, make sure you have all the necessary new parts, gaskets and seals as well as the following items on hand:

> Common hand tools
> A 1/2-inch drive torque wrench
> Piston ring installation tool
> Piston ring compressor
> Plastigage set
> Feeler gauges
> A fine-tooth file
> New engine oil
> Engine assembly lube or moly-base grease
> Gasket sealant
> Thread locking compound

2   In order to save time and avoid problems, engine reassembly must be done in the following general order:

> Piston rings
> Crankshaft and main bearings
> Piston/connecting rod assemblies
> Rear main oil seal housing
> Front case and oil pump assembly
> Oil pan
> Cylinder head assembly
> Water pump
> Timing belt and sprockets
> Timing belt cover
> Intake and exhaust manifolds
> Rocker arm cover
> Flywheel/driveplate

22   Piston rings - installation

Refer to illustrations 22.3, 22.4, 22.5, 22.9a, 22.9b and 22.12

1   Before installing the new piston rings, the ring end gaps must be checked. It's assumed that the piston ring side clearance has been checked and verified correct (see Section 18).

2   Lay out the piston/connecting rod assemblies and the new ring sets so the ring sets will be matched with the same piston and cylinder during the end gap measurement and engine assembly.

3   Insert the top (number one) ring into the first cylinder and square it up with the cylinder walls by pushing it in with the top of the piston **(see illustration)**. The ring should be near the bottom of the cylinder, at the lower limit of ring travel.

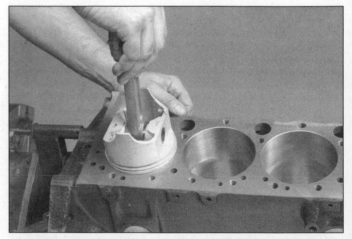

22.3 When checking piston ring end gap, the ring must be square in the cylinder bore (this is done by pushing the ring down with the top of a piston as shown)

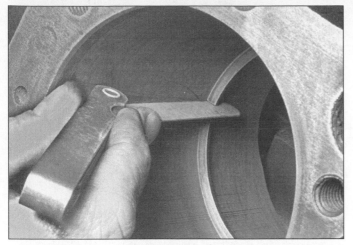

22.4 With the ring square in the cylinder, measure the end gap with a feeler gauge

22.5 If the end gap is too small, clamp a file in a vise and file the ring ends (from the outside end of the file in towards the vise only) to enlarge the gap slightly

4   To measure the end gap, slip feeler gauges between the ends of the ring until a gauge equal to the gap width is found **(see illustration)**. The feeler gauge should slide between the ring ends with a slight amount of drag. Compare the measurement to this Chapter's Specifications. If the gap is larger or smaller than specified, double-check to make sure you have the correct rings before proceeding.

5   If the gap is too small, it must be enlarged or the ring ends may come in contact with each other during engine operation, which can cause serious damage to the engine. The end gap can be increased by filing the ring ends very carefully with a fine file. Mount the file in a vise equipped with soft jaws, slip the ring over the file with the ends contacting the file face and slowly move the ring to remove material from the ends. When performing this operation, file only by pushing the ring from the outside end of the file towards the vise **(see illustration)**.

6   Excess end gap isn't critical unless it's greater than 0.039-inch. Again, double-check to make sure you have the correct rings for your engine.

7   Repeat the procedure for each ring that will be installed in the first cylinder and for each ring in the remaining cylinders. Remember to keep rings, pistons and cylinders matched up.

8   Once the ring end gaps have been checked/corrected, the rings can be installed on the pistons.

9   The oil control ring (lowest one on the piston) is usually installed first. It's composed of three separate components. Slip the spacer/expander into the groove **(see illustration)**. If an anti-rotation

tang is used, make sure it's inserted into the drilled hole in the ring groove. Next, install the lower side rail. Don't use a piston ring installation tool on the oil ring side rails, as they may be damaged. Instead, place one end of the side rail into the groove between the spacer/expander and the ring land, hold it firmly in place and slide a finger around the piston while pushing the rail into the groove **(see illustration)**. Next, install the upper side rail in the same manner.

10   After the three oil ring components have been installed, check to make sure that both the upper and lower side rails can be turned smoothly in the ring groove.

11   The number two (middle) ring is installed next. It's usually stamped with a mark which must face up, toward the top of the piston. **Note:** *Always follow the instructions printed on the ring package or box - different manufacturers may require different approaches. Do not mix up the top and middle rings, as they have different cross-sections.*

12   Use a piston ring installation tool and make sure the identification mark is facing the top of the piston, then slip the ring into the middle groove on the piston **(see illustration)**. Don't expand the ring any more than necessary to slide it over the piston.

13   Install the number one (top) ring in the same manner. Make sure the mark is facing up. Be careful not to confuse the number one and number two rings.

14   Repeat the procedure for the remaining pistons and rings.

22.9a Installing the spacer/expander in the oil control ring groove

22.9b DO NOT use a piston ring installation tool when installing the oil ring side rails

22.12 Install the compression rings with a ring expander - the mark on the ring must face up

2B

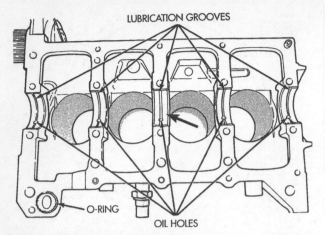

23.5 Install the main bearing inserts into each main bearing saddle in the block. The thrust bearing insert must be installed in the No. 3 (center) bearing position (arrow)

23.11 Lay the Plastigage strips (arrow) on the main bearing journals, parallel to the crankshaft centerline

23 Crankshaft installation and main bearing oil clearance check

1   Crankshaft installation is the first step in engine reassembly. It's assumed at this point that the engine block and crankshaft have been cleaned, inspected and repaired or reconditioned.
2   Position the engine block with the bottom facing up.
3   Remove the mounting bolts and lift out the main bearing cap/bed frame assembly.
4   If they're still in place, remove the original bearing inserts from the block and the main bearing cap/bed frame assembly Wipe the bearing surfaces of the block and assembly with a clean, lint-free cloth. They must be kept spotlessly clean.

Main bearing oil clearance check

Refer to illustrations 23.5, 23.11 and 23.15
5   Clean the back sides of the new main bearing inserts and lay one in each main bearing saddle in the block. Each *upper bearing* has an oil groove and oil hole in it. The thrust bearing insert must be installed in the No. 3 (center) bearing position **(see illustration)**. Lay the lower bearing insert from each set in the corresponding location in the main bearing cap/bed frame assembly. Make sure the tab on the bearing insert fits into the recess in the block or bed frame assembly. **Caution:** *The oil holes in the block must line up with the oil holes in the upper bearing inserts. Do not hammer the bearing insert into place and don't nick or gouge the bearing faces. No lubrication should be used at this time.*
6   Clean the faces of the bearing inserts in the block and the crankshaft main bearing journals with a clean, lint-free cloth.
7   Check or clean the oil holes in the crankshaft, as any dirt here can go only one way - straight through the new bearings.
8   Once you're certain the crankshaft is clean, carefully lay it in position in the cylinder block.
9   Before the crankshaft can be permanently installed, the main bearing oil clearance must be checked.
10   Make sure the three locating dowels are in place on the cylinder block. This is necessary for proper alignment of the main bearing cap/bed plate assembly to the cylinder block and crankshaft.
11   Cut several pieces of the appropriate size Plastigage (they must be slightly shorter than the width of the main bearing journal) and place one piece on each crankshaft main bearing journal, parallel with the journal axis **(see illustration)**.
12   Clean the faces of the bearing inserts in the bed frame assembly. Hold the bearing inserts in place and install this assembly onto the crankshaft and cylinder block. Don't disturb the Plastigage.
13   Apply clean engine oil to all bolt threads prior to installation, then

23.15 Compare the width of the crushed Plastigage to the scale on the envelope to determine the main bearing oil clearance (always take the measurement at the widest point of the Plastigage) - be sure to use the correct scale; standard and metric scales are included

install all bolts finger-tight. Tighten the outer three 8-mm bolts where the locating dowels are located until the bed plate contacts the cylinder block, then tighten these bolts to 22-ft-lbs. At this time the bed plate should be completely seated around the entire perimeter of the cylinder block. Tighten the ten center 11-mm bolts (over the crankshaft bearings). Starting with the center bolts and working out toward the ends, tighten these bolts in three steps, to the torque listed in this Chapter's Specifications. Don't rotate the crankshaft at any time during this operation.
14   Remove the bolts in the reverse order of tightening and carefully lift straight up and off the main bearing cap/bed frame assembly. Don't disturb the Plastigage or rotate the crankshaft. If the main bearing cap/bed frame assembly is difficult to remove, tap it gently from side-to-side with a soft-face hammer to loosen it.
15   Compare the width of the crushed Plastigage on each journal to the scale printed on the Plastigage envelope to obtain the main bearing oil clearance **(see illustration)**. Check the Specifications listed in this Chapter to make sure it's correct.
16   If the clearance is not as specified, the bearing inserts may be the wrong size (which means different ones will be required). Before deciding if different inserts are needed, make sure that no dirt or oil was between the bearing inserts and the cap assembly or block when the clearance was measured. If the Plastigage was wider at one end than the other, the crankshaft journal may be tapered (refer to Section 19). If the clearance still exceeds the limit specified, the bearing insert(s) will

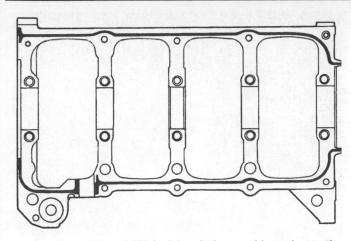

23.21 Apply a 0.059 to 0.078-inch bead of anaerobic sealant to the cylinder block only in the indicated areas

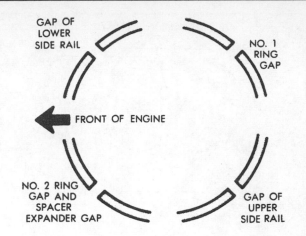

24.5 Position the piston ring end gaps as shown before installing the pistons in the engine block

have to be replaced with an undersize bearing insert(s). **Caution:** *When installing a new crankshaft always use a standard bearing insert set.*

17   Carefully scrape all traces of the Plastigage material off the main bearing journals and/or the bearing insert faces. Be sure to remove all residue from the oil holes. Use your fingernail or the edge of a credit card - don't nick or scratch the bearing faces.

Final crankshaft installation

Refer to illustration 23.21

18   Carefully lift the crankshaft out of the cylinder block.
19   Clean the bearing insert faces in the cylinder block, then apply a thin, uniform layer of moly-base grease or engine assembly lube to each of the bearing surfaces. Be sure to coat the thrust faces as well as the journal face of the thrust bearing. **Caution:** *Be sure to install the thrust bearing insert in the No. 3 journal (see illustration 23.5).*
20   Install a new oil control O-ring seal and make sure the three locating dowels are in place on the cylinder block. The dowels are necessary for proper alignment of the main bearing cap/bed plate assembly to the cylinder block and crankshaft.
21   **Caution:** *Use only the specified anaerobic sealer on the bedplate or damage may occur to the engine.* Clean the bedplate-to-cylinder block mating surface on the block of any oil residue. Apply a 0.059 to 0.078-inch bead of Mopar Torque Cure Gasket Maker to the cylinder block in the indicated areas **(see illustration)**.
22   Make sure the crankshaft journals are clean, then lay the crankshaft back in place in the cylinder block.
23   Clean the bearing insert faces in the main bearing cap/bed frame assembly, then apply the same lubricant to them. **Caution:** *Do not get any lubricant on the bedplate-to-cylinder block mating surface as it will inhibit the sealing ability of the sealant applied to the cylinder block in Step 21.*
24   Hold the bearing inserts in place and install the assembly onto the crankshaft and cylinder block. Push the assembly down until it contacts the locating dowels.
25   Apply clean engine oil to all bolt threads prior to installation, then install all bolts finger-tight.
26   Tighten the outer three 8-mm bolts where the locating dowels are located until the bed plate contacts the cylinder block, then tighten these three bolts to 22-ft-lbs. At this time the bed plate should be completely seated around the entire perimeter of the cylinder block.
27   Tighten the ten center 11-mm bolts (over the crankshaft bearings). Starting with the center bolts and working out toward the ends, tighten these bolts in three steps, to the torque listed in this Chapter's Specifications.
28   Tighten the remaining 8-mm perimeter bolts, starting with the center bolts and working out toward the ends. Tighten these bolts in three steps, to the torque listed in this Chapter's Specifications.
29   Tap the ends of the crankshaft forward and backward with a lead

or brass hammer to line up the main bearing and crankshaft thrust surfaces.
30   Rotate the crankshaft a number of times by hand to check for any obvious binding. It should rotate with a torque of 50 in-lbs or less. If rotation is restricted, correct the problem at this time.
31   Recheck the crankshaft endplay with a feeler gauge or a dial indicator as described in Section 19. The endplay should be correct if the crankshaft thrust faces aren't worn or damaged and new bearings have been installed.
32   Refer to Chapter 2A and install the new rear main oil seal.

24   Pistons and connecting rods - installation and rod bearing oil clearance check

Refer to illustrations 24.5, 24.10, 24.12, 24.13 and 24.16

1   Before installing the piston/connecting rod assemblies, the cylinder walls must be perfectly clean, the top edge of each cylinder bore must be chamfered, and the crankshaft must be in place.
2   Remove the cap from the end of the number one connecting rod (refer to the marks made during removal). Remove the original bearing inserts and wipe the bearing surfaces of the connecting rod and cap with a clean, lint-free cloth. They must be kept spotlessly clean.

Connecting rod bearing oil clearance check

3   Clean the back side of the new upper bearing insert, then lay it in place in the connecting rod. Make sure the tab on the bearing fits into the recess in the rod. Don't hammer the bearing insert into place and be very careful not to nick or gouge the bearing face. Don't lubricate the bearing at this time.
4   Clean the back side of the other bearing insert and install it in the rod cap. Again, make sure the tab on the bearing fits into the recess in the cap, and don't apply any lubricant. It's critically important that the mating surfaces of the bearing and connecting rod are perfectly clean and oil free when they're assembled.
5   Position the piston ring gaps at 90-degree intervals around the piston as shown **(see illustration)**.
6   Lubricate the piston and rings with clean engine oil and attach a piston ring compressor to the piston. Leave the skirt protruding about 1/4-inch to guide the piston into the cylinder. The rings must be compressed until they're flush with the piston.
7   Rotate the crankshaft until the number one connecting rod journal is at BDC (bottom dead center) and apply a coat of engine oil to the cylinder walls.
8   With the weight designation mark, or arrow, on top of the piston facing the front (timing belt end) of the engine, gently insert the piston/connecting rod assembly into the number one cylinder bore and

24.10 The piston can be driven gently into the cylinder bore with the end of a wooden or plastic hammer handle

24.12 Lay the Plastigage strips on each rod bearing journal, parallel to the crankshaft centerline

rest the bottom edge of the ring compressor on the engine block. **Note:** *The connecting rod also has a mark on it that must face the front (timing belt end) of the engine (if it faces the opposite direction, the piston and connecting rod have been assembled improperly.*

9   Tap the top edge of the ring compressor to make sure it's contacting the block around its entire circumference.

10   Gently tap on the top of the piston with the end of a wooden or plastic hammer handle **(see illustration)** while guiding the end of the connecting rod into place on the crankshaft journal. The piston rings may try to pop out of the ring compressor just before entering the cylinder bore, so keep some downward pressure on the ring compressor. Work slowly, and if any resistance is felt as the piston enters the cylinder, stop immediately. Find out what's hanging up and fix it before proceeding. Do not, for any reason, force the piston into the cylinder - you might break a ring and/or the piston.

11   Once the piston/connecting rod assembly is installed, the connecting rod bearing oil clearance must be checked before the rod cap is permanently bolted in place.

12   Cut a piece of the appropriate size Plastigage slightly shorter than the width of the connecting rod bearing and lay it in place on the number one connecting rod journal, parallel with the journal axis **(see illustration)**.

13   Clean the connecting rod cap bearing face and install the rod cap. Make sure the mating mark on the cap is on the same side as the mark on the connecting rod **(see illustration)**. **Note:** *Check to make sure the identification mark on the connecting rod faces toward the front (timing belt) end of the engine.*

14   Install the old rod bolts, at this time, and tighten them to the torque listed in this Chapter's Specifications, working up to it in three steps. **Note:** *Use a thin-wall socket to avoid erroneous torque readings that can result if the socket is wedged between the rod cap and bolt. If the socket tends to wedge itself between the nut and the cap, lift up on it slightly until it no longer contacts the cap. Do not rotate the crankshaft at any time during this operation.*

15   Remove the bolts and detach the rod cap, being very careful not to disturb the Plastigage. Discard the cap bolts at this time as they cannot be reused.

16   Compare the width of the crushed Plastigage to the scale printed on the Plastigage envelope to obtain the oil clearance **(see illustration)**. Compare it to the Specifications (listed in this Chapter) to make sure the clearance is correct.

17   If the clearance is not as specified, the bearing inserts may be the wrong size (which means different ones will be required). Before deciding that different inserts are needed, make sure that no dirt or oil was between the bearing inserts and the connecting rod or cap when the clearance was measured. Also, recheck the journal diameter. If the Plastigage was wider at one end than the other, the journal may be tapered (refer to Section 19). If the clearance still exceeds the limit specified, the bearing will have to be replaced with an undersize bearing. **Caution:** *When installing a new crankshaft always use a standard bearing.*

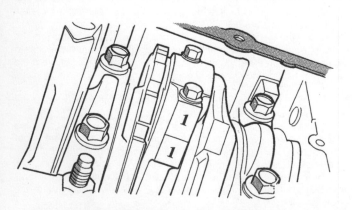

24.13 Install the cap onto the rod and make sure the mating marks are on the same side

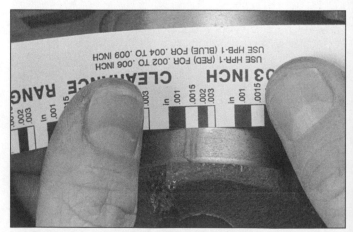

24.16 Compare the width of the crushed Plastigage to the scale on the envelope to determine the rod bearing oil clearance (always take the measurement at the widest point of the Plastigage) - be sure to use the correct scale; standard and metric scales are included

Final connecting rod installation

18   Carefully scrape all traces of the Plastigage material off the rod journal and/or bearing face. Be very careful not to scratch the bearing - use your fingernail or the edge of a credit card.

19   Make sure the bearing faces are perfectly clean, then apply a uniform layer of clean moly-base grease or engine assembly lube to both of them. You'll have to push the piston into the cylinder to expose the face of the bearing insert in the connecting rod.

20   **Caution:** *New connecting rod cap bolts must be installed at this time. Do not reuse the old bolts as they have stretched and cannot be reused.* Slide the connecting rod back into place on the journal, install the rod cap, install new bolts and tighten the bolts to the torque listed in this Chapter's Specifications. Again, work up to the torque in three steps.

21   Repeat the entire procedure for the remaining pistons/connecting rods.

22   The important points to remember are:

a) *Keep the back sides of the bearing inserts and the insides of the connecting rods and caps perfectly clean when assembling them.*

b) *Make sure you have the correct piston/rod assembly for each cylinder.*

c) *The mark on the piston must face the front (timing belt end) of the engine.*

d) *Lubricate the cylinder walls with clean oil.*

e) *Lubricate the bearing faces when installing the rod caps after the oil clearance has been checked.*

23   After all the piston/connecting rod assemblies have been properly installed, rotate the crankshaft a number of times by hand to check for any obvious binding.

24   As a final step, the connecting rod endplay must be checked. Refer to Section 13 for this procedure.

25   Compare the measured endplay to the Specifications to make sure it's correct. If it was correct before disassembly and the original crankshaft and rods were reinstalled, it should still be right. If new rods or a new crankshaft were installed, the endplay may be inadequate. If so, the rods will have to be removed and taken to an automotive machine shop for resizing.

25   Initial start-up and break-in after overhaul

Warning: *Have a fire extinguisher handy when starting the engine for the first time.*

1   Once the engine has been installed in the vehicle, double-check the engine oil and coolant levels. Add transaxle fluid as needed.

2   With the spark plugs out of the engine and the ignition system disabled (disconnect the primary [low voltage] electrical connector from the coil pack), crank the engine until the oil pressure light goes out.

3   Install the spark plugs, hook up the plug wires and restore the ignition system functions.

4   Start the engine. It may take a few moments for the fuel system to build up pressure, but the engine should start without a great deal of effort. **Note:** *If backfiring occurs through the throttle body, recheck the valve timing.*

5   After the engine starts, it should be allowed to warm up to normal operating temperature. Try to keep the engine speed at approximately 2000 rpm. While the engine is warming up, make a thorough check for fuel, oil and coolant leaks. Check the automatic transaxle fluid level (if so equipped).

6   Shut the engine off and recheck the engine oil and coolant levels.

7   Drive the vehicle to an area with minimum traffic, accelerate from 30 to 50 mph, then allow the vehicle to slow to 30 mph with the throttle closed. Repeat the procedure 10 or 12 times. This will load the piston rings and cause them to seat properly against the cylinder walls. Check again for oil and coolant leaks.

8   Drive the vehicle gently for the first 500 miles (no sustained high speeds) and keep a constant check on the oil level. It is not unusual for an engine to use oil during the break-in period.

9   At approximately 500 to 600 miles, change the oil and filter.

10   For the next few hundred miles, drive the vehicle normally. Do not pamper it or abuse it.

11   After 2000 miles, change the oil and filter again and consider the engine broken in.

2B

Notes

Chapter 3
Cooling, heating and air conditioning systems

Contents

Specifications

General

Radiator cap pressure	14 to 18 psi
Thermostat rating (opening temperature)	192 to 199-degrees F
Cooling system capacity	See Chapter 1
Refrigerant type	R-134a
Refrigerant capacity	28 ounces

Torque specifications

Thermostat cover mounting bolts	105 in-lbs
Water pump mounting bolts	105 in-lbs

1 General information

Engine cooling system

All vehicles covered by this manual employ a pressurized engine cooling system with thermostatically controlled coolant circulation. An impeller type water pump mounted on the timing belt end of the block pumps coolant through the engine. The coolant flows around each cylinder and toward the transaxle end of the engine. Cast-in coolant passages direct coolant around the intake and exhaust ports, near the spark plug areas and in close proximity to the exhaust valve guides.

A wax pellet type thermostat is located in a coolant outlet housing on the engine. During warm up, the closed thermostat prevents coolant from circulating through the radiator. As the engine nears normal operating temperature, the thermostat opens and allows hot coolant to travel through the radiator, where it's cooled before returning to the engine.

The cooling system is sealed by a pressure type radiator cap, which raises the boiling point of the coolant and increases the cooling efficiency of the radiator. If the system pressure exceeds the cap pressure relief value, the excess pressure in the system forces the spring-loaded valve inside the cap off its seat and allows the coolant to escape through the overflow tube into a coolant reservoir. When the system cools, the excess coolant is automatically drawn from the reservoir back into the radiator.

The coolant reservoir serves as both the point at which fresh coolant is added to the cooling system to maintain the proper fluid level and as a holding tank for overheated coolant.

This type of cooling system is known as a closed design because coolant that escapes past the pressure cap is saved and reused.

Heating system

The heating system consists of a blower fan and heater core located in the heater box, the hoses connecting the heater core to the engine cooling system and the heater/air conditioning control head on the dashboard. Hot engine coolant is circulated through the heater core. When the heater mode is activated, a flap opens to expose the heater box to the passenger compartment. A fan switch on the control head activates the blower motor, which forces air through the core, heating the air.

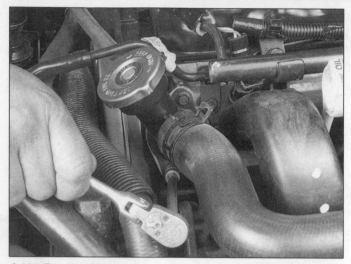

3.11a Remove the bolts from the housing cover and separate the cover and thermostat (SOHC engine)

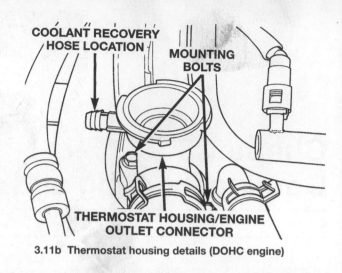

3.11b Thermostat housing details (DOHC engine)

Air conditioning system

The air conditioning system consists of a condenser mounted in front of the radiator, an evaporator mounted adjacent to the heater core, a compressor mounted on the engine, a receiver-drier which contains a high pressure relief valve and the plumbing connecting all of the above components.

A blower fan forces the warmer air of the passenger compartment through the evaporator core (sort of a radiator-in-reverse), transferring the heat from the air to the refrigerant. The liquid refrigerant boils off into low pressure vapor, taking the heat with it when it leaves the evaporator.

2   Antifreeze - general information

Warning: *Do not allow antifreeze to come in contact with your skin or painted surfaces of the vehicle. Rinse off spills immediately with plenty of water. Antifreeze is highly toxic if ingested. Never leave antifreeze lying around in an open container or in puddles on the floor; children and pets are attracted by it's sweet smell and may drink it. Check with local authorities about disposing of used antifreeze. Many communities have collection centers which will see that antifreeze is disposed of safely.*

The cooling system should be filled with a water/ethylene glycol based antifreeze solution, which will prevent freezing down to at least - 20-degrees F, or lower if local climate requires it. It also provides protection against corrosion and increases the coolant boiling point.

The cooling system should be drained, flushed and refilled at the specified intervals (see Chapter 1). Old or contaminated antifreeze solutions are likely to cause damage and encourage the formation of corrosion and scale in the system. Use distilled water with the antifreeze solution. **Note:** *Check with local authorities about disposing of used antifreeze. Many communities have collection centers which will see that antifreeze is disposed of safely.*

Before adding antifreeze, check all hose connections, because antifreeze tends to leak through very minute openings. Engines don't normally consume coolant, so if the level goes down, find the cause and correct it.

The exact mixture of antifreeze-to-water which you should use depends on the relative weather conditions. The mixture should contain at least 50-percent antifreeze, but should never contain more than 70-percent antifreeze. Consult the mixture ratio chart on the antifreeze container before adding coolant. Hydrometers are available at most auto parts stores to test the coolant. Use antifreeze which meets the vehicle manufacturer's specifications.

3   Thermostat - check and replacement

Warning: *Do not remove the radiator cap, drain the coolant or replace the thermostat until the engine has cooled completely. Do not allow antifreeze to come in contact with your skin or painted surfaces of the vehicle. Rinse off spills immediately with plenty of water. Antifreeze is highly toxic if ingested. Never leave antifreeze lying around in an open container or in puddles on the floor; children and pets are attracted by it's sweet smell and may drink it. Check with local authorities about disposing of used antifreeze. Many communities have collection centers which will see that antifreeze is disposed of safely.*

Check

1   Before assuming the thermostat is to blame for a cooling system problem, check the coolant level and temperature gauge operation.

2   If the engine seems to be taking a long time to warm up (based on heater output or temperature gauge operation), the thermostat is probably stuck open. Replace the thermostat with a new one.

3   If the engine runs hot, use your hand to check the temperature of the upper radiator hose. If the hose isn't hot, but the engine is, the thermostat is probably stuck closed, preventing the coolant inside the engine from escaping to the radiator. Replace the thermostat. **Caution:** *Don't drive the vehicle without a thermostat. The computer may stay in open loop, causing emissions and fuel economy to suffer.*

4   If the upper radiator hose is hot, it means that the coolant is flowing and the thermostat is open. Consult the Troubleshooting section at the front of this manual for cooling system diagnosis.

Replacement

Refer to illustrations 3.11a, 3.11b, 3.14 and 3.15

5   Disconnect the cable from the negative terminal of the battery.

6   Drain the cooling system (see Chapter 1). If the coolant is relatively new or in good condition, save it in a clean container and reuse it.

7   Follow the upper radiator hose to the engine to locate the thermostat cover.

8   Disconnect the coolant recovery hose from the thermostat cover.

9   Loosen the hose clamp and detach the hose from the fitting. If the hose is stuck, grasp it near the end with a pair of adjustable pliers and twist it to break the seal, then pull it off. If the hose is old or deteriorated, cut it off and install a new one.

10   If the outer surface of the large fitting that mates with the hose is deteriorated (corroded, pitted, etc.) it may be damaged further by hose removal. If it is, the thermostat cover will have to be replaced.

11   Remove the bolts and detach the thermostat cover **(see illustrations)**. If the cover is stuck, tap it with a soft-face hammer to jar it loose. Be prepared for some coolant to spill as the gasket seal is broken.

3.14 Make sure the rubber gasket is positioned correctly on the thermostat

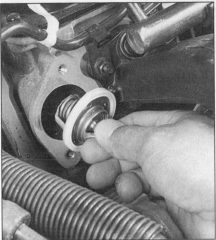

3.15 Install the new thermostat into the cylinder head and, on models so equipped, align the vent with the notch in the cylinder head

4.4a The coolant temperature sensor (arrow) is located in the cylinder head on SOHC engines or . . .

12 Note the position of the air bleed vent and how the thermostat is installed, then remove the thermostat and O-ring.
13 Clean the sealing surface of the housing and the engine of any coolant residue.
14 Make sure the gasket is in place on the thermostat **(see illustration)**.
15 Install the new thermostat into the cylinder head. On models so equipped, align the vent with the notch in the cylinder head **(see illustration)**.
16 Install the thermostat cover and bolts. Tighten the bolts to the torque listed in this Chapter's Specifications.
17 Reattach the radiator hose and coolant recovery hose to the fittings and tighten the hose clamp securely.
18 Refill the cooling system (see Chapter 1).
19 Start the engine and allow it to reach normal operating temperature, then check for leaks and proper thermostat operation (as described in Steps 3 and 4).

***

4   Engine cooling fan and circuit - check and component replacement

***

Warning: *To avoid possible injury or damage, DO NOT operate the engine with a damaged fan. Do not attempt to repair fan blades - replace a damaged fan with a new one.*
Note: *Always be sure to check for a blown fuse before attempting to diagnose an electrical circuit problem.*

Check

Refer to illustrations 4.4a and 4.4b
1   The cooling fan(s) operation is controlled by two different conditions. Whenever the air conditioner is running, the cooling fans will always be operating. The fan(s) will also run when the coolant reaches a specified temperature on information sent to the Power Control Module (PCM) from the engine coolant temperature sensor. The PCM then turns the fan On for the various engine coolant temperatures and vehicle speed combinations.
2   If the engine is overheating and the cooling fan is not coming on, unplug the electrical connector at the base of the fan motor and use a fused jumper wire to connect the fan directly to the battery. If the fan still doesn't run, replace the motor, test each motor separately on models so equipped.
3   If the motor is okay, but the cooling fan doesn't come on when the engine gets hot, the fault may be in the coolant temperature sen-

sor, the fan relay in the PCM, the PCM, or the wiring that connects the components.
4   The coolant temperature sensor is located in the cylinder head on SOHC engines or in the intake manifold on DOHC engines **(see illustrations)**. As the coolant temperature varies the sensor's resistance changes sending a different input signal to the PCM and also to the instrument cluster temperature gauge.
5   Check all wiring and connections. If no obvious problems are found, further diagnosis should be done by a dealer service department or repair shop with a SCAN tool.

Fan replacement

Refer to illustrations 4.9, 4.11, 4.12 and 4.13
6   Disconnect the negative battery cable, then unplug the fan motor electrical connector if you haven't already done so.
7   Drain the cooling system (see Chapter 1). If the coolant is relatively new or in good condition, save it in a clean container and reuse it.
8   Remove the upper hose from the radiator and move it out of the way.

FUEL RAIL

COOLANT TEMPERATURE SENSOR

4.4b . . . on in the intake manifold on DOHC engines - make sure the electrical connector is securely connected

3

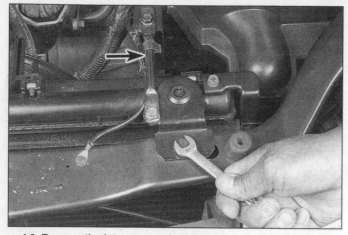

4.9 Remove the interconnecting strut (arrow) attached to the battery case and the upper radiator mounting bracket on each side

4.11 The fan shroud is attached to the top of the radiator with bolts (arrows) - remove all of the bolts (the number of bolts varies among the different models)

9   Remove the upper radiator mounting bolt on each side, then remove both brackets **(see illustration)**.

10   Remove the interconnecting strut on the left (driver's) side **(see illustration 4.9)**.

11   Remove the bolts attaching the top of the fan shroud to the radiator **(see illustration)**.

12   Carefully lift up on the fan shroud and disengage it from the lower retaining clips, then carefully lift the fan shroud assembly out of the engine compartment **(see illustration)**.

13   To detach the fan blade from the motor, support the fan motor from underneath, then remove the clip or nut from the motor shaft **(see illustration)**. **Note:** *It may be necessary to clean small burrs off the motor shaft prior to removing the fan blade. If the fan blade is stuck, apply a little penetrating oil to the end of the shaft and fan bushing, let it sit for awhile and try again.*

14   Installation is the reverse of removal. **Note:** *Some models are equipped with flapper doors on the shroud. When installing the fan shroud assembly, make sure the flapper doors are still in place - without them, the cooling system may not work efficiently.*

---

5   Radiator - removal and installation

Warning: *Do not start this procedure until the engine is completely*

cool. *Do not allow antifreeze to come in contact with your skin or painted surfaces of the vehicle. Rinse off spills immediately with plenty of water. Antifreeze is highly toxic if ingested. Never leave antifreeze lying around in an open container or in puddles on the floor; children and pets are attracted by it's sweet smell and may drink it. Check with local authorities about disposing of used antifreeze. Many communities have collection centers which will see that antifreeze is disposed of safely.*

Removal

Refer to illustrations 5.7a, 5.7b and 5.8

1   Disconnect the cable from the negative terminal of the battery.

2   Drain the cooling system (see Chapter 1). If the coolant is relatively new or in good condition, save it in a clean container and reuse it.

3   Loosen the upper and lower radiator hose clamps, then detach the radiator hoses from the fittings. If they're stuck, grasp each hose near the end with a pair of adjustable pliers and twist it to break the seal, then pull it off - be careful not to damage the radiator fittings! If the hoses are old or deteriorated, cut them off and install new ones.

4   Remove the cooling fan(s) and shroud assembly (see Section 4).

5   If the vehicle is equipped with an automatic transaxle, disconnect the transmission fluid cooler lines and plug the lines and fittings.

6   If the vehicle is equipped with an engine block heater, disconnect the electrical connector.

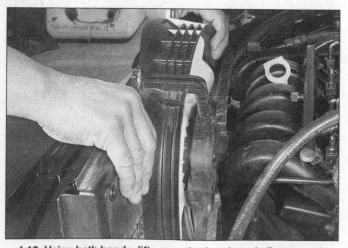

4.12 Using both hands, lift up on the fan shroud, disengage it from the lower retaining clips, then carefully lift the fan shroud assembly out of the engine compartment - do not damage the radiator

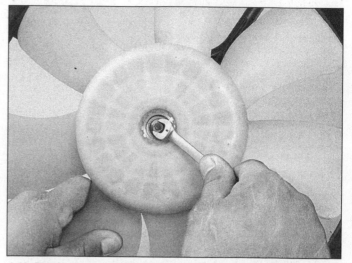

4.13 The fan blade is attached to the fan motor shaft with either a clip or nut - remove the fastener and remove the fan blade

5.7a If equipped, remove the air conditioning condenser top mounting screws . . .

5.7b . . . and the lower mounting screws at the front of the radiator - carefully move the condenser away from the radiator

7   If the vehicle is equipped with air conditioning, remove the condenser mounting screws at the front of the radiator (see illustrations). Carefully pull the condenser away from the radiator - it is not necessary to disconnect the condenser lines.

8   Carefully lift out the radiator (see illustration). Don't spill coolant on the vehicle or scratch the paint.

9   With the radiator removed, it can be inspected for leaks and damage. If it needs repair, have a radiator shop or dealer service department perform the work, as special techniques are required.

10   Bugs and dirt can be removed from the radiator with a garden hose (aimed at the backside of the radiator core) and/or a soft brush. Don't bend the cooling fins.

Installation

11   Installation is the reverse of the removal procedure. Be sure the rubber cushions are seated properly at the base of the radiator.

12   After installation, fill the cooling system with the proper mixture of antifreeze and water (see Chapter 1).

13   Start the engine and check for leaks. Allow the engine to reach normal operating temperature, indicated by the upper radiator hose becoming hot. Recheck the coolant level and add more if required.

14   If you're working on an automatic transaxle equipped vehicle, check and add fluid as needed (see Chapter 1).

6   Coolant reservoir - removal and installation

Refer to illustration 6.3

Warning: *Do not start this procedure until the engine is completely cool. Do not allow antifreeze to come in contact with your skin or painted surfaces of the vehicle. Rinse off spills immediately with plenty of water. Antifreeze is highly toxic if ingested. Never leave antifreeze lying around in an open container or in puddles on the floor; children and pets are attracted by it's sweet smell and may drink it. Check with local authorities about disposing of used antifreeze. Many communities have collection centers which will see that antifreeze is disposed of safely.*

1   Disconnect the coolant reservoir hose from the thermostat cover.

2   Follow the hose from the thermostat cover to the neck of the reservoir cap and lift the cap off the coolant reservoir and withdraw the overflow hose.

3   Remove the holddown bolt and remove the reservoir from the engine compartment (see illustration).

4   Pour out the residual coolant in the reservoir and dispose of properly. Wash the inside and outside of the reservoir and check for cracks or damage. Replace if necessary.

5   Installation is the reverse of removal. Refill the reservoir.

5.8 Using both hands, carefully lift out the radiator - don't spill any residual coolant from the radiator on the vehicle or scratch the paint. Immediately clean off any spilled coolant from painted surfaces

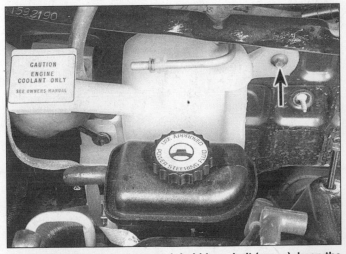

6.3 Remove the coolant reservoir holddown bolt (arrow), keep the reservoir upright and remove it from the engine compartment

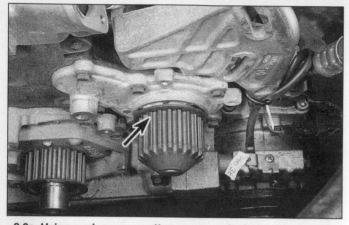

8.6a Using a criss-cross pattern, remove the bolts securing the water pump (arrow) . . .

8.6b . . . and detach the water pump from the engine - if necessary, gently tap it with a soft faced hammer to break the seal

7   Water pump - check

1   A failure in the water pump can cause serious engine damage due to overheating.

2   There are two ways to check the operation of the water pump while it's installed on the engine. If the pump is defective, it should be replaced with a new or rebuilt unit.

3   Remove the timing belt cover (see Chapter 2A). The water pump is equipped with a weep or vent holes. If a failure occurs in the pump seal, coolant will leak from the hole. In most cases you'll need a flashlight to find the hole on the water pump from underneath to check for leaks.

4   If the water pump shaft bearings fail there may be a howling sound at the timing belt end of the engine while it's running. With the engine off, shaft wear can be felt if the water pump pulley is rocked up-and-down. Don't mistake drivebelt slippage, which causes a squealing sound, for water pump bearing failure.

8   Water pump - replacement

Refer to illustrations 8.6a, 8.6b and 8.9

Warning: *Wait until the engine is completely cool before beginning this procedure. Do not allow antifreeze to come in contact with your skin or painted surfaces of the vehicle. Rinse off spills immediately with plenty of water. Antifreeze is highly toxic if ingested. Never leave antifreeze lying around in an open container or in puddles on the floor; children and pets are attracted by it's sweet smell and may drink it. Check with local authorities about disposing of used antifreeze. Many communities have collection centers which will see that antifreeze is disposed of safely.*

1   Disconnect the negative battery cable from the battery.

2   Drain the cooling system (see Chapter 1). If the coolant is relatively new or in good condition, save it in a clean container and reuse it.

3   Remove the timing belt front cover (see Chapter 2A).

4   Remove the timing belt (see Chapter 2A).

5   Remove the timing belt rear cover (see Chapter 2A).

6   Remove the water pump mounting bolts and detach the water pump from the engine **(see illustrations)**. If the water pump is stuck, gently tap it with a soft faced hammer to break the seal.

7   Clean the bolt threads and the threaded holes in the engine to remove corrosion and sealant. Remove all traces of old gasket material from the sealing surfaces.

8   Compare the new pump to the old one to make sure they're identical.

9   Install a new O-ring seal, then apply a thin film of RTV sealant to hold the seal in place during installation **(see illustration)**. **Caution:** *Make sure the O-ring seal is properly seated in the water pump groove to avoid a coolant leak.* Carefully mate the pump to the engine.

10   Install the bolts. Tighten them to the torque listed in this Chapter's

8.9 Remove the old O-ring seal, install a new one, then apply a thin film of RTV sealant to hold the seal in place during installation - make sure the O-ring seal is properly seated in the water pump and that it stays in place during pump installation

Specifications. Don't over-tighten them or the pump may be damaged.

11   Reinstall all parts removed for access to the pump.

12   Refill the cooling system (see Chapter 1) and check the timing belt tension (see Chapter 2A). Run the engine and check for leaks.

9   Coolant temperature sending unit - check and replacement

Check

Refer to illustration 9.6

1   The coolant temperature indicator system is composed of a light or temperature gauge mounted in the instrument cluster and a coolant temperature sending unit mounted on the engine. On this system, there is only one coolant temperature sensor/sending unit, which sends input signals to the PCM and also to the instrument cluster temperature gauge.

2   If an overheating indication occurs, check the coolant level in the system and then make sure the wiring between the sending unit and light or gauge are secure and the fuses are okay.

3   If the temperature gauge shows excessive temperature after running awhile, see the Troubleshooting section in the front of the manual.

4   If the temperature gauge indicates Hot shortly after the engine is started cold, disconnect the electrical connector from the temperature

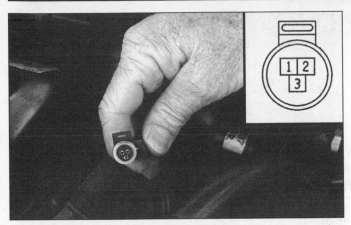

9.6 Disconnect the electrical connector. Use a fused jumper wire, ground the temperature sensor pin No. 3 (purple/yellow wire) on the wiring harness connector, then turn the ignition switch On - the temperature gauge should be at the highest setting

sending unit located on the engine (see illustrations 4.11a or 4.11b).

5   Turn the ignition switch On. The temperature gauge should be at the lowest setting. Turn the ignition switch Off.

6   Use a fused jumper wire and ground the temperature sensor pin No. 3 (purple/yellow wire) (see illustration), then turn the ignition switch On. The temperature gauge should be at the highest setting. After the seat belt lamp goes out, the instrument cluster should chime for about eight seconds. If okay, check the temperature sending unit connector for proper connection. If the connections are okay, replace the sending unit. If not okay, and the high temperature chime sounds and the gauge shows cold, replace the temperature gauge assembly. If the gauge is still not operating correctly, replace the printed circuit board.

Replacement

Warning: *Wait until the engine is completely cool before beginning this procedure. Do not allow antifreeze to come in contact with your skin or painted surfaces of the vehicle. Rinse off spills immediately with plenty of water. Antifreeze is highly toxic if ingested. Never leave antifreeze lying around in an open container or in puddles on the floor; children and pets are attracted by it's sweet smell and may drink it. Check with local authorities about disposing of used antifreeze. Many communities have collection centers which will see that antifreeze is disposed of safely.*

7   Slowly remove the radiator fill cap to release any pressure within the cooling system, then reinstall the cap. This will reduce coolant loss when the sending unit is removed.

8   Disconnect the electrical connector from the sending unit (see illustrations 4.11a or 4.11b).

9   Place a drip pan on the ground directly under the sending unit to catch any expelled coolant.

10   Unscrew the sending unit from the engine. Be prepared for some coolant to drain from the engine.

11   Wrap the new sending unit threads with Teflon tape to prevent coolant leakage.

12   Install the new sending unit and tighten securely.

13   Connect the electrical connector.

14   Check the coolant level after replacement unit has been installed and top up the system, if necessary (see Chapter 1). Check now for proper operation of the gauge and the sending unit. Observe the system for leaks after the engine has warmed up.

10   Blower motor and circuit - check and replacement

Check

Refer to illustrations 10.3 and 10.4

1   Check the fuse and all connections in the circuit for looseness and corrosion. Make sure the battery is fully charged.

2   Remove the heater air conditioner control panel and disconnect the electrical connector (see Section 13).

3   For models equipped with heater only (no air conditioning), test the blower motor control switch with an ohmmeter. Move the Blower and Mode knobs to the indicated positions and check for continuity between the following terminals (see illustration):

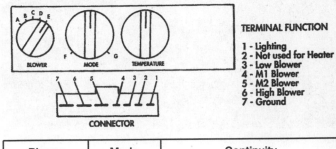

TERMINAL FUNCTION

1 - Lighting
2 - Not used for Heater
3 - Low Blower
4 - M1 Blower
5 - M2 Blower
6 - High Blower
7 - Ground

Blower position	Mode position	Continuity between pins
A	F	Pin 1 to pin 7
B	F	Pin 1 to pin 7, pin 3 to pin 7
C	F	Pin 1 to pin 7, pin 4 to pin 7
D	F	Pin 1 to pin 7, pin 5 to pin 7
E	F	Pin 1 to pin 7, pin 6 to pin 7

10.3 Test the blower motor function with the Blower and Mode knobs in the indicated positions - check for continuity between the terminals (model without air conditioning)

4   For models equipped with heater and air conditioning, test the blower motor control switch with an ohmmeter. Move the Blower and Mode knobs to the indicated positions and check for continuity between the following terminals (see illustration):

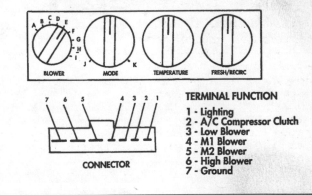

TERMINAL FUNCTION

1 - Lighting
2 - A/C Compressor Clutch
3 - Low Blower
4 - M1 Blower
5 - M2 Blower
6 - High Blower
7 - Ground

Blower position	Mode position	Continuity between pins
A	J	Pin 1 to pin 7, pin 2 to pin 7, pin 6 to pin 7
B	J	Pin 1 to pin 7, pin 2 to pin 7, pin 5 to pin 7
C	J	Pin 1 to pin 7, pin 2 to pin 7, pin 4 to pin 7
D	J	Pin 1 to pin 7, pin 2 to pin 7, pin 3 to pin 7
E	J	Pin 1 to pin 7
F	J	Pin 1 to pin 7, pin 3 to pin 7
G	J	Pin 1 to pin 7, pin 4 to pin 7
H	J	Pin 1 to pin 7, pin 5 to pin 7
I	J	Pin 1 to pin 7, pin 6 to pin 7
I	K	Pin 1 to pin 7, pin 2 to pin 7, pin 6 to pin 7

10.4 On models with air conditioning, test the blower motor function with the Blower and Mode knobs in the indicated positions - check for continuity between the terminals

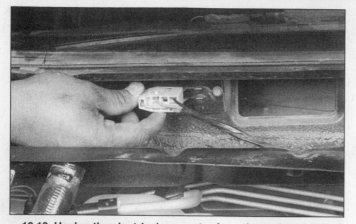

10.10 Unplug the electrical connector from the resistor block

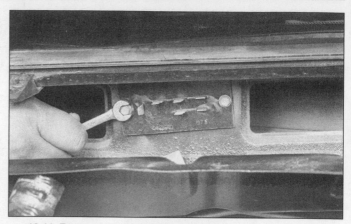

10.11 Remove the mounting screws and the resistor block

11.4 Working under the instrument panel, disconnect the electrical connector from the blower motor

11.6a On models with air conditioning, remove the three mounting screws . . .

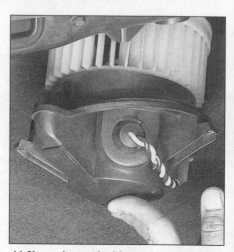

11.6b . . . lower the blower motor and fan from the housing and remove it from the vehicle

5   If the switch fails any part of the continuity check between the ter-minals, other than pin 1 to pin 7, replace the heater control assembly (see Section 13). If there is no continuity between pin 1 to pin 7, check for a blown illumination lamp(s).

6   If the blower motor control switch are okay, check the blower motor operation.

7   Disconnect the blower motor electrical connector and hook one side to the chassis ground and the other to a fused source of battery voltage. If the blower motor doesn't operate, it is faulty and must be replaced (see Section 11).

Resistor block replacement

Refer to illustrations 10.10 and 10.11

8   Disconnect the cable from the negative battery terminal.
9   Remove the cowl assembly (see Chapter 11).
10   Unplug the electrical connector from the resistor block **(see illus-tration)**.
11   Remove the mounting screws and the resistor block **(see illustra-tion)**.
12   Installation is the reverse of removal.

---

11   Heater and air conditioning blower motor - removal and installation

Refer to illustrations 11.4, 11.6a and 11.6b

1   Disconnect the cable from the negative battery terminal.

2   Remove the right (passenger) side scuff plate, then pull back the carpet.
3   On models with air conditioning, carefully cut the wheel housing silencer in line with the blower motor wiring.
4   Disconnect the blower motor electrical connector **(see illustra-tion)**.
5   On models without air conditioning, pull down on the tab, grasp the motor and rotate it about one-eight of a turn counterclockwise. Lower the blower motor and fan from the housing and remove it.
6   On models with air conditioning, remove the three mounting screws and lower the blower motor and fan from the housing and remove it **(see illustrations)**.
7   The fan is balanced with the motor, and is available only as an assembly. If the fan and/or the motor are damage, the fan and motor must be replaced as an assembly.
8   Installation is the reverse of removal.

---

12   Heater core - replacement

Refer to illustrations 12.5a, 12.5b, 12.5c, 12.5d, 12.9a, 12.9b, 12.10, 12.11, 12.12, 12.13, 12.14, 12.15, 12.16 and 12.17

Warning 1: *These models have airbags. Always disconnect the nega-tive battery cable and wait two minutes before working in the vicinity of the impact sensors, steering column or instrument panel to avoid the possibility of accidental deployment of the airbag, which could cause personal injury (see Chapter 12).*

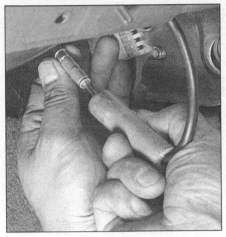

12.5a Working under the instrument panel, disconnect the radio antenna . . .

12.5b . . . cut the tie-wrap securing the blue multi-pin connector and disconnect the connector . . .

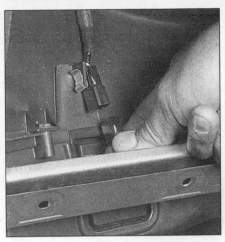

12.5c . . . in the glove box area disconnect the electrical connector . . .

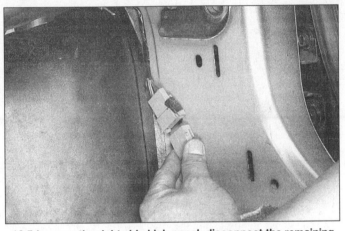

12.5d . . . on the right side kick panel, disconnect the remaining electrical connector

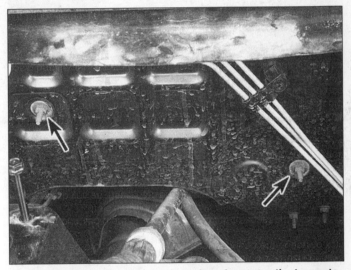

12.9a Working in the engine compartment, remove the two nuts from the air distribution module mounting studs on the left side . . .

Warning 2: *The air conditioning system is under high pressure. DO NOT disassemble any part of the system (hoses, compressor, line fittings, etc.) until after the system has been evacuated and the refrigerant recovered by a dealer service department or air conditioning service station.*

1   Heater core removal on these models is a difficult undertaking for the home mechanic. The procedure requires, removal of the entire instrument panel and related trim panels as well as the partial removal of the steering column and removal the air distribution module containing the heater core. If you attempt it at home, keep track of the assemblies by taking notes and keeping screws and other hardware in small, marked plastic bags for reassembly.

2   Have the air conditioning system discharged (see **Warning 2** above).

3   Disconnect the cable from the negative terminal of the battery. Wait at least two minutes before proceeding.

4   Drain the cooling system (see Chapter 1).

5   Working under the instrument panel, disconnect the radio antenna and the electrical connectors (**see illustrations**).

6   Remove the instrument panel (see Chapter 11).

7   Remove the suction line at the expansion valve, then remove the expansion valve from the evaporator (see Section 18). Cover the ends of the lines to prevent the entry of moisture and debris.

8   Remove the rubber drain tube extension from the condensation drain tube.

9   In the engine compartment, remove the nuts from the air distribution module mounting studs (**see illustrations**).

12.9b . . . then remove the nut on the right side

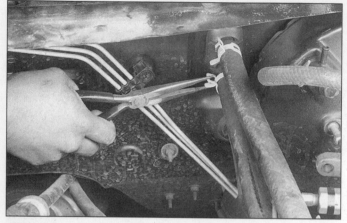

12.10 Using pliers, loosen the hose clamps, slide the clamps onto the hoses then disconnect both heater hoses from the fittings - there may be residual coolant in the hoses

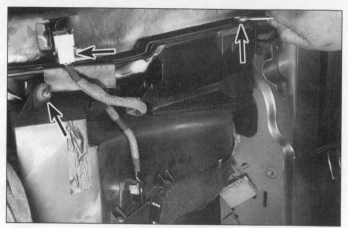

12.11 Disconnect the electrical connector (arrow), then remove the mounting bolt and nut (arrows)

12.12 Carefully pull the air distribution module away from the firewall and remove it from the vehicle - there may be residual coolant in the module

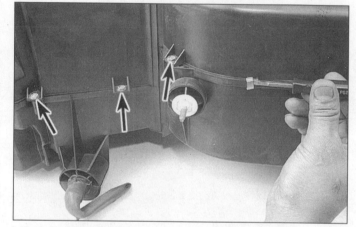

12.13 Remove the bolts and the clips holding the air distribution module halves together

10   In the engine compartment, disconnect the heater hoses where they enter the firewall (see illustration).

11   Remove the right side mounting bolt, the dash panel stud nut and disconnect the electrical connector (see illustration). Note: *The module electrical harness will remain with the air distribution module.*

12   Carefully pull the air distribution module away from the firewall and remove it from the vehicle (see illustration).

13   Remove the perimeter bolts and clips holding the air distribution module together (see illustration).

14   Carefully pull the heater core inlet and outlet tube seal away from

12.14 Carefully pull the heater core inlet and outlet tube seal away from the module

12. 15 Carefully pull straight up and separate the module upper half from the lower half

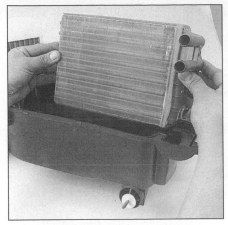

12.16 Lift up and remove the heater core from the lower half

12.17 If necessary, remove the air conditioning evaporator from the lower half

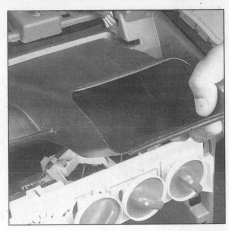

13.7 Carefully remove the air duct from above the control panel

the module (see illustration).

15   Carefully separate module halves and remove the upper half (see illustration).

16   Lift up and remove the heater core (see illustration).

17   The air conditioning evaporator (if equipped) can also be removed at this time (see illustration).

18   Reinstall the heater core (and air conditioner evaporator, if removed) and install the air distribution box by reversing these steps.

19   Refill the cooling system (see Chapter 1), reconnect the battery and run the engine. Check the system for proper operation. Check the operation of all electrical components of the instrument panel. Have the air conditioning system recharged.

13   Heater and air conditioning control assembly - removal and installation

Refer to illustrations 13.7, 13.8, 13.9a, 13.9b, 13.11a and 13.11b

1   Disconnect the cable from the negative battery terminal.

2   Remove the instrument panel top cover (see Chapter 11).

3   Carefully reach down and disconnect the wiring connector at the rear window defogger and/or fog lamp switches.

4   Remove the left (driver) and right (passenger) side trim panels (see Chapter 11).

5   Remove the center bezel (see Chapter 11).

6   Remove the radio (see Chapter 12).

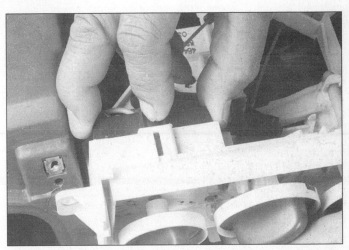

13.8 Release the catch and disconnect the wiring connector from the backside of the control panel

7   Remove the air duct (see illustration).

8   Disconnect the wiring connector (see illustration).

9   Remove the control assembly mounting screws (see illustrations).

10   Carefully pull the control assembly forward.

13.9a Remove the upper mounting screw (arrow) . . .

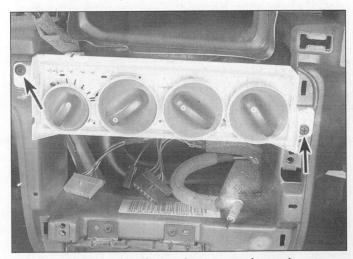

13.9b . . . then the two front screws (arrows)

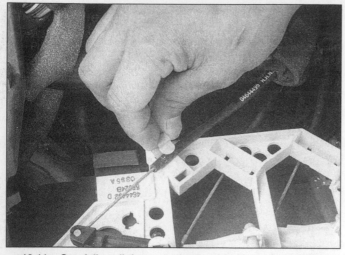

13.11a Carefully pull the control assembly forward out of the instrument panel, disconnect the control cable attachment clips . . .

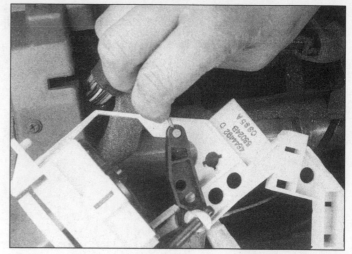

13.11b . . . disconnect the cables from the levers and remove the control assembly

11   Disconnect the control cables from the attachment clips and disconnect the cables from the control assembly **(see illustrations)**. Remove the control assembly.

12   Installation is the reverse of removal.

14   Air conditioning system - check and maintenance

Warning: *The air conditioning system is under high pressure. Do not loosen any hose fittings or remove any components until after the system has been discharged by a dealer service department or service station. Always wear eye protection when disconnecting air conditioning system fittings.*

1   The following maintenance checks should be performed on a regular basis to ensure the air conditioner continues to operate at peak efficiency.

  a) *Check the compressor drivebelt. If it's worn or deteriorated, replace it (see Chapter 1).*
  b) *Check the drivebelt tension and, if necessary, adjust it (see Chapter 1).*
  c) *Check the system hoses. Look for cracks, bubbles, hard spots and deterioration. Inspect the hoses and all fittings for oil bubbles and seepage. If there's any evidence of wear, damage or leaks, replace the hose(s).*
  d) *Inspect the condenser fins for leaves, bugs and other debris. Use a "fin comb" or compressed air to clean the condenser.*
  e) *Make sure the system has the correct refrigerant charge.*
  f) *Check the evaporator housing drain tube for blockage.*

2   It's a good idea to operate the system for about 10 minutes at least once a month, particularly during the winter. Long term non-use can cause hardening, and subsequent failure, of the seals.

3   Because of the complexity of the air conditioning system and the special equipment necessary to service it, in-depth troubleshooting and repairs are not included in this manual (refer to the *Haynes Automotive Heating and Air Conditioning Repair Manual*). However, simple checks and component replacement procedures are provided in this Chapter.

4   The most common cause of poor cooling is simply a low system refrigerant charge. If a noticeable drop in cool air output occurs, the following quick check will help you determine if the refrigerant level is low.

Checking the refrigerant charge

5   Warm the engine up to normal operating temperature.

6   Place the air conditioning temperature selector at the coldest setting and the blower at the highest setting. Open the doors (to make sure the air conditioning system doesn't cycle off as soon as it cools the passenger compartment).

7   With the compressor engaged - the clutch will make an audible click and the center of the clutch will rotate. If the compressor discharge line feels warm and the compressor inlet pipe feels cool, the system is properly charged.

8   Place a thermometer in the dashboard vent nearest the evaporator and monitor the system. If the ambient (outside) air temperature is very high, say 110 degrees F, the duct air temperature may be as high as 60 degrees F, but generally the air conditioning is 30 to 40 degrees F cooler than the ambient air, down to approximately 40 degrees F. **Note:** *Humidity of the ambient air also affects the cooling capacity of the system. Higher ambient humidity lowers the effectiveness of the air conditioning system.*

Adding refrigerant

Refer to illustrations 14.9 and 14.12

9   Buy an automotive charging kit at an auto parts store **(see illustration)**. A charging kit includes a 14-ounce can of refrigerant, a tap valve and a short section of hose that can be attached between the tap valve and the system low side service valve. Because one can of refrigerant may not be sufficient to bring the system charge up to the proper level, it's a good idea to buy a couple of additional cans. Make sure

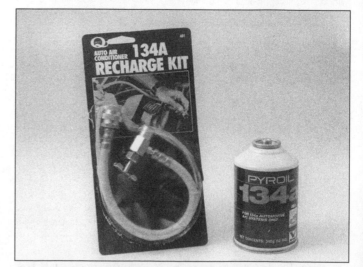

14.9 A basic charging kit is available at most auto parts stores - it must say R-134a (not R-12) and so must the can of refrigerant

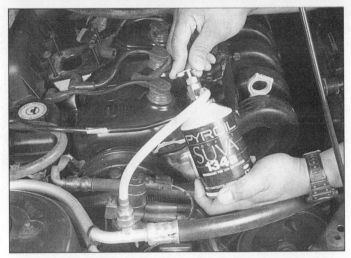

14.12 Add R-134a refrigerant to the low-side port only - the procedure is easier if you wrap the can with a warm, wet towel to prevent icing

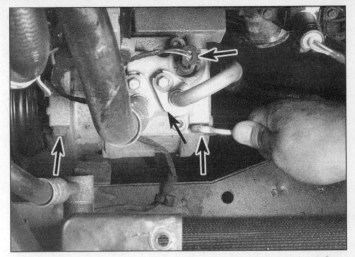

15.3 Unplug the electrical connector (arrow) from the compressor clutch - unbolt the upper bolts (arrows)

that one of the cans contains red refrigerant dye. If the system is leaking, the red dye will leak out with the refrigerant and help you pinpoint the location of the leak. **Caution:** *There are two types of refrigerant, R-12, used on vehicles up to 1992, and the more environmentally-friendly R-134a used in all the models covered by this manual. These two refrigerants (and their appropriate refrigerant oils) are not compatible and must never be mixed or components will be damaged. Use only R-134a refrigerant in the models covered by this manual.* **Warning:** *Never add more than two cans of refrigerant to the system.*

10   Hook up the charging kit by following the manufacturer's instructions. **Warning:** *DO NOT hook the charging kit hose to the system high side! The fittings on the charging kit are designed to fit **only** on the low side of the system.*

11   Back off the valve handle on the charging kit and screw the kit onto the refrigerant can, making sure first that the O-ring or rubber seal inside the threaded portion of the kit is in place. **Warning:** *Wear protective eyewear when dealing with pressurized refrigerant cans.*

12   Remove the dust cap from the low-side charging connection and attach the quick-connect fitting on the kit hose **(see illustration)**.

13   Warm up the engine and turn on the air conditioner. Keep the charging kit hose away from the fan and other moving parts. **Note:** *The charging process requires the compressor to be running. Your compressor may cycle off if the pressure is low due to a low charge. If the clutch cycles off, you can pull the low-pressure cycling switch plug and attach a jumper wire. This will keep the compressor ON.*

14   Hold the can upright, turn the valve handle on the kit until the stem pierces the can, then back the handle out to release the refrigerant. You should be able to hear the rush of gas. Add refrigerant to the low side of the system until both the receiver-drier surface and the evaporator inlet pipe feel about the same temperature. Allow stabilization time between each addition.

15   When the can is empty, turn the valve handle to the closed position and release the connection from the low-side port. Replace the dust cap.

16   Remove the charging kit from the can and store the kit for future use with the piercing valve in the UP position, to prevent inadvertently piercing the can on the next use.

---

15 Air conditioning compressor - removal and installation

Refer to illustrations 15.3 and 15.6

Warning: *The air conditioning system is under high pressure. DO NOT disassemble any part of the system (hoses, compressor, line fittings, etc.) until after the system has been evacuated and the refrigerant*

recovered by a dealer service department or air conditioning service station.

Note: *The filter-drier/receiver-drier (see Section 16) should be replaced whenever the compressor is replaced.*

1   Have the system discharged (see **Warning** above).

2   Disconnect the negative cable from the battery.

3   Unplug the electrical connector from the compressor clutch **(see illustration)**.

4   Remove the drivebelt (see Chapter 1).

5   Disconnect the refrigerant lines from the compressor. Plug the open fittings to prevent entry of dirt and moisture.

6   Unbolt the compressor from the mounting bracket **(see illustration)** and lift it out of the vehicle.

7   If a new compressor is being installed, pour out the oil from the old compressor into a graduated container and add that amount of new refrigerant oil to the new compressor. Follow the directions included with the new compressor.

8   The clutch may have to be transferred from the original to the new compressor.

9   Installation is the reverse of removal. Replace all O-rings with new ones specifically made for use with R-134a refrigerant and lubricate them with R-134a-compatible refrigerant oil.

10   Have the system evacuated, recharged and leak tested by the shop that discharged it.

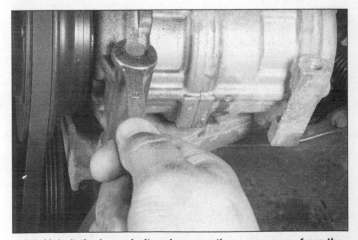

15.6 Unbolt the lower bolt and remove the compressor from the mounting bracket

16.4 Using an appropriate size wrench, disconnect both refrigerant lines from the receiver-drier

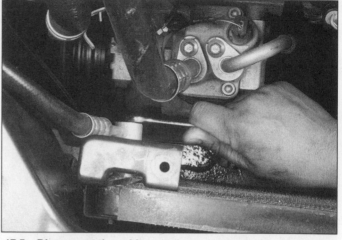

17.5a Disconnect the refrigerant line mounting bracket bolt from one side of the condenser . . .

16   Air conditioning receiver and drier - removal and installation

Refer to illustration 16.4

Warning: *The air conditioning system is under high pressure. DO NOT disassemble any part of the system (hose, compressor, line fittings, etc.) until after the system has been evacuated and the refrigerant recovered by a dealer service department or service station.*

Caution: *Replacement filter-drier/receiver-drier units are so effective at absorbing moisture that they can quickly saturate upon exposure to the atmosphere. When installing a new unit, have all tools and supplies ready for quick reassembly to avoid having the system open any longer than necessary.*

1   The receiver-drier acts as a reservoir for the system refrigerant. It's located on the right (passenger) side of the engine compartment, next to the radiator and condenser.
2   Have the system discharged (see the **Warning** at the beginning of this Section).
3   Disconnect the cable from the negative terminal of the battery.
4   Disconnect the refrigerant lines from the receiver-drier **(see illustration)**.
5   Plug the open fittings to prevent entry of dirt and moisture.
6   Remove the receiver/drier from the large rubber mount and remove it.
7   Installation is the reverse of removal. If a new receiver-drier is being installed add one ounce of R-134a compatible refrigerant oil to it before installation.
8   Take the vehicle back to the shop that discharged it. Have the system evacuated, recharged and leak tested.

17   Air conditioning condenser - removal and installation

Refer to illustrations 17.5a and 17.5b

Warning: *The air conditioning system is under high pressure. DO NOT disassemble any part of the system (hose, compressor, line fittings, etc.) until after the system has been evacuated and the refrigerant recovered by a dealer service department or service station.*

1   Have the system discharged (see the Warning at the beginning of this Section).
2   Disconnect the negative battery cable, then unplug the fan motor electrical connector if you haven't already done so.
3   Drain the cooling system (see Chapter 1). If the coolant is relatively new or in good condition, save it in a clean container and reuse it.
4   Remove the cooling fan and radiator assemblies.

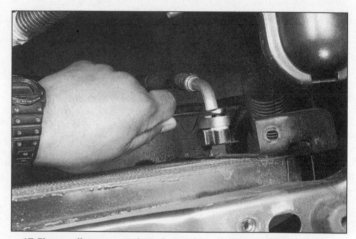

17.5b . . . disconnect the other refrigerant line - plug the open ends of the condenser and the disconnected refrigerant lines to prevent the entry of dirt and moisture

5   Disconnect the refrigerant lines from the condenser **(see illustrations)**. Plug the ends of the open ends of the condenser and the disconnected refrigerant lines to prevent the entry of dirt and moisture.
6   Carefully remove the condenser from the engine compartment.
7   If the original condenser is to be reinstalled, store it with the line fittings on top to prevent oil from draining out. If a new condenser is being installed, pour one ounce of R-134a compatible refrigerant oil into it prior to installation.
8   Reinstall all components in the reverse order of removal.
9   Take the vehicle back to the shop that discharged it. Have the system evacuated, recharged and leak tested.

18   Air conditioning evaporator and expansion valve - removal and installation

Evaporator

The removal of the air conditioning evaporator is performed along with the heater core (see Section 12).

Expansion valve

Refer to illustrations 18.3, 18.4, 18.5, 18.7a and 18.7b
Warning: *The air conditioning system is under high pressure. DO NOT disassemble any part of the system (hose, compressor, line fittings,*

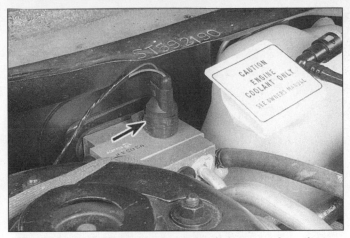

18.3 Disconnect the boot-type electrical connector from the top of the pressure cut-off switch

18.4 Remove the center bolt securing the refrigerant line-sealing plate

etc.) until after the system has been evacuated and the refrigerant recovered by a dealer service department or service station.

1   Have the system discharged (see the **Warning** at the beginning of this Section).

2   Disconnect the negative battery cable.

3   Disconnect the boot-type electrical connector at the pressure cut-off switch **(see illustration)**.

4   Remove the refrigerant line-sealing plate center bolt **(see illustration)**.

5   Carefully pull the refrigerant line-sealing plate assembly from the expansion valve toward the front of the vehicle **(see illustration)**. **Caution:** *Do not scratch the sealing surfaces of either part.*

6   Cover the openings on the sealing plate to prevent the entry of dirt and moisture.

7   Remove the two expansion valve to evaporator sealing plate mounting screws **(see illustration)**. Remove the expansion valve and discard the aluminum sealing gasket **(see illustration)**.

8   Reinstall all components in the reverse order of removal. Install a new aluminum sealing gasket.

9   Take the vehicle back to the shop that discharged it. Have the system evacuated, recharged and leak tested.

18.5 Carefully pull the refrigerant line-sealing plate assembly from the expansion valve toward the front of the vehicle and move it out of the way - cover the openings to prevent the entry of dirt and moisture

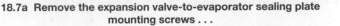

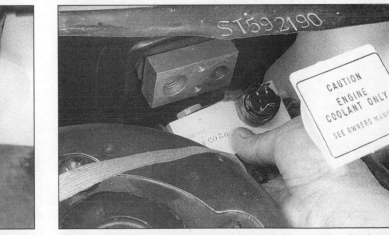

18.7a Remove the expansion valve-to-evaporator sealing plate mounting screws . . .

18.7b . . . then remove the expansion valve. Discard the aluminum sealing gasket as a new one must be installed

Notes

Chapter 4
Fuel and exhaust systems

Contents

4

Specifications

General
Fuel pressure	49 psi (approximate)
Fuel injector coil resistance	12 ohms

Torque specifications
Ft-lbs (unless otherwise noted)
Throttle body mounting bolts	200 inch-lbs
Fuel rail mounting bolts	195 inch-lbs

---

1   General information

The vehicles covered by this manual are equipped with a sequential Multi Port Fuel Injection (MPFI) system. This system uses timed impulses to sequentially inject the fuel directly into the intake ports of each cylinder. The injectors are controlled by the Powertrain Control Module (PCM). The PCM monitors various engine parameters and delivers the exact amount of fuel, in the correct sequence, into the intake ports.

All models are equipped with an electric fuel pump, mounted in the fuel tank. It is necessary to remove the fuel tank for access to the fuel pump. The fuel level sending unit is an integral component of the fuel pump and it must be removed from the fuel tank in the same manner. These systems are equipped with a "returnless" fuel system. The fuel pressure regulator is mounted on top of the fuel pump/fuel level sending unit module. Regulated fuel is sent to the fuel rail and excess fuel is bled off into the tank.

The exhaust system consists of exhaust manifolds, a catalytic converter, an exhaust pipe and a muffler. Each of these components is replaceable. For further information regarding the catalytic converter, refer to Chapter 6.

2.2 Remove the cap from the fuel pressure test port (arrow) located on the fuel rail

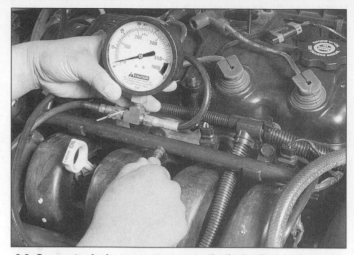

2.3 Connect a fuel pressure gauge to the fuel rail at the test port and use the valve to bleed off the excess fuel into an approved fuel container

2   Fuel pressure relief procedure

Refer to illustrations 2.2 and 2.3

Warning: *Gasoline is extremely flammable, so take extra precautions when you work on any part of the fuel system. Don't smoke or allow open flames or bare light bulbs near the work area, and don't work in a garage where a natural gas-type appliance (such as a water heater or a clothes dryer) with a pilot light is present. Since gasoline is carcinogenic, wear latex gloves when there's a possibility of being exposed to fuel, and, if you spill any fuel on your skin, rinse it off immediately with soap and water. Mop up any spills immediately and do not store fuel-soaked rags where they could ignite. The fuel system is under constant pressure, so, if any fuel lines are to be disconnected, the fuel pressure in the system must be relieved first. When you perform any kind of work on the fuel system, wear safety glasses and have a Class B type fire extinguisher on hand.*

1   Detach the cable from the negative battery terminal. Unscrew the fuel filler cap to relieve pressure built up in the fuel tank.

2   Remove the cap from the fuel pressure test port located on the fuel rail **(see illustration)**.

3   Use one of the two following methods:

a) *Attach a fuel pressure gauge equipped with a bleeder hose (commonly available at auto parts stores) to the test port Schrader valve on the fuel rail* **(see illustration)**. *Place the gauge bleeder hose in an approved fuel container. Open the valve on the gauge to relieve pressure.*

b) *Locate the fuel pressure test port and carefully place several shop towels around the test port and the fuel rail. Remove the cap and, using the tip of a screwdriver, depress the Schrader valve and let the fuel drain into the shop towels. Be careful to catch any fuel that might spray up by using another shop towel.*

4   Unless this procedure is followed before servicing fuel lines or connections, fuel spray (and possible injury) may occur.

5   Install the cap onto the fuel pressure test port and the fuel filler cap.

3   Fuel pump/fuel pressure - check

Warning: *Gasoline is extremely flammable, so take extra precautions when you work on any part of the fuel system. Don't smoke or allow open flames or bare light bulbs near the work area, and don't work in a garage where a natural gas-type appliance (such as a water heater or a clothes dryer) with a pilot light is present. Since gasoline is carcinogenic, wear latex gloves when there's a possibility of being exposed to fuel, and, if you spill any fuel on your skin, rinse it off immediately with*

soap and water. Mop up any spills immediately and do not store fuel-soaked rags where they could ignite. The fuel system is under constant pressure, so, if any fuel lines are to be disconnected, the fuel pressure in the system must be relieved first (see Section 2 for more information). When you perform any kind of work on the fuel system, wear safety glasses and have a Class B type fire extinguisher on hand.

Note: *These systems are equipped with a "returnless" fuel system. The fuel pressure regulator is part of the fuel pump module on 1995 models and on 1996 and later models it is mounted on top of the fuel pump/fuel level sending unit module and is an integral part of the fuel filter assembly.*

Preliminary check

Refer to illustration 3.2

Note: *On all models, the fuel pump is located inside the fuel tank (see Section 7).*

1   If you suspect insufficient fuel delivery, first inspect all fuel lines to ensure that the problem is not simply a leak in a line.

2   Set the parking brake and have an assistant turn the ignition switch to the ON position while you listen to the fuel pump (inside the fuel tank). You should hear a "whirring" sound, lasting for a couple of seconds. Start the engine. The whirring sound should now be continuous (although harder to hear with the engine running). If there is no sound, either the fuel pump fuse **(see illustration)**, fuel pump, fuel pump relay, ASD relay or related circuits are defective (proceed to Step 10).

3.2 Check to make sure the fuel pump fuse is not blown

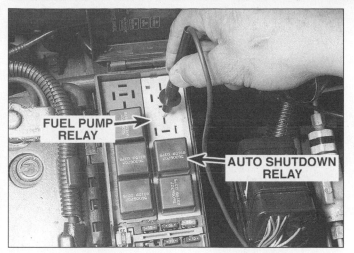

3.11 Locate the fuel pump relay in the Power Distribution Center and check for battery voltage to the relay

Pressure check

3   Relieve the fuel pressure (see Section 2).

4   Remove the cap from the fuel pressure test port on the fuel rail and attach a fuel pressure gauge.

5   Start the engine and check the pressure on the gauge, comparing your reading with the pressure listed in this Chapter's Specifications.

6   If the pressure is higher or lower than specified, inspect the fuel filter - make sure it isn't clogged (see Chapter 1). **Note:** *Because the fuel pressure regulator/fuel filter is mounted on top of the fuel pump/sending unit assembly, access makes testing very difficult. The fuel pump and fuel pressure regulator/fuel filter work together to deliver the proper amount of fuel pressure to the fuel injection system. If fuel pressure is high, the fuel pressure regulator/fuel filter is the cause. However, if the fuel pressure is low, the problem could be the fuel pump and/or fuel pressure regulator/fuel filter. It is recommended that the home mechanic replace both the fuel pump and fuel pressure regulator/fuel filter in the event of low fuel pressure. The fuel pump replacement procedure is located in Section 7 and the fuel pressure regulator/fuel filter replacement procedure is located in Section 14.*

7   If there is no fuel pressure, check the fuel pump (see following).

Component checks

Fuel pump

8   If you suspect a problem with the fuel pump, verify the pump actually runs. Have an assistant turn the ignition switch to ON - you

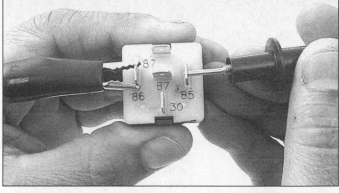

3.13 Check the resistance between terminals number 86 and number 85 - it should be approximately 75 ohms

should hear a brief "whirring" noise as the pump comes on and pressurizes the system.

9   If the pump does not come on (makes no sound), proceed to the next step and check the fuel pump circuit and relays for proper operation.

Main relays

Refer to illustrations 3.11, 3.13, 3.14, 3.15 and 3.16

Note: *The Automatic Shutdown (ASD) relay and the fuel pump relay must both be tested to insure proper fuel pump operation. Testing procedures for the ASD relay and the fuel pump relay are identical.*

10   To test a relay, first remove it from its location in the engine compartment Power Distribution Center. Turn the relay over and note the terminal numbers on the bottom.

11   Verify that there is battery voltage at the terminal on the panel that corresponds with terminal 30 of the relay **(see illustration)**. This terminal should have voltage present with or without the ignition key turned On. Now check the terminal on the panel that corresponds with terminal 86 on the relay - it should have voltage present only with the ignition key turned On.

12   If there is no voltage, check the fuel pump fuse. If voltage is not present at the fuse, check the wiring and connectors to the fuse panel.

13   Connect the probes of an ohmmeter to terminals 86 and 85 and check the resistance. There should be approximately 75 ohms resistance **(see illustration)**.

14   Now connect the ohmmeter probes to terminals 30 and 87A and check for continuity. Continuity should be present **(see illustration)**.

15   Check for continuity between terminals 30 and 87 **(see illustration)**. There should be no continuity.

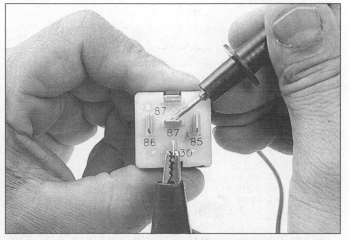

3.14 Also check the resistance between terminals 30 and 87A - continuity should be present

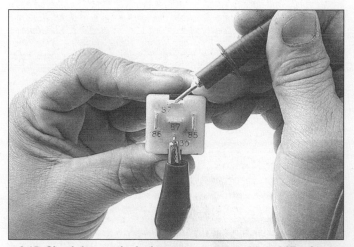

3.15 Check for continuity between terminals 30 and 87 - there should be no continuity

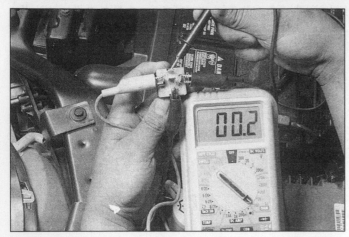

3.16 Using jumper wires, connect battery voltage to terminal 86 and ground terminal 85 - there should be continuity between the terminals 87 and 30

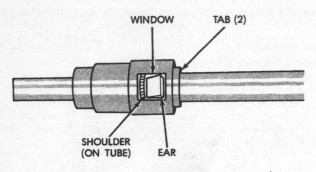

4.11b Plastic tab type quick connect fitting with a window style body

16   Using jumper wires, connect battery voltage to the no. 86 terminal, ground the number 85 terminal and verify that there's continuity between the terminals 87 and 30 **(see illustration)**. If there isn't, replace the relay.

4   Fuel lines and fittings - repair and replacement

Warning: *Gasoline is extremely flammable, so take extra precautions when you work on any part of the fuel system. Don't smoke or allow open flames or bare light bulbs near the work area, and don't work in a garage where a natural gas-type appliance (such as a water heater or a clothes dryer) with a pilot light is present. Since gasoline is carcinogenic, wear latex gloves when there's a possibility of being exposed to fuel, and, if you spill any fuel on your skin, rinse it off immediately with soap and water. Mop up any spills immediately and do not store fuel-soaked rags where they could ignite. The fuel system is under constant pressure, so, if any fuel lines are to be disconnected, the fuel pressure in the system must be relieved first (see Section 2). When you perform any kind of work on the fuel system, wear safety glasses and have a Class B type fire extinguisher on hand.*

1   Always relieve the fuel pressure before servicing fuel lines or fittings (see Section 2).

2   The fuel feed and vapor lines extend from the fuel tank to the engine compartment. The lines are secured to the underbody with clip and screw assemblies. These lines must be occasionally inspected for leaks, kinks and dents.

3   If evidence of dirt is found in the system or fuel filter during disassembly, the line should be disconnected and blown out. Check the fuel strainer on the fuel gauge sending unit (see Section 8) for damage and deterioration.

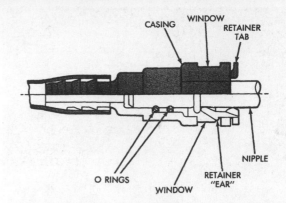

4.11a Cross-sectional view of a two-tab quick connect fuel line fitting

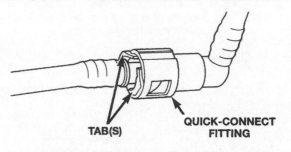

4.11c Plastic two-tab type quick disconnect fitting

Steel tubing

4   If replacement of a fuel line or emission line is called for, use tubes/hoses meeting Chrysler specification or its equivalent.

5   Don't use copper or aluminum tubing to replace steel tubing. These materials cannot withstand normal vehicle vibration.

6   Because fuel lines used on fuel-injected vehicles are under high pressure, they require special consideration.

7   Some fuel lines have threaded fittings with O-rings. Any time the fittings are loosened to service or replace components:

  a) *Use a backup wrench while loosening and tightening the fittings.*
  b) *Check all O-rings for cuts, cracks and deterioration. Replace any that appear hardened, worn or damaged.*
  c) *If the lines are replaced, always use original equipment parts, or parts that meet the original equipment standards specified in this Section.*

Flexible hose

Warning: *Use only original equipment replacement hoses or their equivalent. Others may fail from the high pressures of this system.*

8   Don't route fuel hose within four inches of any part of the exhaust system or within ten inches of the catalytic converter. Metal lines and rubber hoses must never be allowed to chafe against the frame. A minimum of 1/4-inch clearance must be maintained around a line or hose to prevent contact with the frame.

Removal and installation

Refer to illustrations 4.11a, 4.11b, 4.11c, 4.11d and 4.11e

9   Relieve the fuel pressure.

10   Remove all fasteners attaching the lines to the vehicle body.

11   There are various methods depending upon the type of quick-disconnect fitting used on the fuel line **(see illustrations)**. Carefully remove the fuel lines from the chassis. **Caution:** *The plastic ring type fittings are not serviced separately. Do not attempt to service these types of fuel lines in the event the clip or line becomes damaged. Replace the entire fuel line as an assembly.*

12   Installation is the reverse of removal. Be sure to use new O-rings.

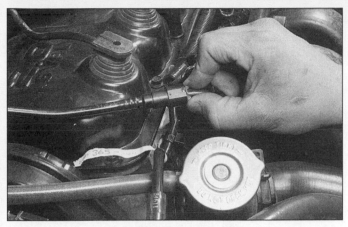

4.11d Depress the plastic tabs . . .

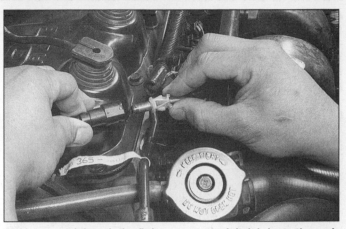

4.11e . . . and detach the fitting - to reattach it, lubricate the end with a little bit of clean engine oil, then push on the fitting until it clicks into place. Tug on it to ensure the connection is locked into place

Repair

13   In the event of any fuel line damage (metal or flexible lines) it is necessary to replace the damaged lines with factory replacement parts. Others may fail from the high pressures of this system.

5   Fuel tank - removal and installation

Refer to illustrations 5.5a, 5.5b, 5.5c, 5.6, 5.7a, 5.7b, 5.9 and 5.10

Warning: *Gasoline is extremely flammable, so take extra precautions when you work on any part of the fuel system. Don't smoke or allow open flames or bare light bulbs near the work area, and don't work in a garage where a natural gas-type appliance (such as a water heater or a clothes dryer) with a pilot light is present. Since gasoline is carcinogenic, wear latex gloves when there's a possibility of being exposed to fuel, and, if you spill any fuel on your skin, rinse it off immediately with soap and water. Mop up any spills immediately and do not store fuel-soaked rags where they could ignite. The fuel system is under constant pressure, so, if any fuel lines are to be disconnected, the fuel pressure in the system must be relieved first (see Section 2 for more information). When you perform any kind of work on the fuel system, wear safety glasses and have a Class B type fire extinguisher on hand.*

Note: *The following procedure is much easier to perform if the fuel tank is empty. Some tanks have a drain plug for this purpose. If the tank does not have a drain plug, the fuel can be siphoned from the tank using a siphoning kit, available at most auto parts stores. NEVER start the siphoning action with your mouth!*

1   Remove the fuel tank filler cap to relieve fuel tank pressure.
2   Relieve the fuel system pressure (see Section 2).

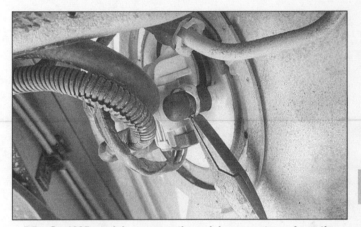

5.5a On 1995 models, remove the quick connect cap from the fuel pump module

3   Detach the cable from the negative terminal of the battery.
4   Raise the rear of the vehicle and support it securely on jackstands.
5   Remove the quick connect cap from the fuel pump module on 1995 models **(see illustration)** or from the fuel tank on 1996 and later models **(see illustration)**. Push a drain hose into the drain port and drain the fuel into an approved gasoline container **(see illustration)**.

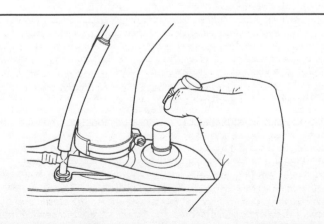

5.5b On 1996 and later models, remove the cap from the fuel tank drain port

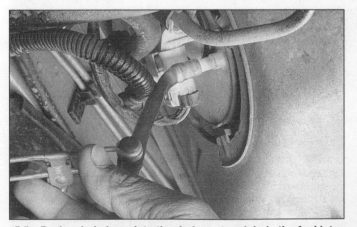

5.5c Push a drain hose into the drain port and drain the fuel into an approved gasoline container

4

5.6 Use needlenose pliers to disconnect the quick disconnect fuel line fitting(s) from the fuel pump module

5.7a Remove the plastic locking pin . . .

5.7b . . . and disconnect the electrical connector from the fuel pump module

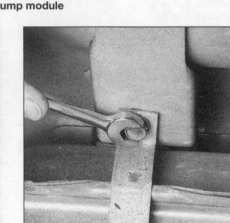

5.9 Remove the fuel tank strap bolts and both fuel tank straps - slightly lower the fuel tank

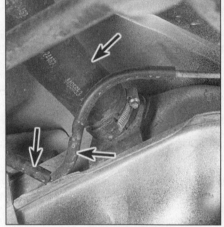

5.10 Disconnect the fuel tank filler tube, filler vent tube from the filler hose and vapor relief tube

6   Disconnect the quick disconnect fuel line fitting(s) from the fuel pump module **(see illustration)**.

7   On the right (passenger) side of the fuel tank, remove the locking pin **(see illustration)** and disconnect the electrical connector from the fuel pump module **(see illustration)**.

8   Support the fuel tank with a floor jack. Place a piece of wood between the jack head and the fuel tank to protect the tank.

9   Remove the fuel tank strap bolts and the fuel tank straps **(see illustration)**. Slightly lower the fuel tank.

10   Disconnect the fuel filler tube, filler vent tube from the filler hose and vapor relief tube from the tee fitting at the fuel tank **(see illustration)**.

11   Remove the tank from the vehicle.

12   Installation is the reverse of removal.

6   Fuel tank cleaning and repair - general information

1   The fuel tanks installed in the vehicles covered by this manual are made of plastic and are not repairable.

2   If the fuel tank is removed from the vehicle, it should not be placed in an area where sparks or open flames could ignite the fumes coming out of the tank. Be especially careful inside a garage where a natural gas-type appliance is located, because the pilot light could cause an explosion.

7   Fuel pump - removal and installation

Refer to illustrations 7.5 and 7.6

Warning 1: *Gasoline is extremely flammable, so take extra precautions when you work on any part of the fuel system. Don't smoke or allow open flames or bare light bulbs near the work area, and don't work in a garage where a natural gas-type appliance (such as a water heater or a clothes dryer) with a pilot light is present. Since gasoline is carcinogenic, wear latex gloves when there's a possibility of being exposed to fuel, and, if you spill any fuel on your skin, rinse it off immediately with soap and water. Mop up any spills immediately and do not store fuel-soaked rags where they could ignite. The fuel system is under constant pressure, so, if any fuel lines are to be disconnected, the fuel pressure in the system must be relieved first (see Section 2) for more information). When you perform any kind of work on the fuel system, wear safety glasses and have a Class B type fire extinguisher on hand.*

Warning 2: *The fuel reservoir in the fuel pump module does not empty when the fuel tank is drained. This fuel will drain out when the fuel pump module is removed from the fuel tank - protect yourself accordingly.*

Caution: *Be sure to change the fuel pump module O-ring gasket and locknut whenever the fuel pump/sending unit assembly is removed for servicing.*

1   Relieve the fuel system pressure (see Section 2).

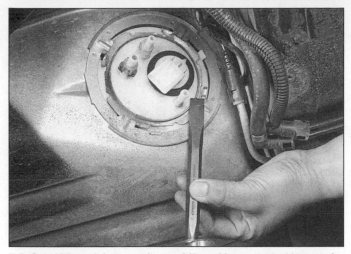

7.5 On 1995 models, use a brass drift and hammer and loosen the lock ring in a counterclockwise direction. On 1996 and later models, turn the locknut counterclockwise to remove it. If the assembly is difficult to turn, use a large pair of pliers to loosen it

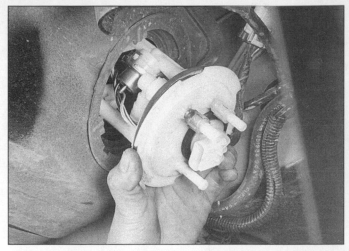

7.6 Slightly angle the unit and remove the fuel pump/fuel level sending unit from the tank

2   Detach the cable from the negative battery terminal.
3   Remove the fuel tank from the vehicle (see Section 5).
4   On 1995 models, mark the location of the fuel drain fitting on the module on the fuel tank with a permanent marker pen. Use this alignment mark during installation.
5   On 1995 models, use a brass drift and hammer and tap the fuel pump module lock ring in a counterclockwise direction (see illustration). On 1996 and later models, turn the locknut counterclockwise to remove it. If the assembly is difficult to turn, use a large pair of pliers to loosen it. Caution: *Do not overtighten the pliers on the nut or damage to the nut and a leak will result.*
6   Remove the fuel pump/fuel level sending unit from the tank (see illustration). Angle the assembly slightly to avoid damaging the fuel level sending unit float.
7   The electric fuel pump is not serviceable. In the event of failure, the complete assembly must be replaced.
8   Installation is the reverse of removal.

8   Fuel level sending unit - check and replacement

Warning: *Gasoline is extremely flammable, so take extra precautions*

when you work on any part of the fuel system. Don't smoke or allow open flames or bare light bulbs near the work area, and don't work in a garage where a natural gas-type appliance (such as a water heater or a clothes dryer) with a pilot light is present. Since gasoline is carcinogenic, wear latex gloves when there's a possibility of being exposed to fuel, and, if you spill any fuel on your skin, rinse it off immediately with soap and water. Mop up any spills immediately and do not store fuel-soaked rags where they could ignite. The fuel system is under constant pressure, so, if any fuel lines are to be disconnected, the fuel pressure in the system must be relieved first (see Section 2). When you perform any kind of work on the fuel system, wear safety glasses and have a Class B type fire extinguisher on hand.

Check
Refer to illustrations 8.2, 8.3 and 8.4
1   Remove the fuel pump/fuel level sending unit assembly (see Section 7).
2   Connect the probes of an ohmmeter to the two center terminals of the fuel level sending unit electrical connector and check for resistance (see illustration).
3   First, check the resistance of the sending unit with the fuel tank completely full. Move the float to the up position. The resistance of the sending unit should be between 1,020 to 1,080 ohms (see illustration).

8.2 Check the resistance between the two center terminals

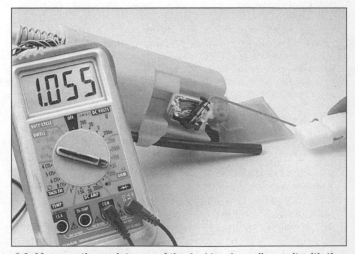

8.3 Measure the resistance of the fuel level sending unit with the float raised (tank full) . . .

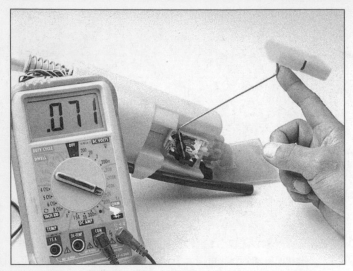

8.4 . . . and then with the float lowered (tank empty)

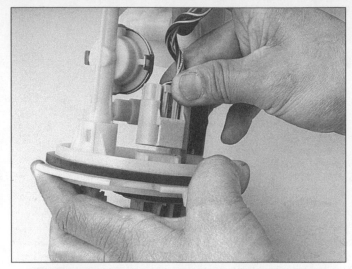

8.6 Disconnect the electrical connector from the module

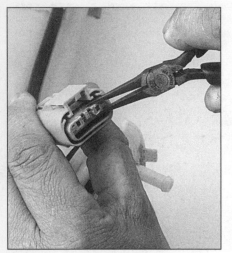

8.7 Use needlenose pliers and carefully pull out and remove the blue locking wedge

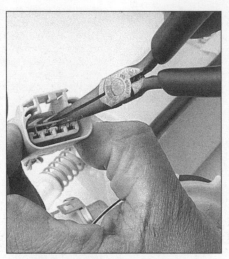

8.8 Use a small screwdriver, or needlenose pliers, and lift the locking fingers away from the terminal, then carefully push the terminal out of the connector

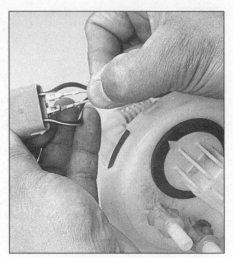

8.9 Pull the level sensor signal and ground terminals out of the connector

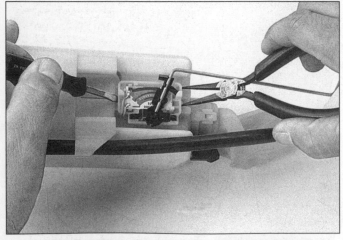

8.11 Slide the sensor wires through the module opening, then slide the sensor out of the channel in the module

4　Position the float in the down (empty) position. The resistance should be between 50 to 90 ohms (see illustration).

5　If the readings are incorrect or there is very little change in resistance as the float travels from full to empty, replace the fuel level sending unit assembly.

Replacement

Refer to illustrations 8.6, 8.7, 8.8, 8.9, 8.11 and 8.12

6　Disconnect the fuel level sensor electrical connector from the module connector (see illustration).

7　Pull out and remove the blue locking wedge (see illustration).

8　Use a small screwdriver, or needlenose pliers, and lift the locking fingers away from the terminal, then push the terminal out of the connector (see illustration) .

9　Pull the level sensor signal and ground terminals out of the connector (see illustration).

10　Insert a screwdriver between the module and the top of the level sensor and push the sensor down slightly.

11　Slide the sensor wires through the module opening, then slide the sensor out of the channel in the module (see illustration).

12　Installation is the reverse of removal. Feed the wires into the guide

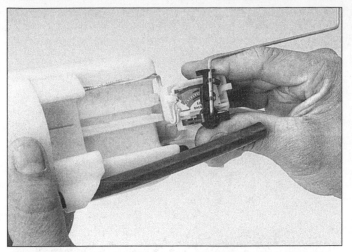

8.12 Feed the wires into the guide grooves, then slide the sensor up the channel until it snaps into place - tug on it to ensure the sensor is locked into place

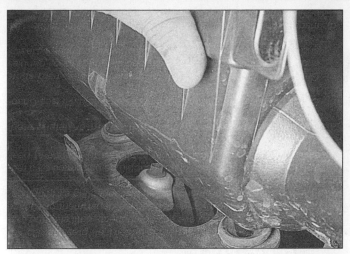

9.3 On models so equipped, remove the bolts then remove the air filter lower housing from the mounting bracket

10.2a Remove the mounting bolt . . .

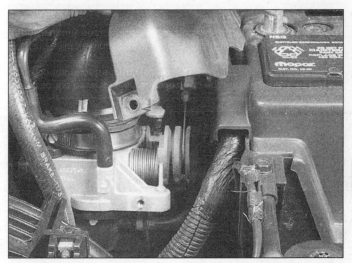

10.2b . . . then remove the throttle cable shield

grooves, then slide the sensor up the channel until it snaps into place **(see illustration).**

9 Air filter assembly - removal and installation

Refer to illustration 9.3
1   Detach the cable from the battery negative terminal.
2   Remove the air cleaner cover and filter element (see Chapter 1).
3   Remove the bolts (if equipped) securing the air filter lower housing to the engine compartment **(see illustration)**.
4   Lift the housing up and remove it from the engine compartment.
5   Installation is the reverse of removal.

10 Accelerator cable - replacement

Refer to illustrations 10.2a, 10.2b, 10.3, 10.4, 10.5a and 10.5b
1   Detach the cable from the negative battery terminal.
2   In the engine compartment, remove the throttle cable shield mounting bolt, then remove the shield **(see illustrations)**.
3   Rotate the throttle body cam and disconnect the throttle cable from the slot in the throttle body cam **(see illustration)**.

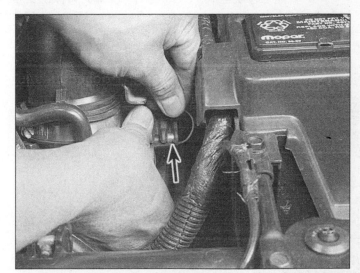

10.3 Disconnect the throttle cable from the slot in the throttle body cam

10.4 Use needlenose pliers, push in on the tab and release the accelerator cable retainer and cable from the bracket

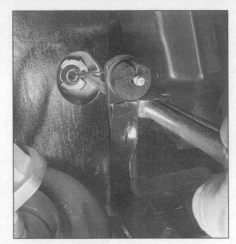

10.5a Pull the throttle cable into the passenger compartment to create slack in the cable . . .

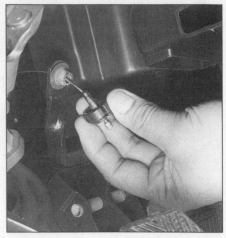

10.5b . . . remove the cable retainer clip from the cable . . .

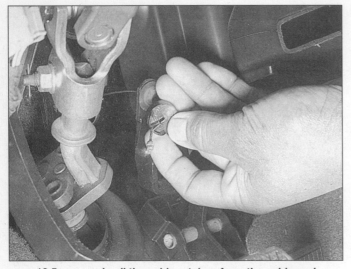

10.5c . . . and pull the cable retainer from the cable end

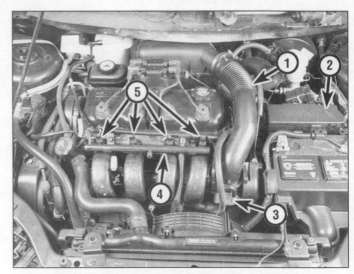

11.1 Fuel injection component location on the SOHC engine

1	Air intake duct	3	Throttle body
2	Powertrain Control	4	Fuel rail
	Module (PCM)	5	Fuel injectors

4   Push in on the tab and release the accelerator cable retainer from the bracket **(see illustration 10.3 and 10.4)**.

5   Working underneath the dash, use needlenose pliers and pull on the throttle cable to create slack in the cable **(see illustration)**. Remove the cable retainer clip from the cable at the accelerator pedal **(see illustration)**. Pull the cable retainer from the accelerator pedal and remove the retainer from the cable end **(see illustrations)**.

6   Push the cable through the firewall and into the engine compartment.

7   Installation is the reverse of removal.

11   Fuel injection system - general information

Refer to illustration 11.1

The sequential Multi Port Fuel Injection (MPFI) system consists of three sub-systems: air intake, electronic control and fuel delivery. The system uses a Powertrain Control Module (PCM) along with the sensors (coolant temperature sensor, Throttle Position Sensor (TPS), Manifold Absolute Pressure (MAP) sensor, oxygen sensor, etc.) to determine the proper air/fuel ratio under all operating conditions **(see illustration)**.

The fuel injection system and the emissions and engine control system are closely linked in function and design. For additional information, refer to Chapter 6.

Air intake system

The air intake system consists of the air filter, the air intake ducts, the throttle body, the idle control system, the air intake plenum and the intake manifold.

A throttle position sensor is attached to the throttle shaft to monitor changes in the throttle opening. The MAP sensor is attached to the intake manifold.

When the engine is idling, the idle speed is controlled by the idle air control system, which consists of the Powertrain Control Module (PCM) and the Idle Air Control (IAC) valve. The IAC valve is controlled by the PCM and is opened and closed depending upon the running conditions of the engine (air conditioning system, power steering, cold and warm running etc.). This valve regulates the amount of airflow past the throttle plate and into the intake manifold, thus increasing or decreasing the engine idle speed. The PCM receives information from the sensors (vehicle speed, coolant temperature, air conditioning, power steering mode etc.) and adjusts the idle according to the demands of the engine and driver.

12.7 Use a stethoscope to determine if the injectors are working properly - they should make a steady clicking sound that rises and falls with engine speed changes

12.8 Measure the resistance of each injector. It should be approximately 12 ohms

Electronic emissions and engine control system

The electronic emissions and engine control system is explained in detail in Chapter 6.

Fuel delivery system

The fuel delivery system consists of these components: The fuel pump, the pressure regulator, the fuel rail and the fuel injectors.

The fuel pump, located within the fuel tank, is an in-line, direct-drive type. Fuel is drawn through a filter into the pump, flows past the armature through the one-way valve, passes through another filter and is delivered to the injectors. A relief valve prevents excessive pressure build-up by opening in the event of a blockage in the discharge side and allowing fuel to flow from the high to the low pressure side.

The pressure regulator maintains a constant fuel pressure to the injectors. Excess fuel is routed back to the fuel tank through the fuel pressure regulator. **Note:** *These systems are equipped with a return-less fuel system. The fuel pressure regulator is mounted on top of the fuel pump/fuel level sending unit module.*

The injectors are solenoid-actuated pintle types consisting of a solenoid, plunger, needle valve and housing. When current is applied to the solenoid coil, the needle valve raises and pressurized fuel squirts out the nozzle. The injection quantity is determined by the length of time the valve is open (the length of time during which current is supplied to the solenoid coils).

The Automatic Shutdown (ASD) relay and the fuel pump relay are contained within Power Distribution Center, which is located in the left (driver) side of the engine compartment. The ASD relay connects battery voltage to the fuel injectors and the ignition coil while the fuel pump relay connects battery voltage only to the fuel pump. If the PCM senses there is NO signal from the camshaft or crankshaft sensors while the ignition key is RUN or cranking, the PCM will de-energize both relays.

12 Fuel injection system - check

Refer to illustrations 12.7, 12.8 and 12.9
Note: *The following procedure is based on the assumption that the fuel pressure is adequate (see Section 3).*

1   Check all electrical connectors that are related to the system. Check the ground wire connections on the intake manifold for tightness. Loose connectors and poor grounds can cause many problems that resemble more serious malfunctions.

2   Check to see that the battery is fully charged, as the control unit and sensors depend on an accurate supply voltage in order to properly meter the fuel.

3   Check the air filter element - a dirty or partially blocked filter will severely impede performance and economy (see Chapter 1).

4   If a blown fuse is found, replace it and see if it blows again. If it does, search for a grounded wire in the harness to the fuel pump.

5   Check the air intake duct to the intake manifold for leaks. Also check the condition of all vacuum hoses connected to the intake manifold.

6   Remove the air intake duct from the throttle body and check for dirt, carbon or other residue build-up. If it's dirty, clean it with carburetor cleaner spray and a toothbrush.

7   With the engine running, place an automotive stethoscope against each injector, one at a time, and listen for a clicking sound, indicating operation **(see illustration)**. If you don't have a stethoscope, place the tip of a screwdriver against the injector and listen through the handle.

8   Unplug the injector electrical connectors and test the resistance of each injector **(see illustration)**. Compare the values to the Specifications listed in this Chapter.

9   Install an injector test light ("noid" light) into each injector electrical connector, one at a time **(see illustration)**. Crank the engine over. Confirm that the light flashes evenly on each connector. This will test for voltage to the injector.

10   The remainder of the system checks can be found in the following Sections.

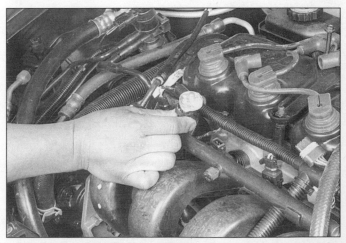

12.9 Install the "noid" light (available at most auto part stores) into each injector electrical connector and confirm that it blinks when the engine is cranking or running

4

13.1 Disconnect the canister purge control hose (arrow) from the top of the throttle body

13 Throttle body - check, removal and installation

Check

Refer to illustration 13.1

1   On top of the throttle body, locate the vacuum hose that goes to the canister purge control solenoid **(see illustration)**. Detach it from the throttle body and attach a vacuum gauge in its place.

2   Start the engine and warm it to its normal operating temperature. Verify the gauge indicates no vacuum.

3   Open the throttle slightly from idle and verify that the gauge indicates vacuum. If the gauge indicates no vacuum, check the port to make sure it is not clogged. Clean it with carburetor cleaner spray if necessary.

4   Stop the engine and verify the accelerator cable and throttle valve operate smoothly without binding or sticking.

5   If the accelerator cable or throttle valve binds or sticks, check for a build-up of sludge on the cable or throttle shaft.

6   If a build-up of sludge is evident, try removing it with carburetor cleaner or a similar solvent.

7   If cleaning fails to remedy the problem, replace the throttle body.

Removal and installation

Refer to illustrations 13.13 and 13.14

Warning: *Wait until the engine is completely cool before beginning this procedure.*

8   Detach the cable from the negative battery terminal.

9   Remove the air filter assembly (see Section 9).

10   Unplug the TPS and IAC sensor connectors from the throttle body.

11   Label and detach all vacuum hoses from the throttle body.

12   Detach the accelerator cable (see Section 10), speed control cable and, if equipped, the automatic transmission throttle valve cable (see Chapter 7B).

13   Unscrew the accelerator and speed control cable bracket bolts and move the bracket out of the way **(see illustration)**.

14   Remove the mounting bolts and remove the throttle body and O-ring gasket **(see illustration)**.

15   Installation is the reverse of removal. Be sure to install the re-usable O-ring gasket. Tighten the throttle body mounting bolts to the torque listed in this Chapter's Specifications. Adjust the accelerator cable (see Section 10) and, if equipped, the throttle valve cable (see Chapter 7B).

14 Fuel pressure regulator/fuel filter - replacement

Warning: *Gasoline is extremely flammable, so take extra precautions*

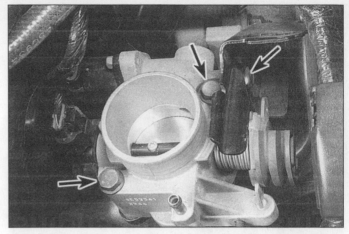

13.13 Remove the accelerator and speed control cable bracket bolts (right arrow) and move the bracket out of the way. Remove the throttle body mounting bolts (left arrows) and remove the throttle body and O-ring gasket.

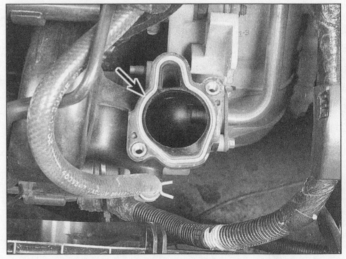

13.14 Install the re-usable O-ring gasket (arrow) into the intake manifold groove - make sure it is properly seated

when you work on any part of the fuel system. Don't smoke or allow open flames or bare light bulbs near the work area, and don't work in a garage where a natural gas-type appliance (such as a water heater or a clothes dryer) with a pilot light is present. Since gasoline is carcinogenic, wear latex gloves when there's a possibility of being exposed to fuel, and, if you spill any fuel on your skin, rinse it off immediately with soap and water. Mop up any spills immediately and do not store fuel-soaked rags where they could ignite. The fuel system is under constant pressure, so, if any fuel lines are to be disconnected, the fuel pressure in the system must be relieved first (see Section 2). When you perform any kind of work on the fuel system, wear safety glasses and have a Class B type fire extinguisher on hand.

Note: *These engines are equipped with a "returnless" fuel system. The fuel pressure regulator is mounted on top of the fuel pump/fuel level sending unit assembly.*

1995 models

Refer to illustrations 14.3a, 14.3b, 14.4a and 14.4b

1   Relieve the fuel system pressure (see Section 2).

2   Remove the fuel pump module (see Section 7).

3   Spread the tangs on the pressure regulator retainer from the tabs and remove the retainer, then carefully pry the pressure regulator out

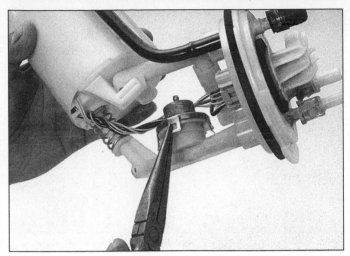

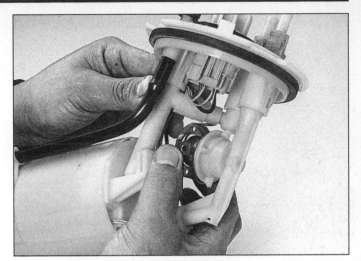

14.3a Spread the tangs on the pressure regulator retainer away from the tabs

14.3b Remove the retainer and carefully pry the pressure regulator out of the fuel pump module housing

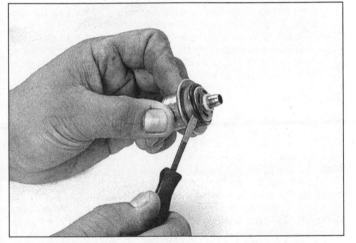

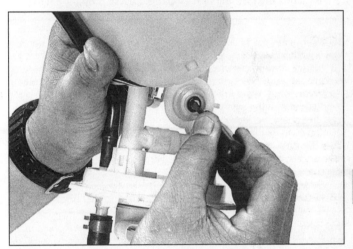

14.4a Remove the O-rings from the pressure regulator . . .

14.4b . . . apply clean engine oil to the O-rings and install them into the fuel pump module. Make sure they are properly seated

of the fuel pump module housing **(see illustrations)**. Ensure that both upper and lower O-rings came out with the regulator.

4   Apply clean engine oil to the O-rings and install them in the receptacle in the fuel pump module. Ensure they are properly seated **(see illustrations)**.

5   Push the pressure regulator into place and make sure it is properly seated.

6   Fold the regulator tangs onto the fuel pump module tabs.

7   Install the fuel pump module (see Section 7).

1996 and later models

Refer to illustrations 14.11 and 14.13

8   Relieve the fuel system pressure (see Section 2).

9   Raise the rear of the vehicle and support it securely on jackstands.

10   On the right (passenger's) side of the fuel tank, wrap a cloth around the fuel line to catch the residual fuel (which may still be under slight pressure) and disconnect the hose. Disconnect the hose from the filter/regulator by using a small wrench to push the black plastic ring on the quick-disconnect fitting.

11   Depress the spring tab on the side of the fuel filter/pressure regulator, then rotate the unit 90-degrees counterclockwise and pull it out **(see illustration). Note:** *Make sure you remove the upper and lower O-rings along with the unit. Do not leave them in the receptacle in the fuel pump module.*

FUEL FILTER/PRESSURE REGULATOR

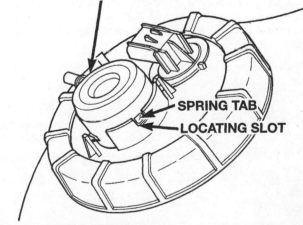

14.11 On 1996 and later models, depress the spring tab on the side of the fuel filter/pressure regulator, rotate the unit 90-degrees counterclockwise and pull it out

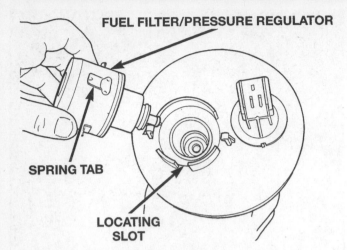

14.13 Align the two hold down tabs with the flange, push down and rotate the filter/regulator clockwise until the spring tab engages the locating slot - make sure it is properly seated

12   Lubricate the filter/regulator's upper and lower O-rings and the fuel line fitting with clean engine oil.
13   Place the new filter/regulator into the opening in the fuel pump module, align the two hold down tabs with the flange **(see illustration)**. Push down and rotate the filter/regulator clockwise until the spring tab is engaged with the locating slot.
14   Insert the fuel line onto the filter/regulator fitting, then connect the quick disconnect fitting into place until it locks in place.
15   Start the engine and check carefully for leaks at the hose connections.

15   Fuel injectors - check, removal and installation

Warning: *Gasoline is extremely flammable, so take extra precautions when you work on any part of the fuel system. Don't smoke or allow open flames or bare light bulbs near the work area, and don't work in a garage where a natural gas-type appliance (such as a water heater or a clothes dryer) with a pilot light is present. Since gasoline is carcinogenic, wear latex gloves when there's a possibility of being exposed to fuel, and, if you spill any fuel on your skin, rinse it off immediately with soap and water. Mop up any spills immediately and do not store fuel-soaked rags where they could ignite. The fuel system is under constant pressure, so, if any fuel lines are to be disconnected, the fuel pressure in the system must be relieved first (see Section 2). When you perform any kind of work on the fuel system, wear safety glasses and have a Class B type fire extinguisher on hand.*

Check

1   Start the engine and warm it to normal operating temperature.
2   With the engine idling, unplug each injector one-at-a-time, note the change in idle speed then reconnect the injector. If the idle speed drop is approximately the same for each cylinder, the injectors are operating correctly. If unplugging a particular injector fails to change the idle speed, proceed to the next step.
3   Turn the engine off. Remove the connector from the injector, and measure the resistance between the two terminals of the injector **(see illustration 12.8)**.
4   The resistance should be approximately 12 to 15 ohms. If not, replace it with a new injector.
5   If the resistance is as specified, connect a high-impedance voltmeter or a special injector harness test light (noid light), (available at most auto parts stores) to the electrical connector **(see illustration 12.9)**.

15.9 Detach the fuel line (arrow) at the fuel rail and move it out of the way - plug the end to prevent the entry of foreign matter

a) *If the voltage fluctuates between zero and two volts (or the light flashes), the injector is receiving proper voltage.*
b) *If there is no voltage, check the wiring harness (see Chapter 12).*
c) *If the wiring harness is not damaged or shorted, check the wiring between the PCM and the injector(s) for a short circuit, or a break in the wire or bad connection.*

Removal

Refer to illustrations 15.9, 15.10, 15.11a, 15.11b, 15.12a and 15.12b
6   Detach the cable from the negative battery terminal.
7   On 1995 models, remove the air inlet tube from the air filter cover. On 1996 and later models, remove the screw and lift off the air inlet duct.
8   Relieve the fuel pressure (see Section 2).
9   Detach the fuel line from the fuel rail **(see illustration)**.
10   Unplug the injector electrical connectors **(see illustration)**. Clearly label and remove any vacuum hoses or electrical wiring that will interfere with the fuel rail removal.
11   Remove the mounting bolts **(see illustration)** and lift the fuel rail assembly along with the fuel injectors from the engine compartment **(see illustration)**.
12   Remove the injector(s) from the fuel rail assembly remove and discard the O-rings **(see illustrations)**. **Note:** *Whether you're replacing an injector or a leaking O-ring, it's a good idea to remove all the injectors from the fuel rail and replace all the O-rings.*

15.10 Unplug the electrical connectors from each fuel injector

15.11a Remove the mounting bolts . . .

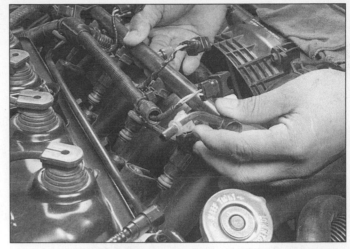

15.11b . . . and carefully lift the fuel rail assembly along with the fuel injectors from the intake manifold

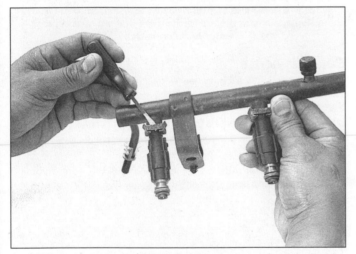

15.12a Release the retaining clip(s) and remove the injector(s) from the fuel rail assembly

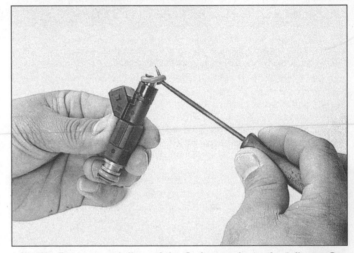

15.12b Remove and discard the O-rings - always install new O-rings whenever the fuel injectors are removed

Installation

Refer to illustration 15.13

13   Coat the new O-rings with clean engine oil and install them onto the injector(s), then insert each injector into its corresponding bore in the fuel rail and install the retaining clip **(see illustration)**.

14   Install the injector and fuel rail assembly on the intake manifold. Make sure the injectors are fully seated, then tighten the fuel rail mounting bolts to the torque listed in this Chapter's Specifications.

15   The remainder of installation is the reverse of removal.

16   After the injector/fuel rail assembly installation is complete, turn the ignition switch to ON, but don't operate the starter (turning the switch on activates the fuel pump for about two seconds, which builds up fuel pressure in the fuel lines and the fuel rail). Repeat this about two or three times, then check the fuel lines, rail and injectors for fuel leakage.

16   Exhaust system servicing - general information

Refer to illustration 16.1

Warning: *Inspection and repair of exhaust system components should be done only after enough time has elapsed after driving the vehicle to*

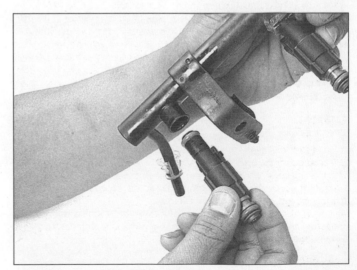

15.13 Coat the new O-rings with clean engine oil and install them onto the injector(s), then insert each injector into its corresponding bore in the fuel rail - make sure the injector is correctly seated in the fuel rail

allow the system components to cool completely. Also, when working under the vehicle, make sure it is securely supported on jackstands.

1   The exhaust system consists of the exhaust manifold, the catalytic converter, the exhaust pipe, muffler and all brackets, hangers and clamps. The exhaust system is attached to the body with mounting brackets and rubber hangers **(see illustration)**. If any of the parts are improperly installed, excessive noise and vibration will be transmitted to the body.

Muffler and pipes

2   Conduct regular inspections of the exhaust system to keep it safe and quiet. Look for any damaged or bent parts, open seams, holes, loose connections, excessive corrosion or other defects which could allow exhaust fumes to enter the vehicle. Also check the catalytic converter when you inspect the exhaust system (see following). Deteriorated exhaust system c omponents should not be repaired; they should be replaced with new parts.

3   If the exhaust system components are extremely corroded or rusted together, welding equipment will probably be required to remove them. The convenient way to accomplish this is to have a muffler repair shop remove the corroded sections with a cutting torch. If, however, you want to save money by doing it yourself (and you don't have a welding outfit with a cutting torch), simply cut off the old components with a hacksaw. If you have compressed air, special pneumatic cutting chisels can also be used. If you do decide to tackle the job at home, be sure to wear safety goggles to protect your eyes from metal chips and work gloves to protect your hands.

4   Here are some simple guidelines to follow when repairing the exhaust system:

   a) *Work from the back to the front when removing exhaust system components.*

   b) *Apply penetrating oil to the exhaust system component fasteners to make them easier to remove.*

   c) *Use new gaskets, hangers and clamps when installing exhaust systems components.*

   d) *Apply anti-seize compound to the threads of all exhaust system fasteners during reassembly.*

   e) *Be sure to allow sufficient clearance between newly installed parts and all points on the underbody to avoid overheating the floor pan and possibly damaging the interior carpet and insulation. Pay particularly close attention to the catalytic converter and heat shield.*

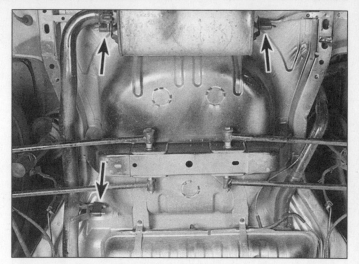

16.1 Inspect the exhaust system mounting brackets and rubber hangers (arrows) - if any of the parts are improperly installed, excessive noise and vibration will be transmitted to the body. Replace any of the rubber hangers that are starting to deteriorate or harden

Catalytic converter

Warning: *The converter gets very hot during operation. Make sure it has cooled down before you touch it.*

Note: *See Chapter 6 for more information on the catalytic converter.*

5   Periodically inspect the heat shield for cracks, dents and loose or missing fasteners.

6   Remove the heat shield and inspect the converter for cracks or other damage.

7   If the converter must be replaced, remove the front mounting shoulder bolts and springs from the flange. Loosen the rear band clamp and separate the converter from the exhaust system (you should be able to push the exhaust pipe out of the way to clear the converter outlet fitting).

8   Installation is the reverse of removal. Be sure to use new gaskets and tighten the bolts securely.

Chapter 5
Engine electrical systems

Contents

Specifications

Ignition system

Ignition coil resistance (at 70-degrees F)
  Primary resistance
    1995 through 1998 .... 0.45 to 0.65 ohms
    1999
      Weastec (steel towers) .... 0.45 to 0.65 ohms
      Diamond (brass towers) .... 0.53 to 0.65 ohms
  Secondary resistance
    1995 through 1998 .... 7,000 to 15,800 ohms @ 70 to 80-degrees F
    1999
      Weastec (steel towers) .... 11,500 to 13,500 ohms
      Diamond (brass towers) .... 10,900 to 14,700 ohms

Torque specifications

Ft-lbs
Starter mounting bolts 40

1 General information

The engine electrical systems include all ignition, charging and starting components. Because of their engine-related functions, these components are discussed separately from chassis electrical devices such as the lights, the instruments, etc., which are included in Chapter 12.

Always observe the following precautions when working on the electrical systems:

a) *Be extremely careful, when servicing engine electrical components. They are easily damaged if checked, connected or handled improperly.*
b) *Never leave the ignition switch on for long periods of time with the engine off.*
c) *Don't disconnect the battery cables while the engine is running.*
d) *Maintain correct polarity when connecting a battery cable from another vehicle during jump starting.*
e) *Always disconnect the negative cable first and hook it up last or the battery may be shorted by the tool being used to loosen the cable clamps.*

It's also a good idea to review the safety-related information regarding the engine electrical systems located in the *Safety First* section near the front of this manual before beginning any operation included in this Chapter.

2 Battery - emergency jump starting

Refer to the Booster battery (jump) starting procedure at the front of this manual.

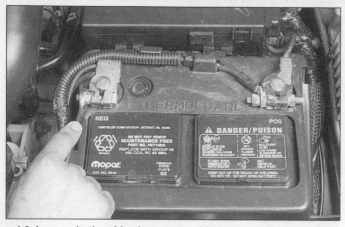

4.2 Loosen both cable clamp nuts with a wrench, then remove the cable from the negative terminal followed by the positive battery cable

4.3a Remove the thermoguard . . .

3   Battery cables - check and replacement

1   Periodically inspect the entire length of each battery cable for damage, cracked or burned insulation and corrosion. Poor battery cable connections can cause starting problems and decreased engine performance.

2   Check the cable-to-terminal connections at the ends of the cables for cracks, loose wire strands and corrosion. The presence of white, fluffy deposits under the insulation at the cable terminal connection is a sign that the cable is corroded and should be replaced. Check the terminals for distortion, missing mounting bolts and corrosion.

3   When removing the cables, always disconnect the negative cable first and hook it up last or the battery may be shorted by the tool used to loosen the cable clamps. Even if only the positive cable is being replaced, be sure to disconnect the negative cable from the battery first (see Chapter 1 for further information regarding battery cable removal).

4   Disconnect the old cables from the battery, then trace each of them to their opposite ends and detach them from the starter solenoid and ground terminals. Note the routing of each cable to ensure correct installation.

5   If you are replacing either or both of the old cables, take them with you when buying new cables. It is vitally important that you replace the cables with identical parts. Cables have characteristics that make them easy to identify: positive cables are usually red and larger in cross-section; ground cables are usually black and smaller in cross-section.

6   Clean the threads of the solenoid or ground connection with a wire brush to remove rust and corrosion. Apply a light coat of battery terminal corrosion inhibitor, or petroleum jelly, to the threads to prevent future corrosion.

7   Attach the cable to the solenoid or ground connection and tighten the mounting nut/bolt securely.

8   Before connecting a new cable to the battery, make sure that it reaches the battery post without having to be stretched.

9   Connect the positive cable first, followed by the negative cable.

4   Battery - removal and installation

Refer to illustrations 4.2, 4.3a, 4.3b and 4.5

1   Disconnect both cables from the battery terminals. **Caution:** *Always disconnect the negative cable first and hook it up last or the battery may be shorted by the tool being used to loosen the cable clamps.*

2   Loosen the cable clamp nuts with a wrench, being careful to remove the negative cable first, and slide them off the terminals **(see illustration)**.

3   Remove the thermoguard and disconnect the hold-down clamp nut, then remove the clamp **(see illustrations)**.

4   Lift out the battery. Be careful - it's heavy. **Note:** *Battery straps and handlers are available at most auto parts stores for a reasonable price. They make it easier to remove and carry the battery.*

5   While the battery is out, remove and inspect the carrier (tray) for corrosion **(see illustration)**.

4.3b . . . remove the hold-down clamp nut and the clamp from the battery tray

4.5 Inspect the battery carrier (tray) for corrosion

6.3 To use a calibrated ignition tester, simply disconnect a spark plug wire, connect it to the tester, clip the tester to a convenient ground and crank the engine over - if there's enough power to fire the plug, sparks will be visible between the electrode tip and the tester body

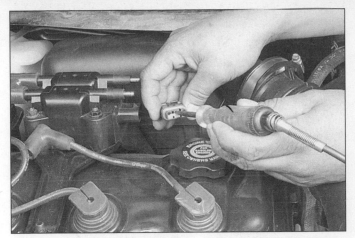

6.8 Touch the probe of an LED test light to the dark blue/tan and black/gray coil driver circuits and observe that the test light flashes while the engine is cranked over

6   If corrosion has leaked down to the battery support, remove the bolts and lift the battery tray out. Use baking soda to clean the deposits from the tray and all metal supports to prevent the support from further oxidation.

7   If you are replacing the battery, make sure you get one that's identical, with the same dimensions, amperage rating, cold cranking rating, etc. Make sure it is fully charged prior to installation in the vehicle.

8   Installation is the reverse of removal. Position the battery with the positive (+) terminal toward the left (driver's) side and reinstall the battery back into the battery carrier. Make sure that no parts or wires are laying on the carrier during installation of the battery.

9   Install the thermoguard, then install a pair of specially treated felt washers around the terminals (available at auto parts stores), then coat the terminals and the cable clamps with petroleum jelly or grease to prevent further corrosion. Install the cable clamps and tighten the nuts, being careful to install the negative cable last.

5   Ignition system - general information

All models are equipped with a distributorless ignition system (DIS). The entire ignition system consists of the ignition switch, the battery, the coil pack, the primary (low voltage) and secondary (high voltage) wiring circuits, the ignition wires and spark plugs, the camshaft position sensor, the crankshaft position sensor and the Powertrain Control Module (PCM). The PCM controls the ignition timing, spark and advance characteristics for the engine. The ignition timing is not adjustable. The crankshaft and camshaft sensors are both Hall Effect timing devices. Refer to Chapter 6 for testing and replacement procedures for the crankshaft sensor and camshaft sensor.

The crankshaft sensor and camshaft sensor generate pulses that are input to the Powertrain Control Module. The PCM determines crankshaft position from these two sensors. The PCM calculates injector sequence and ignition timing from the crankshaft position.

The PCM regulates the ignition system. The PCM supplies battery voltage to the ignition coil pack through the Automatic Shutdown Relay (ASD). The PCM also controls the ground circuit for the ignition coil.

The computerized ignition system provides complete control of the ignition timing by determining the optimum timing using a micro computer in response to engine speed, coolant temperature, throttle position and vacuum pressure in the intake manifold. These parameters are relayed to the PCM by the camshaft position sensor, crankshaft position sensor, the Throttle Position Sensor (TPS), coolant temperature sensor and Manifold Absolute Pressure (MAP) sensor. Ignition timing is altered during warm-up, idling and warm running conditions by the PCM.

Refer to a dealer parts department or auto parts store for any questions concerning the availability of the ignition parts and assemblies. Testing the camshaft position sensor and the crankshaft position sensor is covered in Chapter 6.

6   Ignition system - check

Refer to illustrations 6.3 and 6.8

Warning: *Because of the very high voltage generated by the ignition system (40,000 volts), extreme care should be taken whenever an operation is performed involving ignition components. This not only includes the coil and spark plug wires, but related items connected to the system as well, such as the electrical connectors, tachometer and any test equipment.*

1   With the ignition switch turned to the "ON" position, a glowing instrument panel "Battery" light or "Oil Pressure" light is a basic check for battery supply to the ignition system and PCM.

2   Check all ignition wiring connections for tightness, cuts, corrosion or any other signs of a bad connection.

3   Use a calibrated ignition tester (available at most auto parts stores or specialty tool companies) to verify adequate secondary voltage at each spark plug **(see illustration)**. Make sure you use an ignition tester calibrated for electronic ignition systems. A faulty or poor connection at that plug could also result in a misfire. Also, check for carbon deposits inside the spark plug boot.

4   If NO spark or INTERMITTENT sparks occur, disconnect the coil pack electrical connector and check for battery voltage to the ignition coil pack on the center (orange wire) with the ignition On. You may have to cycle the ignition key on and off several times to make this check because the computer shuts off the ignition feed if it senses the engine is not cranking.

5   Using an ohmmeter, check the resistance between the coil terminals (see Section 7). If an open is found (verified by an infinite reading), replace the coil pack.

6   Using an ohmmeter, check the resistance of the spark plug wires. Refer to the specified resistance values in this Chapter's Specifications.

7   Check the operation of the camshaft position sensor (see Chapter 6) and the crankshaft position sensor (see Chapter 6).

8   If all the checks are correct, check the coil driver circuits from the computer. Using a test light (an LED-type test light works best for this check) connected to the positive battery terminal, disconnect the coil pack electrical connector and probe the dark blue/tan and black/gray connector terminals while an assistant cranks the engine **(see illustration).** Caution: *Do not touch the dark green/orange wire terminal with the test light connected to the positive battery terminal or damage to*

5

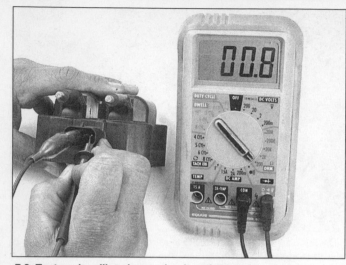

7.3 Test each coil's primary circuit resistance by connecting one probe of the ohmmeter to the center terminal and the other probe to each end terminal. The primary resistance of each coil should be within specifications

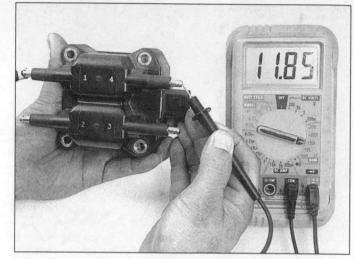

7.4 Connect the ohmmeter probes to the secondary tower for each coil pack pair. Each coil pair should fall within the secondary resistance specification value

the PCM may result. If the circuits are functioning properly, the light will rapidly blink on and off as the PCM grounds the circuit. If there is no flashing from the test light, most likely the computer is defective. Have the PCM diagnosed by a dealer service department.

9   Additional checks should be performed by a dealer service department or an automotive repair shop.

7   Ignition coil - check and replacement

Check

Refer to illustrations 7.3 and 7.4

1   Clearly label the four spark plug wires, then detach them from the coil pack. Measure the resistance of each cable and compare your measurements with those listed in this Chapter's Specifications. Replace any cable not within the specified range.

2   Unplug the electrical connector from the coil pack.

3   Working on the coil pack connector, measure the resistance on the primary side of each coil terminal with a digital ohmmeter **(see illustration)**. At the coil, connect an ohmmeter between the center pin (B+) and each end pin, in turn. Compare your readings with the primary resistance value listed in this Chapter's Specifications.

4   Measure the secondary resistance of the coil between the paired high tension towers of each coil **(see illustration)**. Compare your readings with the secondary resistance value listed in this Chapter's Specifications.

5   If either coil in the coil pack fails any of the above tests, replace the coil pack.

Replacement

Refer to illustration 7.8

6   Clearly label the four spark plug wires, then detach them from the coil pack.

7   Unplug the electrical connector from the coil pack.

8   Remove the coil pack mounting nuts **(see illustration)** and lift the coil pack from the mounting bracket on the valve cover.

9   Installation is the reverse of removal.

8   Charging system - general information and precautions

The charging system includes the alternator, a charge indicator

7.8 Remove the coil pack mounting nuts (arrows) and lift the coil from the engine compartment

light, the battery, the Powertrain Control Module (PCM), the ASD relay, a fusible link and the wiring between all the components. The charging system supplies electrical power to maintain the battery at its full charge capacity. The alternator is driven by a drivebelt on the front of the engine.

The alternator control system within the PCM varies the voltage generated at the alternator in accordance with driving conditions. Depending on electric load, vehicle speed, engine coolant temperature, battery temperature sensor, accessories (air conditioning system, radio, cruise control etc.) and the intake air temperature, the system will adjust the amount of voltage generated, creating less load on the engine.

The purpose of the voltage regulator is to limit the alternator's voltage to a preset value. This prevents power surges, circuit overloads, etc., during peak voltage output. The voltage regulator is contained within the PCM and in the event of failure, the PCM must be replaced as a single unit.

These models are equipped with a Mitsubishi (MELCO) 83 amp alternator. The alternator must be replaced as a single unit in the event of failure.

The charging system doesn't ordinarily require periodic maintenance. However, the drivebelt, battery, harness wires and connections should be inspected at the intervals outlined in Chapter 1.

The dashboard warning light should come ON when the ignition

9.2 To measure battery voltage, attach the voltmeter leads to the battery terminals (engine OFF) - to measure charging voltage, start the engine

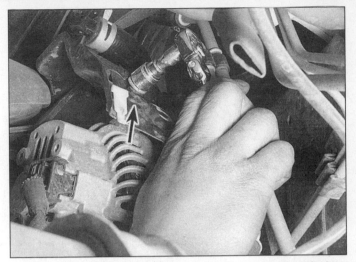

10.2 Remove the mounting bolt and the lower plastic splash shield (arrow)

key is turned to ON, but it should go off immediately after the engine is started. If it remains on, there is a malfunction in the charging system (see Section 9).

Be very careful when making electrical circuit connections to a vehicle equipped with an alternator and note the following:

a) *When reconnecting wires to the alternator from the battery, be sure to note the polarity.*

b) *Before using arc welding equipment to repair any part of the vehicle, disconnect the wires from the alternator and the battery terminals.*

c) *Never start the engine with a battery charger connected.*

d) *Always disconnect both battery cables before using a battery charger.*

e) *The alternator is turned by an engine drivebelt which could cause serious injury if your hands, hair or clothes become entangled in it with the engine running.*

f) *Because the alternator is connected directly to the battery, it could arc or cause a fire if overloaded or shorted out.*

g) *Wrap a plastic bag over the alternator and secure it with rubber bands before steam cleaning the engine.*

9 Charging system - check

Refer to illustration 9.2
Note: *These vehicles are equipped with an On Board Diagnostic (OBD-II) system that is useful for detecting charging system problems. Refer to Chapter 6 for the trouble code extracting procedures.*

1   If a malfunction occurs in the charging circuit, do not immediately assume that the alternator is causing the problem. First check the following items:

a) *The battery cables where they connect to the battery. Make sure the connections are clean and tight.*

b) *The battery electrolyte specific gravity. If it is low, charge the battery.*

c) *Check the external alternator wiring and connections.*

d) *Check the drivebelt condition and tension (see Chapter 1).*

e) *Check the alternator mounting bolts for tightness.*

f) *Run the engine and check the alternator for abnormal noise.*

2   Using a voltmeter, check the battery voltage with the engine off. It should be approximately 12-volts **(see illustration)**.

3   Start the engine and check the battery voltage again. It should now be approximately 13 to 15-volts.

4   If the indicated voltage reading is less or more than the specified

charging voltage, have the PCM checked at a dealer service department. The voltage regulator on these models is contained within the PCM and it cannot be adjusted, removed or tampered with in any way.

5   Due to the special equipment necessary to test or service the alternator, it is recommended that if a fault is suspected, the vehicle be taken to a dealer or a shop with the proper equipment. Because of this, the home mechanic should limit maintenance to checking connections and the inspection and replacement of the alternator.

6   The charge light on the instrument panel illuminates with the key on and engine not running, and should go out when the engine runs.

7   If the charge light remains on, there is a fault in the system. Before replacing the alternator, the battery condition, alternator belt tension and electrical cable connections should be checked.

10 Alternator - removal and installation

Refer to illustrations 10.2, 10.3, 10.5 and 10.6

1   Detach the cable from the negative terminal of the battery.

2   Remove the mounting bolt and the lower plastic splash shield located under the engine **(see illustration)**.

3   Mark and detach the electrical connectors from the alternator **(see illustration)**.

4   Loosen the drivebelt adjustment bolts and nut, then detach the alternator drivebelt (see Chapter 1).

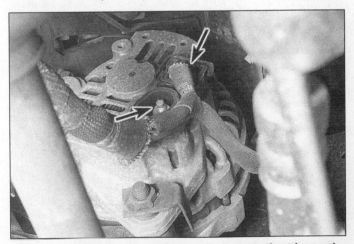

10.3 Disconnect the alternator electrical connections (arrows)

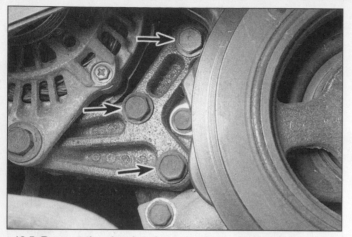

10.5 Remove the pivot bracket mounting bolts (arrows) and the mounting bracket

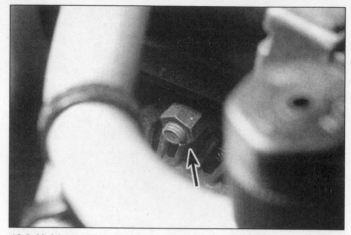

10.6 Hold onto the alternator, remove the adjustment nut (arrow), slide alternator off the T-bolt and separate it from the engine

5   Remove the pivot bracket mounting bolts **(see illustration)**. Remove the pivot bolt and the mounting bracket.
6   Hold onto the alternator, remove the adjustment nut **(see illustration)**, slide alternator off the T-bolt and separate it from the engine.
7   If you are replacing the alternator, take the old one with you when purchasing a replacement unit. Make sure the new/rebuilt unit looks identical to the old alternator. Look at the terminals - they should be the same in number, size and location as the terminals on the old alternator. Finally, look at the identification numbers - they will be stamped into the housing or printed on a tag attached to the housing. Make sure the numbers are the same on both the old and new alternators.
8   Many new/rebuilt alternators do not have a pulley installed, so you may have to switch the pulley from the old unit to the new/rebuilt one. When buying an alternator, find out the shop's policy regarding pulleys; some shops will perform this service free of charge.
9   Installation is the reverse of removal.
10   After the alternator is installed, adjust the drivebelt tension (see Chapter 1).
11   Check the charging voltage to verify proper operation of the alternator (see Section 9).

11   Starting system - general information and precautions

The starter motor assembly is a light-weight design that uses a planetary gear reduction drive. This starter/solenoid assembly is made by Bosch and provides higher rotational speeds for starting. This unit is sold strictly as a complete assembly. Check with your local dealer parts department before disassembly.
The starting system consists of the battery, the starter motor, the starter solenoid and the wires connecting them. The solenoid is mounted directly on the starter motor.
The solenoid/starter motor assembly is installed on the upper part of the engine, next to the transmission bellhousing.
When the ignition key is turned to the Start position, the starter solenoid is actuated through the starter control circuit which includes a starter relay located in the Power Distribution Center. The starter solenoid then connects the battery to the starter. The battery supplies the electrical energy to the starter motor, which does the actual work of cranking the engine.
Always observe the following precautions when working on the starting system:

a)   *Excessive cranking of the starter motor can overheat it and cause serious damage. Never operate the starter motor for more than 15 seconds at a time without pausing to allow it to cool for at least two minutes.*
b)   *The starter is connected directly to the battery and could arc or cause a fire if mishandled, overloaded or shorted out.*

c)   *Always detach the cable from the negative terminal of the battery before working on the starting system.*

12   Starter motor - in-vehicle check

Refer to illustration 12.7
Note: *Before diagnosing starter problems, make sure the battery is fully charged.*
1   If the starter motor does not turn at all when the switch is operated, make sure the shift lever is in Neutral or Park.
2   Make sure the battery is charged and all cables, both at the battery and starter solenoid terminals, are clean and secure.
3   If the starter motor spins but the engine is not cranking, the overrunning clutch in the starter motor is slipping and the starter motor must be replaced. Also, the ring gear on the flywheel or driveplate may be worn.
4   If, when the switch is actuated, the starter motor does not operate at all but the solenoid clicks, the problem lies with either the battery, the main solenoid contacts or the starter motor itself (or the engine is seized).
5   If the solenoid plunger cannot be heard when the switch is actuated, the battery is faulty, the fusible link is burned (the circuit is open) or the solenoid itself is defective.
6   To check the solenoid, connect a remote starter switch between the battery and the ignition switch wire terminal (the small terminal) on the solenoid. If the starter motor operates when the remote switch is activated, the solenoid is OK and the problem is in the ignition switch, neutral start switch, starter relay or the interconnecting wiring.
7   Locate the starter relay in the power distribution center **(see illustration)**. Remove the relay and perform the identical tests as for the Automatic Shutdown Relay (ASD) and the fuel pump relay in Chapter 4, Section 3. Refer to **illustrations 3.13a, 3.13b and 3.14** in Chapter 4.
8   If the starter motor still does not operate, remove the starter/solenoid assembly for replacement as a complete unit.
9   If the starter motor cranks the engine at an abnormally slow speed, first make sure that the battery is fully charged and that all terminal connections are clean and tight. If the engine is partially seized, or has the wrong viscosity oil in it, it will crank slowly.
10   Run the engine until normal operating temperature is reached, then remove the fuel pump relay from the power distribution center to keep the engine from starting.
11   Connect a voltmeter positive lead to the positive battery post and connect the negative lead to the negative post.
12   Crank the engine and take the voltmeter readings as soon as a steady figure is indicated. Do not allow the starter motor to turn for more than l5 seconds at a time. A reading of nine volts or more, with the starter motor turning at normal cranking speed, is normal. If the

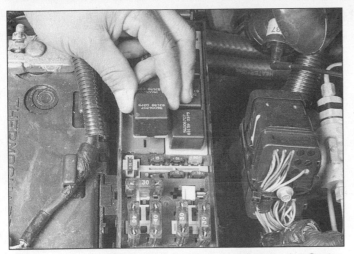

12.7 Remove the starter relay from the Power Distribution Center, with the ignition key OFF

13.3 Remove the engine front mount bolt from the front crossmember mounting bracket

13.4 Remove the electrical connectors (arrows) from the starter solenoid

13.5 Remove the mounting bolts (and ground wire) (arrow) and detach the starter from the transaxle housing

5

reading is nine volts or more but the cranking speed is slow, the motor, solenoid contacts or circuit connections are faulty. If the reading is less than nine volts and the cranking speed is slow, the starter motor is probably bad.

13   Starter motor - removal and installation

Refer to illustrations 13.3, 13.4 and 13.5

1   Detach the cable from the negative terminal of the battery.
2   Raise the front of the vehicle and support it securely on jackstands.
3   On air conditioning equipped models, support the engine and

transaxle assembly so It will not rotate in either direction. Remove the engine front mount bolt from the front crossmember mounting bracket **(see illustration)**. Lower the front of the engine, rotate the engine forward to allow easy access to the starter motor assembly.
4   Clearly label, then disconnect the wires from the terminal on the starter motor solenoid **(see illustration)**.
5   Remove the mounting bolts (and ground wire) and detach the starter from the transaxle housing **(see illustration)**. Partially move the starter assembly away from the transaxle housing to gain access to the wiring connectors.
6   Position the starter vertically and remove it through the bottom of the vehicle. Carefully move the air conditioning lines out of the way.
7   Installation is the reverse of removal. Tighten the starter mounting bolts to the torque listed in this Chapter's Specifications.

Notes

Chapter 6
Emissions and engine control systems

Contents

Specifications

Torque specifications

Ft-lbs (unless otherwise indicated)

Crankshaft sensor retaining bolt	70 in-lbs
Camshaft sensor	
Sensor retaining bolt	80 in-lbs
Target magnet retaining bolt	30 in-lbs
EGR tube mounting nuts	96 in-lbs
EGR valve bolts	200 in-lbs
Knock sensor	96 in-lbs

1 General information

Refer to illustration 1.5

To prevent pollution of the atmosphere from incompletely burned and evaporating gases, and to maintain good driveability and fuel economy, a number of emission control systems are incorporated. The principal systems are:

Positive Crankcase Ventilation (PCV) system
Evaporative Emission Control (EVAP) system
Exhaust Gas Recirculation (EGR) system
Oxygen sensor (O2) system
Catalytic converter (TWC)
Powertrain Control Module (PCM) (computer) and information sensors

The Sections in this Chapter include general descriptions, checking procedures within the scope of the home mechanic and component replacement procedures (when possible) for each of the systems listed above.

Before assuming an emissions control system is malfunctioning, check the fuel and ignition systems carefully. The diagnosis of some emission control devices requires specialized tools, equipment and

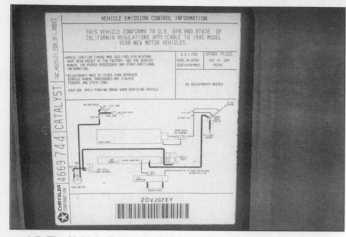

1.5 The Vehicle Emission Control Information (VECI) label is located on the underside of the hood and contains information on idle speed adjustment, ignition timing, location of the emissions control devices on your vehicle, vacuum line routing, etc.

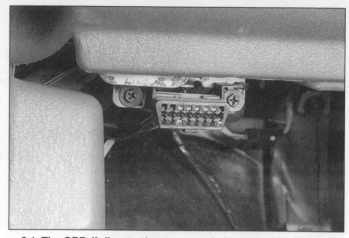

2.1 The OBD-II diagnostic connector is located under the left (driver's) side of the instrument panel

training. If checking and servicing become too difficult or if a procedure is beyond your ability, consult a dealer service department. Remember, the most frequent cause of emissions problems is simply a loose or broken vacuum hose or wire, so always check the hose and electrical connections that interconnect the components within each system first.

This doesn't mean, however, that emission control systems are particularly difficult to maintain and repair. You can quickly and easily perform many checks and do most of the regular maintenance at home with common tune-up and hand tools. **Note:** *Because of a Federally mandated extended warranty which covers the emission control system components, check with your dealer about warranty coverage before working on any emissions-related systems. Once the warranty has expired, you may wish to perform some of the component checks and/or replacement procedures in this Chapter to save money.*

Pay close attention to any special precautions outlined in this Chapter. A Vehicle Emissions Control Information (VECI) label is located in the engine compartment **(see illustration)**. This label contains important emissions specifications and adjustment information. When servicing the engine or emissions systems, the VECI label in your particular vehicle should always be checked for up-to-date information.

2   On Board Diagnosis (OBD-II) system - description and trouble code access

Refer to illustration 2.1
Note: *On the models covered by this manual the CHECK ENGINE light or Malfunction Indicator Light (MIL) located in the instrument panel flashes on for three seconds as a bulb test when the engine is started. The light comes on and stays on when there's a problem in the engine control system and a trouble code is stored in memory. All models are equipped with the OBD-II system. On 1995 through 1998 models the trouble codes can be accessed using the ignition key but it will be necessary to use a SCAN tool to read and interpret the various levels of diagnostic information. On models since 1999, the only way to access the trouble codes is with the special factory SCAN tool or OBD-II code reader. These tools are available from auto parts stores and specialty equipment manufacturers. Before outputting the trouble codes, thoroughly inspect ALL electrical connectors and hoses. Make sure all electrical connections are tight, clean and free of corrosion; make sure all hoses are properly connected, fit tightly and are in good condition (no cracks or tears).*

1   The self-diagnosis information contained in the PCM (computer) can be accessed either by the ignition key or by using a special tool called the Diagnostic Readout Box (DRB-II). This tool is attached to the

diagnostic connector **(see illustration)** located under the left (driver's) side of the instrument panel in the passenger compartment and reads the codes and parameters on the digital display screen. The tool is expensive and most home mechanics prefer to use the alternate method. The drawback with the ignition key method is that it does not access all the available codes for display. Most problems can be solved or diagnosed quite easily and if the information cannot be obtained readily, have the vehicle's self-diagnosis system analyzed by a dealer service department or other qualified repair shop.

2   To obtain the codes using the ignition key method, first set the parking brake and put the shift lever in Park. Raise the engine speed to approximately 2,500 rpm and slowly let the speed down to idle. Also cycle the air conditioning system (on briefly, then off). Next, with your foot on the brake, select each position on the transmission (Reverse, Drive, Low etc.), finally bring the shifter back to Park and turn off the engine. This will allow the computer to obtain any fault codes that might be linked to any of the sensors controlled by the transmission, engine speed or air conditioning system.

3   To display the codes on the dashboard (CHECK ENGINE light or Malfunction Indicator Light), with the engine NOT running, turn the ignition key ON, OFF, ON, OFF and finally ON (must be done within 5 seconds). The codes will begin to flash. The light will blink the number of the first digit then pause and blink the number of the second digit. For example: Code 23, air temperature sensor circuit, would be indicated by two flashes, pause, three flashes.

4   Certain criteria must be met for a fault code to be entered into the PCM's memory. The criteria might be a specific range of engine rpm, engine temperature or input voltage to the PCM. It's possible that a fault code for a particular monitored circuit may not be entered into the memory despite a malfunction. This may happen because one of the fault code criteria has not been met. For example, the engine must be operating between 750 and 2,000 rpm in order to monitor the MAP sensor circuit correctly. If the engine speed is raised above 2,400 rpm, the MAP sensor output circuit shorts to ground and will not allow a fault code to be entered into the memory. Then again, the exact opposite could occur: A code is entered into the memory that suggests a malfunction within another component that is not monitored by the computer. For example, a fuel pressure problem cannot register a fault directly but instead, it will cause a rich or lean fuel mixture problem. Consequently, this will cause an oxygen sensor malfunction resulting in a stored code in the computer for the oxygen sensor. Be aware of the interrelationship of the sensors and circuits and the overall relationship of the emissions control and fuel injection systems.

5   The accompanying table is a list of the typical trouble codes which may be encountered while diagnosing the system. Also included are simplified troubleshooting procedures. If the problem persists after these checks have been made, more detailed service procedures will have to be performed by a dealer service department or other qualified repair shop.

Trouble codes

Note: *Not all trouble codes apply to all models.*

Code 11   No distributor reference signal detected during engine cranking. Check the circuit between the distributor and the PCM.

Code 12   Problem with the battery connection. Direct battery input to PCM disconnected within the last 50 ignition key-on cycles.

Code 13**   Indicates a problem with the MAP sensor vacuum system.

Code 14**   MAP sensor voltage too low or too high.

Code 15**   A problem with the Vehicle Speed Sensor signal. No Vehicle Speed Sensor signal detected during road load conditions.

Code 17   Engine is cold too long. Engine coolant temperature remains below normal operating temperatures during operation (check the thermostat).

Code 21**   Problem with oxygen sensor signal circuit. Sensor voltage to computer not fluctuating.

Code 22**   Coolant sensor voltage too high or too low. Test coolant temperature sensor.

Code 23**   Indicates that the air temperature sensor input is below the minimum acceptable voltage or sensor input is above the maximum acceptable voltage.

Code 24**   Throttle position sensor voltage high or low. Test the throttle position sensor.

Code 25**   Idle Air Control (IAC) valve circuits. A shorted condition is detected in one or more of the IAC valve circuits. Or a vacuum leak is detected.

Code 27   One of the injector control circuit output drivers does not respond properly to the control signal. Check the circuits.

Code 31**   Problem with the canister purge solenoid circuit.

Code 32**   An open or shorted condition detected in the EGR solenoid circuit. Possible air/fuel ratio imbalance not detected during diagnosis.

Code 33   Air conditioning clutch relay circuit. An open or shorted condition detected in the compressor clutch relay circuit.

Code 34   Open or shorted condition detected in the speed control vacuum or vent solenoid circuits.

Code 35   Open or shorted condition detected in the radiator fan low speed relay circuit.

Code 37**   An open or shorted condition detected in the torque converter part throttle unlock solenoid control circuit.

Code 41***   Problem with the charging system. An open or shorted condition detected in the generator field control circuit.

Code 42   Fuel pump relay or auto shutdown relay (ASD) control circuit indicates an open or shorted circuit condition.

Code 43**   Multiple cylinder missfire detected. Peak primary circuit current not achieved with the maximum dwell time.

Code 44   Battery temperature sensor volts malfunction. Problem with the battery temperature voltage circuit in the PCM.

Code 46***   Charging system voltage too high. Computer indicates that the battery voltage is not properly regulated.

Code 47***   Charging system voltage too low. Battery voltage sense input below target charging voltage during engine operation and no significant change in voltage detected during active test of alternator output.

Code 51**   Oxygen sensor signal input indicates lean fuel/air ratio condition during engine operation.

Code 52**   Oxygen sensor signal input indicates rich fuel/air ratio condition during engine operation.

Code 53**   Internal PCM failure detected.

Code 54**   No camshaft position sensor signal from distributor. Problem with the distributor synchronization circuit.

Code 55   Completion of fault code display on CHECK ENGINE lamp. This is an end of message code.

Code 62   Unsuccessful attempt to update EMR mileage in the controller EEPROM.

Code 63**   Controller failure. EEPROM write denied. Check the PCM.

Code 65**   Power steering switch failure.

Code 72**   Catalytic converter efficiency failure. Catalyst efficiency below required level.

*** These codes illuminate the CHECK ENGINE light on the instrument panel during engine operation once the trouble code has been recorded.*

*** These codes illuminate the CHARGE SYSTEM light on the instrument panel during engine operation once the trouble code has been recorded.*

6

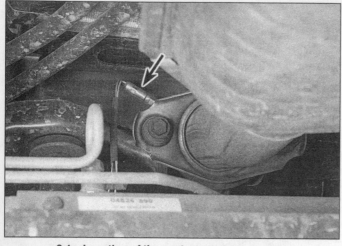

3.1a Location of the upstream oxygen sensor near the exhaust manifold

3   Information sensors and output actuators

Note: *All models are equipped with the OBD-II system. The engine codes can be accessed using the ignition key but it will be necessary to use a special factory SCAN tool (DRB-II) to read and interpret the various levels of diagnostic information. Have the vehicle diagnosed by a dealer service department if following the sensor checking procedures fail to turn up a problem. After performing checking procedures to any of the information sensors, be sure to clear the PCM of all trouble codes by disconnecting the cable from the negative terminal of the battery for at least ten seconds.*

Oxygen sensor

General description

Refer to illustrations 3.1a and 3.1b

1   All models are equipped with two oxygen sensors, an upstream oxygen sensor, which is located in the exhaust manifold and a downstream oxygen's sensor, which is located at the outlet pipe of the catalytic converter **(see illustrations)**. The two sensors monitor the deterioration of the catalytic converter due to age and they also monitor the oxygen content of the exhaust gas stream. The oxygen content in the exhaust reacts with the oxygen sensor to produce a voltage output which varies from 0.1-volt (high oxygen, lean mixture) to 0.9-volts (low oxygen, rich mixture). The PCM constantly monitors this variable voltage output to determine the ratio of oxygen to fuel in the mixture. The PCM

3.1b Location of the downstream oxygen sensor on the exhaust pipe after the catalytic converter

alters the air/fuel mixture ratio by controlling the pulse width (open time) of the fuel injectors. A mixture ratio of 14.7 parts air to 1 part fuel is the ideal mixture ratio for minimizing exhaust emissions, thus allowing the catalytic converter to operate at maximum efficiency. It is this ratio of 14.7 to 1 which the PCM and the oxygen sensor attempt to maintain at all times. Both sensors are equipped with a heating element that keeps the sensors at proper operating temperature during all operating modes.

2   The oxygen sensor produces no voltage when it is below its normal operating temperature of about 600-degrees F. During this initial period before warm-up, the PCM operates in OPEN LOOP mode.

3   When there is a problem with the oxygen sensor or its circuit, the PCM operates in the open loop mode - that is, it controls fuel delivery in accordance with a programmed default value instead of feedback information from the oxygen sensor.

4   The proper operation of the oxygen sensors depends on four conditions:

a) *Electrical - The low voltages generated by the sensors depend upon good, clean connections which should be checked whenever a malfunction of the sensor(s) is suspected or indicated.*

b) *Outside air supply - The sensors are designed to allow air circulation to the internal portion of the sensor. Whenever the sensor is removed and installed or replaced, make sure the air passages are not restricted.*

c) *Proper operating temperature - The PCM will not react to the sensor signal until the sensor reaches approximately 600-degrees F. This factor must be taken into consideration when evaluating the performance of the sensor.*

d) *Unleaded fuel - The use of unleaded fuel is essential for proper operation of the sensors. Make sure the fuel you are using is of this type.*

5   In addition to observing the above conditions, special care must be taken whenever the sensor(s) is serviced.

a) *The oxygen sensors have a permanently attached pigtail and electrical connector which should not be removed from the sensor. Damage or removal of the pigtail or electrical connector can adversely affect operation of the sensor(s).*

b) *Grease, dirt and other contaminants should be kept away from the electrical connector and the louvered end of the sensor(s).*

c) *Do not use cleaning solvents of any kind on the oxygen sensors.*

d) *Do not drop or roughly handle the sensors.*

Check

6   Locate the oxygen sensor electrical connector. Using an ohmmeter, check the resistance of the oxygen sensor heater elements. Unplug the oxygen sensor electrical connectors and attach the leads of an ohmmeter to the wire terminals. The resistance should be approximately 5 to 7 ohms. If not, replace the sensor(s).

Replacement

Note: *Because they are installed in the exhaust manifold and catalytic converter, which contracts when cool, the oxygen sensors may be very difficult to loosen when the engine is cold. Rather than risk damage to the sensor (assuming you are planning to reuse it in another manifold or pipe), start and run the engine for a minute or two, then shut it off. Be careful not to burn yourself during the following procedure.*

7   Disconnect the cable from the negative battery terminal.

8   Raise the vehicle and place it securely on jackstands.

9   Carefully disconnect the electrical connector from the sensor and unscrew the sensor from the exhaust manifold or catalytic converter **(see illustrations 3.1a and 3.1b)**.

10   Anti-seize compound must be used on the threads of the sensor to facilitate future removal. The threads of new sensors will already be coated with this compound, but if an old sensor is removed and reinstalled, recoat the threads.

11   Install the sensor and tighten it securely.

12   Reconnect the electrical connector of the pigtail lead to the main engine wiring harness.

13   Lower the vehicle, take it on a test drive and check to see that no trouble codes set.

3.14a MAP sensor location on the SOHC engine

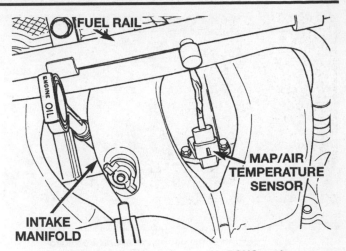

3.14b MAP sensor location on the DOHC engine

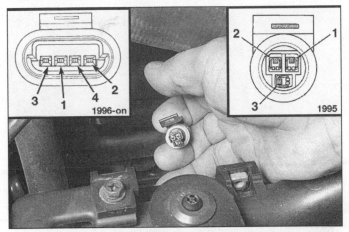

3.17 Using a voltmeter, check for reference voltage to the MAP sensor between the voltage supply and sensor ground terminals. It should be approximately 4.0 to 5.0 volts.

1	Voltage supply	4	IAT output voltage
2	Sensor ground		(1996-on only)
3	MAP output voltage		

Manifold Absolute Pressure (MAP) sensor

General description

Refer to illustrations 3.14a and 3.14b

14 The Manifold Absolute Pressure (MAP) sensor monitors the intake manifold pressure changes resulting from changes in engine load and speed and converts the information into a voltage output. The PCM uses the MAP sensor to control fuel delivery and ignition timing. The PCM will receive information as a voltage signal that will vary from 1.0 to 1.5 volts at closed throttle (high vacuum) and 4.0 to 4.5 volts at wide open throttle (low vacuum). The MAP sensor is located on the side of the intake manifold plenum **(see illustrations)**.

15 A failure in the MAP sensor circuit should set a Code 13 or a Code 14.

Check

Refer to illustration 3.17

16 Check the electrical connector at the sensor for a snug fit. Check the terminals in the connector and the wires leading to it for looseness and breaks. Repair as required.

17 To check the MAP sensor supply voltage; disconnect the electrical connector, turn the ignition key ON (engine not running) and check for voltage between the voltage supply (violet/white wire) and the sensor ground (black/light blue wire) terminals at the sensor connector **(see illustration)**. There should be approximately 4.5 to 5.5 volts.

18 To check the MAP sensor output voltage; reconnect the connector

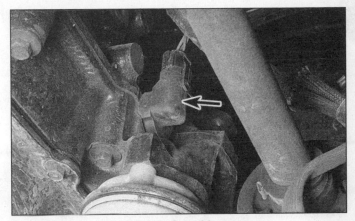

3.24 Crankshaft position sensor

to the sensor, turn the ignition key ON (engine not running) and check for voltage by backprobing the sensor ground (black/light blue wire) and the MAP output voltage (dark green/red wire) terminals at the sensor connector. There should be approximately 4 to 5 volts. Start the engine, the voltage should drop to 1.5 to 2.1 volts with the engine idling.

19 If the MAP sensor voltage readings are incorrect, replace the MAP sensor.

Replacement

20 Disconnect the electrical connector from the MAP sensor.

21 Remove the MAP sensor mounting bolts and detach the sensor from the intake plenum.

22 Installation is the reverse of removal.

Crankshaft position sensor

General description

23 The crankshaft position sensor determines the timing for the fuel injection and ignition on each cylinder. It also detects engine RPM. The crankshaft position sensor is a Hall-Effect device that is mounted on the cylinder block behind the alternator and detects two sets of four timing notches in the crankshaft's second counterweight. The engine will not operate if the PCM does not receive a crankshaft position sensor input.

Check

Refer to illustration 3.24

24 Check the reference voltage to the crankshaft sensor from the PCM. Locate the crankshaft sensor electrical connector **(see illustration)** on cylinder block behind the alternator, remove the connector and with the ignition key ON (engine not running) install the positive probe of the voltmeter to the orange wire terminal (+). There should be 8.0 to 9.0 volts.

6

3.29a Location of the coolant temperature sensor on the SOHC engine

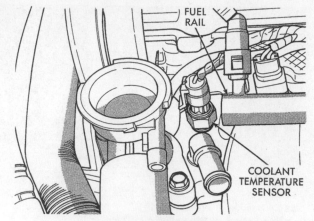

3.29b Location of the coolant temperature sensor on the DOHC engine

25   If reference voltage is present, check for the crank sensor signal. Install the electrical connector onto the crank sensor, backprobe the gray/black wire terminal (+) using a pin or paper clip and monitor the voltage changes as you turn the engine over slowly using a socket and wrench on the crankshaft pulley or by tapping the ignition key without starting the engine. The voltage will fluctuate from less than 0.5 (metal under sensor) to as high as 5.0 volts (slots under sensor).

Replacement

26   Disconnect the crankshaft sensor wiring harness connector.
27   Remove the crankshaft sensor mounting bolt. Use only the original bolt to mount the sensor, they are machined to correctly space the sensor to the cylinder block.
28   Installation is the reverse of removal. Tighten the bolt(s) to the torque listed in this Chapter's Specifications.

Engine Coolant Temperature (ECT) sensor

General description

Refer to illustrations 3.29a and 3.29b

29   The coolant temperature sensor is a thermistor (a resistor which varies the value of its resistance in accordance with temperature changes) **(see illustrations)**. The change in the resistance values will directly affect the voltage signal from the coolant thermosensor. As the sensor temperature DECREASES, the resistance values will INCREASE. As the sensor temperature INCREASES, the resistance values will DECREASE. A failure in the coolant sensor circuit should set either a Code 14 or a Code 15. These codes indicate a failure in the coolant temperature circuit, so the appropriate solution to the problem will be either repair of a wire or replacement of the sensor. The sensor can also be checked with an ohmmeter, by measuring its resistance when cold, then warming up the engine and taking another measurement.

Check

30   To check the sensor, release the locking tab, unplug the electrical connector. Check the resistance values of the coolant temperature sensor with the engine cold (70-degrees F = 7,000 to 13,000 ohms).Next, start the engine and warm it up until it reaches operating temperature. The resistance should be lower (200-degrees F = 700 to 1,000 ohms). **Note:** *Since the coolant sensor is difficult to access, it may be easier to remove the sensor and perform the tests in a pan of heated water.*

Replacement

Warning: *Wait until the engine is completely cool before beginning this procedure.*
31   Drain the cooling system until the coolant level is below the sensor. Release the locking tab, unplug the electrical connector, then carefully unscrew the sensor. **Caution:** *Handle the coolant sensor with care. Damage to this sensor will affect the operation of the entire fuel injection system.*
32   Before installing the new sensor, wrap the threads with Teflon

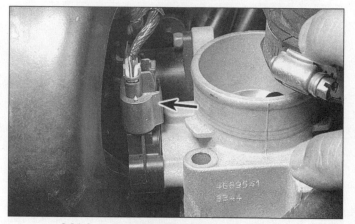

3.34 Location of the Throttle Position Sensor

sealing tape to prevent leakage and thread corrosion.
33   Installation is the reverse of removal. Refill the cooling system.

Throttle Position Sensor (TPS)

General description

Refer to illustration 3.34

34   The Throttle Position Sensor (TPS) is located on the end of the throttle shaft on the throttle body **(see illustration)**. By monitoring the output voltage from the TPS, the PCM can determine fuel delivery based on throttle valve angle (driver demand). A broken or loose TPS can cause intermittent bursts of fuel from the injectors and an unstable idle because the PCM thinks the throttle is moving.

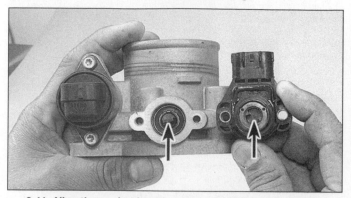

3.41 Align the socket locating tangs (arrow) on the throttle position sensor with the throttle shaft (arrow) in the throttle body, then install the TPS

3.43 Location of the Intake Air Temperature sensor (IAT) on 1995 models. On 1996 and later models, the Intake Air Temperature sensor is combined with the MAP sensor

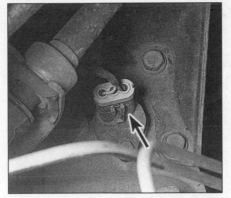

3.48 Location of the Vehicle Speed Sensor on the transaxle

3.53a Location of the camshaft position sensor on SOHC engines

Check

35   Locate the Throttle Position Sensor (TPS) on the throttle body.

36   With the electrical connector connected to the TPS, check the TPS signal voltage. Connect the positive probe (+) of the voltmeter onto the center terminal and the negative probe to ground. and observe the TPS sensor voltage. With the throttle valve fully closed, the voltage should read approximately 0.4 to 1.2 volts. Gradually open the throttle valve and observe an increase in voltage as the sensor travels from idle to full throttle. The voltage should increase to approximately 3.0 to 4.5 volts at wide open throttle. If the readings are incorrect, replace the TPS sensor.

Replacement

Refer to illustration 3.41

37   Disconnect the evaporation purge hose from the throttle body.
38   Disconnect the electrical connector from the TPS.
39   Remove the throttle body from the intake manifold (see Chapter 4).
40   Remove the mounting screws from the TPS and remove the TPS from the throttle body.
41   When installing the TPS, be sure to align the socket locating tangs on the TPS with the throttle shaft in the throttle body **(see illustration)**.
42   Installation is the reverse of removal. Be sure the throttle valve is fully closed once the TPS is mounted. If it isn't, rotate the TPS to allow complete closure (idle) before tightening the mounting screws.

Intake Air Temperature (IAT) sensor

General information

Refer to illustration 3.43

Note: *The 1995 models are equipped with a separate IAT sensor. On 1996 and later models, the IAT sensor is combined with the MAP sensor into a single sensor. Both types are mounted on the intake manifold.*

43   The Intake Air Temperature sensor is located in the intake manifold **(see illustration)**. This sensor operates as a negative temperature coefficient (NTC) device. As the sensor temperature DECREASES, the resistance values will INCREASE. As the sensor temperature INCREASES, the resistance values will DECREASE. Most cases, the appropriate solution to the problem will be either repair of a wire or replacement of the sensor.

Check

44   To check the sensor, unplug the electrical connector. Check the resistance values of the IAT sensor while it is at room temperature (70-degrees F = 7,000 to 13,000 ohms).Next, start the engine and warm it up until it reaches operating temperature. The resistance should be lower (200-degrees F = 700 to 1,000 ohms).

Replacement

45   Unplug the electrical connector from the air temperature sensor.

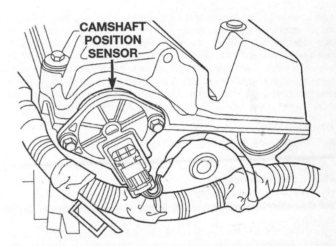

CAMSHAFT POSITION SENSOR

3.53b Location of the camshaft position sensor on DOHC engines

46   Unscrew the sensor from the intake manifold and remove the air temperature sensor.
47   Installation is the reverse of removal.

Vehicle Speed Sensor (VSS)

General description

Refer to illustration 3.48

48   The Vehicle Speed Sensor (VSS) is located on the transaxle depending upon the model and equipment package **(see illustration)**. This sensor is a permanent magnetic variable reluctance sensor that produces a pulsing voltage whenever vehicle speed is over 3 mph. These pulses are translated by the PCM and provided to other systems for fuel and transmission shift control.

Check

49   In the event of Vehicle Speed Sensor failure, have the system checked with a SCAN tool at a dealer service department.

Replacement

50   To replace the VSS, disconnect the electrical connector from the VSS.
51   Remove the retaining bolt and lift the VSS from the transaxle.
52   Installation is the reverse of removal.

Camshaft position sensor

General description

Refer to illustrations 3.53a and 3.53b

53   The camshaft position sensor **(see illustrations)** provides cylinder identification to the PCM to synchronize the fuel system with the

6

3.61 Location of the knock sensor on the cylinder block

4.4 Remove the PCM mounting screws

**4.5 Completely loosen the electrical connector retaining screw -
the screw will not come out of the connector**

spark system. The synchronizing signal is generated from a rotating target magnet attached to the rear of the camshaft. The target magnet has four different poles arranged in a symmetrical pattern. As the target magnet rotates, the sensor senses the changes in polarity and generates pulses. The change in polarity sends the low voltage pulses (approximately 0.5 volts) and then the high voltage increases to about 5.0 volts. These voltage pulses are in turn processed by the PCM which in turn determines ignition timing.

Check
54   In the event of camshaft position sensor failure, have the system checked with a SCAN tool at a dealer service department.

Replacement
55   Disconnect the negative terminal from the battery.
56   Remove the filtered air tube from the throttle body and air filter housing.
57   On SOHC engines, remove the air inlet tube. Disconnect the electrical connector from the engine coolant sensor and camshaft position sensor. Remove the brake booster hose and electrical connectors from the holders on the end of the valve cover.
58   Remove the bolt from the camshaft sensor and lift the sensor from the rear of the cylinder head.
59   If necessary, remove the target magnet mounting screw and remove the magnet.
60   Installation is the reverse of removal. If removed, align the locating pins on the backside of the target magnet with the locating holes in the rear of the camshaft and tighten the screw securely.

Knock sensor

General information
Refer to illustration 3.61
61   The engine is equipped with a single knock sensor mounted on the cylinder block **(see illustration)**. If the knock sensor detects a knock in the cylinder during the combustion process it sends an electrical signal to the PCM. The PCM, in turn, retards the ignition timing by a certain amount to reduce the uncontrolled detonation. The knock sensor consists of a small amount of piezoelectric material that oscillates with engine vibration. If the engine detonation supersedes the normal limit, the vibration causes an increase in the voltage signal from the knock sensor

Check
62   In the event of knock sensor failure, have the system checked with a SCAN tool at a dealer service department.

Replacement
63   Disconnect the electrical connector and unscrew the knock sensor from the engine block.
64   Installation is the reverse of removal. Tighten the knock sensor to

the torque listed in this Chapters Specifications. **Note:** *Over or under tightening of the sensor effects the knock sensors performance, possibly causing improper spark control.*

Park/Neutral position switch
65   Refer to Chapter 7 for all the checks and replacement procedures for the Park/Neutral position switch.

---

4   Powertrain Control Module (PCM) - replacement

Refer to illustrations 4.4, 4.5, 4.6a and 4.6b
Caution: *To avoid electrostatic discharge damage to the PCM, handle the PCM only by its case. Do not touch the electrical terminals during removal and installation. If available, ground yourself to the vehicle with an anti-static ground strap, available at computer supply stores.*
1   Disconnect the cables from the negative battery terminal, then from the positive battery terminal.
2   Remove the neck from the windshield washer bottle.
3   Carefully squeeze the tabs on the Power Distribution Center (PDC) unit while pulling up and remove it from its mounting bracket. Move the PDC aside to gain access to the PCM bracket screws.
4   Remove the PCM mounting screws **(see illustration)**.
5   Loosen the electrical connector retaining screw **(see illustration)**.
6   Partially lift the PCM up, release the clips and detach the electrical connector **(see illustrations)**.
7   Remove the PCM
8   Installation is the reverse of removal.

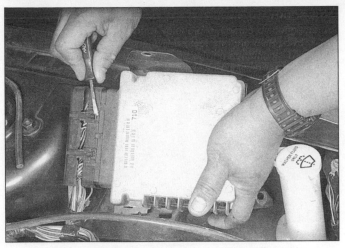

4.6a Partially lift the PCM up, release the clips with a screwdriver . . .

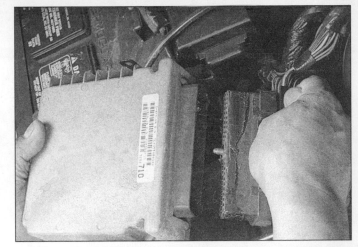

4.6b . . . detach the electrical connector and remove the unit

6.6 Install a hand-held vacuum pump onto the EGR valve, apply 5 in-Hg of vacuum, and observe that the valve diaphragm moves up and down freely without any binding - the engine idle speed should drop or the engine should stall with vacuum applied

5   Positive Crankcase Ventilation (PCV) system

1   The Positive Crankcase Ventilation (PCV) system reduces hydrocarbon emissions by scavenging crankcase vapors. It does this by circulating fresh air from the air cleaner through the crankcase, where it mixes with blow-by gases and is then rerouted through a PCV valve to the intake manifold.

2   The main components of the PCV system are the PCV valve and the vacuum hoses connecting these two components with the engine.

3   To maintain idle quality, the PCV valve restricts the flow when the intake manifold vacuum is high. If abnormal operating conditions (such as piston ring problems) arise, the system is designed to allow excessive amounts of blow-by gases to flow back through the crankcase vent tube into the air cleaner to be consumed by normal combustion.

4   Checking and replacement of the PCV valve is covered in Chapter 1.

6   Exhaust Gas Recirculation (EGR) system

Note: *If the EGR valve control solenoid becomes disconnected or damaged, the electrical signal will be lost and the EGR valve will be open at all times during warm-up and driving conditions. The symptoms will be poor performance, rough idle and driveability problems.*

General description

1   The EGR system reduces oxides of nitrogen by recirculating exhaust gas through the EGR valve and intake manifold into the combustion chambers.

2   The EGR system consists of the EGR valve, the Electrical EGR Transducer (EET), the Powertrain Control Module (PCM) and various sensors. The PCM memory is programmed to produce the ideal EGR valve lift for each operating condition. An EGR valve lift sensor detects the amount of EGR valve lift and sends this information to the PCM. The PCM then compares It with the ideal EGR valve lift, which is determined by data received from the other sensors. If there's any difference between the two, the PCM signals the Electrical EGR Transducer to reduce the amount of vacuum applied to the EGR valve.

Check

Refer to illustration 6.6

3   Start the engine and warm it to its normal operating temperature.

4   Check the condition of all the EGR system hoses and tubes for leaks, cracks, kinks or hardening of the rubber hoses. Make sure all the hoses are intact before proceeding with the EGR check.

5   Check the Vehicle Emission Control Information (VECI) label in Section 1 for the correct EGR system hose routing. Reroute the hoses if necessary.

6   Detach the vacuum hose from the EGR valve and attach a hand-held vacuum pump to the valve **(see illustration)**.

7   Start the engine and apply 5 in-Hg. of vacuum to the EGR valve with the engine at idle speed. The idle speed should drop considerably or even stall as vacuum is applied. This indicates that the EGR system is operating properly.

8   If the engine speed does not change, this indicates a possible faulty EGR valve, blocked or plugged EGR tube or passages in the intake and exhaust manifolds that may be plugged with carbon.

9   Remove the EGR valve. Apply vacuum to the EGR valve and observe the stem on the EGR valve for movement. If the valve opens and closes correctly the EGR valve is operating correctly. The problem is in either a plugged EGR tube or plugged passageways at the intake or exhaust manifold. If the stem did not move, replace the EGR valve.

10   Remove the EGR tube and check for plugged ports in the manifolds, bent tubes or other problems. If necessary replace the EGR tube with a new part. **Note:** *If the EGR valve is severely plugged with carbon deposits, do not attempt to scrape them out. Replace the unit.*

Component replacement

Refer to illustration 6.14

Note: *The EGR valve and Electrical EGR Transducer (EET) must be replaced together, as a unit.*

11   Disconnect the electrical connector and vacuum hoses from the Electrical EGR Transducer (EET).

6

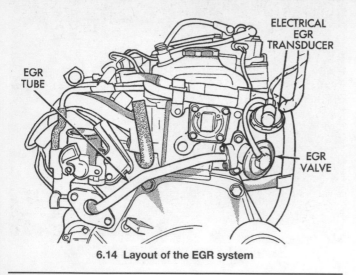

6.14 Layout of the EGR system

7.5 Location of the EVAP canister

12   Remove the air inlet duct.

13   Remove the EGR tube mounting bolts from the EGR valve.

14   Remove the screws that secure the EGR valve and detach the EGR valve **(see illustration)**. Lift the EGR valve and the EET out as a single unit.

15   Clean the mating surfaces of the EGR valve and adapter.

16   Install the EGR valve, using a new gasket. Tighten the screws securely.

17   Connect the vacuum hoses and electrical connector to the Electrical EGR Transducer (EET).

7   Evaporative emissions control (EVAP) system

General description

Refer to illustrations 7.5 and 7.6

1   The fuel evaporative emissions control system absorbs fuel vapors and, during engine operation, releases them into the engine intake where they mix with the incoming air-fuel mixture and are burned.

2   Every evaporative system employs a canister filled with activated charcoal to absorb fuel vapors.

3   The fuel filler cap is fitted with a two-way valve as a safety device. The valve vents fuel vapors to the atmosphere if the evaporative control system fails.

4   Another fuel cut-off valve (fuel tank rollover valve), mounted on the fuel tank, regulates fuel vapor flow from the fuel tank to the charcoal canister, based on the pressure or vacuum caused by temperature changes.

5   After passing through the two-way valve, fuel vapor is carried by vent hoses to the charcoal canister located on the right (passenger) side of the vehicle behind the front facia **(see illustration)**. The activated charcoal in the canister absorbs and stores these vapors.

6   When the engine is running and warmed to a pre-set temperature, a purge control solenoid **(see illustration)**, allows a purge control diaphragm valve in the charcoal canister to be opened by intake manifold vacuum. Fuel vapors from the canister are then drawn through the purge control diaphragm valve by intake manifold vacuum. The duty cycle of the EVAP purge control solenoid regulates the rate of flow of the fuel vapors from the canister to the throttle body. The PCM controls the purge control solenoid. During cold running conditions and hot start time delay, the PCM does not energize the solenoid (NO PURGING VAPORS). After the engine has warmed up to the correct operating temperatures the PCM purges the vapors into the throttle body according to the running conditions of the engine. The PCM will cycle (ON then OFF) the purge control solenoid about 5 to 10 times per second. The flow rate will be controlled by the pulse width or length of time the solenoid is allowed to be energized.

7   1997 models are also equipped with a leak detection pump that is used to detect a leak in the evaporative system.

Check

Note: *The evaporative control system, like all emission control systems, is protected by a Federally-mandated extended warranty (5 years or 50,000 miles at the time this manual was written). The EVAP system probably won't fail during the service life of the vehicle; however, if it does, the hoses or charcoal canister are usually to blame.*

8   Always check the hoses first. A disconnected, damaged or missing hose is the most likely cause of a malfunctioning EVAP system. Refer to the Vacuum Hose Routing Diagram (located on the under side of the hood) to determine whether the hoses are correctly routed and attached. Repair any damaged hoses or replace any missing hoses as necessary. **Note:** *Be sure to replace with approved fuel resistant hoses.*

9   Checking of the operation of the system must be tested by a dealer service department.

Component replacement

Canister

10   Raise the vehicle and place it securely on jackstands. Remove the front right wheel and the splash shield.

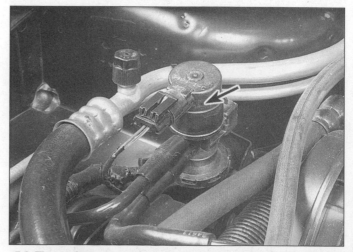

7.6 The canister purge control solenoid (arrow) is located in the right side corner of the engine compartment

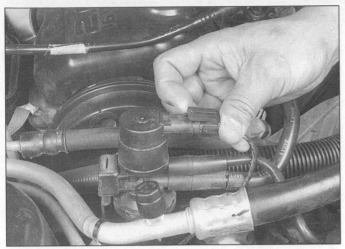

7.14a Release the clip and unplug the electrical connector from the solenoid . . .

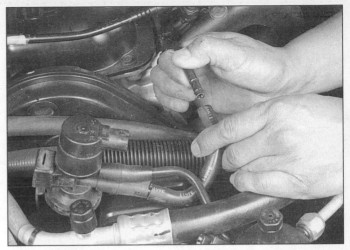

7.14b . . . disconnect the vacuum lines from the purge control solenoid . . .

7.14c . . . remove the mounting bolt and remove the solenoid and bracket assembly from the engine mount

11   To replace the canister, disconnect the vacuum hose(s), unsnap the clamp and remove the canister from the mounting bracket **(see illustration 7.5)**.
12   Installation is the reverse of removal.

Canister purge control solenoid

Refer to illustrations 7.14a, 7.14b and 7.14c
13   The purge control solenoid is mounted on the right (passenger) side of the engine compartment on the engine mount.
14   Unplug the electrical connector, disconnect the vacuum hose(s), remove the mounting bolt and remove the solenoid and bracket assembly from the engine mount **(see illustrations)**.
15   Installation is the reverse of removal.

Leak detector pump (1997 and later models)

16   Raise the vehicle and place it securely on jackstands. Remove the front right wheel and the splash shield.
17   Disconnect the vacuum hose from the canister.
18   Release the locking tab and disconnect the electrical connector from the pump.
19   Remove the 3 nuts from the canister and remove the pump and bracket as an assembly.
20   Installation is the reverse of removal.

Fuel tank rollover valves

Refer to illustration 7.23
21   There are two rollover valves, one located in the fuel filler tube and the other on the top of the fuel tank.
22   Open the fuel filler cap to relieve pressure in the fuel tank.
23   To remove the fuel filler tube valve, disconnect the vapor tube from the valve **(see illustration)**. Remove the valve by prying one side up and rolling the grommet out of the filler tube.
24   To remove the fuel tank valve, remove the fuel tank (see Chapter 4). Disconnect the vapor tube from the valve. Remove the valve by prying one side up and rolling the grommet out of the tank along with the valve.
25   Installation is the reverse of removal.

8   Catalytic converter system

Note: *Because of a Federally mandated extended warranty which covers emissions-related components such as the catalytic converter, check with a dealer service department before replacing the converter at your own expense.*

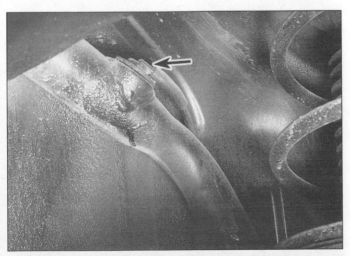

7.23 The fuel tank pressure relief/rollover valve is located on fuel filler neck

6

General description

Refer to illustration 8.1

1   The catalytic converter **(see illustration)** is an emission control device added to the exhaust system to reduce pollutants from the exhaust gas stream. There are two types of converters. The conventional oxidation catalyst reduces the levels of hydrocarbon (HC) and carbon monoxide (CO). The three-way catalyst lowers the levels of oxides of nitrogen (NOx) as well as hydrocarbons (HC) and carbon monoxide (CO).

8.1 Location of the catalytic converter in the exhaust system

Check

2   The test equipment for a catalytic converter is expensive and highly sophisticated. If you suspect that the converter on your vehicle is malfunctioning, take it to a dealer or authorized emissions inspection facility for diagnosis and repair.

3   Whenever the vehicle is raised for servicing of underbody components, check the converter for leaks, corrosion, dents and other damage. Check the welds/flange bolts that attach the front and rear ends of the converter to the exhaust system. If damage is discovered, the converter should be replaced.

4   Although catalytic converters don't often fail, they can become plugged. The easiest way to check for a restricted converter is to use a vacuum gauge to diagnose the effect of a blocked exhaust on intake vacuum.

   a) *Open the throttle until the engine speed is about 2000 rpm.*
   b) *Release the throttle quickly.*
   c) *If there is no restriction, the gauge will quickly drop to not more than 2 in-Hg or more above its normal reading.*
   d) *If the gauge does not show 5 in-Hg or more above its normal reading, or seems to momentarily hover around its highest reading for a moment before it returns, the exhaust system, or the converter, is plugged (or an exhaust pipe is bent or dented, or the core inside the muffler has shifted).*

Replacement

5   Refer to the exhaust system removal and installation Section in Chapter 4.

Chapter 7 Part A
Manual transaxle

Contents

Specifications

Torque specifications

	Ft-lbs (unless otherwise indicated)
Backup light switch	18
Crossover cable adjust screw	70 in-lbs
Drain plug	22
Front engine mount-to-transaxle	80
Front mount through bolt	45
Front mount-to-motor bolts	40
Lateral strut-to-engine	40
Lateral strut-to-transaxle	40
Left mount through bolt	80
Left mount-to-transaxle bolt	40
Torque damper	
Bracket-to-frame	40
Bracket-to-transaxle	40
Shift cable bracket-to-transaxle bolts	21
Transaxle case bolts	21
Transaxle-to-engine bolt	70
Transaxle-to-engine intake bracket bolts	70

1 General information

The vehicles covered by this manual are equipped with either a 5-speed manual or a 3-speed automatic transaxle. Information on the manual transaxle is included in this part of Chapter 7. Service procedures for the automatic transaxle are contained in Chapter 7, Part B.

Both the manual transaxle and the differential are housed in a compact, lightweight, two-piece aluminum alloy housing.

The procedures in this Chapter tell you how to replace and adjust those parts of the transaxle that can be serviced at home, as well as how to remove and install the transaxle itself. Because of the complexity of the transaxle internals, the difficulty of obtaining replacement parts and the special tools needed to service those parts, we don't recommend repairing the transaxle at home.

2 Shift cables - removal, installation and adjustment

Warning: *These vehicles are equipped with air bags. Always disconnect the negative battery cable and wait two minutes before working in the vicinity of the impact sensors, steering column or instrument panel to avoid the possibility of accidental deployment of the airbag(s), which could cause personal injury (see Chapter 12).*

Removal

Refer to illustrations 2.5, 2.6, 2.7, 2.9, 2.10, 2.11 and 2.13

1 In the event of hard shifting, disconnect both cables at the transaxle and operate the shifter from the driver's seat. If the shift lever moves smoothly through all positions with the cables disconnected, the crossover cable should be adjusted as described at the end of this

2.5 Use two flat blade screwdrivers and carefully pry the selector cable from the select lever

2.6 Use two flat blade screwdrivers and carefully pry the crossover cable from the crossover lever

2.7 Using pliers, remove the cable bracket retaining clip (arrow) and remove the cable from the bracket

Section. To remove and install the shift cables, perform the following.

2   Raise the hood and place a blanket over the left (driver's) fender to protect it.

3   On 1996 and later models, remove the screw and lift off the air fil-ter inlet duct.

4   Remove the battery and battery tray (see Chapter 5).

5   Using two flat blade screwdrivers, carefully pry the selector cable from the select lever **(see illustration)**. **Caution:** *To avoid damage to the cable isolator bushings, pry up with equal force on both sides of the shifter.*

6   Using two flat blade screwdrivers, carefully pry the crossover cable from the crossover lever **(see illustration)**. Discard the cable retaining clips.

7   Remove the cable bracket retaining clips on the transaxle and remove the cables from the bracket **(see illustration)**. Discard the retaining clips.

8   Remove the center console (see Chapter 11).

9   Remove the floor pan grommet mounting nuts **(see illustration)**.

10   Remove both cable retaining clips at the shifter and remove the cables from the bracket **(see illustration)**. Discard the retaining clips.

11   Use a flat blade screwdriver and carefully pry the selector cable and the crossover cable from the shifter **(see illustration)**. Discard the cable retaining clips. **Caution:** *To avoid damage to the cable isolator bushings, pry up with equal force on both sides of the shifter.*

12   Raise the front of the vehicle and place it securely on jackstands.

13   Remove the screws securing the grommet plate mounting to the underbody heat shield and floor pan **(see illustration)**.

14   Detach both cables from the cable support clip on the tunnel

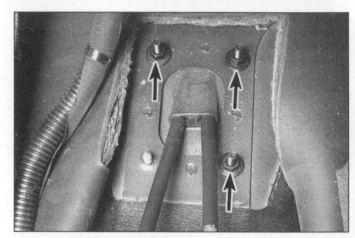

2.9 Remove the shift cable floor pan grommet mounting nuts (arrows)

above the catalytic converter.

15   Remove the cable assembly from the vehicle.

Installation

16   Installation is the reverse of removal. Install new cable retaining clips at all locations and make sure they are properly seated in the cable grooves.

17   Adjust the crossover cable.

2.10 Use needle-nose pliers to remove both cable retaining clips at the shifter

2.11 Use a flat blade screwdriver to carefully pry the selector cable and the crossover cable from the shifter

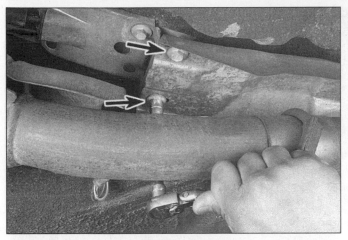

2.13 Working under the vehicle, remove the screws (arrows) securing the grommet plate mounting to the underbody heat shield and floor pan

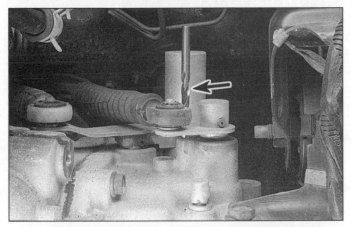

2.19 Align the hole in the crossover lever with the hole in the transaxle raised boss. Insert a 1/4-inch drill bit arrow) through the lever and into the raised boss at least 1/2-inch

Adjustment

Refer to illustrations 2.18 and 2.19

Note: *Only the crossover cable can be adjusted. There are no provisions for adjustment for the selector cable.*

18   Loosen the crossover cable adjusting screw **(see illustration)**.
19   Align the hole in the crossover lever with the hole in the transaxle raised boss. Insert a 1/4-inch drill bit through the lever and into the

2.18 Loosen the crossover cable adjust screw

raised boss **(see illustration)**. Make sure the drill bit goes into the transaxle hole at least 1/2-inch.
20   Place the shifter lever in the neutral position (allow the shifter to self-center in this position).
21   Tighten the crossover cable adjusting screw to the torque listed in this Chapter's Specifications. The shift lever must stay in the self-centered position while tightening the screw.
22   Remove the 1/4-inch drill bit from the lever and transaxle.
23   Shift the transaxle into all gear positions to make sure the cable is functioning properly. Readjust if necessary.

3   Shift lever - removal and installation

Refer to illustrations 3.2 and 3.6
Warning: *These vehicles are equipped with air bags. Always disconnect the negative battery cable and wait two minutes before working in the vicinity of the impact sensors, steering column or instrument panel to avoid the possibility of accidental deployment of the airbag(s), which could cause personal injury (see Chapter 12).*
1   Remove the center console assembly (see Chapter 11).
2   Remove the shifter boot **(see illustration)**.
3   Disconnect the shift cables (see Section 2).
4   Remove the parking brake mechanism (see Chapter 9).
5   Remove the airbag control module (see Chapter 12).
6   Remove the shift lever bracket nuts **(see illustration)** and remove the shift lever assembly.
7   Installation is the reverse of removal. Be sure to adjust the crossover shift cable when you're done (see Section 3).

7A

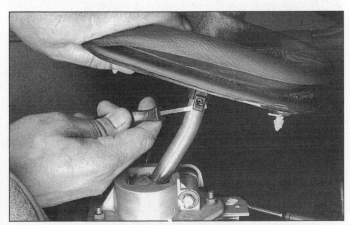

3.2 Use a screwdriver to release the clamp and remove the shifter boot

3.6 Remove all four of the shift lever bracket mounting nuts (only two are visible), then remove the shift lever assembly

4.1 The back-up light switch is located on top of the transaxle, near the left (driver's side) front corner of the housing

5.2a Use a flat blade screwdriver and release the clips securing the Power Distribution Center to the battery holding bracket

5.2b Carefully pull the Power Distribution Center up and move it out of the way

4   Back-up light switch - check and replacement

Check

Refer to illustration 4.1

1   The backup light switch **(see illustration)** is located on top of the transaxle, near the left (driver's side) front corner of the housing.

2   Turn the ignition key to the On position and move the shift lever to the Reverse position. The backup light switch should turn on the backup lights.

3   If it doesn't, check the 10A backup light fuse (fuse number 8) in the fuse box under the instrument panel on the driver's side (see Chapter 12).

4   If the fuse is okay, verify that there's voltage available on the battery side of the switch (white wire) (with the ignition turned to the On position).

5   If there's no voltage on the battery side of the switch, check the wire between the fuse and the switch; if there is voltage, put the shift lever in Reverse and see if there's voltage on the lamp side of the switch (violet/black wire).

6   If there's no voltage on the lamp side of the switch, replace the switch (see below); if there is voltage, note whether only one or both back-up light bulbs are out.

7   If only one bulb is out, replace it; if they're both out, it could be the bulbs but it's more likely that the wire between the switch and the bulbs has an open somewhere.

Replacement

8   Unplug the electrical connector from the backup light switch.

9   Unscrew the switch.

10   Wrap the switch threads with Teflon tape, or equivalent, screw in the new switch and tighten to the torque listed in this Chapter's Specifications.

11   Plug in the connector.

12   Check the operation of the backup lights to be sure the switch is working correctly.

5   Manual transaxle - removal and installation

Refer to illustrations 5.2a, 5.2b, 5.16, 5.19, 5.21, 5.27, 5.28a, 5.28b and 5.30

Removal

1   Detach both battery cables (negative cable first). Remove the battery and the battery tray (see Chapter 5).

2   Carefully pull the Power Distribution Center up and out of its hold-

5.17 Support the transaxle with a transmission jack

ing bracket and move it out of the way **(see illustrations)**.

3   Disconnect the electrical connector for the cruise control (if equipped).

4   Unplug the electrical connectors for the speed sensor and the back-up light switch.

5   Disconnect the shift cables from the transaxle (see Section 2).

6   Remove the clutch housing vent cap.

7   Disconnect the clutch cable from the bellhousing (see Chapter 8).

8   Remove the shift cable mounting bracket **(see illustration 2.7)**.

9   Remove the accelerator cable shield (if equipped).

10   Remove the intake manifold support bracket (if equipped).

11   Remove the starter motor upper bolt.

12   Remove the bellhousing upper bolts.

13   Loosen the front wheel lug nuts. Raise the vehicle and place it securely on jackstands. Remove both front wheels.

14   On models so equipped, remove the structural collar from the oil pan and transaxle (see Section 15, Chapter 2A).

15   Support the engine from above with a hoist (see Chapter 2), or place a jack and a wood block under the oil pan to spread the load.

16   Drain the transaxle fluid (see Chapter 1).

17   Support the transaxle with a transmission jack, if available, or with a floor jack **(see illustration)**. Safety chains will help steady the transaxle on the jack.

18   Remove any exhaust components which will interfere with transaxle removal (see Chapter 4).

19   Remove both driveaxle assemblies (see Chapter 8).

20   Remove the torque damper and bracket **(see illustration)**.

21   Remove the starter motor lower bolt and ground strap. Remove the starter motor.

5.20 Remove the torque damper mounting bolts and bracket

5.22 Remove the transaxle-to-rear lateral support bracket

5.28 Remove the left transaxle mount through bolt, then remove the mount from the transaxle

5.29a Remove all of the transaxle-to-engine mounting bolts . . .

5.29b . . . only four bolts are shown - remove all of them

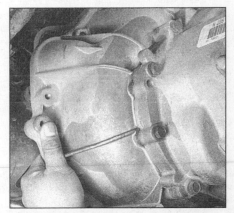

5.31 Once the transaxle input shaft is clear, securely hold onto the unit, lower the transaxle and remove it from under the vehicle

22   Remove the transaxle to rear lateral support bracket (see illustration).

23   Remove any remaining chassis or suspension components which will interfere with transaxle removal.

24   Remove the front motor mount through-bolt. Remove the front motor mount bolts from the engine and the transaxle.

25   Remove the bolts and the dust shield.

26   On 1995 models and 1996 and later models manufactured in Toluca, Mexico, the clutch assembly remains attached to the engine. Note: On 1996 and later models manufactured in Toluca, Mexico, the 11th digit of the VIN will be T. On 1996 and later models manufactured in Belvidere, Michigan, the 11th digit of the VIN will be D.

27   On 1996 and later models manufactured in Belvidere, Michigan, perform the following:

a) Make an alignment mark on the clutch drive plate and the clutch pressure plate. This will ensure proper alignment during installation.

b) Remove the four driveplate-to-modular clutch bolts. Rotate the engine crankshaft using the damper pulley clockwise to expose the bolts. Remove all four bolts.

c) Push the modular clutch assembly into the transaxle bellhousing. This is necessary for ease of transaxle removal.

28   Remove the left transaxle mount through bolt, then remove the mount from the transaxle (see illustration).

29   Remove all of the transaxle-to-engine mounting bolts (see illustrations). Note: Only four bolts are shown - remove all of them.

30   Make a final check that all wires and hoses have been disconnected from the transaxle, then move the transaxle and jack toward the side of the vehicle until the transaxle is clear of the engine. Make sure you keep the transaxle level as you do this.

31   Once the transaxle input shaft is clear, lower the transaxle and remove it from under the vehicle (see illustration).

32   Inspect the clutch components (see Chapter 8). In most cases, the clutch components should be replaced whenever the transaxle is removed.

Installation

33   Install the clutch components if you removed them (see Chapter 8).

34   With the transaxle secured to the jack, raise it into position and carefully slide it forward, engaging the input shaft with the clutch splines. Do not use excessive force to install the transaxle - if the input shaft doesn't slide into place, readjust the angle of the transaxle so it's level. You may also need to turn the input shaft so the splines are properly engaged with the clutch.

35   Install the left transaxle mount and the through bolt through the frame rail (see illustration 5.28). Tighten the bolt to the to the torque listed in this Chapter's Specifications.

36   On 1996 and later models manufactured in Belvidere, Michigan, align the driveplate-to-modular clutch, referring to the mark made in Step 25. Install the new four driveplate-to-modular clutch bolts. Rotate the engine crankshaft clockwise to expose the bolt holes. Tighten the bolts in a crisscross pattern to the to the torque listed in Chapter 8 Specifications.

37   Install the dust shield and bolts. Tighten the bolts securely.

38   Install the front motor mount bolts and the through bolt. Tighten the bolts to the to the torque listed in this Chapter's Specifications.

39   Install any chassis or suspension components that were removed.

40   Install the transaxle to rear lateral support bracket (see illustration 5.21). Tighten the bolts to the to the torque listed in this Chapter's Specifications.

7A

7.4 Using a large screwdriver or prybar, carefully pry the oil seal out of the transaxle (if you can't remove the oil seal with a screwdriver or prybar, you may need to obtain a special seal removal tool - available at most auto parts stores - to do the job)

7.6 Using a seal installer, large section of pipe or a large deep socket as a drift, drive the new seal squarely into the bore and make sure that it's completely seated; lubricate the lip of the new seal with multi-purpose grease

41   Install the starter motor, the ground strap and the lower bolt. Do not tighten the bolt at this time.
42   Install the torque damper and bracket **(see illustration 5.19)**. Tighten the bolts and nuts to the torque listed in this Chapter's Specifi-cations.
43   Install both driveaxle assemblies (see Chapter 8).
44   Install any exhaust components that were removed (see Chapter 4).
45   Remove any jacks or wood blocks from under the transaxle.
46   On models so equipped, install the structural collar (see Sec-tion 15, Chapter 2A).
47   Install the wheels and lug nuts. Lower the vehicle, and tighten the lug nuts to the torque listed in the Chapter 1 Specifications.
48   Install the bellhousing upper bolts. Tighten the bolts to the torque listed in this Chapter's Specifications.
49   Install the starter motor upper bolt. Tighten both the upper and lower bolts to the torque listed in Chapter 5 Specifications.
50   Install the intake manifold support bracket (if equipped).
51   Install the accelerator cable shield (if equipped).
52   Install the shift cable mounting bracket **(see illustration 5.8)**. Tighten the bolts to the to the torque listed in this Chapter's Specifica-tions.
53   Connect the clutch cable onto the bellhousing (see Chapter 8).
54   Install the clutch housing vent cap.
55   Connect the shift cables onto the transaxle (see Section 2).
56   Connect the electrical connectors for the speed sensor and the back-up lamp switch.
57   Connect the electrical connector for the cruise control (if so equipped).
58   Move the Power Distribution Center back into its holding bracket **(see illustration 5.2)**.
59   Install the battery tray, the battery and attach the battery cables (see Chapter 5).
60   Adjust the shift cable (see Section 2).
61   Fill the transaxle (see Chapter 1). Road test the vehicle and check for proper transaxle operation and check for fluid leaks. Shutoff the engine and recheck the fluids.

6   Manual transaxle overhaul - general information

1   Overhauling a manual transaxle is a difficult job for the do-it-your-selfer. It involves the disassembly and reassembly of many small parts. Numerous clearances must be precisely measured and, if necessary, changed with select fit spacers and snap-rings. As a result, if transaxle problems arise, it can be removed and installed by a competent do-it-yourselfer, but overhaul should be left to a transmission repair shop.

Rebuilt transaxles may be available - check with your dealer parts department and auto parts stores. At any rate, the time and money involved in an overhaul is almost sure to exceed the cost of a rebuilt unit.
2   Nevertheless, it's not impossible for an inexperienced mechanic to rebuild a transaxle if the special tools are available and the job is done in a deliberate step-by-step manner so nothing is overlooked.
3   The tools necessary for an overhaul include internal and external snap-ring pliers, a bearing puller, a slide hammer, a set of pin punches, a dial indicator and possibly a hydraulic press. In addition, a large, sturdy workbench and a vise or transaxle stand will be required.
4   During disassembly of the transaxle, make careful notes of how each piece comes off, where it fits in relation to other pieces and what holds it in place - actually noting how they are installed when you remove the parts will make it much easier to get the transaxle back together. **Note:** *The output shaft cannot be disassembled.*
5   Before taking the transaxle apart for repair, it will help if you have some idea what area of the transaxle is malfunctioning. Certain prob-lems can be closely tied to specific areas in the transaxle, which can make component examination and replacement easier. Refer to the *Troubleshooting* Section at the front of this manual for information regarding possible sources of trouble.

7   Driveaxle seal replacement

Refer to illustrations 7.4 and 7.6
1   Oil leaks frequently occur at the driveaxle seals. Replacing these seals is relatively easy, since you don't have to remove the transaxle to get to them.
2   The driveaxle seals are located in the sides of the transaxle, where the splined inner ends of the driveaxles mate with the differential side gears. If you suspect that one of these seals is leaking, raise the vehicle and support it securely on jackstands. If these seal is in fact leaking, you'll see lubricant running down the side of the transaxle below the seal.
3   Remove the driveaxle (see Chapter 8).
4   Using a large screwdriver or prybar, carefully pry the oil seal out of the transaxle **(see illustration)**.
5   If you can't remove the oil seal with a screwdriver or pry bar, you may need to obtain a special seal removal tool (available at most auto parts stores) to do the job.
6   Using a large section of pipe or a large deep socket as a drift, install the new oil seal **(see illustration)**. Drive it into the bore squarely and make sure that it's completely seated. Lubricate the lip of the new seal with multi-purpose grease.
7   Install the driveaxle (see Chapter 8). Be careful not to damage the lip of the new seal.

Chapter 7 Part B
Automatic transaxle

Contents

Specifications

General
Fluid type and capacity	See Chapter 1

Torque specifications
	Ft-lbs
Cooler lines-to-transaxle connectors	21
Motor mount bolts	
Front bolt	40
Left mount bolts	40
Neutral start switch	24
Starter-to-transaxle bolts	40
Torque converter-to-driveplate bolts	50
Transaxle-to-engine bolts	70

1 General information

All vehicles covered in this manual come equipped with either a 5-speed manual or a 3-speed automatic transaxle. All information on the automatic transaxle is included in this Part of Chapter 7. Information for the manual transaxle can be found in Part A of this Chapter.

Due to the complexity of the automatic transaxle covered in this manual and to the specialized equipment necessary to perform most service operations, this Chapter contains only those procedures related to general diagnosis, routine maintenance, adjustment and removal and installation.

If the transaxle requires major repair work, it should be left to a dealer service department or an automotive or transmission repair shop. You can, however, remove and install the transaxle yourself and save the expense, even if the repair work is done by a transmission shop.

2 Diagnosis - general

Note: *Automatic transaxle malfunctions may be caused by five general conditions: poor engine performance, improper adjustments, hydraulic malfunctions, mechanical malfunctions or malfunctions in the computer or its signal network. Diagnosis of these problems should always begin with a check of the easily repaired items: fluid level and condition (see Chapter 1), shift cable adjustment and shift lever installation. Next, perform a road test to determine if the problem has been corrected or if more diagnosis is necessary. If the problem persists after the preliminary tests and corrections are completed, additional diagnosis should be done by a dealer service department or transmission repair shop. Refer to the Troubleshooting section at the front of this manual for information on symptoms of transaxle problems.*

Preliminary checks

1   Drive the vehicle to warm the transaxle to normal operating temperature.

2   Check the fluid level as described in Chapter 1:

  a) *If the fluid level is unusually low, add enough fluid to bring the level within the designated area of the dipstick, then check for external leaks (see following).*

  b) *If the fluid level is abnormally high, drain off the excess, then check the drained fluid for contamination by coolant. The presence of engine coolant in the automatic transmission fluid indicates that a failure has occurred in the internal radiator walls that separate the coolant from the transmission fluid (see Chapter 3).*

  c) *If the fluid is foaming, drain it and refill the transaxle, then check for coolant in the fluid, or a high fluid level.*

3   Check the engine idle speed. **Note:** *If the engine is malfunctioning, do not proceed with the preliminary checks until it has been repaired and runs normally.*

4   Check and adjust the throttle pressure and shift cables, if necessary (see Sections 4 and 5).

5   Inspect the shift lever linkage under the console (see Section 6) and the manual lever on the transaxle (see Section 6). Make sure that both are operating properly and smoothly.

Fluid leak diagnosis

6   Most fluid leaks are easy to locate visually. Repair usually consists of replacing a seal or gasket. If a leak is difficult to find, the following procedure may help.

7   Identify the fluid. Make sure it's transmission fluid and not engine oil or brake fluid (automatic transmission fluid is a deep red color).

8   Try to pinpoint the source of the leak. Drive the vehicle several miles, then park it over a large sheet of cardboard. After a minute or two, you should be able to locate the leak by determining the source of the fluid dripping onto the cardboard.

9   Make a careful visual inspection of the suspected component and the area immediately around it. Pay particular attention to gasket mating surfaces. A mirror is often helpful for finding leaks in areas that are hard to see.

10   If the leak still cannot be found, clean the suspected area thoroughly with a degreaser or solvent, then dry it.

11   Drive the vehicle for several miles at normal operating temperature and varying speeds. After driving the vehicle, visually inspect the suspected component again.

12   Once the leak has been located, the cause must be determined before it can be properly repaired. If a gasket is replaced but the sealing flange is bent, the new gasket will not stop the leak. The bent flange must be straightened.

13   Before attempting to repair a leak, check to make sure that the following conditions are corrected or they may cause another leak. **Note:** *Some of the following conditions cannot be fixed without highly specialized tools and expertise. Such problems must be referred to a transmission shop or a dealer service department.*

Gasket leaks

14   Check the pan periodically. Make sure the bolts are tight, no bolts are missing, the gasket is in good condition and the pan is flat (dents in the pan may indicate damage to the valve body inside).

15   If the pan gasket is leaking, the fluid level or the fluid pressure may be too high, the vent may be plugged, the pan bolts may be too tight, the pan sealing flange may be warped, the sealing surface of the transaxle housing may be damaged, the gasket may be damaged or the transaxle casting may be cracked or porous. If sealant instead of gasket material has been used to form a seal between the pan and the transaxle housing, it may be the wrong sealant.

Seal leaks

16   If a transaxle seal is leaking, the fluid level or pressure may be too high, the vent may be plugged, the seal bore may be damaged, the seal itself may be damaged or improperly installed, the surface of the shaft protruding through the seal may be damaged or a loose bearing

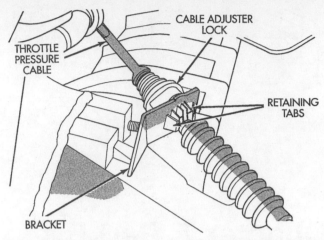

4.3 Pull the throttle pressure cable adjuster lock upward and release the lock on the throttle pressure cable assembly

may be causing excessive shaft movement.

17   Make sure the dipstick tube seal is in good condition and the tube is properly seated. Periodically check the area around the speedometer sensor for leakage. If transmission fluid is evident, check the O-ring for damage.

Case leaks

18   If the case itself appears to be leaking, the casting is porous and will have to be repaired or replaced.

19   Make sure the oil cooler hose fittings are tight and in good condition.

Fluid comes out vent pipe or fill tube

20   If this condition occurs the possible causes are, the transaxle is overfilled, there is coolant in the fluid, the case is porous, the dipstick is incorrect, the vent is plugged or the drain-back holes are plugged.

---

3   Driveaxle seal replacement

      For the procedures relating to the replacement of the drive axle oil seals within the transaxle, refer to Chapter 7A.

---

4   Throttle pressure cable - adjustment and replacement

Adjustment

Refer to illustrations 4.3, 4.5 and 4.10

1   Drive the vehicle several miles, making frequent starts and stops to allow the transaxle to shift through all gears and to reach normal operating temperature. Shut off the engine.

2   Raise the hood and place a blanket over the left (driver's) fender to protect it.

3   Pull the cable adjuster lock upward and release the lock on the throttle pressure cable assembly **(see illustration)**.

4   After the cross-lock is released, the cable must be free to slide all the way toward the engine, against its stop. This is necessary for proper adjustment.

5   Move the transaxle throttle control lever fully clockwise, against its internal stop **(see illustration)**. Press the cable adjuster lock downward into the locked position.

6   The cable backlash is now automatically adjusted. To check cable operation, move the throttle control lever forward (counterclockwise), then slowly release the lever and check that it returns fully rearward (clockwise). **Note:** *It is not necessary to lubricate this cable, nor any component of this system.*

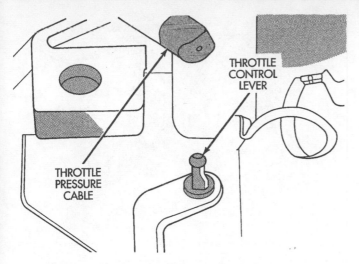

4.5 Move the throttle control lever fully clockwise, against its internal stop, then press the cable adjuster lock downward into the locked position

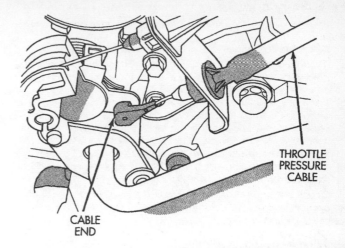

4.10 Unsnap the cable end from the throttle linkage cam while squeezing in on the retaining tabs, then remove the cable from the mounting bracket

Replacement

7   Raise the hood and place a blanket over the left (driver's) fender to protect it.

8   Unsnap and remove the end of the throttle pressure cable from the throttle control lever (see illustration 4.5).

9   Squeeze in on the retaining tabs and remove the cable from the mounting bracket at the transaxle.

10   Unsnap the cable end from the throttle linkage cam. Squeeze in on the retaining tabs and remove the cable from the mounting bracket at the throttle linkage (see illustration).

11   Remove the cable.

12   Install by reversing this procedure. Adjust the cable as previously described.

5   Shift cable - removal, installation and adjustment

Warning: *These vehicles are equipped with air bags. Always disconnect the negative battery cable and wait two minutes before working in the vicinity of the impact sensors, steering column or instrument panel to avoid the possibility of accidental deployment of the airbag(s), which could cause personal injury (see Chapter 12).*

Removal

Refer to illustrations 5.5, 5.10, 5.11, 5.13 and 5.15

1   In the event of hard shifting, disconnect the cable at the transaxle and operate the shifter from the driver's seat. If the shift lever moves smoothly through all positions with the cable disconnected, then the cable should be adjusted as described at the end of this Section. To remove and install the shift cable, perform the following.

2   Raise the hood and place a blanket over the left (driver's) fender to protect it.

3   Remove the battery and battery tray (see Chapter 5).

4   Remove the cruise control servo (if equipped).

5   Remove the shift cable bracket screw on the transaxle. Lift up and disconnect the shift cable from the shift lever post (see illustration).

6   Squeeze the three metal tabs and disconnect the shift cable from the bracket.

7   Remove the center console (see Chapter 11).

8   Remove shift knob set screw and remove knob from shifter.

9   Remove gearshift indicator lamp from the shift trim bezel.

10   Remove the shift trim bezel screws and the bezel (see illustration).

7B

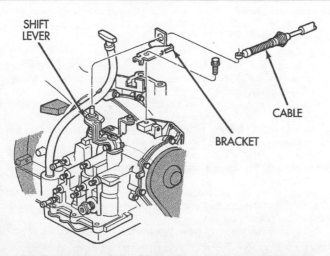

5.5 Remove the shift cable bracket screw, then lift up and disconnect the shift cable from the shift lever post

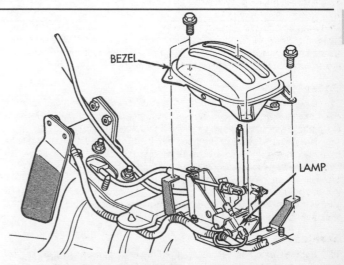

5.10 Remove the screws and shift trim bezel

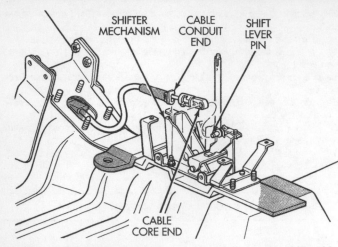

5.11 Use a flat-blade screwdriver and carefully pry the shift cable core end from the shift lever pin. Carefully pry the cable conduit end tabs away from the shift mechanism, then pull up and remove the cable conduit end from the groove in the shifter bracket

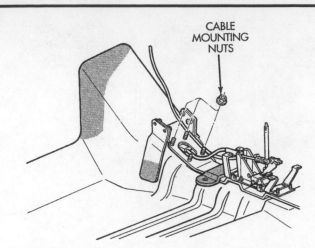

5.13 Remove the nuts securing the shift cable grommet plate

11   Use a flat-blade screwdriver and carefully pry the shift cable core end from the shift lever pin (see illustration).

12   Use a small screwdriver and carefully pry the cable conduit end tabs away from the shift mechanism. Pull up and remove the cable conduit end from the groove in the shifter bracket (see illustration 5.11).

13   Remove the shift cable grommet plate mounting nuts (see illustration).

14   Raise the vehicle and support it securely on jackstands.

15   Working under the vehicle, remove the shift cable retainer plate. Remove the shift cable grommet plate screws and grommet plate (see illustration).

16   Carefully remove the shift cable out through the underbody floor opening while unfolding the cable retainer clips.

17   Remove the shift cable assembly from the vehicle.

Installation

18   Route the new cable into the engine compartment and through the opening in the underbody floor.

19   Working under the vehicle, install the shift cable grommet plate and tighten the screws securely. Install the shift cable retainer plate and screw, tighten the screw securely.

20   Lower the vehicle.

21   Install the shift cable grommet plate mounting nuts and tighten them securely.

22   Install the cable conduit end into the shift bracket and push it all the way down until the end tabs are locked in place.

23   Install the shift cable core end onto the shift lever pin. Make sure it snaps into place.

24   Install the shift trim bezel and screws. Install the gearshift indicator lamp assembly.

25   Install the shift knob and tighten the set screw securely.

26   Install the center console (see Chapter 11).

27   Working under the hood, install the shift cable onto the bracket, make sure the three metal tabs are locked into place.

28   Connect the shift cable onto the shift lever post. Make sure it snaps into place.

29   Install the shift cable bracket onto the transaxle and tighten the screw.

30   Install the cruise control servo (if so equipped).

31   Install the battery tray and the battery (see Chapter 5).

32   Adjust the shift cable as described in the following.

Adjustment

Refer to illustration 5.36

33   Remove the center console (see Chapter 11).

34   Place the shift lever in the Park position.

35   Make sure the shift lever at the transaxle is in the Park position. The park sprag must be engaged when adjusting the cable. Rock the vehicle back and forth to ensure that the Park sprag is fully engaged.

36   Push down on the tab and unsnap the collar at the shifter cable (see illustration).

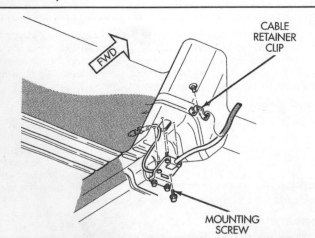

5.15 Working under the vehicle, first remove the shift cable retainer plate, then the shift cable grommet plate screws and grommet plate

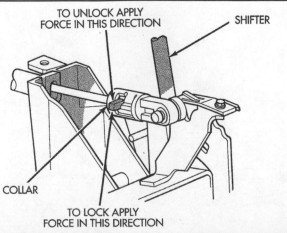

5.36 Push the tab down and unsnap the collar at the shifter cable. Rotate the collar on the shift cable adjuster until it seats against the plastic housing to the fully detented lock position

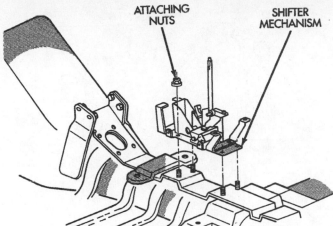

6.7 Remove the nuts securing the shift lever base and remove the shift lever assembly

37   Rotate the collar on the shift cable adjuster until it seats against the plastic housing to the fully detained lock position **(see illustration 5.36)**. With the collar in this position, the shift linkage is now properly adjusted. **Note:** *If you cannot rotate the collar to the fully detained lock position, rotate the collar back to its initial unlocked position. Make sure the transaxle is still in the Park position. Slightly move the shift lever fore and aft, while rotating the collar to the lock position against the plastic housing. The collar must seat against the plastic housing to be in the required detented lock position.*
38   Install the center console (see Chapter 11).
39   Check the shift lever for proper operation. It should operate smoothly without binding. The engine should start only in the Park or Neutral positions.
40   Shift the transaxle into all gear positions to make sure the cable is functioning properly. Readjust if necessary.

6   Shift lever - removal and installation

Refer to illustration 6.7
Warning: *These vehicles are equipped with air bags. Always disconnect the negative battery cable and wait two minutes before working in the vicinity of the impact sensors, steering column or instrument panel to avoid the possibility of accidental deployment of the airbag(s), which could cause personal injury (see Chapter 12).*
1   Remove the center console (see Chapter 11).

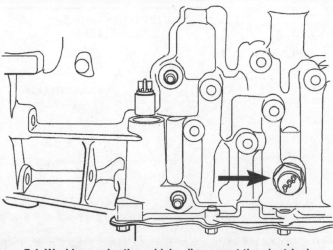

7.4 Working under the vehicle, disconnect the electrical connector from the switch

2   Loosen the shift knob set screw and remove the knob from the shifter.
3   Remove the gearshift indicator lamp from the shift trim bezel.
4   Remove the shift trim bezel screws and the bezel **(see illustration 5.10)**.
5   Disconnect the shift cable from the shifter mechanism (see Section 5).
6   Disconnect the shift/interlock cable from the shifter mechanism (see Section 8).
7   Remove the shift lever base attaching nuts and remove the shift lever assembly **(see illustration)**.
8   Installation is the reverse of removal. Be sure to adjust the shift cable when you're finished (see Section 5).

7   Neutral start switch - check and replacement

Check

Refer to illustration 7.4
Note: *Before performing this procedure, be sure the shift cable is correctly adjusted.*
1   Raise the vehicle and place it securely on jackstands.
2   Working under the vehicle, disconnect the electrical connector from the switch.
3   Place the shift lever in the Park or Neutral position.
4   Working on the switch connector, test for continuity between the switch center pin and ground **(see illustration)**. Continuity should exist only with the transaxle in Park or Neutral.
5   If the switch fails this test, replace the switch.

Replacement

6   Working under the vehicle, disconnect the electrical connector from the switch.
7   Place a drain container under the transaxle and unscrew the switch, some fluid loss will occur. Discard the seal.
8   Look into the switch opening in the transaxle. Have an assistant shift the transaxle from Park to Neutral. Check that the internal operating fingers are centered in the switch opening.
9   Install a new seal and the switch into the transaxle and tighten the switch to the torque listed in this Chapter's Specifications.
10   Retest the switch (see Step 1 through 5).
11   Reconnect the switch electrical connector and lower the vehicle.
12   Check the transaxle fluid and add, if necessary (see Chapter 1).

8   Shift/ignition interlock system - description, check and cable replacement

7B

Warning: *These vehicles are equipped with air bags. Always disconnect the negative battery cable and wait two minutes before working in the vicinity of the impact sensors, steering column or instrument panel to avoid the possibility of accidental deployment of the airbag(s), which could cause personal injury (see Chapter 12).*

Description

1   The shift/ignition interlock system connects the automatic transaxle shift lever and the ignition lock system. With the ignition switch in the Off or Accessory position, the interlock system holds the transmission shift lever in Park. When the key is in the Off or Run position, the shift lever is unlocked and can be moved to any position. And if the shift lever is not in Park, the system prevents the operator from turning the ignition switch to the Off or Start positions.

Check

2   Place the shift lever in the Park position. The ignition switch should rotate freely from Off to the Lock position. Move the shift lever to the Drive position. The ignition switch should not be able to rotate from Off to the Lock position.

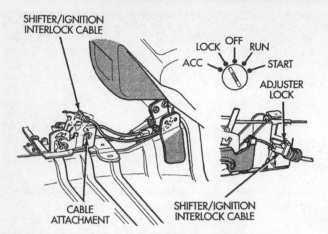

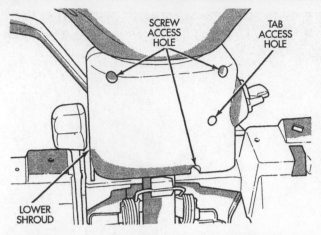

8.9 Use a small screwdriver to carefully pry out the adjuster lock on the shifter/interlock cable. Unsnap the shifter/interlock cable end fitting from the groove in the shifter bracket, then pull the cable out of the shifter mechanism

8.11 Insert a screwdriver into the tab in the lower shroud access hole. Depress the lock cylinder button while using the key to rotate the lock cylinder between the On and Start positions, then pull the lock cylinder from the steering column - remove the key

3   With the ignition switch in the Off or Run position, you should be able to move the shift lever out of the Park position. With the ignition switch in the Lock or Accessory position, you should not be able to move the shift lever from the Park position.

4   If you are able to move the shift lever in any way other than previously described, the interlock system requires service.

Cable replacement

Refer to illustrations 8.9, 8.11 and 8.13

5   Remove the center console (see Chapter 11).

6   Loosen the shift knob set screw and remove the knob from the shifter.

7   Remove the gearshift indicator lamp from the shift trim bezel.

8   Remove the shift trim bezel screws and the bezel **(see illustration 5.10)**.

9   Use a small screwdriver and carefully pry out the adjuster lock on the shifter/interlock cable. Unsnap the shifter/interlock cable end fitting from the groove in the shifter bracket **(see illustration)**. Pull the cable out of the shifter mechanism.

10   Remove the steering column covers (see Chapter 11).

11   Insert a screwdriver into the tab access hole in the lower shroud **(see illustration)**. Depress the lock cylinder button while rotating the lock cylinder with the key between the On and Start positions, then pull the lock cylinder from the steering column. Remove the key from the lock cylinder.

12   Remove the lower shroud screws and the shroud.

13   At the ignition key lock cylinder, squeeze the interlock cable clip and disconnect it, then pull the cable from the lock cylinder housing **(see illustration)**.

14   Unhook the cable retaining clip from the wiring harness and remove the interlock cable from under the center console mounting bracket and the front dash panel.

15   Route the interlock cable down the steering column and down to the shift lever assembly.

16   Install the lock cylinder and make sure it locks into place. Turn the key to the Run position.

17   Insert the interlock cable into the lock cylinder and make sure it snaps into place in the housing.

18   Reattach the interlock cable to the shift lever base. The cable housing is fully seated when it snaps into place.

19   Adjust the interlock cable (see Steps 21 through 25).

20   The remainder of the installation is the reverse of removal.

Adjustment

Refer to illustration 8.24

21   If the ignition switch cannot be turned from the Lock position with the shifter in Park, the interlock cable may require adjustment. Place the shift lever in the Park position.

22   Turn the ignition switch to the Lock or Accessory position. If you are unable to turn the ignition switch to either of these positions; grasp the slug on the end of the cable with needle nose pliers and pull back

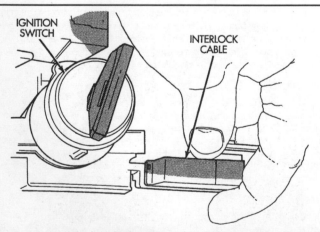

8.13 Squeeze the interlock cable clip and disconnect it, then pull the cable from the lock cylinder housing

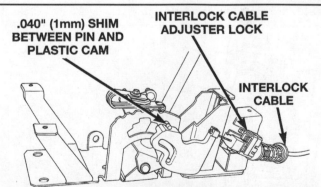

8.24 To adjust the interlock cable, pry up on the adjuster lock, and place a 0.04-inch shim between the larger portion of the shifter gate pin and the plastic cam. The interlock spring should now automatically compensate for the slack in the adjuster. Snap the interlock adjuster lock onto the cable and remove the shim - don't leave the shim in place

9.3a To gain access to the long through bolt, remove the rubber plug from the panel . . .

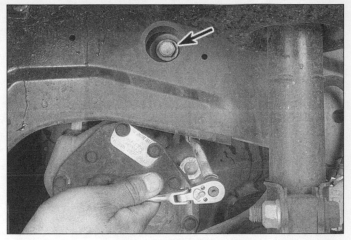

9.3b . . . then remove the mounting bolts, raise the jack slightly and remove the left mount

on the cable. Now turn the ignition switch to the Lock or Accessory position.

23   Check that the cable end slug is completely seated into the shifter interlock lever. Also make sure the ignition switch is still in the Lock or Accessory position.

24   Pry up on the adjuster lock on the interlock cable. Place a 0.04-inch shim between the larger portion of the shifter gate pin and the plastic cam **(see illustration)**. The interlock spring should automatically compensate for the slack in the adjuster.

25   Snap the interlock adjuster lock onto the cable and remove the shim. **Note:** *Do not leave the shim in place.*

9   Transaxle mount - check and replacement

Check

1   Insert a large screwdriver or prybar between the mount bracket and the rubber portion of the mount and pry up.

2   The transaxle should not move excessively away from the mount. If it does, or if the rubber is torn or badly cracked, replace the mount.

Replacement

Refer to illustrations 9.3a and 9.3b

3   To replace the mount, remove the rubber plug and the long through bolt **(see illustrations)**.

4   Support the transaxle with a jack, remove the two mounting bolts **(see illustration 9.3b)**, raise the jack slightly and remove the left

mount. **Warning:** *Never place your hands between the transaxle and the frame as the jack could slip and serious injury could result. Use a long screwdriver or other tool to remove the mount.*

5   Installation is the reverse of removal. Tighten the bolts to the torque specification listed in this Chapter's Specifications.

10   Automatic transaxle - removal and installation

Removal

Refer to illustrations 10.7, 10.8, 10.10, 10.11, 10.18, 10.25a and 10.25b

1   Detach both battery cables (negative cable first). Remove the battery and the battery tray (see Chapter 5).

2   Carefully pull the Power Distribution Center up and out of its holding bracket and move it out of the way (see Chapter 7A).

3   Disconnect the electrical connector for the cruise control (if so equipped).

4   Unplug the electrical connectors for the speed sensor, back-up lamp switch and torque converter clutch.

5   Disconnect the shift cable from the transaxle lever (see Section 5).

6   Disconnect the throttle pressure control cable from the transaxle lever (see Section 4).

7   Remove the shift cable bracket bolt and bracket **(see illustration)**.

8   Remove the throttle pressure control cable bracket bolt and bracket **(see illustration)**.

7B

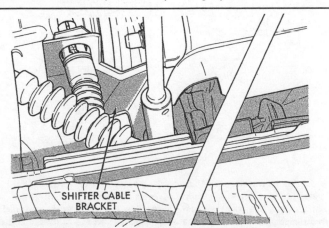

10.7 Remove the mounting bolt and the shift cable bracket

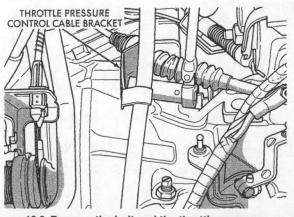

10.8 Remove the bolt and the throttle pressure control cable bracket

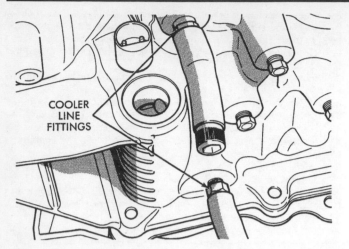

10.10 Disconnect the cooler line fittings from the transaxle and plug the ends to avoid contamination

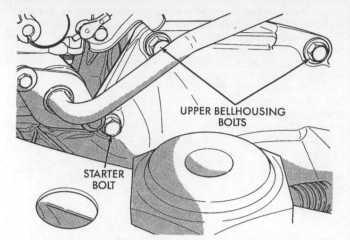

10.11 Remove the bolts from the upper bellhousing and the upper bolt on the starter motor

9   Remove the dipstick tube.

10   Disconnect the transaxle cooler lines at the transaxle (see illustration). Plug the ends to avoid contamination.

11   Remove the upper bellhousing bolts and the starter motor upper bolt (see illustration).

12   Loosen the front wheel lug nuts. Raise the vehicle and place it securely on jackstands. Remove both front wheels.

13   Drain the transaxle fluid (see Chapter 1).

14   Support the engine from above with a hoist (see Chapter 2).

15   Support the transaxle with a transmission jack, if available, or with a floor jack. Safety chains will help steady the transaxle on the jack.

16   Remove any exhaust components which will interfere with transaxle removal (see Chapter 4).

17   Remove both driveaxle assemblies (see Chapter 8).

18   Remove the transaxle to rear lateral support bracket (see illustration).

19   On models so equipped, remove the structural collar from the oil pan and transaxle (see Section 15, Chapter 2A).

20   Remove the engine front bracket through bolt and the mounting bolts. Remove the bracket.

21   Remove the starter motor lower bolt and ground strap. Remove the starter motor.

22   Remove the bolts and the dust shield.

23   Remove any remaining chassis or suspension components which will interfere with transaxle removal.

24   Remove the front motor mount through-bolt. Remove the front

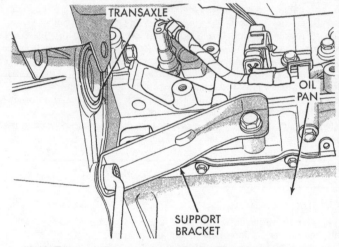

10.18 Remove the mounting bolts and the transaxle-to-rear lateral support bracket

motor mount bolts from the engine and the transaxle.

25   Make an alignment mark on the torque converter and the drive plate. This will ensure proper alignment during installation.

26   Remove the four driveplate-to-torque converter bolts. Rotate the

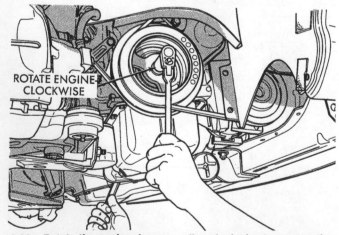

10.26a Rotate the engine damper pulley clockwise to expose the four driveplate-to-torque converter bolts

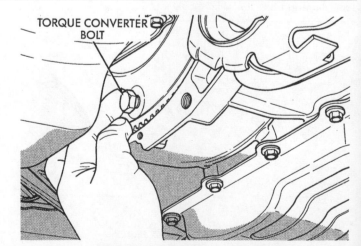

10.26b Be sure to remove all four bolts

engine crankshaft by turning the damper pulley clockwise to expose the bolts **(see illustration)**. Remove all four bolts **(see illustration)**.

27 Remove the transmission mount through-bolt **(see illustration 9.3b)**.

28 Support the transaxle with a jack, remove the two mounting bolts, raise the jack slightly and remove the left mount.

29 Remove the lower rear transaxle-to-engine bolt.

30 Make a final check that all wires and hoses have been disconnected from the transaxle, then move the transaxle and jack toward the side of the vehicle until the transaxle is clear of the engine locating dowels. Make sure you keep the transaxle level as you do this. **Note:** *As soon as the transaxle clears the engine, attach a small C-clamp to hold the torque converter to the transaxle housing during the remainder of the removal procedure.*

31 Lower the transaxle and remove it from under the vehicle.

Installation

32 With the transaxle secured to the jack, raise it into position and carefully slide it forward. Remove the C-clamp and rotate the torque converter to align the torque converter bolt holes with the driveplate bolt holes. Install the bolts but do not tighten at this time. Do not use excessive force to install the transaxle - if so something binds and the transaxle won't mate with the engine, alter the angle of the transaxle slightly until it does mate. **Caution:** *Do NOT use the transaxle-to-engine bolts to force the transaxle to the engine. Doing so could crack or damage major components. If you experience difficulties, have an assistant help line up the dowel pins on the engine block with the transaxle. Some wiggling of the engine and/or transaxle will probably be necessary to secure proper alignment of the two components.*

33 Install the lower rear transaxle-to-engine bolt, the two left mount bracket bolts, and the transmission mount through-bolt **(see illustration 9.3b)**. Tighten the bolts to the torque listed in this Chapter's Specifications.

34 Tighten the four driveplate-to-torque converter bolts to the torque listed in this Chapter's Specifications.

35 Install the dust shield and bolts. Tighten the bolts securely.

36 Install any chassis or suspension components that were removed.

37 Install the engine front bracket and mounting bolts. Tighten the bolts to the torque listed in this Chapter's Specifications.

38 On models so equipped, install the structural collar (see Section 15, Chapter 2A).

39 Install the starter motor, the ground strap and the lower bolt. Do not tighten the bolt at this time.

40 Install both driveaxle assemblies (see Chapter 8).

41 Install any exhaust components that were removed (see Chapter 4).

42 Remove any jacks or wood blocks from under the transaxle.

43 Install the wheels and lug nuts. Lower the vehicle, and tighten the lug nuts to the torque listed in the Chapter 1 Specifications.

44 Install the bellhousing upper bolts. Tighten the bolts to the to the torque listed in this Chapter's Specifications.

45 Install the starter motor upper bolt. Tighten both the upper and lower bolts to the to the torque listed in this Chapter's Specifications.

46 Install the dipstick tube.

47 Connect the transaxle cooler lines at the transaxle and tighten to the torque listed in this Chapter's Specifications.

48 Install the throttle pressure control cable bracket and bolt. Tighten the bolt securely.

49 Install the shift cable bracket and bolt. Tighten the bolt securely.

50 Connect the throttle pressure control cable onto the transaxle lever (see Section 4).

51 Connect the shift cable to the transaxle lever (see Section 5).

52 Connect the electrical connectors for the speed sensor and the back-up lamp switch.

53 Connect the electrical connector for the cruise control (if equipped).

54 Move the Power Distribution Center back into its holding bracket.

55 Install the battery tray and the battery. Attach the battery cables (positive first, then negative) (see Chapter 5).

56 Fill the transaxle with lubricant (see Chapter 1).

57 Adjust the shift cable (see Section 5).

58 Road test the vehicle and check for proper transaxle operation and check for fluid leaks. Shut off the engine and recheck the fluids.

Notes

Chapter 8
Clutch and driveaxles

Contents

Specifications

Torque specifications
	Ft-lbs (unless otherwise noted)
Clutch pressure plate-to-flywheel bolts	250 in-lbs
Modular clutch-to-driveplate	55
Driveaxle/hub nut	135
Wheel lug nuts	See Chapter 1

1 General information

The information in this Chapter deals with the components from the rear of the engine to the front wheels, except for the transaxle, which is dealt with in Chapter 7A and 7B. For the purposes of this Chapter, these components are grouped into two categories: Clutch and driveaxles. Separate Sections within this Chapter offer general descriptions and checking procedures for both groups.

Since nearly all the procedures covered in this Chapter involve working under the vehicle, make sure it's securely supported on sturdy jackstands or a hoist where the vehicle can be easily raised and lowered.

2 Clutch - description and check

1 All vehicles with a manual transaxle use a single dry plate, diaphragm spring type clutch. The clutch disc has a splined hub which allows it to slide along the splines of the transaxle input shaft. The clutch and pressure plate are held in contact by spring pressure exerted by the diaphragm in the pressure plate. The vehicles manufactured in the Toluca, Mexico assembly plant are equipped with a conventional clutch assembly while the vehicles manufactured from 1996-on in the Belvidere, Michigan plant have the modular clutch assembly that includes a clutch assembly where the clutch pressure plate and friction disc are an integral unit.

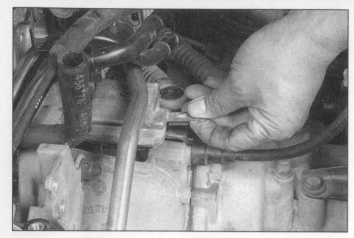

3.3 Pull off the rubber clutch inspection cover

3.4 Grab onto the cable housing and pull the clutch cable from the groove in the bellhousing, then disconnect it from the release lever

2   The clutch release system is cable-actuated. The system consists of the clutch pedal, the cable, a clutch release lever and the clutch release (or throw-out) bearing.

3   When pressure is applied to the clutch pedal to release the clutch, the cable moves the release lever, which pivots, moving the release bearing. The bearing pushes against the fingers of the diaphragm spring of the pressure plate assembly, which in turn releases the clutch plate. The clutch cable on these models is self-adjusting and requires no routine maintenance or adjustment.

4   Terminology can be a problem regarding the clutch components because common names have in some cases changed from that used by the manufacturer. For example, the driven plate is also called the clutch plate or disc, the pressure plate assembly is sometimes referred to as the clutch cover, the clutch release bearing is sometimes called a throw-out bearing, and so on.

5   Other than replacing components that have obvious damage, some preliminary checks should be performed to diagnose a clutch system failure:

a) *To check "clutch spin down time," run the engine at normal idle speed with the transaxle in Neutral (clutch pedal up - engaged). Disengage the clutch (pedal down), wait several seconds and shift the transaxle into Reverse. No grinding noise should be heard. A grinding noise would most likely indicate a problem in the pressure plate or the clutch disc.*

b) *To check for complete clutch release, run the engine (with the*

parking brake applied to prevent movement) and hold the clutch pedal approximately 1/2-inch from the floor. Shift the transaxle between 1st gear and Reverse several times. If the shift is not smooth, component failure is indicated.

c) *Visually inspect the clutch pedal bushings at the top of the clutch pedal to make sure there is no sticking or excessive wear.*

3   Clutch cable - removal and installation

Removal

Refer to illustrations 3.3, 3.4, 3.5a, 3.5b, 3.5c and 3.6

1   Raise the hood and place a blanket over the left (driver's) fender to protect it.

2   Carefully pull the Power Distribution Center up and out of its holding bracket and move it out of the way.

3   Remove the clutch cable inspection cover from the bellhousing **(see illustration)**.

4   Pull back on the clutch cable housing and disengage it from the groove in the bellhousing, then disconnect it from the release lever **(see illustration)**.

5   At the clutch pedal, slightly depress the clutch pedal to allow access to the clutch cable. Remove the clip securing the up

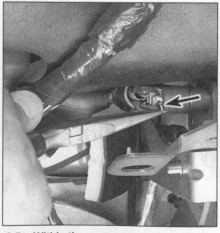

3.5a Within the passenger compartment, slightly depress the clutch pedal to allow access to the clutch cable, then remove the clip securing the up/stop spacer to the clutch pedal pivot pin . . .

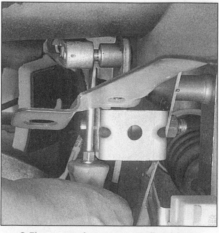

3.5b . . . wedge a narrow flat-blade screwdriver between the clutch pedal pivot pin and the up stop/spacer, then pull the up stop/spacer from the pivot pin . . .

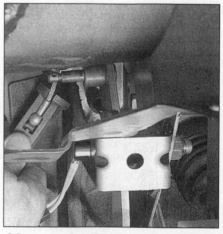

3.5c . . . remove the up stop/spacer from the clutch cable end

3.6 Within the engine compartment, free the grommet from the firewall, then pull on the grommet and carefully remove the clutch cable and grommet from the firewall

4.6 Using a diagonal pattern, slowly loosen the clutch cover-to-flywheel bolts, loosening each bolt a little at a time until all spring pressure is relieved. Then hold the clutch cover securely and completely remove the bolts

stop/spacer to the clutch pedal pivot pin **(see illustration)**. Wedge a narrow flat-blade screwdriver between the clutch pedal pivot pin and the up stop/spacer, then pull the up stop/spacer from the pivot pin **(see illustration)**. Remove the up stop/spacer from the clutch cable end **(see illustration)**.

6   **Caution:** *Do not pull on the clutch cable while removing it from the dash panel as the cable self-adjuster may be damaged.* Within the engine compartment, hold onto the grommet and, using a slight twisting motion, carefully remove the clutch cable grommet free from the firewall and clutch bracket. If necessary, carefully use a screwdriver to free the grommet from the firewall opening **(see illustration)**. Remove the clutch cable assembly.

Installation

7   Within the engine compartment, using a slight twisting motion. insert the self-adjusting end of the clutch cable through the grommet in the firewall and the clutch bracket.

8   In the passenger compartment, seat the cylindrical part of the grommet into the firewall opening and clutch bracket. Make sure the self-adjuster is firmly seated against the clutch bracket to ensure the adjuster will function properly.

9   Connect the clutch cable end onto the up stop/spacer and install the spacer onto the clutch pedal pivot pin. Install the clip and make sure it properly seated.

10   Within the engine compartment, using slight pressure, pull the clutch cable end to draw the cable taut. Push the cable housing toward the firewall with less than 25-lbs of pressure. The cable housing should move about 1-inch - this indicates proper adjustment. If the does not adjust, determine if the mechanism is properly seated on the bracket.

11   Guide the cable through the slot in the bellhousing and connect it to the release lever seating the cupped washer securely in the release lever tangs.

12   Pull back on the clutch cable housing and insert it into the bell-housing.

13   Install the clutch cable inspection cover onto the bellhousing.

4   Clutch components - removal, inspection and installation

Warning: *Dust produced by clutch wear and deposited on clutch components may contain asbestos, which is hazardous to your health. DO NOT blow it out with compressed air and DO NOT inhale it. DO NOT use gasoline or petroleum-based solvents to remove the dust. Brake system cleaner should be used to flush the dust into a drain pan. After the clutch components are wiped clean with a rag, dispose of the contaminated rags and cleaner in a labeled, covered container.*

Removal

1   **Note:** *The vehicles manufactured in the Toluca, Mexico assembly plant are equipped with a conventional clutch assembly while the vehicles manufactured from 1996-on in the Belvidere, Michigan have the modular clutch assembly. Before beginning work on the clutch assembly, check the 11th character on the VIN plate (upper driver's side corner of instrument panel, visible through windshield) to ensure where the vehicle was manufactured. The letter "D" indicates vehicles manufactured in Belvidere, Michigan and the letter "T" indicates vehicles manufactured in Toluca, Mexico.* If working on a vehicle equipped with a modular clutch, and replacement parts are required, the "Modular Clutch Service Package" contains the following parts:

a) *One modular clutch assembly.*
b) *One drive plate.*
c) *One backing plate assembly.*
d) *Four drive plate-to-clutch bolts.*
e) *Eight drive plate-to-crankshaft bolts.*

On 1996 and later models manufactured in Belvidere, if only the clutch disc requires replacement, it can be replaced separately. If the clutch pressure plate or flywheel requires replacement, the Modular Clutch Service Package must be obtained and installed as a set. Separate components are not available from the dealers service department.

2   Access to the clutch components is normally accomplished by removing the transaxle, leaving the engine in the vehicle. If, of course, the engine is being removed for major overhaul, then the opportunity should always be taken to check the clutch for wear and replace worn components as necessary. However, the relatively low cost of the clutch components compared to the time and labor involved in gaining access to them warrants their replacement any time the engine or transaxle is removed, unless they are new or in near-perfect condition. The following procedures assume that the engine will stay in place.

All 1995 models and 1996 and later Toluca-built models

Refer to illustrations 4.6, 4.7 and 4.8

3   Remove the transaxle from the vehicle (see Chapter 7, Part A). Support the engine while the transaxle is out. Preferably, an engine hoist should be used to support it from above. However, if a jack is used underneath the engine, make sure a piece of wood is used between the jack and oil pan to spread the load.

4   The clutch release fork and release bearing can remain attached to the transaxle for the time being.

5   Make an alignment mark on the flywheel and the clutch pressure plate. This will ensure proper alignment during installation.

6   Slowly loosen the clutch cover-to-flywheel bolts **(see illustration)**. Work in a diagonal pattern and loosen each bolt a little at

8

4.7 Use a prybar or flat-blade screwdriver to carefully pry the clutch cover free of the locating dowels on the flywheel (1995 models and later Toluca-built models)

4.8 Hold onto the clutch disc and pull it away from the flywheel, then remove the clutch cover and the clutch disc (1995 models and later Toluca-built models)

a time until all spring pressure is relieved. Then hold the clutch cover securely and completely remove the bolts.

7   Use a prybar or flat blade screwdriver and carefully pry the clutch cover free from the locating dowels on the flywheel **(see illustration)**.

8   Hold onto the clutch disc and remove the clutch cover **(see illustration)**, followed by the clutch disc. **Caution:** *Do not touch the clutch disc facing with your oily or dirty hands as the clutch surface will become contaminated.*

1996 and later Belvidere-built models

9   Remove the transaxle from the vehicle (see Chapter 7, Part A).

10   Remove the modular clutch assembly from the transaxle input shaft. **Caution:** *Do not touch the clutch disc facing with your oily or dirty hands as the clutch surface will become contaminated.*

Inspection (Toluca-built models only)

Refer to illustrations 4.13, 4.15a and 4.15b

11   **Note:** *Chrysler does not provide any service inspection procedures for the modular clutch assemblies used on vehicles manufactured in Belvidere. Ordinarily, when a problem occurs in the clutch, it can be attributed to wear of the clutch driven plate assembly (clutch disc). However, all components should be inspected at this time.*

12   Inspect the flywheel for cracks, heat checking, score marks and other damage. If the imperfections are slight, a machine shop can

resurface it. **Note:** *This flywheel is not machined flat, but has a slight concave surface with the inner diameter 0.001 to 0.0039-inch below the outer diameter.* If the flywheel must be resurfaced it must be machined as noted - not totally flat. Refer to Chapter 2A for flywheel removal procedures.

13   Inspect the lining on the clutch disc. There should be at least 1/16-inch of lining above the rivet heads. Check for loose rivets, distortion, cracks, broken springs and other obvious damage **(see illustration)**. As mentioned above, ordinarily the clutch disc is replaced as a matter of course, so if in doubt about its condition, replace it with a new one.

14   The release bearing should be replaced along with the clutch disc (see Section 4).

15   Check the machined surface and the diaphragm spring fingers of the pressure plate **(see illustrations)**. If the surface is grooved or otherwise damaged, replace the pressure plate assembly. Also check for obvious damage, distortion, cracking, etc. Light glazing can be removed with emery cloth or sandpaper. If a new pressure plate is indicated, new or factory rebuilt units are available.

Installation

All 1995 models and 1996 and later Toluca-built models

Refer to illustrations 4.17a, 4.17b, 4.18a and 4.18b

16   Before installation, carefully wipe the flywheel and pressure plate

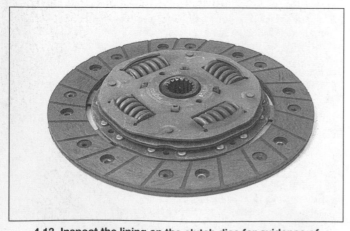

4.13 Inspect the lining on the clutch disc for evidence of excessive wear, such as smeared friction material, damaged rivets, worn hub splines and distorted or damaged damper cushions or springs (1995 models and later Toluca-built models)

4.15a Inspect the pressure plate friction surface for score marks, cracks and evidence of overheating (1995 models and later Toluca built models)

NORMAL FINGER WEAR

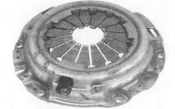

EXCESSIVE
WEAR

EXCESSIVE FINGER WEAR

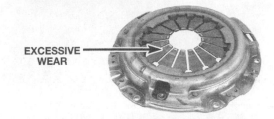

BROKEN OR BENT FINGERS

4.15b Replace the pressure plate if any of these conditions are noted (1995 models and later Toluca-built models)

4.17a Position and center the clutch disc onto the flywheel and hold it in place . . .

4.17b . . . hold the clutch disc in place and install the pressure plate against the flywheel while aligning the plate to the flywheel dowel pins. Insert your thumb through the spring fingers of the pressure plate to keep the clutch centered and move the pressure plate against the flywheel and onto the dowel pins (1995 models and later Toluca-built models)

machined surfaces clean with brake system cleaner. It's important that no oil or grease is on these surfaces or the lining of the clutch disc. Handle these parts only with clean hands.

17   Position the clutch disc against the flywheel and center it **(see illustration)**, while holding the disc in place, install the pressure plate against the flywheel **(see illustration)**.

18   Hold the pressure plate in place and install the mounting bolts and tighten only finger tight at this time **(see illustration)**. Install an alignment tool **(see illustration)**. Make sure it's installed properly (most

4.18a Hold the pressure plate in place and install the mounting bolts, tightening only finger tight at this time (1995 models and later Toluca-built models)

4.18b Center the clutch disc in the pressure plate with a clutch alignment tool (1995 models and later Toluca-built models)

8

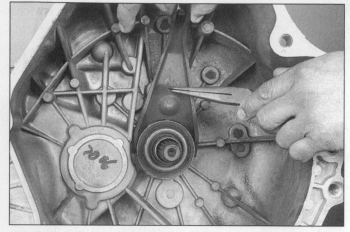

5.3 Secure the spring clip in place with a screwdriver or needle-nose pliers

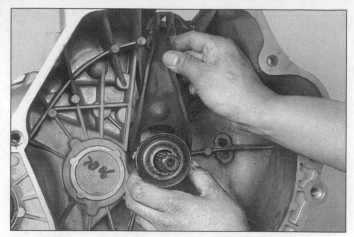

5.4 Hold the release bearing in place, disengage the clip and pull the release lever from the pivot stud. Then slide the release lever up to disengage it from the release bearing

5.5 Slide the release bearing off the input shaft

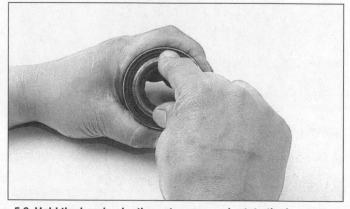

5.6 Hold the bearing by the outer race and rotate the inner race while applying pressure - if the bearing doesn't turn smoothly or if it's noisy, it must be replaced (it's a good idea to replace the bearing even if it checks out good)

replacement clutch plates will be marked "flywheel side" or something similar - if not marked, install the clutch disc with the damper springs or cushions toward the transaxle).

19   Center the clutch disc by ensuring the alignment tool is through the splined hub and into the recess in the crankshaft. Wiggle the tool up, down or side-to-side as needed to bottom the tool. Tighten the pressure plate-to-flywheel bolts a little at a time, working in a criss-cross pattern to prevent distortion of the cover. After all of the bolts are snug, tighten them to the torque listed in this Chapter's Specifications. Remove the alignment tool.

20   Using high-temperature grease, lubricate the inner groove of the release bearing (see Section 5). Also place a light coat of grease on the release lever contact areas, the input shaft splines and the input shaft bearing retainer.

21   Install the clutch release bearing (see Section 5).

22   Install the transaxle and all components removed previously, tightening all fasteners to the proper torque specifications.

1996 and later Belvidere-built models

23   Install the modular clutch assembly onto the transaxle input shaft. **Caution:** *Do not touch the clutch disc facing with your oily or dirty hands as the clutch surface will become contaminated.*

24   Install the transaxle onto the vehicle (see Chapter 7, Part A). **Note:** *Be sure to install new bolts when attaching the modular clutch to the driveplate. Tighten the bolts to the torque listed in this Chapter's specifications.*

5   Clutch release bearing and lever - removal, inspection and installation

Warning: *Dust produced by clutch wear and deposited on clutch components may contain asbestos, which is hazardous to your health. DO NOT blow it out with compressed air and DO NOT inhale it. DO NOT use gasoline or petroleum-based solvents to remove the dust. Brake system cleaner should be used to flush it into a drain pan. After the clutch components are wiped clean with a rag, dispose of the contaminated rags and cleaner in a labeled, covered container.*

Removal

Refer to illustrations 5.3, 5.4 and 5.5

1   Disconnect the negative cable from the battery.

2   Remove the transaxle (see Chapter 7 Part A).

3   **Caution:** *Do not use a screwdriver or pry bar to disengage the lever as the spring clip will be damaged.* Move the lever and bearing so the lever is at right angles to the input shaft. Secure the spring clip in place with a screwdriver or needle-nose pliers **(see illustration)**.

4   Hold the release bearing in place and pull the release the lever from the pivot stud and remove it **(see illustration)**.

5   Slide the release bearing off the input shaft **(see illustration)**.

Inspection

Refer to illustrations 5.6, 5.7a, 5.7b and 5.7c

6   Hold the bearing by the outer race and rotate the inner race while

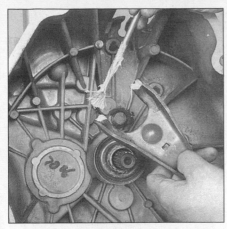

5.7a Using high-temperature grease, lubricate the release lever ends . . .

5.7b . . . the inner splines of the release bearing . . .

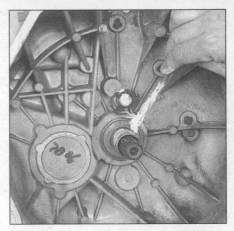

5.7c . . . and the sleeve around the input shaft

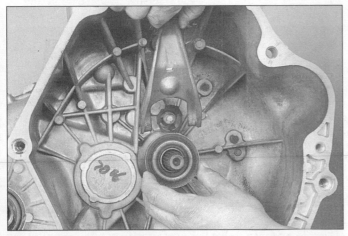

5.9 Install the release bearing over the input shaft, then install the release lever fingers onto the release bearing and onto the pivot ball. Make sure the lever is properly seated and that the spring clip is inserted through the release lever slot

applying pressure **(see illustration)**. If the bearing doesn't turn smoothly or if it's noisy, replace the bearing assembly with a new one. Wipe the bearing with a clean rag and inspect It for damage, wear and cracks. Don't immerse the bearing in solvent - it's sealed for life and to do so would ruin it. Also check the release lever and fork for cracks and bends. **Note:** *Because of the difficulty involved in removing the transaxle for release bearing replacement, we recommend routinely replacing the release bearing when the clutch components are replaced.*

7   Check the release lever for wear or damage especially in the area where the lever contacts the release bearing **(see illustration)**. Also be sure to clean any dirt off the pivot ball stud and stud pocket in the release fork. Lubricate the release lever ends, the inner diameter of the release bearing and the input shaft **(see illustrations). Caution:** *The pivot stud ball is Teflon coated - don't apply any lubrication to it or its pocket in the release fork as this would break down the Teflon coating.*

Installation

Refer to illustration 5.9

8   Install the release bearing onto the input shaft **(see illustration 5.5)**.

9   Install the release lever fingers onto the release bearing and onto the pivot ball **(see illustration)**. Snap the lever into place on the pivot ball. Make sure it is properly seated and that the spring clip is inserted through the release lever slot.

10   Install the transaxle (see Chapter 7 Part A).

6   Clutch start switch - check, replacement and adjustment

Check

1   Verify that the engine will not start when the clutch pedal is released.

2   Verify that the engine will start when the clutch pedal is depressed all the way.

3   If the engine won't start with the pedal depressed, or starts with the pedal released, unplug the electrical connector to the switch (located near the top of the clutch pedal) and check continuity between the connector terminals with the clutch pedal depressed.

4   If there's continuity between the terminals with the pedal depressed, the switch is okay; if there's no continuity between the terminals with the pedal depressed, replace the switch. If there's continuity between the terminals when the clutch pedal is released, replace the switch.

Replacement

5   The non-adjustable switch is mounted vertically at the upper end of the clutch pedal lever.

6   Unplug the switch electrical connector, if you haven't already done so.

7   Depress the wing tabs on the switch and push the switch out of the mounting bracket.

8   Remove the switch and wires out of the slot in the bracket.

9   Installation is the reverse of removal.

7   Driveaxles - general information and inspection

1   Power is transmitted from the transaxle to the wheels through a pair of driveaxles. The inner end of each driveaxle is splined to the differential side gears. The driveaxles can be pulled out to replace the oil seals (see Chapter 7A). The outer ends of the driveaxles are splined to the front hubs and locked in place by a large nut.

2   Each driveaxle assembly consists of an inner and outer constant velocity (CV) joint connected together by an driveaxle shaft. The inner ends of the driveaxles are equipped with a tripot on all models. The design is capable of both angular and axial motion. In other words, the inner CV joints are free to slide in-and-out as the driveaxle moves up-and-down with the wheel. These joints can be disassembled and cleaned in the event of a boot failure, but if any parts are damaged, the entire driveaxle assembly must be replaced as a unit (see Section 8).

3   The outer CV joints on all models, is a ball-and-socket design, are capable of angular - but not axial - movement. These joints can be cleaned and repacked if an outer boot is torn, but if any parts are dam-

8

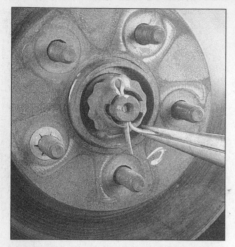

8.2a Use pliers to remove the hub nut cotter pin (discard it after removal)

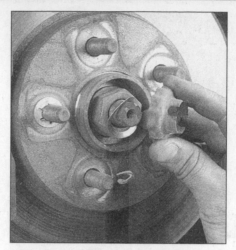

8.2b Remove the driveaxle hub nut lock, spring washer and hub nut

8.3 To prevent the hub from turning while you're loosening the driveaxle hub nut, wedge a prybar between two of the wheel studs

8.8 To loosen the driveaxle from the hub splines, tap the end of the driveaxle with a soft-faced hammer

8.9 Pull out on the steering knuckle and detach the driveaxle from the hub

aged, the entire driveaxle assembly must be replaced as a unit (see Section 8).

4   The boots should be inspected periodically for damage and leaking lubricant. Torn tripot and CV joint boots must be replaced immediately or the tripot or CV joints can be damaged. Boot replacement involves removal of the driveaxle (see Section 8). **Note:** *Some auto parts stores carry "split" type replacement boots, which can be installed without removing the driveaxle from the vehicle. This is a convenient alternative; however, the driveaxle should be removed and the CV joint disassembled and cleaned to ensure the joint is free from contaminants such as moisture and dirt which will accelerate CV joint wear.* The most common symptom of worn or damaged CV joints, besides lubricant leaks, is a clicking noise in turns, a clunk when accelerating after coasting and vibration at highway speeds. To check for wear in the CV joints and driveaxle shafts, grasp each axle (one at a time) and rotate it in both directions while holding the CV joint housings, feeling for play indicating worn splines or sloppy CV joints. Also check the axleshafts for cracks, dents and distortion.

8   Driveaxle - removal and installation

Removal

Refer to illustrations 8.2a, 8.2b, 8.3, 8.8, 8.9, 8.11, 8.12a and 8.12b

1   Disconnect the cable from the negative terminal of the battery.
2   Remove the hub nut cotter pin and discard it **(see illustration)**.

Discard the old cotter pin - you'll need a new one for reassembly. Remove the driveaxle hub nut lock and spring washer **(see illustration)**.

3   Set the parking brake, place the transmission in gear and have an assistant apply the brakes firmly, then loosen the hub/driveaxle nut with a large socket and breaker bar **(see illustration)**. Do not remove the nut at this time - only loosen it.
4   Loosen the front wheel lug nuts, raise the vehicle and support it securely on jackstands. Remove the wheel. Remove the driveaxle hub nut.
5   It's not absolutely necessary that you drain the transaxle lubricant prior to removing a driveaxle, but if the mileage on the odometer indicates that the transaxle is nearing the lubricant-change interval prescribed in Chapter 1, now is a good time to do it.
6   Remove the nut securing the tie-rod end stud to the steering knuckle, then remove the tie-rod (see Chapter 10).
7   Remove the bolt and nut securing the balljoint to the steering knuckle then pry the lower control arm down to separate the components (see Chapter 10).
8   To loosen the driveaxle from the hub splines, tap the end of the driveaxle with a soft-faced hammer **(see illustration)**. If the driveaxle is stuck in the hub splines and won't move, it may be necessary to push it from the hub with a puller.
9   Pull out on the steering knuckle and detach the driveaxle from the hub **(see illustration)**. Suspend the outer end of the driveaxle on a Bungee cord or piece of wire.
10   Before you remove the driveaxle, look for lubricant leakage in the

8.11 To remove the right (passenger's side) driveaxle, position the prybar against the inner tripot joint and carefully pry the joint out of the transaxle

8.12a To remove the left (driver's side) driveaxle, position a prybar against the inner tripot joint and carefully pry the joint off the transaxle side gear and retaining clip

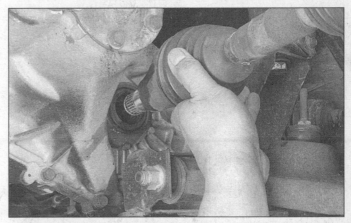

8.12b Pull straight out on the driveaxle to avoid damage to the transaxle oil seal - be careful not to over-extend the inner tripot joint or damage the axleshaft boots

area around the differential seal. If there's evidence of a leak, you'll want to replace the seal after removing the driveaxle (see Chapter 7 Part A).

11   To remove the right (passenger's side) driveaxle, position the pry-bar against the inner tripot joint and carefully pry the joint off the transaxle side gear and retaining clip **(see illustration)**. Do not use the driveaxle to pull the on the inner tripot joint. Doing so might damage the inner joint components. Pry straight out on the driveaxle to avoid damage to the transaxle oil seal. Remove the driveaxle assembly, being careful not to over extend the inner tripot joint or damage the axleshaft boots.

12   To remove the left (driver's side) driveaxle, position a pry bar against the inner tripot joint and carefully pry the joint off the transaxle side gear and retaining clip **(see illustration)**. Do not use the driveaxle to pull the on the inner tripot joint. Doing so might damage the inner joint components. Pull straight out on the driveaxle to avoid damage to the transaxle oil seal **(see illustration)**. Remove the driveaxle assembly, being careful not to over extend the inner tripot joint or damage the axleshaft boots.

13   Should it become necessary to move the vehicle while the driveaxle is out, place a large bolt with two large washers (one on each side of the hub) through the hub and tighten the nut securely.

14   If you noted evidence of a leaking driveaxle seal, refer to Chapter 7A for the seal replacement procedure.

Installation

15   Installation is the reverse of removal, but with the following additional points:

 a) Apply an even bead of multi-purpose grease around the splines of the inner tripot.

 b) When installing the driveaxle, hold the driveaxle straight out, push it in sharply to seat the driveaxle snap ring into the groove in the transaxle side gear. To make sure the circlip is properly seated in the gear groove, attempt to pull the driveaxle out of the transaxle by hand. If the snap-ring is properly seated the inner tripot will not move out.

 c) Clean all foreign matter from the driveaxle outer CV joint threads. Install the spring washer and the nut. Tighten the nut securely but not to the specified torque specification at this time.

 d) Install the wheel and lug nuts, lower the vehicle.

 e) Tighten the hub nut to the torque listed in this Chapter's specifications. Install the nut lock and a NEW cotter pin. Bend the ends over completely.

 f) Tighten the wheel lug nuts to the torque listed in the Chapter 1 Specifications.

 g) Add transaxle/differential lubricant (see Chapter 1).

 h) Have the front wheels aligned by a qualified wheel alignment shop.

9   Driveaxle boot replacement and CV joint inspection

Caution: The inner tripot joint boots on the vehicles covered in this manual are constructed from different materials for different temperature applications. High-temperature applications use silicone rubber that is soft and pliable. Standard temperature applications use Hytrel plastic that is stiff and rigid. The replacement boots must be the same type of material as the sealing boot that was removed.

Note: If the CV joints are be damaged (usually due to torn boots), replacement parts are not available. The complete driveaxle, new or rebuilt, must be replaced as an assembly and are available on an exchange basis.

1   Remove the driveaxle (see Section 8).

2   Mount the driveaxle in a vice with wood lined jaws (to prevent damage to the axleshaft). Check the CV joint for excessive play in the radial direction, which indicates worn parts. Check for smooth operation throughout the full range of motion for each CV joint. If a boot is torn, the recommended procedure is to disassemble the joint, clean the components and inspect for damage due to loss of lubrication and possible contamination by foreign matter. If the CV joint is in good condition, lubricate it with CV joint grease provided with the new boot kit and install a new boot.

Outer CV joint

Disassembly

Refer to illustrations 9.3a, 9.3b and 9.4

3   Using a small screwdriver or chisel, pry up on the boot clamp

8

9.3a Pry up the retaining tabs on the boot clamps . . .

9.3b . . . then open the clamps and remove them from the boot

9.4 Pry the edge of the boot loose from the CV joint and pull it off the joint

9.10 Wrap the axleshaft splines with tape to prevent damage to the boot when installing it

9.11 To install the outer CV joint onto the axleshaft, place the axleshaft in a bench vise and tap the joint onto the shaft splines with a hammer and a brass punch

retaining tabs to loosen them and slide both clamps off **(see illustrations)**.

4   Pry up on the edge of the boot and pull it off the CV joint **(see illustration)**.

5   Carefully drive the CV joint off the axleshaft with a soft face hammer. Strike the inner race only - be careful not to damage the splines or the cage.

6   Remove the boot.

Check

7   Clean the CV joint thoroughly with solvent to remove all grease. Blow the solvent out of the joint with compressed air, if available. **Warning:** *Wear eye protection!* Check for cracks, pitting, scoring and other signs of wear.

8   If there's any sign of damage or excessive wear, replace the outer CV joint as an assembly. There are no parts available separately, so it can't be overhauled.

Installation

Refer to illustrations 9.10 and 9.11

9   Pack the CV joint with the CV joint grease included in the boot kit.

10   Slide the new boot and small clamp onto the axleshaft. It's a good idea to wrap the splined end of the axleshaft with tape to protect the small end of the new boot from damage **(see illustration)**. Partially fill the boot with CV joint grease. Place the large boot clamp onto the axleshaft.

11   Install the CV joint assembly onto the axleshaft and, using a brass

hammer, drive the joint onto the shaft **(see illustration)**.

12   Wipe any excess grease from the axle boot groove on the outer race. Seat the small diameter of the boot in the recessed area on the axleshaft. Push the other end of the boot onto the CV joint housing and move the race in or out until there's no deformation (distortion or dents) in the boot.

13   Equalize the pressure in the boot by inserting a dull screwdriver between the boot and the outer race **(see illustration 9.22a)**. Don't damage the boot with the tool.

14   Install the boot clamps **(see illustrations 9.22b and 9.22c)**.

Inner tripot joint

Disassembly

Refer to illustrations 9.15, 9.16, 9.17 and 9.18

15   After removing the boot clamps **(see illustrations 9.3a and 9.3b)**, pull the boot back from the inner tripot joint and slide the joint housing off **(see illustration)**.

16   Use a centerpunch to mark the tripot and axleshaft to ensure that they are reassembled properly **(see illustration)**.

17   Remove the snap-ring from the end of the axleshaft with a pair of snap-ring pliers **(see illustration)**.

18   Use a hammer and a brass punch to drive the tripot joint from the driveaxle **(see illustration)**.

Check

19   Clean all components with solvent to remove the grease, and check for cracks, pitting, scoring and other signs of wear.

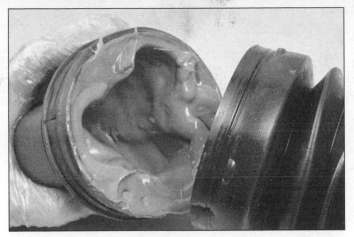

9.15 Once the boot is detached from the inner tripot housing, the housing can be removed

9.16 Use a center-punch to place marks (arrows) on the tripot and the driveaxle to ensure that they're properly reassembled

9.17 Remove the snap-ring from the groove in the end of the axleshaft

9.18 Drive the tripot joint from the axleshaft with a brass punch and hammer - make sure you don't damage the bearing surfaces or the splines on the shaft

Reassembly

Refer to illustrations 9.20, 9.22a, 9.22b and 9.22c

20   Slide the clamps and boot onto the axleshaft. It's a good idea to wrap the axleshaft splines with tape to prevent damaging the boot **(see illustration 9.10)**. Position the tripot with the chamfered side going on first, slide it onto the shaft **(see illustration)** and install the

snap-ring. Apply grease to the tripot assembly, the inside of the joint housing and the inside of the boot.

21   Slide the boot into place, making sure both ends seat in their grooves.

22   Equalize the pressure in the boot, then tighten and secure the boot clamps **(see illustrations)**. Proceed to Step 23.

9.20 Install the tripot with the chamfered (tapered) ends of the splines facing toward the axleshaft

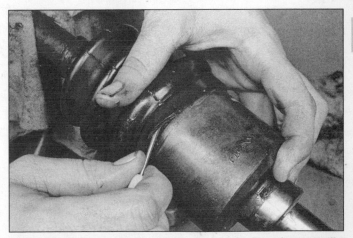

9.22a Equalize the pressure inside the boot by inserting a small, DULL screwdriver between the boot and the CV joint housing

8

9.22b To install the new clamps, bend the tang down and . . .

9.22c . . . tap the tabs down to hold it in place

Driveaxle installation

23   Install a new circlip on the inner CV joint stub axle.
24   Install the driveaxle (see Section 8).

Chapter 9   Brakes

Contents

Specifications

General
Brake fluid type ... See Chapter 1

Disc brakes
Brake pad minimum thickness	See Chapter 1
Disc lateral runout limit	0.005 inch
Disc minimum thickness	Cast into disc
Thickness variation	0.0005 inch

Drum brakes
Minimum brake lining thickness	See Chapter 1
Maximum drum diameter	Cast into drum

Torque specifications
Brake booster mounting nuts	250 in-lbs
Brake hose banjo bolt-to-caliper	24 ft-lbs
Caliper guide pin bolts	192 in-lbs
Master cylinder-to-brake booster mounting nuts	250 in-lbs
Parking brake pedal assembly mounting bolts	250 in-lbs
Wheel cylinder-to-brake backing plate mounting nuts	75 in-lbs

1   General information

General

All models covered by this manual are equipped with a hydraulically operated brake system. All front brakes are discs; rear brakes are either drums or discs. All brakes are self-adjusting. Disc brakes automatically compensate for pad wear, while drum brakes incorporate an adjustment mechanism which is activated as the brakes are applied.

The hydraulic system is split diagonally - the left front and right rear brakes are on one circuit; the right front and left rear on the other. If one circuit fails, the other circuit will remain functional and a warning indicator will light up on the dashboard when a substantial amount of brake fluid is lost, showing that a failure has occurred.

Calipers

All disc brakes used by the vehicles covered in this manual are equipped with a double-pin floating caliper, a single-piston design that "floats" on two steel guide pins. When the brake pedal is depressed, hydraulic pressure pushing on the piston is transmitted to the inner brake pad and against the inner surface of the brake disc. As the force against the disc from the inner pad is increased, the caliper assembly moves in, sliding on the guide pins and pulling the outer pad against the disc, providing a pinching force on the disc.

Master cylinder

The master cylinder is located under the hood on the driver's side, and can be identified by the large fluid reservoir on top. The master cylinder has two separate circuits to accommodate the diagonally split system.

Power brake booster

The power brake booster uses engine manifold vacuum to provide assistance to the brakes. It is mounted on the firewall in the engine compartment, directly behind the master cylinder.

Parking brake system

The parking brake pedal actuates the rear brakes via two cables. The parking brake cables pull on a lever attached to the brake shoe assembly, causing the shoes to expand against the drum (or, on rear disc brake models, a pair of small brake shoes inside the disc/hub assembly).

Precautions

There are some general precautions and warnings related to the brake system:

a) *Use only brake fluid conforming to DOT 3 specifications.*
b) *The brake pads and linings may contain asbestos fibers which are hazardous to your health if inhaled. Whenever you work on brake system components, DO NOT blow it out with compressed air and DO NOT inhale it. DO NOT use gasoline or petroleum-based solvents to remove the dust. Brake system cleaner should be used to flush the dust into a drain pan. After the brake components are wiped clean with a rag, dispose of the contaminated rags and cleaner in a labeled, covered container. Do not allow the fine dust to become airborne.*
c) *Safety should be paramount whenever any servicing of the brake components is performed. Do not use parts or fasteners which are not in perfect condition, and be sure all clearances and torque specifications are adhered to. If you are at all unsure about a certain procedure, seek professional advice. Upon completion of any brake system work, test the brakes carefully in a controlled area before driving the vehicle in traffic.*
d) *If a problem is suspected in the brake system, don't drive the vehicle until it's fixed.*

---

2   Anti-lock Brake System (ABS) - general information

Description

The Bendix ABX-4, or Teves Mark 20, Anti-lock Brake System (ABS) prevents wheel lock-up under heavy braking conditions on virtually any road surface. Preventing the wheels from locking up maintains vehicle maneuverability, preserves directional stability, and allows optimal deceleration. How does ABS work? Basically, by monitoring the rotational speed of the wheels and controlling the brake line pressure to the calipers/wheel cylinders at each wheel during braking.

Principle components

Controller Anti-lock Brake (CAB)

The CAB consists of a pair of microprocessors which monitor wheel speeds and control the anti-lock and traction control functions. The CAB receives two identical signals and process the information independently of one another. The results are compared to make sure that they agree. If they don't, the CAB turns off the ABS and traction control functions, and turns on the warning lights.

Hydraulic control unit

The Hydraulic Control Unit (HCU) is located in the engine compartment on the left frame rail, just below and ahead of the master cylinder. The HCU contains the valve block assembly, the pump/motor assembly and the fluid accumulator.

Valve block assembly

The valve block assembly contains eight valve/solenoids: four inlet valves and four outlet valves. The inlet valves are spring-loaded in the open position and the outlet valves are spring-loaded in the closed position. During ABS operation, these valves are cycled to maintain the proper slip ratio for each channel. If a wheel locks, the inlet valve is closed to prevent a further increase in pressure. Simultaneously, the outlet valve is opened to release the pressure back to the accumulators until the wheel is no longer slipping. Once the wheel no longer slips, the outlet valve closes and the inlet valve opens to allow pressure to the wheel caliper or wheel cylinder.

Pump/motor assembly

The pump/motor assembly consists of an electric motor and a dual-piston pump. The pump provides high-pressure brake fluid to the hydraulic control unit when the ABS system is activated.

Fluid accumulators

The two fluid accumulators in the HCU are for the primary and secondary hydraulic circuits, respectively. The accumulators temporarily store brake fluid that is blocked during ABS operation. This fluid is re-routed to the pump.

Proportioning valves

See Section 9.

Wheel speed sensors

A speed sensor is mounted at each wheel. The speed sensors send variable voltage signals to the HCU. These analog voltage outputs are proportional to the speed of rotation of each wheel.

Diagnosis and repair

The ABS system has self-diagnostic capabilities. Each time the ignition key is turned to On, the system runs a self-test. If it finds a problem, the ABS and traction control warning lights come on and remain on. If there's no problem with the system, the lights go out after a second or two.

If the ABS and traction control warning lights come on and stay on during vehicle operation, there is a problem in the ABS system. Two things now happen: The controller stores a diagnostic trouble code (which can be displayed with a DRB II scanner at the dealer) and the ABS system is shut down. Once the ABS system is disabled, it will remain disabled until the problem is fixed and the trouble code is erased. However, the regular brake system will continue to function normally.

Although a DRB II (a special electronic tester) is necessary to properly diagnose the system, you can make a few preliminary checks before taking the vehicle to a dealer:

a) *Make sure the brake calipers are in good condition.*
b) *Check the electrical connector at the controller.*
c) *Check the fuses.*
d) *Follow the wiring harness to the speed sensors and brake light switch and make sure all connections are secure and the wiring isn't damaged.*

If the above preliminary checks don't rectify the problem, the vehicle should be diagnosed by a dealer service department.

---

3   Disc brake pads - replacement

Refer to illustrations 3.3, 3.4a through 3.4l
Warning: *Disc brake pads must be replaced on both front or rear wheels at the same time - never replace the pads on only one wheel. Also, the dust created by the brake system may contain asbestos, which is harmful to your health. Never blow it out with compressed air and don't inhale any of it. An approved filtering mask should be worn when working on the brakes. Do not, under any circumstances, use petroleum-based solvents to clean brake parts. Use brake system cleaner only!*
Note: *This procedure applies to both the front and the rear disc brakes.*
1   Loosen the front wheel lug nuts, raise the front of the vehicle and support it securely on jackstands. Apply the parking brake. Remove the front wheels (or the rear wheels, if you're working on a vehicle with rear discs).
2   Remove about two-thirds of the fluid from the master cylinder

3.3 Use a C-clamp to depress the piston into its bore; this aids in removal of the caliper and installation of the new pads

3.4a Wash down the disc and brake pads with brake cleaner to remove brake dust; DO NOT blow brake dust off with compressed air

3.4b To remove the front caliper, remove these guide pin bolts (arrows)

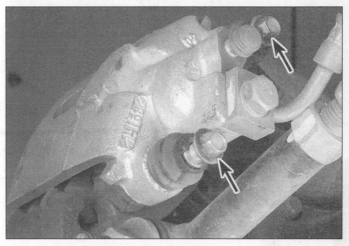

3.4c To remove the rear caliper, remove these guide pin bolts (arrows)

reservoir and discard it. Position a drain pan under the brake assembly and clean the caliper and surrounding area with brake system cleaner.

3   Push the piston back into its bore to provide room for the new brake pads with a C-clamp **(see illustration)**. As the piston is depressed to the bottom of the caliper bore, the fluid in the master

cylinder will rise. Make sure it doesn't overflow. If necessary, siphon off some of the fluid.

4   To replace the brake pads, follow the accompanying photos, beginning with **illustration 3.4a**. Be sure to stay in order and read the caption under each illustration.

3.4d Hang the caliper from the strut coil spring with a piece of wire - don't let it hang by the brake hose

3.4e Pry the outer brake pad retaining spring from the caliper . . .

9

3.4f . . . and remove the outer brake pad

3.4g Pull the inner brake pad retaining spring loose from the piston and remove the pad

3.4h Remove the guide pin bushings

3.4i Remove the bushing boots, inspect them for tears and replace as necessary

5   While the pads are removed, inspect the caliper for brake fluid leaks and ruptures of the piston boot. Overhaul or replace the caliper as necessary (see Section 4). Also inspect the brake disc carefully (see Section 5). If machining is necessary, follow the information in that Section to remove the disc.

6   Before installing the caliper guide pin bolts, clean them and check them for corrosion and damage. If they're significantly corroded or damaged, replace them. Be sure to tighten the caliper guide pin bolts to the torque listed in this Chapter's Specifications.

7   Install the brake pads on the opposite wheel, then install the wheels and lower the vehicle. Tighten the lug nuts to the torque listed in the Chapter 1 Specifications. Add brake fluid to the reservoir until it's full (see Chapter 1).

8   Pump the brakes several times to seat the pads against the disc, then check the fluid level again.

9   Carefully test the operation of the brakes before placing the vehicle in normal operation. Try to avoid heavy brake applications until the brakes have been applied lightly several times to seat the pads.

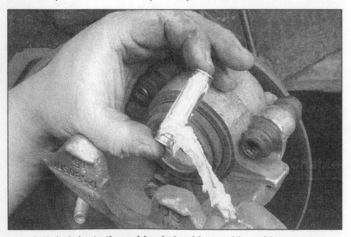

3.4j Lubricate the guide pin bushings with multi-purpose grease before installing them

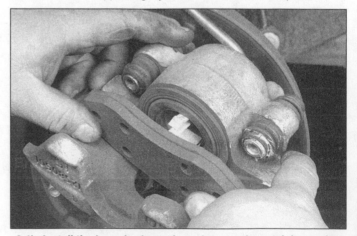

3.4k Install the inner brake pad - make sure the retaining spring is fully seated into its bore in the piston

3.4l Install the outer brake pad - make sure the retaining spring is properly engaged with the caliper body

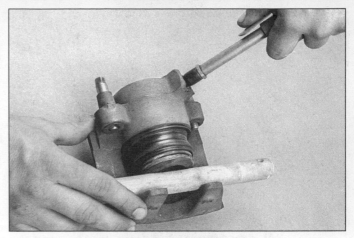

4.4 With a block of wood placed between the piston and the caliper frame, use compressed air to ease the piston out of the bore

4 Disc brake caliper - removal, overhaul and installation

Warning: *Dust created by the brake system may contain asbestos, which is harmful to your health. Never blow it out with compressed air and don't inhale any of it. An approved filtering mask should be worn when working on the brakes. Do not, under any circumstances, use petroleum-based solvents to clean brake parts. Use brake system cleaner only.*

Note: *If an overhaul is indicated (usually because of fluid leaks, a stuck piston or broken bleeder screw) explore all options before beginning this procedure. New and factory rebuilt calipers are available on an exchange basis, which makes this job quite easy. If you decide to rebuild the calipers, make sure rebuild kits are available before proceeding. Always rebuild or replace the calipers in pairs - never rebuild just one of them.*

Removal

1 Loosen the front wheel lug nuts, raise the vehicle and support it securely on jackstands. Remove the front wheels (or the rear wheels, if you're working on a vehicle with rear discs).
2 Unscrew the banjo bolt from the caliper and detach the hose.

Note: *If you're just removing the caliper for access to other components, don't disconnect the hose.* Discard the sealing washers on each side of the fitting and use new ones during installation. Wrap a plastic bag around the end of the hose to prevent fluid loss and contamination.
3 Refer to the first few steps in Section 3 (caliper removal is the first part of the brake pad replacement procedure). Clean the caliper assembly with brake system cleaner. **Warning:** *DO NOT, under any circumstances, use kerosene, gasoline or petroleum-based solvents to clean brake parts!* Be sure to check the pads as well and replace them if necessary (see Section 3).

Overhaul

Refer to illustrations 4.4, 4.5a, 4.5b, 4.6, 4.10, 4.11a, 4.11b and 4.12
4 Place several shop towels or a block of wood in the center of the caliper to act as a cushion, then use compressed air, directed into the fluid inlet, to remove the piston **(see illustration)**. Use only enough air pressure to ease the piston out of the bore. If the piston is blown out, even with the cushion in place, it may be damaged. **Warning:** *Never place your fingers in front of the piston in an attempt to catch or protect it when applying compressed air, as serious injury could occur.*
5 Pry the dust boot from the caliper bore **(see illustrations)**.

9

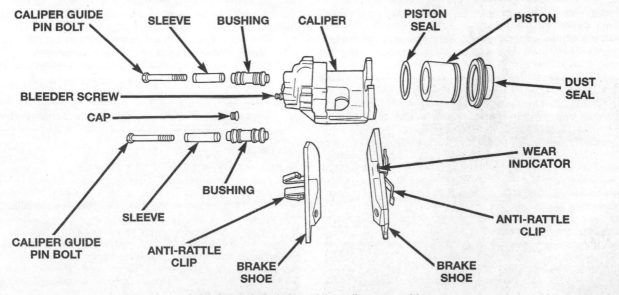

4.5a An exploded view of the caliper assembly

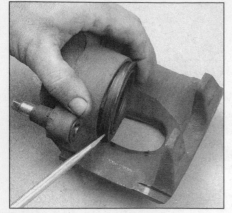

4.5b Carefully pry the dust boot out of the caliper

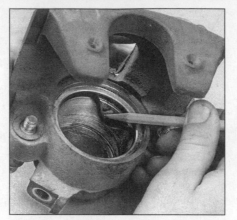

4.6 The piston seal should be removed with a plastic or wooden tool to avoid damage to the bore and the seal groove (a pencil will do the job)

4.10 Position the new seal in the cylinder groove - make sure it isn't twisted

4.11a Slip the boot over the piston

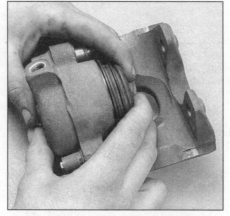

4.11b Push the piston straight into the cylinder - make sure it doesn't become cocked in the bore

4.12 If you don't have a boot installation tool, gently seat the boot with a drift punch

6   Using a wood or plastic tool, remove the piston seal from the groove in the caliper bore **(see illustration)**. Metal tools may cause bore damage.

7   Remove the bleeder screw, then remove and discard the guide pin bushings and sleeves.

8   Clean the remaining parts with brake system cleaner or clean brake fluid, then blow them dry with filtered, unlubricated compressed air.

9   Inspect the surfaces of the piston for nicks and burrs and loss of plating. If surface defects are present, the caliper must be replaced. Check the caliper bore in a similar way. Light polishing with crocus cloth is permissible to remove slight corrosion and stains. Discard the caliper pins if they're severely corroded or damaged.

10   Lubricate the new piston seal with clean brake fluid and position the seal in the cylinder groove using your fingers only **(see illustration)**.

11   Install the new dust boot in the groove in the end of the piston **(see illustration)**. Dip the piston in clean brake fluid and insert it squarely into the cylinder. Depress the piston to the bottom of the cylinder bore **(see illustration)**.

12   Seat the boot in the caliper counterbore using a boot installation tool or a blunt punch **(see illustration)**.

13   Install the new guide pin boots and bushings. Install the bleeder screw and tighten it securely.

14   Install the brake pads in the caliper.

Installation

15   Install the caliper assembly, tightening the caliper guide pin bolts to the torque listed in this Chapter's Specifications.

16   Connect the brake hose to the caliper using new sealing washers. Tighten the banjo bolt to the torque listed in this Chapter's Specifications.

17   Bleed the brakes (see Section 11).

18   Install the wheels and lug nuts. Lower the vehicle and tighten the lug nuts to the torque listed in the Chapter 1 Specifications.

19   After the job has been completed, firmly depress the brake pedal a few times to bring the pads into contact with the disc.

20   Carefully test the operation of the brakes before placing the vehicle in normal operation.

5   Brake disc - inspection, removal and installation

Inspection

Refer to illustrations 5.2, 5.3, 5.4a and 5.4b

1   Loosen the wheel lug nuts, raise the front (or rear) of the vehicle and support it securely on jackstands. Apply the parking brake. Remove the front (or rear)wheels. Reinstall the lug nuts, flat side toward the disc, to hold the disc firmly against the hub.

2   Remove the brake caliper as described in Section 4. Visually inspect the disc surface for score marks and other damage **(see illustration)**. Light scratches and shallow grooves are normal after use and won't affect brake operation. Deep grooves - over 0.015-inch deep - require disc removal and refinishing by an automotive machine shop. Be sure to check both sides of the disc.

3   To check disc runout, place a dial indicator at a point about 1/2-inch from the outer edge of the disc **(see illustration)**. Set the

5.2 The brake pads on this vehicle were obviously neglected, as they wore down to the rivets, then cut deep grooves into the disc, which must be replaced

5.3 Use a dial indicator to check disc runout - if the reading exceeds the specified runout limit, the disc will have to be machined or replaced

5.4a On some models, the minimum thickness is cast into the inside of the disc - on others, it's located on the outside of the disc

5.4b Use a micrometer to measure the thickness of the disc at several points

indicator to zero and turn the disc. The indicator reading should not exceed the runout limit listed in this Chapter's Specifications. If it does, the disc should be refinished by an automotive machine shop. **Note:** *Professionals recommend resurfacing the brake discs regardless of the dial indicator reading (to produce a smooth, flat surface that will eliminate brake pedal pulsations and other undesirable symptoms related to questionable discs). At the very least, if you elect not to have the discs resurfaced, deglaze them with sandpaper or emery cloth.*

4   The disc must not be machined to a thickness less than the specified minimum thickness. The minimum (or discard) thickness is cast into the disc **(see illustration)**. The disc thickness can be checked with a micrometer **(see illustration)**.

Removal and installation

Refer to illustration 5.8

5   Loosen the wheel lug nuts, raise the vehicle and place it securely on jackstands.

6   Remove the wheel. If you're removing a rear disc, block the front wheels and release the parking brake.

7   Remove the caliper (see Section 4).

8   Remove the retaining clips, if present, from the wheel studs **(see illustration)**.

9   Pull the disc off the hub.

10   If you're removing a rear disc and the disc won't come off, remove the plug from the parking brake adjusting access hole. Turn the adjusting star wheel with a suitable tool (such as a screwdriver or brake adjusting tool) and retract the parking brake shoes (see Section 13 for details on the parking brake shoes on models with rear disc brakes).

11   Installation is the reverse of removal. Make sure you tighten the caliper guide pin bolts to the torque listed in this Chapter's Specifications.

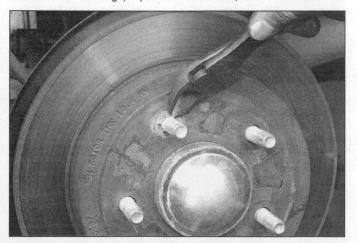

5.8 Cut off and discard the disc retaining washers, if present (it isn't necessary to reinstall them)

9

6.2 Before disassembling the brake shoe assembly, wash it thoroughly with brake system cleaner

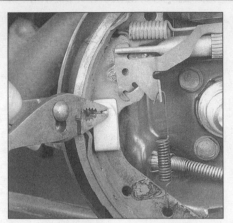

6.4a Twist the hold-down spring pin 90 degrees

6.4b Remove the brake shoe hold-down spring

6.4c Withdraw one of the brake shoes from the wheel cylinder (arrow) to relieve some of the return spring pressure

6.4d Unhook the self-adjuster lever spring

6   Drum brake shoes - replacement

Refer to illustrations 6.2, 6.4a through 6.4x and 6.5

Warning: *Drum brake shoes must be replaced on both wheels at the same time - never replace the shoes on only one wheel. Also, the dust created by the brake system may contain asbestos, which is harmful to*

your health. Never blow it out with compressed air and don't inhale any of it. An approved filtering mask should be worn when working on the brakes. Do not, under any circumstances, use petroleum-based solvents to clean brake parts. Use brake system cleaner only!

Caution: *Whenever the brake shoes are replaced, the hold-down springs should also be replaced. Due to the continuous heating/cooling cycle that the springs are subjected to, they lose their tension over a*

6.4e Remove the self-adjuster lever

6.4f Unhook the upper return spring from both brake shoes

6.4g Remove the self-adjuster from both brake shoes

6.4h Unhook the anchor plate spring from both brake shoes

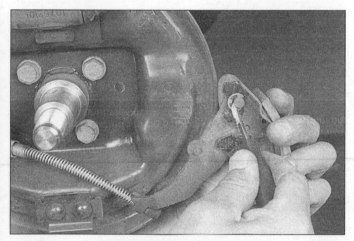

6.4I Remove the E-clip and separate the parking brake arm from the rear brake shoe assembly

6.4j Unhook and detach the parking brake cable from the lever

period of time and may allow the shoes to drag on the drum and wear at a much faster rate than normal.

1   Loosen the wheel lug nuts, raise the rear of the vehicle and support it securely on jackstands. Block the front wheels to keep the vehicle from rolling. Release the parking brake. Remove the wheel. **Note:** *All four front or rear brake shoes must be replaced at the same time, but to avoid mixing up parts, work on only one brake assembly at a time.*

2   Remove the brake drum. **Note:** *If the drum won't come off, retract the brake shoes by inserting a screwdriver or brake adjusting tool through the hole in the backing plate and turning the adjuster screw star wheel. The drum should now come off.* Wash down the brake assembly with brake cleaner **(see illustration).**

3   Remove the hub and bearing assembly (see Chapter 10).

4   Follow **illustrations 6.4a through 6.4x** for the inspection and replacement of the brake shoes. Be sure to stay in order and read the caption under each illustration.

6.4k Apply high-temperature grease to all areas where the brake shoes make contact with the backing plate

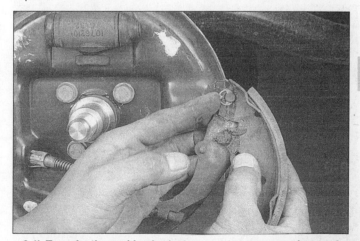

6.4l Transfer the parking brake lever to the new rear shoe and install the E-clip. Make sure the clip is properly seated

9

6.4m Correctly position the rear shoe in place

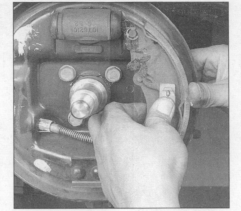

6.4n Install the rear brake shoe hold-down spring

6.4o Twist the hold-down spring pin 90 degrees

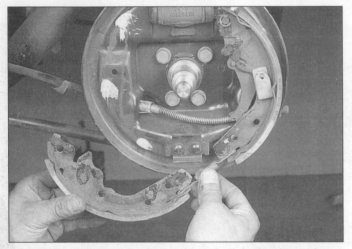

6.4p Attach the anchor plate spring to both brake shoes, then move the front brake shoe up into position. Move the anchor spring into the correct position behind the anchor plate

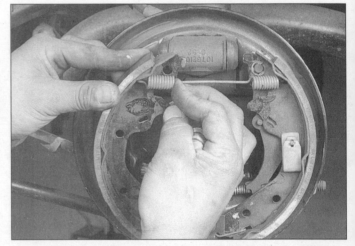

6.4q Attach the return spring first to the rear brake shoe then to the front shoe

5   Before reinstalling the drum it should be checked for cracks, score marks, deep scratches and hard spots, which will appear as small discolored areas. If the hard spots cannot be removed with fine emery cloth or if any of the other conditions listed above exist, the drum must be taken to an automotive machine shop to have it turned. **Note:** *Professionals recommend resurfacing the drums whenever a*

brake job is done. Resurfacing will eliminate the possibility of out-of-round drums. If the drums are worn so much that they can't be resurfaced without exceeding the maximum allowable diameter (stamped into the drum) **(see illustration)**, *then new ones will be required. At the very least, if you elect not to have the drums resurfaced, remove the glazing from the surface with emery cloth or sandpaper using a swirling motion.*

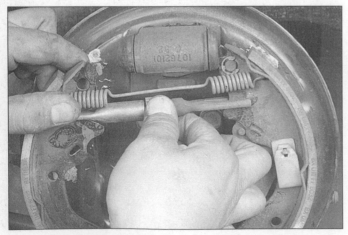

6.4r Engage the self-adjuster with the front shoe, then the rear shoe

6.4s Move the front shoe into position and push the brake shoe assembly against the brake backing plate; make sure both shoes are properly seated against the wheel cylinder pistons

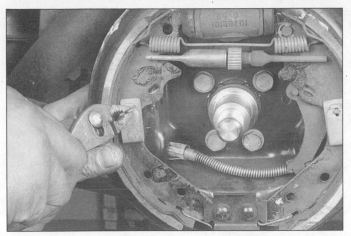

6.4t Install the front brake shoe hold-down spring and turn the spring hold-down pin 90 degrees

6.4u Install the self-adjuster lever onto the front brake shoe and the self-adjuster

6.4v Hook the lower end of the self-adjuster lever spring into its hole (arrow) in the front brake shoe

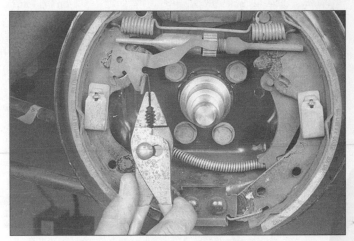

6.4w Hook the upper end of the spring onto the self-adjuster lever

6   Install the hub and bearing assembly (see Chapter 10).

7   Install the brake drum. Pump the brake pedal several times, then turn the adjuster star wheel using a screwdriver inserted through the hole in the backing plate until the brake shoes slightly drag on the drum as the drum is turned. Now, back-off the adjuster until the shoes don't drag on the drum.

8   Mount the wheel, install the lug nuts, then lower the vehicle. Tighten the lug nuts to the torque listed in the Chapter 1 Specifications.

9   Make a number of forward and reverse stops to adjust the brakes until satisfactory pedal action is obtained.

10   Carefully test the operation of the brakes before placing the vehicle in normal operation.

6.4x Install the self-adjuster lever onto its pivot pin; make sure the small lever at the upper left is installed between the adjuster and the front brake shoe as shown

6.5 The maximum allowable diameter is stamped into the drum

9

7.2 To detach the wheel cylinder from the brake backing plate, disconnect the brake line fitting (lower arrow) and remove the wheel cylinder bolts (upper arrows)

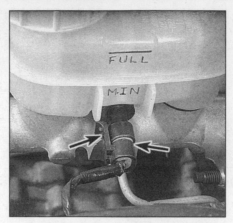

8.3 Unhook the clip and unplug the electrical connector from the brake fluid level sensor, which is located on the left side of the reservoir

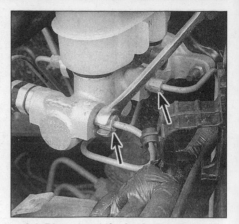

8.4 Disconnect the brake line fittings (arrows) with a flare-nut wrench (ABS-equipped models have two line fittings, while non-ABS models have four)

7   Wheel cylinder - removal, overhaul and installation

Note: *If an overhaul is indicated (usually because of fluid leakage or sticky operation) explore all options before beginning the job. New wheel cylinders are available, which makes this job quite easy. If you decide to rebuild the wheel cylinder, make sure a rebuild kit is available before proceeding. Never overhaul only one wheel cylinder. Always rebuild both of them at the same time.*

Removal

Refer to illustration 7.2

1   Remove the brake shoes (see Section 6).
2   Unscrew the brake line fitting from the rear of the wheel cylinder **(see illustration)**. If available, use a flare-nut wrench to avoid rounding off the corners on the fitting. Don't pull the metal line out of the wheel cylinder - it could bend, making installation difficult.
3   Remove the two bolts securing the wheel cylinder to the brake backing plate.
4   Remove the wheel cylinder.
5   Plug the end of the brake line to prevent the loss of brake fluid and the entry of dirt.

Overhaul

6   To disassemble the wheel cylinder, remove the rubber dust boot from each end of the cylinder, then push out the two pistons, the cups and the cup expanders and spring assembly. Discard the rubber parts and use new ones from the rebuild kit when reassembling the wheel cylinder.
7   Inspect the pistons for scoring and scuff marks. If present, the wheel cylinder should be replaced.
8   Examine the inside of the cylinder bore for score marks and corrosion. If these conditions exist, the cylinder can be honed slightly to restore it, but replacement is recommended.
9   If the cylinder is in good condition, clean it with brake system cleaner. **Warning:** *DO NOT, under any circumstances, use gasoline or petroleum-based solvents to clean brake parts!*
10   Remove the bleeder screw and make sure the hole is clean.
11   Lubricate the cylinder bore with clean brake fluid, then insert one of the new rubber cups into the bore. Make sure the lip on the rubber cup faces in.
12   Install the cup expander and spring assembly from the other side of the cylinder, then install the remaining cup in the cylinder bore.
13   Install the pistons.
14   Install the boots.

Installation

15   Installation is the reverse of removal. Attach the brake line to the

wheel cylinder before installing the mounting bolts and tighten the line fitting after the wheel cylinder mountings bolts have been tightened. If available, use a flare-nut wrench to tighten the line fitting. Make sure you tighten the line fitting securely and the wheel cylinder mounting bolts to the torque listed in this Chapter's Specifications.
16   Install the brake shoes and brake drum (see Section 6).
17   Bleed the brakes (see Section 11). Don't drive the vehicle in traffic until brake operation has been thoroughly tested.

8   Master cylinder - removal, installation and vacuum seal replacement

Removal

Refer to illustrations 8.3, 8.4 and 8.5

1   **Caution:** *On ABS equipped models, the vacuum in the vacuum booster must be pumped down prior to removing the master cylinder, otherwise foreign matter may be sucked into the vacuum booster.* With the ignition switch on the Off position, pump the brake pedal 4 to 5 times until a firm pedal is achieved without the aid of any vacuum assist.
2   Place rags under the brake line fittings and prepare caps or plastic bags to cover the ends of the lines once they're disconnected. **Caution:** *Brake fluid will damage paint. Cover all painted surfaces and avoid spilling fluid during this procedure.*
3   Unhook the clip and unplug the electrical connector from the brake fluid level sensor **(see illustration)**.
4   Loosen the tube nuts at the ends of the brake lines where they enter the master cylinder. To prevent rounding off the flats on these nuts, a flare-nut wrench, which wraps around the nut, should be used **(see illustration)**. Pull the brake lines away from the master cylinder slightly and plug the ends to prevent contamination. Also plug the openings in the master cylinder to prevent fluid spillage.
5   On ABS equipped models, clean the area where the master cylinder attaches to the vacuum booster using a aerosol brake cleaner. Remove the two master cylinder mounting nuts **(see illustration)** and unbolt the bracket. Move the bracket aside slightly, taking care not to kink the hydraulic lines. Remove the master cylinder from the vehicle.
6   Remove the reservoir cap, then discard any fluid remaining in the reservoir.
7   On ABS equipped models, replace the front vacuum seal surrounding the pushrod. Refer to Step 17.

Installation

8   Whenever the master cylinder is removed, the entire hydraulic system must be bled. The time required to bleed the system can be reduced is the master cylinder is filled with fluid and bench bled before

8.5 To detach the master cylinder from the power brake booster, remove these nuts, then pull the master cylinder assembly straight off the mounting studs

8.17 *Carefully* insert a small screwdriver between the pushrod and the vacuum seal and pry out the seal. Note the direction of the seal lip so the new seal can be installed in the same direction

9.1 All non-ABS models have two proportioning valves (arrows), on the right side, that balance braking pressure from front to rear

it's installed on the vehicle. Since you'll have to apply pressure to the master cylinder piston and, at the same time, control flow from the brake line outlets, the master cylinder should be mounted in a vise, with the jaws of the vise clamping on the mounting flange.

9   Insert threaded plugs into the brake line outlet holes and snug them down so that air won't leak past them - but not so tight that they can't be easily loosened.

10   Fill the reservoir with brake fluid of the recommended type (see Chapter 1).

11   Remove one plug and push the piston assembly into the bore to expel the air from the master cylinder. A large Phillips screwdriver can be used to push on the piston assembly.

12   To prevent air from being drawn back into the master cylinder, the plug must be replaced and snugged down before releasing the pressure on the piston.

13   Repeat the procedure until only brake fluid is expelled from the brake line outlet hole. When only brake fluid is expelled, repeat the procedure at the other outlet hole and plug. Be sure to keep the master cylinder reservoir filled with brake fluid to prevent the introduction of air into the system.

14   Since high pressure isn't involved in the bench bleeding procedure, an alternative to the removal and replacement of the plugs with each stroke of the piston assembly is available. Before pushing in on the piston assembly, remove the plug as described in Step 12. Before releasing the piston, however, instead of replacing the plug, simply put

your finger tightly over the hole to keep air from being drawn back into the master cylinder. Wait several seconds for brake fluid to be drawn from the reservoir into the bore, then depress the piston again, removing your finger as brake fluid is expelled. Be sure to put your finger back over the hole each time before releasing the piston, and when the bleeding procedure is complete for that outlet, replace the plug and tighten it before going on to the other port.

15   Carefully install the master cylinder by reversing the removal steps. Tighten the master cylinder mounting nuts to the torque listed in this Chapter's Specifications.

16   Bleed the brake system (see Section 11).

Vacuum Seal Replacement - ABS equipped models

Refer to illustration 8.17

Caution: *On ABS equipped models, the master cylinder is used to create a seal for holding vacuum in the vacuum booster. The seal in the front of the vacuum booster MUST be replaced whenever the master cylinder is removed from the vacuum booster.*

17   *Carefully* insert a small screwdriver between the pushrod and the vacuum seal and pry it out **(see illustration)**. Note the direction of the oil seal so the new seal can be installed is the same direction. **Note:** *Do not insert the screwdriver between the seal and the vacuum booster as this cause a vacuum leak.*

18   Apply Mopar Silicone Dielectric Compound to the exposed length of the pushrod. **Note:** *Use of another type of grease or lubricant will not provide adequate long term lubrication of the pushrod.*

19   Position the new pushrod seal with the notches pointing toward the master cylinder. Install the seal and push it on until it is seated against the master cylinder housing.

9   Proportioning valve - description, check and replacement

Description

Refer to illustrations 9.1 and 9.2

1   All non-ABS models have two proportioning valves **(see illustration)** that balance front to rear braking by controlling the increase in rear system hydraulic pressure above a preset level. Under light pedal pressure, the valve allows full hydraulic pressure to the front and rear brakes. But above a certain pressure - known as the "split point" - the proportioning valve reduces the amount of pressure increase to the rear brakes in accordance with a predetermined ratio. This lessens the chance of rear wheel lock-up and skidding.

9

2   Models equipped with ABS use a screw-in proportioning valve **(see illustration)** in each rear brake hydraulic circuit located at the master cylinder or on the brake lines at the rear of the vehicle. Below a preset level of pressure, the valves do nothing. Above a certain pressure, the valves limit brake pressure to the rear brakes.

Check

3   If either rear wheel skids prematurely under hard braking, it could indicate a defective proportioning valve. If this occurs, drive the vehicle to a dealer immediately and have the system checked out by a competent professional in the dealer service department. A pair of special pressure gauges are required for diagnosing the proportioning valve.

Replacement

Non-ABS models

Caution: *Brake fluid will damage paint. Cover all painted surfaces and avoid spilling fluid during this procedure.*

4   Loosen the brake hydraulic fluid lines from the proportioning valve with a flare-nut wrench to prevent rounding off the corners of the fittings. Back off the fittings and detach the lines. Plug the ends of the lines to prevent loss of brake fluid and the entry of dirt.
5   Unbolt the valve and remove it.
6   Installation is the reverse of removal.
7   Bleed the system after the replacement valve has been installed.

Models with ABS

8   Raise the rear of the vehicle and place it securely on jackstands.
9   Unscrew the proportioning valve from the brake lines. Use a flare-nut wrench to prevent rounding off the corners of the fittings. Back off the fittings and detach the lines. Plug the ends of the lines to prevent loss of brake fluid and the entry of dirt.
10   Installation is the reverse of removal.
11   Bleed the system after the replacement valve has been installed.

---

10   Brake hoses and lines - inspection and replacement

1   About every six months, with the vehicle raised and placed securely on jackstands, the flexible hoses which connect the steel brake lines with the front and rear brake assemblies should be inspected for cracks, chafing of the outer cover, leaks, blisters and other damage. These are important and vulnerable parts of the brake system and inspection should be complete. A light and mirror will be needed for a thorough check. If a hose exhibits any of the above defects, replace it with a new one.

Flexible hose replacement

Refer to illustration 10.3

2   Clean all dirt away from the ends of the hose.
3   Disconnect the brake line from the hose fitting **(see illustration)**. Be careful not to bend the frame bracket or line. If the threaded fitting is corroded, soak it with penetrating oil and allow the penetrate time to loosen it up, then try again. If you try to break loose a brake nut that's frozen, you will kink the metal line, which will then have to be replaced.
4   Separate the metal line from the connection and pull the flexible hose through the bracket. Immediately plug the metal line to prevent excessive fluid loss or contamination.
5   Unscrew the banjo bolt at the caliper and disconnect the hose from the caliper, discarding the sealing washers on either side of the fitting.
6   Using new sealing washers, attach the new brake hose to the caliper. Tighten the banjo bolt to the torque listed this Chapter's Specifications.
7   Insert the other end of the new hose through the bracket. Make sure the hose isn't kinked or twisted, then attach metal line to the hose and tighten the brake line fitting nut securely.
8   Carefully check to make sure the suspension or steering components don't make contact with the hose. Have an assistant push down on the vehicle while you watch to see whether the hose interferes with suspension operation. If you're replacing a front hose, have your assis-

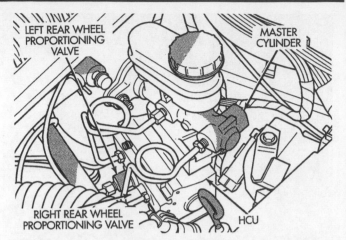

9.2 ABS models have a screw-in proportioning valve in each rear brake hydraulic circuit (typical)

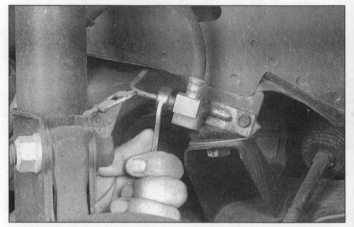

10.3 To disconnect a flexible brake hose from a metal brake line, simply unscrew the threaded fitting nut as shown, but make sure you don't kink the metal line; if the fitting nut is frozen, soak it with penetrant and try again

tant turn the steering wheel lock-to-lock while you make sure the hose doesn't interfere with the steering linkage or the steering knuckle.
9   Bleed the brake system (see Section 11).

Metal brake lines

10   When replacing brake lines, be sure to use the correct parts. Don't use copper tubing for any brake system components. Purchase steel brake lines from a dealer parts department or auto parts store.
11   Prefabricated brake line, with the tube ends already flared and fittings installed, is available at auto parts stores and dealer parts departments. These lines are also sometimes bent to the proper shapes.
12   When installing the new line make sure it's well supported in the brackets and has plenty of clearance between moving or hot components. Make sure you tighten the fittings securely.
13   After installation, check the master cylinder fluid level and add fluid as necessary. Bleed the brake system as outlined in Section 11 and test the brakes carefully before placing the vehicle into normal operation.

---

11   Brake system - bleeding

Refer to illustrations 11.7, 11.8 and 11.10

Warning: *Wear eye protection when bleeding the brake system. If the fluid comes in contact with your eyes, immediately rinse them with water and seek medical attention.*

Note: *Bleeding the brake system is necessary to remove any air that's*

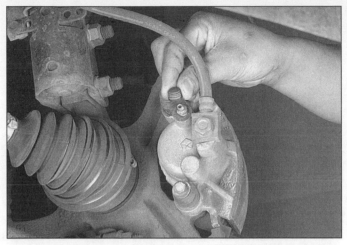

11.7 Remove the cap from each bleeder valve

11.8 When bleeding the brakes, a hose is connected to the bleed screw at the caliper or wheel cylinder and then submerged in brake fluid - air will be seen as bubbles in the tube and container (all air must be expelled before moving to the next wheel)

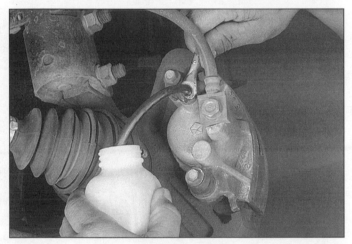

11.10 Open the bleeder screw just enough to allow a flow of fluid to leave the valve

trapped in the system when it's opened during removal and installation of a hose, line, caliper, wheel cylinder or master cylinder.

1   If a brake line was disconnected only at a wheel, then only that caliper or wheel cylinder must be bled.

2   On conventional (non-ABS) brake systems, if air has entered the system due to low fluid level, all four brakes must be bled. **Warning:** *If this has occurred on a model with an Anti-lock Brake System (ABS), or if the lines to the Hydraulic Control Unit (HCU) have been disconnected, the vehicle must be towed to a dealer service department or other repair shop equipped with a DRB II scan tool to have the system properly bled.*

3   If a brake line is disconnected at a fitting located between the master cylinder and any of the brakes, that part of the system served by the disconnected line must be bled.

4   Remove any residual vacuum from the brake power booster (if equipped) by applying the brake several times with the engine off.

5   Remove the master cylinder reservoir cover and fill the reservoir with brake fluid. Reinstall the cover. **Note:** *Check the fluid level often during the bleeding operation and add fluid as necessary to prevent the fluid level from falling low enough to allow air bubbles into the master cylinder.*

6   Have an assistant on hand, as well as a supply of new brake fluid, an empty clear container, a length of 3/16-inch clear plastic or vinyl tubing to fit over the bleeder valve and a wrench to open and close the bleeder valve.

7   Beginning at the right rear wheel, remove the bleeder cap **(see illustration)** loosen the bleeder screw slightly, then tighten it to a point where it's snug but can still be loosened quickly and easily.

8   Place one end of the tubing over the bleeder screw fitting and submerge the other end in brake fluid in the container **(see illustration)**.

9   Have the assistant pump the brakes a few times to get pressure in the system, then hold the pedal firmly depressed.

10   While the pedal is held depressed, open the bleeder screw just enough to allow a flow of fluid to leave the valve **(see illustration)**. Watch for air bubbles to exit the submerged end of the tube. When the fluid flow slows after a couple of seconds, tighten the screw and have your assistant release the pedal.

11   Repeat Steps 9 and 10 until no more air is seen leaving the tube, then tighten the bleeder screw and proceed to the left rear wheel, the right front wheel and the left front wheel, in that order, and perform the same procedure. Be sure to check the fluid in the master cylinder reservoir frequently.

12   Never use old brake fluid. It contains moisture which will deteriorate the brake system components and can even boil if the temperature of the brake fluid rises high enough, which will render the brakes useless.

13   Refill the master cylinder with fluid at the end of the operation. Reinstall the bleeder caps.

14   Check the operation of the brakes. The pedal should feel solid when depressed, with no sponginess. If necessary, repeat the entire process. **Warning:** *Do not operate the vehicle if the pedal feels low or spongy, if the ABS light on the dash won't go off or if you are in doubt about the effectiveness of the brake system.*

---

12   Power brake booster - check, removal and installation

Operating check

1   Depress the brake pedal several times with the engine off and make sure that there is no change in the pedal reserve distance.

2   Depress the pedal and start the engine. If the pedal goes down slightly, operation is normal.

Airtightness check

3   Start the engine and turn it off after one or two minutes. Depress the brake pedal several times slowly. If the pedal goes down farther the first time but gradually rises after the second or third depression, the booster is airtight.

4   Depress the brake pedal while the engine is running, then stop the engine with the pedal depressed. If there is no change in the pedal reserve travel after holding the pedal for 30 seconds, the booster is airtight.

9

Removal

Refer to illustrations 12.8 and 12.9

Note: *On models equipped with ABS, the hydraulic control unit must be removed from the vehicle prior to removing the booster unit. This procedure should be entrusted to a dealer service department or other repair shop.*

5   The power brake booster unit requires no special maintenance apart from periodic inspection of the vacuum hose and the case. Disassembly of the power unit requires special tools and is not ordinarily performed by the home mechanic. If a problem develops, it's recommended that a new or factory rebuilt unit be installed.

6   Remove the master cylinder (see Section 8). It isn't necessary to actually disconnect the brake lines from the master cylinder; simply slide the master cylinder off the mounting studs and push it aside (just make sure you don't kink the metal brake lines).

7   Disconnect the vacuum hose from the power brake booster.

8   Working under the dash, disconnect the power brake pushrod from the top of the brake pedal by prying off the retainer clip **(see illustration)**. Discard the old retainer clip and buy a new clip for reassembly.

9   Remove the nuts attaching the booster to the firewall **(see illustration)**.

10   Carefully lift the booster unit away from the firewall and out of the engine compartment.

Installation

11   To install the booster, place it into position and tighten the retaining nuts to the torque listed in this Chapter's Specifications. Connect the brake pedal. **Warning:** *Use a new retainer clip. Do not re-use the old clip.*

12   Install the master cylinder and vacuum hose.

13   Carefully test the operation of the brakes before placing the vehicle in normal operation.

---

13   Parking brake shoes (models with rear disc brakes) - removal, inspection and installation

---

Warning: *Dust created by the brake system may contain asbestos, which is harmful to your health. Never blow it out with compressed air and don't inhale any of it. An approved filtering mask should be worn when working on the brakes. Do not, under any circumstances, use petroleum-based solvents to clean brake parts. Use brake system cleaner only.*

Note: *Parking brake shoes should be replaced on both wheels at the same time - never replace the shoes on only one wheel.*

Removal

Refer to illustrations 13.6a through 13.6h

1   The parking brake system should be checked as a normal part of driving. With the vehicle parked on a hill, apply the brake, place the

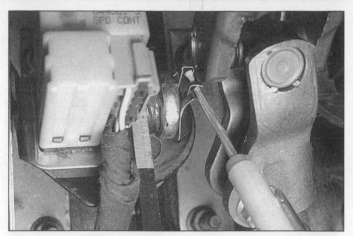

12.8 Pry off the retainer and disconnect the power brake pushrod from the top of the brake pedal. Discard the old retainer clip and buy a new clip for reassembly

12.9 Working up under the dash, disconnect the brake booster pushrod from the brake pedal arm, then remove these four nuts (arrows) and remove the booster

transmission in Neutral and verify that the parking brake alone with hold the vehicle (be sure to stay in the vehicle during this check). Additionally, every 24 months - and any time a fault is suspected - the assembly itself should be visually inspected.

2   Loosen the rear wheel lug nuts, raise the rear of the vehicle and support it securely on jackstands. Block the front wheels and remove

13.6a Remove the front brake shoe hold-down clip by pushing in on the clip and turning the retaining pin 90-degrees

13.6b Remove the rear brake shoe hold-down clip

13.6c Pull the upper end of the rear brake shoe away from the parking brake actuator lever . . .

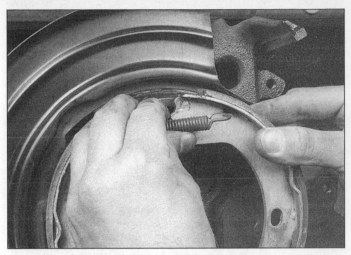

13.6d . . . then unhook the upper spring from the rear shoe

13.6e Disengage the lower end of the rear shoe from the adjuster . . .

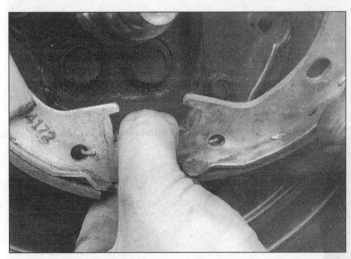

13.6f . . . then unhook the lower spring from the rear shoe and remove the rear shoe

the rear wheels. Release the parking brake.

3   Remove the rear calipers (see Section 4). Support the caliper assemblies with a Bungee cord or heavy wire and don't disconnect the brake line from the caliper.

4   Remove the rear discs (see Section 5). Remove the rear hub and

bearing assemblies (see Chapter 10).

5   Clean the parking brake assembly with brake system cleaner.

6   Follow the accompanying sequence of photos to remove the parking brake shoes **(see illustrations)**. Be sure to stay in order and read the caption under each illustration.

13.6g Unhook the lower spring from the front brake shoe

13.6h Unhook the upper spring from the front brake shoe

9

13.10a Lubricate the friction points on the brake backing plate with high-temperature grease

13.10b Insert the end of the parking brake cable into the parking brake actuator lever, if removed

13.10c Insert the pin for the hold-down clip through the brake backing plate

13.10d Install the front parking brake shoe

Inspection

7   Inspect the lining contact pattern to determine whether the shoes are bent or have been improperly adjusted. The lining should show contact across the entire width, extending from head to toe. Shoes showing contact only on one side should be replaced.

8   Clean the backing plate with a suitable solvent.

9   Inspect the drum (see Section 6).

Installation

Refer to illustrations 13.10a through 13.10l

10   Follow the accompanying sequence of photos to install the new shoes **(see illustrations)**, then install the hub and bearing assemblies (see Chapter 10).

11   Before installing the disc, rotate the star wheel on the adjuster until the distance across the friction surfaces of the parking brake

13.10e Install the front brake shoe hold-down clip

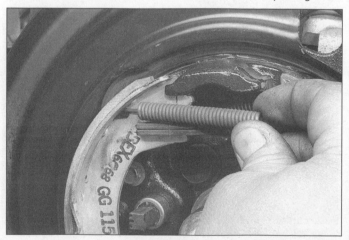

13.10f Hook the upper return spring to the front parking brake shoe

13.10g Hook the lower return spring to the front parking brake shoe

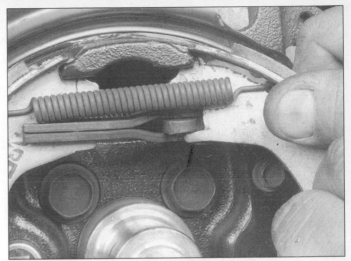

13.10h Hook the upper return spring to the rear parking brake shoe

13.10i Hook the lower return spring to the rear parking brake shoe

13.10j Pull the rear parking brake shoe back and engage it with the actuator lever

13.10k Insert the pin for the rear hold-down clip through the backing plate and install the rear hold-down clip

13.10l Install the adjuster between the parking brake shoes, then turn the adjuster star wheel until the distance across the friction surfaces of the shoes is 6-3/4 inches

9

14.3 To lock the sector into place, insert a 3/16-inch drill bit, Allen wrench or small screwdriver into the parking brake lever mechanism; the tool must go all the way through both sides of the parking brake mechanism

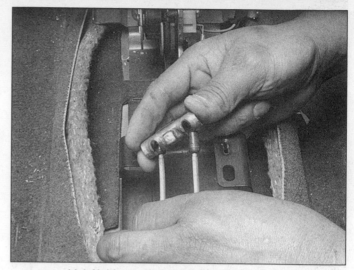

14.4 Hold onto the equalizer and disconnect both rear brake cables

shoes is 6-3/4 inches.

12   Install the disc (see Section 5). Using a screwdriver or brake adjusting tool, turn the star wheel on the parking brake shoe adjuster until the shoes slightly drag as the disc is turned, then back-off the adjuster until the shoes don't drag.

13   Install the caliper (see Section 4).

14   Repeat this sequence for the other parking brake shoes at the other rear wheel.

14   Parking brake lever and automatic adjuster assembly - removal and installation

Removal

Refer to illustrations 14.3, 14.4, 14.5 and 14.6

1   Remove the center console (see Chapter 11).

2   Lower the parking brake lever.

3   **Warning:** *The self-adjusting mechanism of the parking brake lever assembly contains a clock spring loaded to about twenty pounds. Use*

care in handling the parking brake lever assembly. Do not release the self-adjuster lockout device before installing the cables into the equalizer. Keep your hands away from the self-adjuster sector and pawl. Careless handling of the parking brake lever adjuster mechanism could cause serious injury. Grasp the parking brake front output cable and pull it toward the rear. Continue to pull on the front cable until a 3/16-inch drill bit, Allen wrench or small screwdriver can be inserted into the brake handle and the brake sector gear to lock it into place **(see illustration).** *Push the drill bit or Allen wrench all the way trough the mechanism. Locking the sector gear relieves the strain on the rear parking brake cables.*

4   Disconnect both rear brake cables from the parking brake equalizer **(see illustration).**

5   Unplug the electrical connector ground from the brake warning light switch **(see illustration).**

6   Remove the nuts attaching the parking brake lever assembly to the center console bracket **(see illustration).**

7   Remove the parking brake lever, the automatic adjuster and the front output cable as an assembly.

Installation

8   Install the parking brake lever and automatic adjuster assembly onto the center console bracket, install the nuts and tighten securely.

14.5 Unplug the electrical connector from the brake warning light switch

14.6 Remove the bolt attaching the parking brake pedal assembly to the floor pan

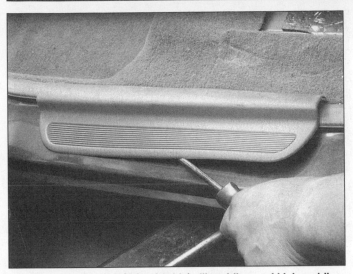

15.8 Remove the left (driver's side) sill molding and kick molding

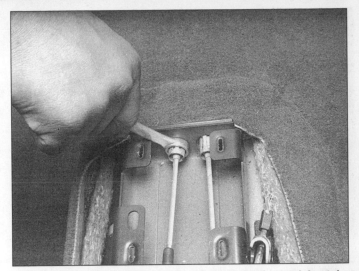

15.10 Use a 1/2-inch box wrench and compress the retaining tabs of the cable housing - then pull the cable through the opening in the center console bracket

9   Reconnect the electrical connector ground onto the brake warning light switch.

10   Insert each parking brake cable through the hole in the equalizer on the front output cable. Make sure the cables are properly installed and are aligned with the cable track in the lever.

11   Using a pair of pliers, pull out the drill bit or Allen wrench installed in the parking brake sector gear mechanism with a firm and quick motion. When the tool is removed from the parking brake pedal adjuster mechanism, the adjuster automatically adjusts the parking brake cables.

12   Apply and release the parking brake lever several times. The rear wheels should rotate freely without the brakes dragging.

13   Install the center console (see Chapter 11).

15   Parking brake cables - replacement

Front cable

Replacement

1   **Note:** *The front output cable is an integral part of the brake lever assembly and cannot be replaced separately. Do not attempt to remove the cable from the lever assembly since it is attached to the clock spring.* Remove the parking brake lever assembly (see Section 14).

2   Install the parking brake lever assembly (see Section 14).

Rear cables

Removal

Refer to illustrations 15.8, 15.10, 15.12, 15.13, 15.14 and 15.15

Note: *Disconnect only one rear parking brake cable from the rear brakes at a time. If you disconnect both cables simultaneously, it will be extremely difficult to connect both of them to the equalizer.*

3   Remove the center console (see Chapter 11).

4   Lower the parking brake lever.

5   **Warning:** *The self-adjusting mechanism of the parking brake lever assembly contains a clock spring loaded to about twenty pounds. Use care in handling the parking brake lever assembly. Do not release the self-adjuster lockout device before installing the cables into the equalizer. Keep your hands away from the self-adjuster sector and pawl. Careless handling of the parking brake lever adjuster mechanism could cause serious injury.* Grasp the parking brake front output cable and pull it toward the rear. Continue to pull on the front cable until a 3/16-inch drill bit or Allen bolt can be inserted into the brake handle and the brake sector gear to lock it into place **(see illustration 14.3)**. Push the drill bit or Allen wrench all the way through the mechanism. Locking

the sector gear relieves the strain on the rear parking brake cables.

6   Disconnect one of the rear brake cables from the parking brake equalizer **(see illustration 14.4)**.

7   Remove the rear seat assembly (see Chapter 11).

8   On four-door models, carefully pry on the retaining clips and remove the rear door sill scuff plate on each side **(see illustration)**.

9   Fold rear carpeting forward to expose the parking brake cables.

10   Compress the retaining tabs of the cable housing with a 1/2-inch box wrench or a pair of pliers **(see illustration)**. Pull the cable through the opening in the center console bracket.

11   Loosen the rear wheel lug nuts, raise the rear of the vehicle and place it securely on jackstands. Remove the rear wheels.

12   On models with rear drum brakes, remove the rear drum (see Section 6) and the rear hub and bearing assembly (see Chapter 10). Disassemble the brake shoe assembly (see Section 6). Disconnect the cable from the parking brake lever **(see illustration)**. Using a small hose clamp, squeeze the cable housing retainer tabs and pull the cable through the brake backing plate. If you don't have a clamp handy, use a 1/2-inch box wrench or a pair of pliers (using pliers isn't as easy).

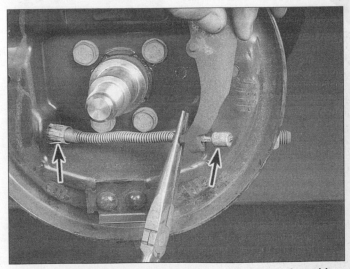

15.12 On models with rear drum brakes, disconnect the cable from the parking brake actuator lever (right arrow), squeeze the retainer tabs (left arrow) on the cable housing and pull the cable through the brake backing plate

9

15.13 On models with rear disc brakes, disconnect the cable from the parking brake actuator lever, then squeeze the retainer tabs on the cable housing and pull the cable through the brake backing plate

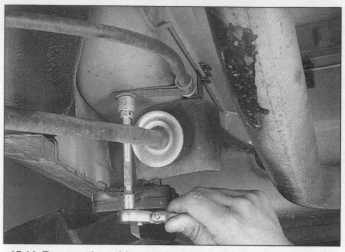

15.14 Remove the cable retaining bolts attaching the rear cable to the floorpan and frame

13   On models with rear disc brakes, remove the rear caliper (see Section 4) and disc (see Section 5). Disassemble the parking brake shoe assembly (see Section 13). Disconnect the cable from the parking brake actuator lever **(see illustration)**, then squeeze the retainer tabs on the cable housing and pull the cable through the backing plate.
14   Remove the cable bracket from the frame rail **(see illustration)**.
15   Remove the cable sealing grommet from the floor pan **(see illustration)**.
16   Remove the cable assembly from the vehicle.

Installation

17   Insert the front end of the rear cable through the hole in the floorpan. Make sure the sealing grommet is installed correctly to ensure a proper seal.
18   Insert the rear end of the new rear cable through the hole in the brake backing plate. Make sure the cable is pulled through the hole far enough to allow the retaining tabs to expand all the way around the cable, locking the cable to the backing plate.
19   Install the cable bracket onto the frame rail and tighten the bolt securely.
20   On models with rear drum brakes, connect the cable to the parking brake lever, reassemble the rear brake assembly (see Section 13), install the rear hub and bearing assembly (see Chapter 10) and install the rear drum.
21   On models with rear disc brakes, connect the cable to the parking brake actuator lever, reassemble the parking brake shoe assembly (see Section 13), install the disc (see Section 5) and install the rear caliper (see Section 4).
22   Install the rear wheels, hand tighten the wheel lug nuts, remove the jackstands and lower the vehicle. Tighten the rear wheel lug nuts to the torque listed in the Chapter 1 Specifications.
23   Grasp the parking brake cable grommet at the floor pan and pull hard to make sure the grommet is fully seated to the floor pan.
24   Route the cable under the carpeting and up to the cable retaining bracket on the floor pan.
25   Install the cable through the cable retaining bracket and make sure the cable retainers have expanded out to hold cable in place in the bracket.
26   Grasp the equalizer firmly, pull it to the rear and connect the rear cable to the equalizer **(see illustration 14.4)**.
27   Repeat this procedure for the other rear cable, if you're replacing both cables.
28   Fold back the carpet and on four-door models, install both rear door opening sill scuff plates. Install the rear seat assembly (see Chapter 11).
29   Install the center console (see Chapter 11).

16   Brake light switch - check and adjustment

Refer to illustration 16.7

1   The brake light switch is a normally-open switch that controls the operation of the vehicle brake lights. The switch is located near the top of the brake pedal and is attached to the bracket. When the brake pedal is applied, a spring-loaded plunger closes the circuit to the left and right brake lights.
2   On models with cruise control, the brake light switch also deactivates the cruise control system when the brake pedal is depressed.

Check

3   If the brake lights don't come on when the brake pedal is applied, check the brake light fuse (see Chapter 12). If the fuse has blown, look for a short in the brake light circuit.
4   If the fuse is okay, use a test light or voltmeter to verify that there's voltage to the switch. If there's no voltage to the switch, look for an open or short in the power wire to the switch. Repair the power wire.
5   If the brake lights still don't come on when the brake pedal is applied, unplug the electrical connector from the brake light switch

15.15 Remove the cable sealing grommet from the floorpan and remove the cable assembly

16.7 Hold the brake pedal down, then rotate the brake light switch about 30-degrees in a counterclockwise direction and remove the switch

and, using an ohmmeter, verify that there's continuity between the switch terminals when the brake pedal is applied, i.e. the switch is closed. If there isn't, replace the switch.

6   If there is continuity between the switch terminals when the brake is applied, but the brake lights don't come on when the brake pedal is applied, check the wiring between the switch and the brake lights for an open circuit.

Replacement

7   Depress and hold the brake pedal, then rotate the brake light switch about 30-degrees in a counterclockwise direction **(see illustration)**.

8   Pull the switch to the rear and remove it from its mounting bracket.

9   Unplug the electrical connector from the switch.

10   Hold onto the switch and pull the plunger outward until it has ratcheted to its fully extended position.

11   Install and adjust the new switch (see following).

Adjustment

12   Depress the brake pedal as far as it will go, then install the switch in the bracket by aligning the index key on the switch with the slot at the top of the square hole in the mounting bracket. **Caution:** *Don't use excessive force when pulling back on the brake pedal to adjust the switch. If you use too much force, you will damage the switch or the striker.* When the switch is fully installed in the bracket, rotate the switch clockwise about 30-degrees to lock the switch into the bracket.

13   Gently pull back on the brake pedal until the pedal stops moving. The switch plunger will ratchet backward to the correct position.

14   Plug the electrical connector into the switch.

9

Notes

Chapter 10
Suspension and steering systems

Contents

Specifications

General
Power steering fluid .... Chapter 1

Torque specifications   Ft-lbs (unless otherwise indicated)

Front suspension
Control arm-to-front crossmember bolt and nut	120
Control arm-to-steering knuckle clamp bolt and nut	70
Stabilizer-to-control arm bolt and nut	21
Stabilizer-to-crossmember bolts	21
Strut/spring top attaching nuts	300 in-lbs
Strut/spring clevis-to-knuckle bolt and nut	40 plus 90 degrees additional
Strut/spring shaft retaining nut	55
Tie-rod end adjusting nut	55
Tie-rod-to-steering knuckle nut	40

Rear suspension
Brake support plate-to-knuckle bolts	50
Lateral arms-to-spindle bolt and nut	70
Lateral arms-to-rear crossmember bolt and nut	70
Rear hub retaining nut	160
Stabilizer-to-link bolt and nut	300 in-lbs
Stabilizer bushing retaining bolts	300 in-lbs
Strut/spring top attaching nuts	300 in-lbs
Strut/spring clevis-to-knuckle bolt and nut	70
Strut/spring shaft retaining nut	55
Trailing arm-to-frame bracket nut	70
Trailing arm-to-spindle nut	70

10

Torque specifications

Ft-lbs (unless otherwise indicated)

Steering system

Airbag module retaining bolts	90 in-lbs
Crossmember-to-underbody bolts	
Preliminary	20 in-lbs
Final	120
Power steering hose bracket bolt	17
Power steering pump bracket mounting bolts	40
Power steering pump mounting bolts	40
Pressure hose banjo bolt	25
Steering gear coupler pinch bolt	250 in-lbs
Steering gear-to-crossmember mounting bolts	50
Steering wheel nut	45
Tie-rod end stud nut	40

1.1 Front steering and suspension components

1	Steering gear assembly	2	Strut assemblies	3	Control arms	4	Stabilizer bar link

1.2 Rear suspension components

| 1 | *Suspension arms (rear)* | 2 | *Strut assemblies* | 3 | *Suspension arms (front)* | 4 | *Strut rods* |

1   General information

Refer to illustrations 1.1 and 1.2

The front suspension is a Macpherson strut design. The upper end of each strut is attached to the vehicle's body strut support. The lower end of the strut is connected to the upper end of the steering knuckle. The steering knuckle is attached to a balljoint mounted on the outer end of the suspension control arm **(see illustration)**.

The rear suspension also utilizes strut/coil spring assemblies. The upper end of each strut is attached to the vehicle body by a strut support. The lower end of the strut is attached to the rear knuckle. The carrier is located by a pair of suspension arms on each side, and a longitudinally mounted strut rod between the body and the knuckle **(see illustration)**.

The power-assisted rack-and-pinion steering gear is attached to the front suspension crossmember. The steering gear actuates the tie-rods, which are attached to the steering knuckles. The steering column is designed to collapse in the event of an accident.

Frequently, when working on the suspension or steering system components, you may come across fasteners which seem impossible to loosen. These fasteners on the underside of the vehicle are continually subjected to water, road grime, mud, etc., and can become rusted or "frozen" in place, making them extremely difficult to remove. In order to unscrew these stubborn fasteners without damaging them (or other components), be sure to use lots of penetrating oil and allow it to soak in for a while. Using a wire brush to clean exposed threads will also ease removal of the nut or bolt and prevent damage to the threads. Sometimes a sharp blow with a hammer and punch will break the bond between a nut and bolt threads, but care must be taken to prevent the punch from slipping off the fastener and ruining the threads. Heating the stuck fastener and surrounding area with a torch sometimes helps too, but isn't recommended because of the obvious dangers associated with fire. Long breaker bars and extension, or "cheater," pipes will increase leverage, but never use an extension pipe on a ratchet - the ratcheting mechanism could be damaged. Sometimes tightening the nut or bolt first will help to break it loose. Fasteners that require drastic measures to remove should always be replaced with new ones.

Since most of the procedures dealt with in this Chapter involve jacking up the vehicle and working underneath it, a good pair of jack-stands will be needed. A hydraulic floor jack is the preferred type of jack to lift the vehicle, and it can also be used to support certain components during various operations. **Warning:** *Never, under any circumstances, rely on a jack to support the vehicle while working on it. Whenever any of the suspension or steering fasteners are loosened or removed they must be inspected and, if necessary, replaced with new ones of the same part number or of original equipment quality and design. Torque specifications must be followed for proper reassembly and component retention. Never attempt to heat or straighten any suspension or steering components. Instead, replace any bent or damaged part with a new one.*

2   Strut assembly (front) - removal and installation

Refer to illustrations 2.3, 2.4, 2.5 and 2.6

1　Loosen the front wheel lug nuts.

2　Raise the vehicle and support it securely on jackstands. Remove the front wheels.

10

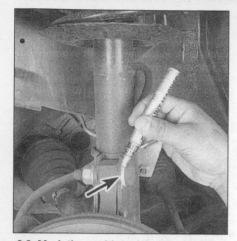

2.3 Mark the position of the camber cam (arrow) in relation to the strut

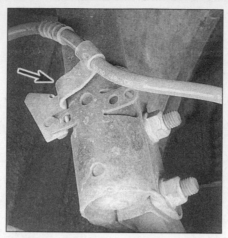

2.4 Remove the bolt and detach the brake hose bracket (arrow) from the strut

2.5 Remove the nuts, bolts, cam and washer plate securing the strut to the steering knuckle

3   **Note:** *If both strut assemblies are going to be removed, mark the assemblies right and left so they will be reinstalled on the correct side. Mark the position of the camber cam* **(see illustration).**

4   Disconnect the brake hose bracket from the strut. On ABS equipped models, the vehicle speed sensor is also attached to the brake hose bracket **(see illustration)**.

5   Remove the strut-to-steering knuckle nuts, bolts, cam and washer plate **(see illustration)**.

6   Remove the upper mounting nuts **(see illustration)**, disengage the strut from the steering knuckle and detach it from the vehicle.

7   Inspect the strut and coil spring assembly for leaking fluid, dents, damage and corrosion. If the strut is damaged, see Section 3.

8   To install the strut, place it in position with the studs extending up through the shock tower. Install the nuts and tighten them to the torque listed in this Chapter's Specifications.

9   Attach the strut to the steering knuckle, then insert the strut-to-steering knuckle bolts through the cam and washer plate. Install the nuts, but don't tighten them yet.

10   Attach the brake hose (and ABS speed sensor) bracket to the strut and tighten the bolt.

11   Install a C-clamp on the strut and knuckle. Tighten it just enough to remove any looseness between the knuckle and strut. Align the marks you made on the cam and strut. **Caution:** *To not turn the bolts as they are serrated and must not be turned - hold the bolt stationary*

and tighten the nut onto the bolt. Tighten the steering knuckle-to-strut bolts and nuts to the torque listed in this Chapter's Specifications.

12   Install the wheels and lower the vehicle.

3   Strut /coil spring - replacement

Note: *You'll need a spring compressor for this procedure. Spring compressors are available on a daily rental basis at most auto parts stores or equipment yards.*

1   If the struts or coil springs exhibit the telltale signs of wear (leaking fluid, loss of damping capability, chipped, sagging or cracked coil springs) explore all options before beginning any work. The strut/shock absorber assemblies are not serviceable and must be replaced if a problem develops. However, strut assemblies complete with springs may be available on an exchange basis, which eliminates much time and work. Whichever route you choose to take, check on the cost and availability of parts before disassembling your vehicle. **Warning:** *Disassembling a strut assembly is a potentially dangerous undertaking and utmost attention must be directed to the job, or serious injury may result. Use only a high-quality spring compressor and carefully follow the manufacturer's instructions furnished with the tool. After removing the coil spring from the strut assembly, set it aside in a safe, isolated area.*

2.6 Remove these three upper mounting nuts (arrows) - DO NOT remove the center nut!

3.3 Mount the strut clevis bracket portion of the strut assembly in a vise

3.4 Install the spring compressor in accordance with the tool manufacturer's instructions and compress the spring until all pressure is removed from the upper suspension support

3.5 Loosen the damper shaft nut with a socket wrench

3.6 Remove the damper shaft nut and suspension support

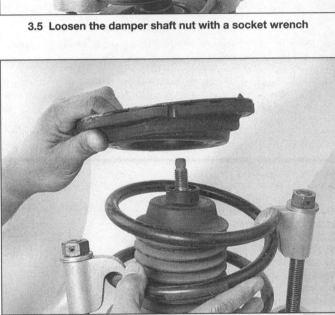

3.7a Remove the upper spring seat . . .

Disassembly

Refer to illustrations 3.3, 3.4, 3.5, 3.6, 3.7a, 3.7b, 3.8 and 3.9

2   Remove the strut and spring assembly (see Section 2).

3   Mount the strut clevis bracket portion of the strut assembly **(see illustration)**. **Caution:** *Do not clamp any other portion of the strut assembly in the vise as it will be damaged.* Line the vise jaws with wood or rags to prevent damage to the unit and don't tighten the vise excessively.

4   Following the tool manufacturer's instructions, install the spring compressor (which can be obtained at most auto parts stores or equipment yards on a daily rental basis) on the spring and compress it sufficiently to relieve all pressure from the upper spring seat **(see illustration)**. This can be verified by wiggling the spring.

5   Loosen the shaft nut with a socket wrench **(see illustration)**.

6   Remove the nut and suspension support **(see illustration)**. Inspect the bearing in the suspension support for smooth operation. If it doesn't turn smoothly, replace the suspension support. Check the rubber portion of the suspension support for cracking and general deterioration. If there is any separation of the rubber, replace it.

7   Remove the upper spring seat and dust boot from the damper shaft **(see illustrations)**. Check the spring seat for cracking and hardness; replace it if necessary.

10

3.7b . . . and the dust boot from the damper shaft

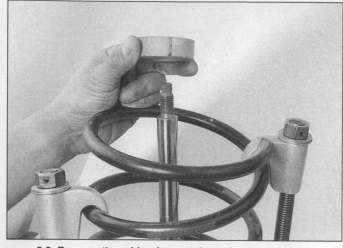

3.8 Remove the rubber bumper from the damper shaft

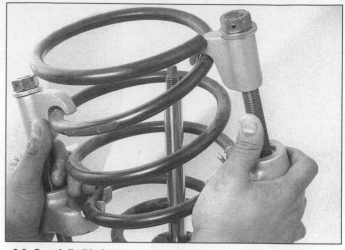

3.9 Carefully lift the compressed spring from the assembly and set it in a safe place - keep the ends of the spring pointed away from your body

8   Slide the rubber bumper off the damper shaft **(see illustration)**.
9   Carefully lift the compressed spring from the assembly **(see illustration)** and set it in a safe place. **Warning:** *When removing the compressed spring, lift it off very carefully and set it in a safe place. Keep the ends of the spring away from your body.* **Note:** *Mark the spring so it can be reinstalled on the same side of the vehicle from which it was removed.*

Reassembly

10   Extend the damper rod to its full length and install the rubber bumper.
11   Position the coil spring with the smaller coils going on first and carefully place the coil onto the damper shaft.
12   Install the rubber bumper onto the damper shaft and push it all the way down until it bottoms out.
13   Install the upper spring seat and dust boot onto the damper shaft.
14   Install the suspension support and align the support notch with the clevis bracket on the strut support. Install the suspension support to the damper shaft.
15   Install the nut and tighten it to the torque listed in this Chapter's Specifications.
16   Equally loosen the coil spring compressors until the top coil is properly seated against the upper spring seat and suspension support. Relieve all tension from the spring compressors and remove them from the coil spring.
17   Install the strut/spring assembly (see Section 2).

4   Stabilizer (sway) bar and bushings (front) - removal and installation

Refer to illustrations 4.2, 4.3 and 4.6
1   Loosen the front wheel lug nuts, raise the front of the vehicle, support it securely on jackstands and remove the front wheels.
2   Remove the stabilizer bar retainer bolts, nuts and retainers from the lower control arms **(see illustration)**.
3   Support the stabilizer bar and remove the stabilizer bar clamp bolts and clamps from the front suspension crossmember **(see illustration)**. Remove the stabilizer bar from the vehicle.
4   Check the bar for damage, corrosion and signs of twisting.
5   Check the clamps, bushings and retainers for distortion, damage and wear. Replace the inner bushings by prying them open at the split and removing them. Install the new bushings with the split facing toward the front of the vehicle. The outer bushings can be removed by cutting them off or hammering them from the bar. Force the new bushings onto the end of the bar until 1/2-inch of the bar is protruding. Silicone spray lubricant will ease this process.
6   Attach the bar to the crossmember so the cutouts in the stabilizer bar bushings are aligned with the raised bead on the crossmember **(see illustration)**. Install the retainers aligning the raised bead on the retainer with the bushing cutouts and install the bolts, but don't tighten

4.2 Remove the stabilizer bar retainer bolts, nuts and retainers from the lower control arms

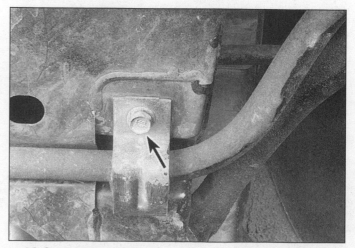

4.3 Support the stabilizer bar and remove both stabilizer bar clamp bolts and clamps from the front suspension crossmember

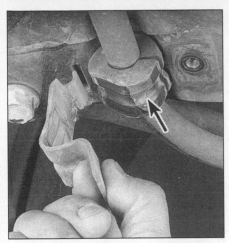

4.6 Install the retainers, aligning the raised bead on the retainer with the bushing cutouts (arrow) and install the retainers and bolts

5.2 Remove the bolt and nut (arrow) to disconnect the control arm from the balljoint

5.4 Separate the control arm from the steering knuckle with a prybar

them completely yet.
7   Raise the control arms to normal ride height and tighten the bolts to the torque listed in this Chapter's Specifications.
8   Install the wheels and lower the vehicle.

5   Control arm - removal, inspection and installation

Removal

Refer to illustrations 5.2, 5.4 and 5.5
1   Loosen the wheel lug nuts on the side to be dismantled, raise the front of the vehicle, support it securely on jackstands and remove the wheel.
2   Remove the balljoint clamping bolt and nut **(see illustration)**.
3   Disconnect the stabilizer bar from the control arms (see Section 4) and rotate the bar down, out of the way.
4   Use a prybar to disconnect the control arm from the steering knuckle **(see illustration)**. Pull the balljoint stud from the steering knuckle. **Caution:** *Do not move the steering knuckle/strut assembly out or you may separate the inner CV joint.*
5   Remove the bolt and nut that attach the front of the control arm to the engine cradle **(see illustration)**.
6   Remove the bolt and nut that attach the rear of the control arm to

the engine cradle **(see illustration 5.5)**.
7   Remove the control arm.

Inspection

8   Make sure the control arm is straight. If it's bent, replace it. Do not attempt to straighten a bent control arm.
9   Inspect the bushings. If they're cracked, torn or worn out, replace the control arm.

Installation

10   Installation is the reverse of removal. Tighten the control arm's front bolt and nut first, then the rear bolt and nut. Be sure to tighten all fasteners to the torque listed in this Chapter's Specifications.
11   Install the wheel and lug nuts, lower the vehicle and tighten the lug nuts to the torque listed in the Chapter 1 Specifications.
12   It's a good idea to have the front wheel alignment checked, and if necessary, adjusted after this job has been performed.

6   Balljoints - check and replacement

Refer to illustration 6.2
1   The suspension balljoints are designed to operate without freeplay.

5.5 To detach the front end of the control arm from the engine cradle, remove these two bolts and nuts (arrows)

6.2 Place a prybar or large screwdriver between the control arm and the underside of the steering knuckle and try to lever the knuckle from side to side and check for play

10

2   To check for wear, place a prybar or large screwdriver between the control arm and the underside of the steering knuckle and try to lever the knuckle from side to side **(see illustration)**. Try to wiggle the grease fitting at the base of the ball joint - it should not move easily.

3   If there is any movement, the balljoint is worn and must be replaced with a new one. Remove the control arm (see Section 5) and take it to a dealer service department or automotive machine shop to have the old balljoint pressed out and a new one pressed in.

7   Steering knuckle, hub and bearing - removal, inspection and installation

Removal

1   With the vehicle weight resting on the front suspension, remove the hub cap, cotter pin, nut lock and spring washer. Loosen, but do not remove, the front hub (driveaxle) nut and wheel lug nuts.

2   Raise the front of the vehicle, support it securely on jackstands and remove the front wheels.

3   Remove the caliper and brake pads (see Chapter 9), then remove the caliper mounting bracket from the steering knuckle. Taking care not to twist the brake hose, hang the caliper out of the way in the wheel well with a piece of wire.

4   Disconnect the tie-rod end from the steering knuckle (see Section 16).

5   Move the tie-rod out of the way and secure it with a piece of wire.

6   Remove the lower control arm ball joint from the steering knuckle (see Section 5).

7   With the knuckle and hub assembly in the straight-ahead position, grasp it securely and pull it directly out and off the driveaxle splines. **Caution:** *Be careful not to pull the driveaxle out or you may disengage the inner CV joint.*
It may be necessary to tap on the axle end with a soft-face hammer to dislodge the driveaxle from the hub. Secure the end of the driveaxle with a piece of wire.

8   Mark the position of the camber cam (see Section 2).

9   Remove the strut-to-steering knuckle nuts, bolts, cam and washer plate **(see illustration 2.5)**. Remove the steering knuckle.

Inspection

10   Place the assembly on a clean work surface and wipe it off with a lint-free cloth. Inspect the knuckle for rust, damage and cracks. Check the bearings by rotating them to make sure they move freely, without excessive noise or looseness. The bearings should be packed with an adequate supply of clean grease. **Note:** *Further disassembly will have to be left to your dealer service department or a repair shop because of the special tools required.*

Installation

11   Prior to installation, clean the CV joint seal and the hub grease seal with solvent (don't get any solvent on the CV joint boot). Lubricate the entire circumference of the CV joint wear sleeve and seal contact surface with multi-purpose grease (see Chapter 8).

12   Carefully place the knuckle and hub assembly in position. Align the splines of the axle and the hub and slide the hub into place.

13   Install the knuckle-to-strut bolts, camber cam, washer plate and nuts, followed by the balljoint pinch bolt and nut. Adjust the position of the camber cam (see Section 2). **Caution:** *To not turn the bolts as they are serrated and must not be turned - hold the bolt stationary and tighten the nut onto the bolt.* Tighten the steering knuckle-to-strut bolts and nuts to the torque listed in this Chapter's Specifications.

14   Reattach the tie-rod end to the steering knuckle and tighten the nut (see Section 16).

15   Install the brake disc, pads and caliper/adapter assembly (see Chapter 9).

16   Reattach the brake hose bracket to the strut.

17   Push the CV joint completely into the hub to make sure it is seated and install the washer and hub nut finger tight.

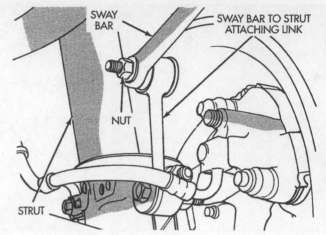

8.2 Detach the stabilizer (sway) bar links from the sway bar - then rotate the stabilizer bar down to clear the bar links

18   Install the wheels, hand tighten the lug nuts, lower the vehicle and tighten the wheel lug nuts to the torque specified in Chapter 1.

19   With an assistant applying the brakes, tighten the hub nut to the torque specified in Chapter 8. Install the spring washer, nut lock and a new cotter pin.

20   With the weight of the vehicle on the suspension, check the steering knuckle and balljoint nuts to make sure they are tightened properly.

21   Have the front end alignment checked and, if necessary, adjusted.

8   Stabilizer(sway) bar and bushings (rear) - removal and installation

Refer to illustrations 8.2 and 8.3

1   Loosen the rear wheel lug nuts. Raise the rear of the vehicle and place it securely on jackstands. Remove the rear wheels.

2   Detach the stabilizer (sway) bar links from the bar **(see illustration)**. Rotate the stabilizer bar down to clear the bar links.

3   Unbolt the stabilizer bar bushing retainers from the body **(see illustration)**.

4   The stabilizer bar can now be removed from the vehicle. Pull the retainers off the stabilizer bar (if they haven't fallen off already) using a rocking motion.

5   Check the bushings for wear, hardness, distortion, cracking and

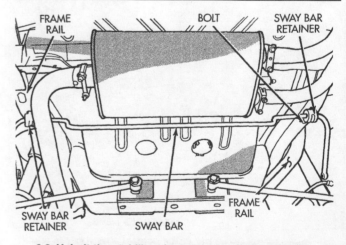

8.3 Unbolt the stabilizer (sway) bar bushing retainers from the body

9.3 Remove the bolt and nut and detach the brake hose bracket (arrow) from the strut. If the vehicle is equipped with ABS, detach the ABS sensor wire from the strut

9.5 Remove the strut-to-knuckle mounting bolts and nuts (arrows)

other signs of deterioration, replacing them if necessary. Also check the link bushings for these signs.

6   Using a wire brush, clean the areas of the bar where the bushings ride.

7   Installation is the reverse of the removal procedure. Install the new bushings with the split facing toward the rear of the vehicle. If necessary, use a light coat of vegetable oil to ease bushing and U-bracket installation (don't use petroleum-based products or brake fluid, as these will damage the rubber).

8   Installation is the reverse of removal.

9   Strut assembly (rear) - removal, inspection and installation

Removal

Refer to illustrations 9.3, 9.5 and 9.7

1   Remove the trunk carpet assembly.

2   Loosen the rear wheel lug nuts, raise the rear of the vehicle and support it securely on jackstands. Remove the wheel.

3   Detach the brake hose bracket from the strut **(see illustration)**. If the vehicle is equipped with ABS, detach the ABS sensor wire from the strut.

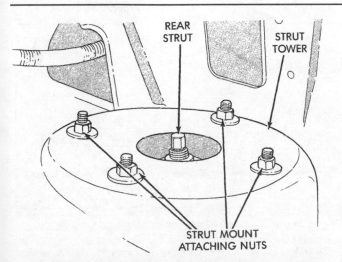

9.7 Remove the strut tower dust shield. Loosen but do not remove the four upper strut mount attaching nuts

4   Secure the rear knuckle, suspension and brake assembly to the body with apiece of wire prior to removing the strut-to-knuckle mounting bolts.

5   Remove the strut-to-knuckle bolts and nuts **(see illustration)**.

6   Install the wheel and lug nuts, lower the vehicle and tighten the lug nuts to the torque listed in the Chapter 1 Specifications.

7   Remove the strut tower dust shield. Loosen but do not remove the four upper strut-to-body mounting nuts **(see illustration)**.

8   Secure the strut assembly with wire or rope, then remove the four nuts and lower the strut assembly.

9   Remove the strut assembly.

Inspection

10   Follow the inspection procedures described in Section 3. If you determine that the strut assembly must be disassembled for replacement of the strut or the coil spring, refer to Section 4.

Installation

11   Maneuver the assembly up into the fenderwell and insert the mounting studs through the holes in the body. Install the nuts, but don't tighten them yet.

12   Connect the strut to the knuckle and install the bolts and nuts. Install a C-clamp on the strut and knuckle. Tighten it just enough to remove any looseness between the knuckle and strut. **Caution:** *To not turn the bolts as they are serrated and must not be turned - hold the bolt stationary and tighten the nut onto the bolt.* Tighten the steering knuckle-to-strut bolts and nuts to the torque listed in this Chapter's Specifications.

13   Attach the brake hose (and ABS speed sensor) bracket to the strut and tighten the bolt.

14   Attach the brake hose bracket to the strut. If the vehicle is equipped with ABS, attach the ABS wire to the strut.

15   Install the wheel and lug nuts, lower the vehicle and tighten the lug nuts to the torque listed in the Chapter 1 Specifications.

16   Tighten the four strut upper mounting nuts to the torque listed in this Chapter's Specifications.

17   Install the trunk carpet assembly.

10   Trailing arms - removal and installation

Removal

Refer to illustrations 10.3 and 10.4

1   Loosen the rear wheel lug nuts, raise the rear of the vehicle and support it securely on jackstands. Remove the wheel.

2   Remove the rear brake drum or caliper assembly (see Chapter 9).

10

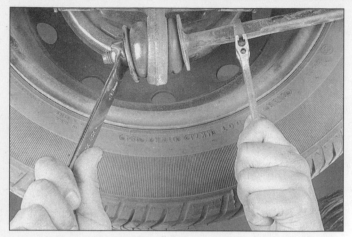

10.3 To keep the trailing arm from turning, secure a large adjustable wrench onto the flat on the rear portion, then remove the rear nut and the strut retainer

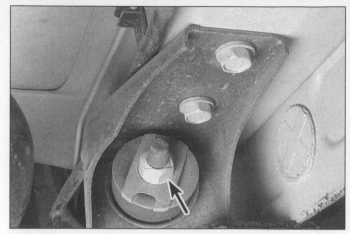

10.4 Attach a large adjustable wrench onto the flat on the front of the trailing arm to keep it from turning. Remove the front nut and the strut retainer at the frame mounting bracket

Taking care not to twist the brake hose, hang the brake assembly or disc/caliper assembly out of the way in the wheel well with a piece of wire.

3   Attach a large adjustable wrench onto the flat on the rear of the trailing arm to keep it from turning. At the knuckle, remove the rear nut and the strut retainer with the small inner hole and strut bushing **(see illustration).**

4   Attach a large adjustable wrench onto the flat on the front of the trailing arm to keep it from turning. At the frame mounting bracket, remove the front nut and the strut retainer with the small inner hole and strut bushing **(see illustration).**

5   Mark the front of the trailing arm so it will be reinstalled in the same direction.

6   Move the rear strut/coil assembly toward the rear and remove the rear portion of the trailing arm from the knuckle. Remove the front portion from the frame mounting bracket.

7   Slide off the bushings and strut retainers with the large inner hole from each end of the trailing arm.

Inspection

8   Make sure the trailing arm is straight. If it's bent, replace it. Do not attempt to straighten a bent trailing arm.

9   Inspect the bushings. If they're cracked, torn or worn out, replace all of them as a set.

Installation

10   Installation is the reverse of removal. Install the trailing arm in the same direction as when removed, see Step 5. Tighten the nuts to the torque listed in this Chapter's Specifications.

11   Install the wheel and lug nuts, lower the vehicle and tighten the lug nuts to the torque listed in the Chapter 1 Specifications.

11   Lateral arms - removal and installation

Removal

Refer to illustration 11.5

1   Raise the rear of the vehicle and support it securely on jack-stands. Block the front wheels.

2   Remove the front and rear lateral arms-to-rear spindle carrier bolt, washer and nut.

3   Mark the position of the toe adjust cams.

4   Mark the front lateral arms (having the same size bushing sleeves) so they will be installed in their original location.

5   **Note:** *Note the installed direction of the mounting bolts, outer bolts installed from the front and inner bolt installed from the rear, also*

the bolts are of different lengths. Remove the lateral arms to the strut/knuckle and frame crossmember bolts, washers, rear toe adjustment cams and nuts **(see illustration).**

6   Remove the front and rear lateral arms.

Installation

7   **Note:** *This short bolt must be installed from the front of the vehicle.* Install the washer on the short bolt, then install the front lateral arm onto the front of the knuckle and install the bolt through the knuckle. Install the rear lateral arm onto the bolt and the knuckle and install the washer and nut. Do not tighten the bolt and nut at this time.

8   **Note:** *This long bolt must be installed from the rear of the vehicle.* Install the toe adjust cam on the long bolt, then move the rear lateral arm up into position on the rear crossmember and push the bolt through both parts. Move the front lateral arm up into position and push the bolt through it and install the washer and nut. Do not tighten the bolt and nut at this time.

9   Install the wheel and lug nuts, then lower the vehicle to the ground. Tighten the lateral arm bolts and nuts to the torque listed in this Chapter's specifications. Tighten the wheel lug nuts to the torque listed in the Chapter 1 Specifications.

10   Have the rear wheel alignment checked by a dealer service department or an alignment shop.

11.5 To disconnect the lateral arms from the strut/knuckle and frame crossmember, remove these nuts (arrows) and knock out the bolts (but don't remove the bolts until after the strut/knuckle is supported by a floor jack - the strut assembly is heavy, so it's a good idea to have an assistant standing by to lend a hand if necessary)

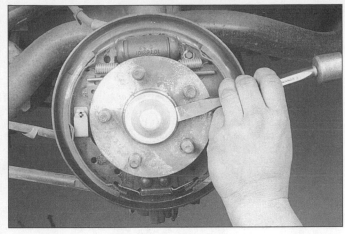
12.3a Remove the dust cap

12.3b Remove the mounting nut

12 Hub and bearing assembly (rear) - removal and installation

Refer to illustrations 12.3a, 12.3b and 12.3c

Warning: *Dust created by the brake system may contain asbestos, which is harmful to your health. Never blow it out with compressed air and don't inhale any of it. Do not, under any circumstances, use petroleum-based solvents to clean brake parts. Use brake system cleaner only.*

1   Loosen the wheel lug nuts, raise the vehicle and support it securely on jackstands. Remove the wheel.

2   On models with rear drum brakes, remove the drum; on models with rear disc brakes, remove the caliper and the brake disc (see Chapter 9).

3   Follow the accompanying photos to remove the hub and bearing assembly **(see illustrations)**. Installation is the reverse of removal. Be sure to tighten the hub-to-spindle nut to the torque listed in this Chapter's Specifications.

4   Install the brake drum, or disc and caliper (see Chapter 9).

5   Install the wheel and hand tighten the wheel lug nuts. Remove the jackstands, lower the vehicle and tighten the lug nuts to the torque listed in the Chapter 1 Specifications.

13 Spindle - removal and installation

Refer to illustrations 13.2a, 13.2b and 13.5

Warning: *Dust created by the brake system may contain asbestos,*

12.3c Remove the hub and bearing assembly

which is harmful to your health. Never blow it out with compressed air and don't inhale any of it. Do not, under any circumstances, use petroleum-based solvents to clean brake parts. Use brake system cleaner only.

1   Loosen the rear wheel lug nuts, raise the vehicle and support it on jackstands. Block the front wheels and remove the rear wheel.

2   On models with ABS, remove the wheel speed sensor from the brake backing plate **(see illustrations)**.

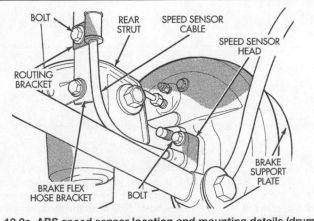
13.2a ABS speed sensor location and mounting details (drum brake models)

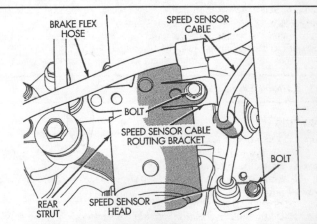
13.2b On disc brake models, the ABS speed sensor (if equipped) is mounted to the caliper bracket

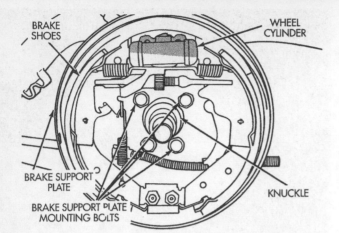

13.5 To remove the brake backing plate, remove these four bolts

3   On models with rear drum brakes, remove the rear brake drum and brake shoe assembly, disconnect the parking brake cable from the parking brake lever and disconnect the brake hose from the wheel cylinder (see Chapter 9). On models with rear disc brakes, remove the caliper and brake disc, remove the parking brake shoes and disconnect the parking brake cable from the actuator lever (see Chapter 9).

4   Remove the rear hub and bearing assembly (see Section 12).

5   On models with rear drum brakes, unbolt the brake backing plate **(see illustration)** and remove it. On models with rear disc brakes unbolt the adapter mounting plate and remove it.

6   Loosen, but do not remove, the rear strut-to-spindle mounting nuts.

7   Secure the lateral links to the body with a piece of wire prior to removing the lateral links-to-spindle mounting bolts. Remove the nut and bolt which attach the lateral links to the spindle **(see illustration 11.5)**. Refer to Section 11 for correct procedure.

8   Remove the nut and washer which attach the trailing arm to the spindle **(see illustration 10.3)**. Refer to Section 10 for correct procedure

9   Remove the rear strut-to-spindle mounting nuts and bolts and slide the spindle down and out of the strut rut clevis bracket.

10   Installation is the reverse of removal. **Note:** *Refer to Sections 10 and 11 for proper bolt and nut tightening procedures.* Be sure to tighten all suspension fasteners to the torque listed in this Chapter's Specifications.

11   Install the wheel and lug nuts. Lower the vehicle and tighten the lug nuts to the torque listed in the Chapter 1 Specifications.

14   Steering system - general information

All models are equipped with rack-and-pinion steering. The steering gear - which is located behind the engine, above the transaxle, in front of the firewall - operates the steering knuckles via tie rods connected to steering arms on the strut assemblies. The tie-rod ends can be replaced by unscrewing them from the inner tie rods. Adjustment sleeves between the inner tie rods and the tie-rod ends are used to adjust front wheel toe.

The power assist system consists of a belt-driven pump and associated lines and hoses. The fluid level in the power steering pump reservoir should be checked periodically (see Chapter 1).

The steering wheel operates the steering shaft, which actuates the steering gear through a short steering column and a couple of universal joints (referred to by Chrysler as the upper and lower intermediate column couplers). Looseness in the steering can be caused by wear in these universal joints, the steering gear, the tie-rod ends and loose retaining bolts.

15   Steering wheel - removal and installation

Removal

Refer to illustrations 15.3, 15.4, 15.5a, 15.5b, 15.5c, 15.6a, 15.6b, 15.7 and 15.8

Warning: *These models have airbags. Always disconnect the negative battery cable and wait two minutes before working in the vicinity of the impact sensors, steering column or instrument panel to avoid the possibility of accidental deployment of the airbag, which could cause personal injury (see Chapter 12).*

1   Make sure the front wheels are in the *straight ahead* position. Lock the steering column as follows: Turn the steering wheel clockwise 1/2-turn from the straight-ahead position, turn the ignition key to the Lock position and remove the key from the key lock cylinder. This ensures that no damage occurs to the airbag clockspring when the steering wheel is removed.

2   Disconnect the cable from the negative terminal of the battery. Wait at least two minutes before proceeding.

3   On models with cruise control, remove the two cruise control screws and switches from the steering wheel to gain access to the airbag module retaining screws. If the vehicle isn't equipped with cruise control, remove the screws and the covers on the each side of the steering wheel for access **(see illustration)**.

4   Remove the airbag module retaining bolt on each side **(see illustration)**.

5   Lift the airbag module off the steering wheel **(see illustration)** and

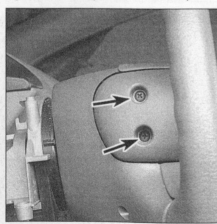

15.3 Remove the cover screws (arrows) and pull off the cover on each side

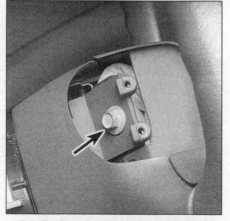

15.4 To detach the airbag module from the steering wheel, remove the two module retaining bolts (left bolt shown, right bolt identical)

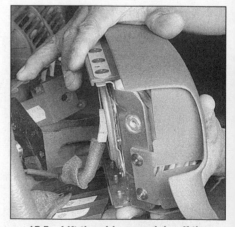

15.5a Lift the airbag module off the steering wheel . . .

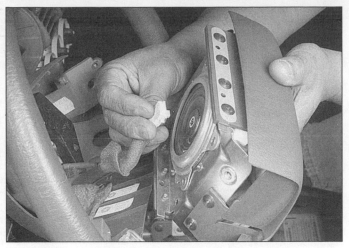

15.5b . . . unplug the module electrical connector . . .

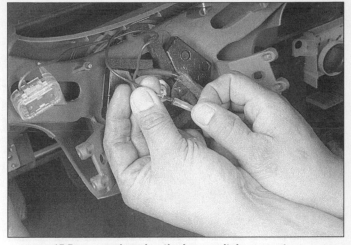

15.5c . . . and unplug the horn switch connector

unplug the airbag electrical connector **(see illustration)**. Also unplug the electrical connector for the horn **(see illustration)**. **Warning:** *Carry the airbag with the trim cover side* **facing away** *from your body to minimize injury if the airbag module accidentally deploys. Set the airbag module aside in a safe, isolated location and set it down with the trim cover side facing up.*

6   Remove the steering wheel retaining nut **(see illustration)**. On models so equipped, remove the weight module **(see illustration)**.

7   Mark the relationship of the steering wheel to the steering shaft **(see illustration)**.

8   Use a puller to disconnect the steering wheel from the shaft **(see illustration)**.

Installation

9   Align the mark on the steering wheel with the mark on the shaft and slip the wheel onto the shaft. Install the nut and tighten it to the torque listed in this Chapter's Specifications.

10   **Warning:** *Do not reconnect the airbag module electrical connector yourself. Take the vehicle to a dealer's service department and have the airbag system checked prior to reconnecting the connector.*

11   Plug in the horn and airbag module electrical connectors.

12   Tighten the module retaining bolts to the torque listed in this Chapter's Specifications.

13   Plug in and install the cruise control switches and tighten the screws securely. On vehicles without cruise control, install the covers.

14   Connect the negative battery cable.

15   From the *passenger side* of the vehicle, turn the ignition switch to

15.6a Remove the steering wheel retaining nut . . .

the Off position, then turn it to the On position. Check that the instrument cluster AIRBAG lamps is illuminated for six to eight seconds and then goes out indicating the airbag system is functioning properly. If the lamp fails to light, blinks on and off or stays on, there is a malfunction in the airbag system. If any of these conditions exist, the vehicle should be diagnosed by a dealer service department.

15.6b . . remove the weight module (models so equipped)

15.7 Mark the relationship of the steering wheel to the steering shaft

15.8 Use a steering wheel puller to remove the wheel from the shaft

10

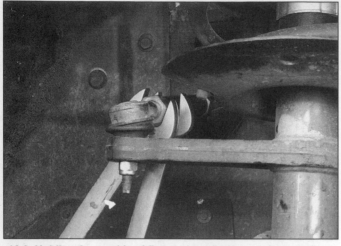

16.3 Holding the machined flat on the adjustment sleeve with an open-end wrench, loosen the tie-rod end jam nut

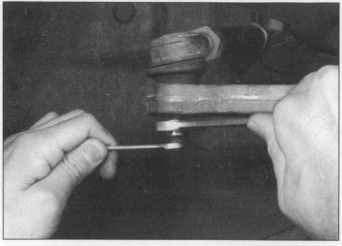

16.4 Prevent the tie-rod end stud from turning by holding it with a wrench, then break the stud nut loose with another wrench, but don't remove it yet

16   Tie-rod ends - removal and installation

Removal

Refer to illustrations 16.3, 16.4 and 16.5

1   Loosen the wheel lug nuts. Raise the front of the vehicle, support it securely on jackstands, block the rear wheels and set the parking brake. Remove the front wheel.

2   Measure the distance from the center of the tie-rod end to the outer edge of the adjustment sleeve and write down this measurement.

3   Hold the adjustment sleeve with a wrench on the machined flat and loosen the jam nut with another wrench **(see illustration)**.

4   Loosen - but don't remove - the nut on the tie-rod end stud **(see illustration)**.

5   Disconnect the tie-rod from the steering arm with a puller **(see illustration)**. Remove the nut and separate the tie-rod.

6   Unscrew the tie-rod end from the adjustment sleeve.

Installation

7   Thread the jam nut onto the new tie-rod end and screw the tie-rod end into the adjustment sleeve until the distance from the center of the new tie-rod end to the outer edge of the adjustment sleeve matches the measurement you made before removing the old tie-rod end.

8   Install the tie-rod end stud into the steering arm, install the stud nut and tighten it to the torque listed in this Chapter's Specifications.

9   Tighten the jam nut securely.

10   Install the wheel and lug nuts. Lower the vehicle and tighten the lug nuts to the torque listed in the Chapter 1 Specifications.

11   Have the front end alignment checked by an alignment shop.

17   Steering gear - removal and installation

Removal

Refer to illustrations 17.3, 17.5, 17.7a, 17.7b, 17.8, 17.9, 17.10, 17.11 and 17.13

Warning: *These models are equipped with airbags. Make sure the steering shaft is not turned while the steering gear is removed or you could damage the airbag system. To prevent the shaft from turning,* **turn the ignition key to the lock position before beginning work or run the seat belt through the steering wheel and clip the seat belt into place.** *Due to the possible damage to the airbag system, we recommend only experienced mechanics attempt this procedure.*

Note: *These models are designed and assembled using* **net build** *front*

16.5 Install a small puller and push the tie-rod end stud out of the steering arm

suspension alignment settings. The front suspension alignment settings are determined as the vehicle is being built by accurately locating the front suspension crossmember to the master gauge holes located in the underbody of the vehicle. Therefore whenever the front crossmember is removed from the vehicle's body it must be reinstalled in the **exact** *same location on the body to maintain correct front end alignment.*

1   Disconnect the negative battery cable.

2   Turn the front wheels of the vehicle to the full-left position, then turn them back until the retaining pin in the coupler is accessible. Turn the ignition key to the Lock position to keep the steering column from rotating after the coupler is disengaged from the steering gear. **Caution:** *Failure to lock the steering shaft could allow it to rotate beyond its normal number of turns in either direction, which will damage the airbag module clockspring. Using paint, mark the relationship of the steering coupler to the steering gear shaft to ensure proper reassembly.*

3   Working in the passenger compartment, disconnect the steering gear coupler from the steering column shaft coupler **(see illustration)**.

4   Loosen the front wheel lug nuts, raise the front of the vehicle and support it securely on jackstands. Remove both wheels.

5   On manual transaxle models, disconnect the power hop damper from the front suspension crossmember **(see illustration)**. Move the damper out of the way - it is not necessary to remove the unit from the transaxle.

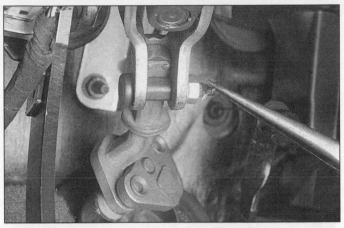

17.3 Using paint, mark the relationship of the steering coupler to the steering gear shaft to ensure proper reassembly, then remove the clip and disconnect the steering gear coupler from the steering column shaft coupler

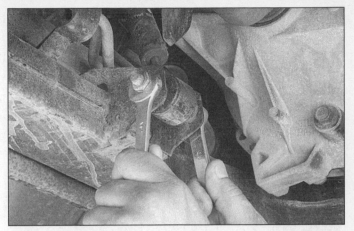

17.5 On manual transaxle models, remove the bolt and nut and disconnect the power hop damper from the front suspension crossmember; move the damper out of the way

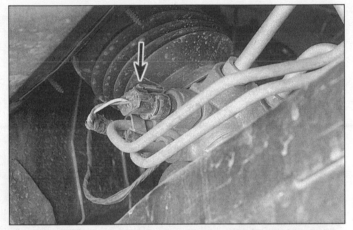

17.7a On power steering models, unhook the clip and disconnect the electrical connector (arrow) from the power steering fluid pressure switch . . .

17.7b . . . then remove the power steering fluid hose bracket (arrow) - leave the bracket attached to the hoses

6   Disconnect the tie-rod ends from the steering spindle (see Section 16).

7   If the vehicle is equipped with power steering, disconnect the electrical connector from the power steering fluid pressure switch **(see illustration)**. Remove the power steering fluid hose bracket - leave the bracket attached to the hoses **(see illustration)**.

8   If the vehicle is equipped with power steering, place a drain pan under the steering gear. Detach the power steering pressure and return lines **(see illustration)** and cap the ends to prevent excessive fluid loss and contamination. Detach the bracket from the top of the steering gear assembly.

9   **Caution:** *Before removing the front crossmember, the exact location of the crossmember must be accurately scribed on the underbody*

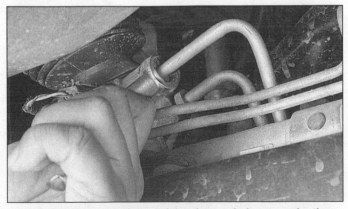

17.8 On power steering models, place a drain pan under the steering gear and detach the power steering pressure and return lines - cap the ends to prevent excessive fluid loss and contamination

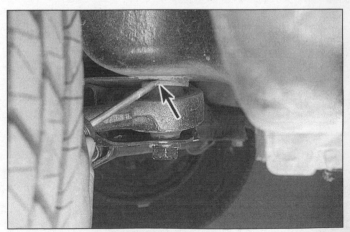

17.9 Using an awl, accurately scribe a line marking the location of front crossmember-to-underbody

10

17.10 Position a transmission jack under the center of the front crossmember to support it

17.11 Loosen the two mounting bolts (arrows) attaching the front crossmember and lower control arms to the underbody

of the vehicle. Using an awl or scribe, accurately scribe a line marking the location of the front crossmember-to-underbody **(see illustration).**

10   Position a transmission jack, or equivalent, under the center of the front crossmember **(see illustration).**

11   Remove the two front mounting bolts which attach the front crossmember to the frame rails of underbody, then loosen the two rear mounting bolts which attach the front crossmember and lower control arms to the underbody **(see illustration).**

12   Continue to loose the rear bolts while lowering the transmission jack and front suspension crossmember - don't remove the rear bolts as they keep the crossmember attached to the control arms. Lower the crossmember sufficiently to remove the bolts securing the steering gear to the crossmember. **Caution:** *Do not allow the crossmember to hang from the lower control arms as they will be damaged - it must be supported by the jack at all times.*

13   Remove the four mounting bolts which attach the steering gear to the crossmember **(see illustration),** slide the steering gear forward in the vehicle to disengage the coupler from the steering gear shaft. Once the steering gear is disengaged, do NOT turn the steering gear shaft or the steering column shaft (see the **Warning** at the beginning of this Section). Remove the steering gear assembly from the vehicle.

Installation

14   Install the steering gear onto the crossmember and install the four mounting bolts **(see illustration 17.13).** Tighten the bolts to the torque listed in this Chapter's Specifications.

15   Slowly raise the steering gear assembly up and engage the coupler onto the steering gear shaft. If you're installing the old steering gear, align the paint mark on the steering coupler with the mark on the steering gear shaft and insert the shaft into the coupler. If you're installing a new steering gear assembly, rotate the steering gear shaft back from its full-left position until the master spline on the steering gear shaft is aligned with the master spline on the coupler, then insert the shaft into the coupler.

16   Continue to raise the crossmember and align the four mounting holes in the crossmember. Install the rear two mounting bolts then the front two mounting bolts. Tighten the four bolts in a crisscross pattern until he crossmember is up against the underbody. Tighten the bolts to the *preliminary* torque listed in this Chapter's Specifications

17   Using a soft face hammer, tap the crossmember into correct alignment with the scribe marks made on the underbody in Step 9 **(see illustration 17.9). Caution:** *This alignment is necessary to maintain the net build front suspension alignment settings.* When the alignment is correct, first tighten the rear two bolts, then the front two bolts to the *final* torque listed in this Chapter's Specifications

18   If the vehicle is equipped with power steering, attach the power steering fluid pressure and return lines to the correct ports on the

17.13 Remove the four mounting bolts attaching the steering gear to the crossmember

steering gear **(see illustration 17.8)** and tighten the tube fittings to the torque listed in this Chapter's Specifications. Connect the electrical connector onto the power steering fluid pressure switch **(see illustration 17.7b).** Install the power steering fluid hose bracket and tighten the bolt securely **(see illustration 17.7a).**

19   Connect the tie-rod ends onto the steering spindle (see Section 16).

20   On manual transaxle models, connect the power hop damper onto the front suspension crossmember and tighten the bolt and nut to the torque listed in this Chapter's Specifications.

21   Install the wheel and lug nuts. Lower the vehicle and tighten the lug nuts to the torque listed in the Chapter 1 Specifications.

22   Working in the passenger compartment, connect the steering gear coupler onto the steering column shaft coupler **(see illustration 17.3).** Tighten the bolt and nut to the torque listed in this Chapter's Specifications. Install the retaining clip onto the bolt.

23   Have the front end alignment checked by an alignment shop.

18   Power steering pump - removal and installation

Refer to illustrations 18.4, 18.5, 18.7, 18.8, 18.9, 18.12a, 18.12b and 18.12c

1   Disconnect the cable from the negative battery terminal.

2   Using a large syringe or suction gun, suck as much fluid out of the

18.4 Unscrew the pressure hose fitting from the power steering pump discharge port - discard the O-ring seals from the banjo bolt and fitting

18.5 Remove the hose clamp from the reservoir-to-power steering pump hose - then detach the hose from the pump

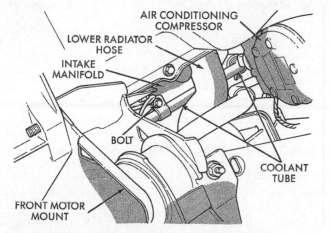

18.7 On DOHC engines, remove the coolant tube bolt - move the coolant tube away from the intake manifold to gain access to the power steering pump mounting bolt

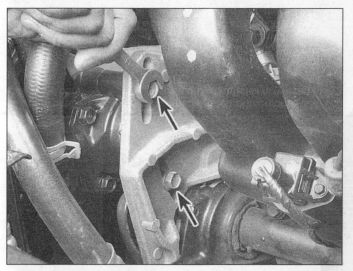

18.8 Remove the two bolts which attach the power steering pump to the engine bracket

power steering fluid reservoir as possible.

3   Place a drain pan under the vehicle to catch any fluid that spills out when the hoses are disconnected.

4   Unscrew the power steering pressure hose fitting from the power steering pump discharge port **(see illustration)**. Discard the O-ring seals from the banjo bolt and fitting.

5   Remove the hose clamp **(see illustration)** from the hose coming from the reservoir to the power steering pump and detach the hose from the pump.

6   Raise the vehicle and support it securely on jackstands.

7   On DOHC engines, remove the coolant tube bolt which is attached to the intake manifold **(see illustration)**. Move the coolant tube away from the intake manifold to gain access to the power steering pump mounting bolt. **Note:** *It is not necessary to disconnect the coolant tube nor drain and of the coolant.*

8   Remove the two bolts which attach the power steering pump to the engine bracket **(see illustration)**.

9   **Note:** *The pump's front mounting bracket is slotted where it attaches to the front engine mount.* Loosen, don't remove, the bolt which attaches pump front mounting bracket to the front engine mount **(see illustration)**.

10   Remove the drivebelt from the pump.

11   Remove the power steering pump, pulley and mounting bracket as an assembly.

18.9 Loosen, don't remove, the bolt attaching the pump front mounting bracket to the front engine mount

10

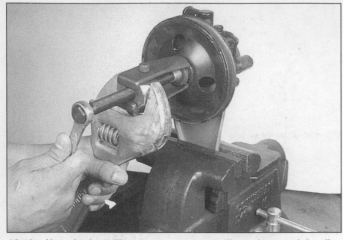

18.12a If you're installing a new pump, you'll need a special puller to remove the pulley from the old pump . . .

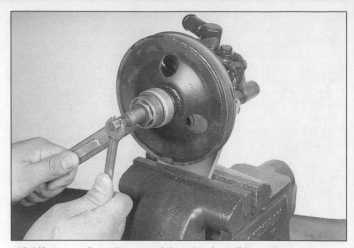

18.12b . . . and another special tool to install it on the new pump

12   If you're installing a new pump, you'll need a special puller **(see illustration)** to remove the pulley from the old pump and another special tool **(see illustration)** to install it on the new pump. These tools are available at most auto parts stores. When the pulley is removed, also remove the mounting bracket from the pump **(see illustration).**
13   Installation is the reverse of removal. Be sure to tighten the power steering pump bolts to the torque listed in this Chapter's Specifications. Install all new O-ring seals on the pressure fitting, then tighten the hose fitting to the torque listed in this Chapter's specifications.
14   Top up the fluid level in the reservoir (see Chapter 1) and bleed the system (see Section 19).
15   Adjust the drive belt (see Chapter 1).

19   Power steering system - bleeding

1   Following any operation in which the power steering fluid lines have been disconnected, the power steering system must be bled to remove all air and obtain proper steering performance.
2   With the front wheels in the straight ahead position, check the power steering fluid level and, if low, add fluid until it reaches the Cold mark on the dipstick.
3   Start the engine and allow it to run at fast idle. Recheck the fluid level and add more if necessary to reach the Cold mark on the dipstick.
4   Bleed the system by turning the wheels from side to side, without hitting the stops. This will work the air out of the system. Keep the

reservoir full of fluid as this is done.
5   When the air is worked out of the system, return the wheels to the straight ahead position and leave the vehicle running for several more minutes before shutting it off.
6   Road test the vehicle to be sure the steering system is functioning normally and noise free.
7   Recheck the fluid level to be sure it is up to the Hot mark on the dipstick while the engine is at normal operating temperature. Add fluid if necessary (see Chapter 1).

20   Wheels and tires - general information

Refer to illustration 20.1
1   All vehicles covered by this manual are equipped with metric-sized fiberglass or steel belted radial tires **(see illustration)**. Use of

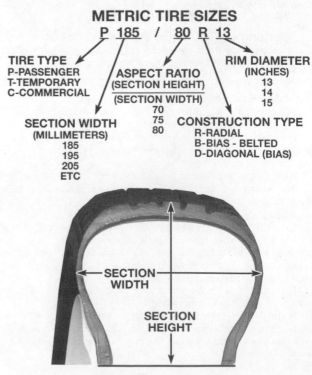

20.1 Metric tire size code

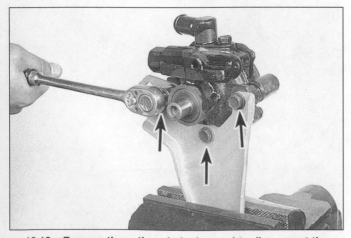

18.12c Remove these three bolts (arrows) to disconnect the mounting bracket from the pump

other size or type of tires may affect the ride and handling of the vehicle. Don't mix different types of tires, such as radials and bias belted, on the same vehicle as handling may be seriously affected. It's recommended that tires be replaced in pairs on the same axle, but if only one tire is being replaced, be sure it's the same size, structure and tread design as the other.

2 Because tire pressure has a substantial effect on handling and wear, the pressure on all tires should be checked at least once a month or before any extended trips (see Chapter 1).

3 Wheels must be replaced if they are bent, dented, leak air, have elongated bolt holes, are heavily rusted, out of vertical symmetry or if the lug nuts won't stay tight. Wheel repairs that use welding or peening are not recommended.

4 Tire and wheel balance is important in the overall handling, braking and performance of the vehicle. Unbalanced wheels can adversely affect handling and ride characteristics as well as tire life. Whenever a tire is installed on a wheel, the tire and wheel should be balanced by a shop with the proper equipment.

21 Wheel alignment - general information

Refer to illustration 21.1

A wheel alignment refers to the adjustments made to the wheels so they are in proper angular relationship to the suspension and the ground. Wheels that are out of proper alignment not only affect vehicle control, but also increase tire wear. The alignment angles normally measured are camber, caster and toe-in **(see illustration)**. Toe-in is the only adjustable angle on the front or the rear. The other angles should be measured to check for bent or worn suspension parts.

Getting the proper wheel alignment is a very exacting process, one in which complicated and expensive machines are necessary to perform the job properly. Because of this, you should have a technician with the proper equipment perform these tasks. We will, however, use this space to give you a basic idea of what is involved with a wheel alignment so you can better understand the process and deal intelligently with the shop that does the work.

Toe-in is the turning in of the wheels. The purpose of a toe specification is to ensure parallel rolling of the wheels. In a vehicle with zero toe-in, the distance between the front edges of the wheels will be the same as the distance between the rear edges of the wheels. The actual amount of toe-in is normally only a fraction of an inch. On the front end, toe-in is controlled by the tie-rod end position on the tie-rod. On the rear end, it's controlled by a threaded adjuster on the rear lateral link. Incorrect toe-in will cause the tires to wear improperly by making them scrub against the road surface.

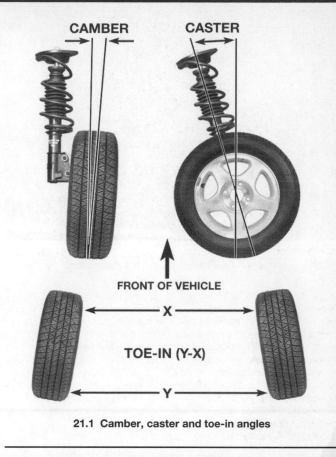

21.1 Camber, caster and toe-in angles

Camber is the tilting of the wheels from vertical when viewed from one end of the vehicle. When the wheels tilt out at the top, the camber is said to be positive (+). When the wheels tilt in at the top the camber is negative (-). The amount of tilt is measured in degrees from vertical and this measurement is called the camber angle. This angle affects the amount of tire tread which contacts the road and compensates for changes in the suspension geometry when the vehicle is cornering or traveling over an undulating surface.

Caster is the tilting of the front steering axis from the vertical. A tilt toward the rear is positive caster and a tilt toward the front is negative caster.

10

Notes

Chapter 11   Body

Contents

1   General information

The models covered by this manual feature a "unibody" layout, using a floor pan with front and rear frame side rails which support the body components, front and rear suspension systems and other mechanical components. Certain components are particularly vulnerable to accident damage and can be unbolted and repaired or replaced. Among these parts are the body moldings, bumpers, front fenders, the hood and trunk lids and all glass. Only general body maintenance practices and body panel repair procedures within the scope of the do-it-yourselfer are included in this chapter.

2   Body - maintenance

1   The condition of the vehicle's body is very important, because the resale value depends a great deal on it. It's much more difficult to repair a neglected or damaged body than it is to repair mechanical components. The hidden areas of the body, such as the wheel wells, the frame and the engine compartment, are equally important, although they don't require as frequent attention as the rest of the body.

2   Once a year, or every 12,000 miles, it's a good idea to have the underside of the body steam cleaned. All traces of dirt and oil will be removed and the area can then be inspected carefully for rust, dam-

aged brake lines, frayed electrical wires, damaged cables and other problems. The front suspension components should be greased after completion of this job.

3   At the same time, clean the engine and the engine compartment with a steam cleaner or water-soluble degreaser.

4   The wheel wells should be given close attention, since undercoating can peel away and stones and dirt thrown up by the tires can cause the paint to chip and flake, allowing rust to set in. If rust is found, clean down to the bare metal and apply an anti-rust paint.

5   The body should be washed about once a week. Wet the vehicle thoroughly to soften the dirt, then wash it down with a soft sponge and plenty of clean soapy water. If the surplus dirt is not washed off very carefully, it can wear down the paint.

6   Spots of tar or asphalt thrown up from the road should be removed with a cloth soaked in solvent.

7   Once every six months, wax the body and chrome trim. If a chrome cleaner is used to remove rust from any of the vehicle's plated parts, remember that the cleaner also removes part of the chrome, so use it sparingly.

3   Vinyl trim - maintenance

Don't clean vinyl trim with detergents, caustic soap or petroleum-based cleaners. Plain soap and water works just fine, with a soft brush to clean dirt that may be ingrained. Wash the vinyl as frequently as the

11

rest of the vehicle. After cleaning, application of a high-quality rubber and vinyl protectant will help prevent oxidation and cracks. The protectant can also be applied to weatherstripping, vacuum lines and rubber hoses, which often fail as a result of chemical degradation, and to the tires.

4   Upholstery and carpets - maintenance

1   Every three months remove the floor mats and clean the interior of the vehicle (more frequently if necessary). Use a stiff whisk broom to brush the carpeting and loosen dirt and dust, then vacuum the upholstery and carpets thoroughly, especially along seams and crevices.

2   Dirt and stains can be removed from carpeting with basic household or automotive carpet shampoos available in spray cans. Follow the directions and vacuum again, then use a stiff brush to bring back the "nap" of the carpet.

3   Most interiors have cloth or vinyl upholstery, either of which can be cleaned and maintained with a number of material-specific cleaners or shampoos available in auto supply stores. Follow the directions on the product for usage, and always spot-test any upholstery cleaner on an inconspicuous area (bottom edge of a back seat cushion) to ensure that it doesn't cause a color shift in the material.

4   After cleaning, vinyl upholstery should be treated with a protectant. **Note:** *Make sure the protectant container indicates the product can be used on seats - some products may make a seat too slippery.* **Caution:** *Do not use a protectant on vinyl-covered steering wheels.*

5   Leather upholstery requires special care. It should be cleaned regularly with saddle soap or leather cleaner. Never use alcohol, gasoline, nail polish remover or thinner to clean leather upholstery.

6   After cleaning, regularly treat leather upholstery with a leather conditioner, rubbed in with a soft cotton cloth. Never use car wax on leather upholstery.

7   In areas where the interior of the vehicle is subject to bright sunlight, cover leather seating areas of the seats with a sheet if the vehicle is to be left out for any length of time.

5   Body repair - minor damage

Repair of scratches

1   If the scratch is superficial and does not penetrate to the metal of the body, repair is very simple. Lightly rub the scratched area with a fine rubbing compound to remove loose paint and built up wax. Rinse the area with clean water.

2   Apply touch-up paint to the scratch, using a small brush. Continue to apply thin layers of paint until the surface of the paint in the scratch is level with the surrounding paint. Allow the new paint at least two weeks to harden, then blend it into the surrounding paint by rubbing with a very fine rubbing compound. Finally, apply a coat of wax to the scratch area.

3   If the scratch has penetrated the paint and exposed the metal of the body, causing the metal to rust, a different repair technique is required. Remove all loose rust from the bottom of the scratch with a pocket knife, then apply rust inhibiting paint to prevent the formation of rust in the future. Using a rubber or nylon applicator, coat the scratched area with glaze-type filler. If required, the filler can be mixed with thinner to provide a very thin paste, which is ideal for filling narrow scratches. Before the glaze filler in the scratch hardens, wrap a piece of smooth cotton cloth around the tip of a finger. Dip the cloth in thinner and then quickly wipe it along the surface of the scratch. This will ensure that the surface of the filler is slightly hollow. The scratch can now be painted over as described earlier in this section.

Repair of dents

See photo sequence

4   When repairing dents, the first job is to pull the dent out until the affected area is as close as possible to its original shape. There is no point in trying to restore the original shape completely as the metal in the damaged area will have stretched on impact and cannot be restored to its original contours. It is better to bring the level of the dent up to a point which is about 1/8-inch below the level of the surrounding metal. In cases where the dent is very shallow, it is not worth trying to pull it out at all.

5   If the back side of the dent is accessible, it can be hammered out gently from behind using a soft-face hammer. While doing this, hold a block of wood firmly against the opposite side of the metal to absorb the hammer blows and prevent the metal from being stretched.

6   If the dent is in a section of the body which has double layers, or some other factor makes it inaccessible from behind, a different technique is required. Drill several small holes through the metal inside the damaged area, particularly in the deeper sections. Screw long, self tapping screws into the holes just enough for them to get a good grip in the metal. Now the dent can be pulled out by pulling on the protruding heads of the screws with locking pliers.

7   The next stage of repair is the removal of paint from the damaged area and from an inch or so of the surrounding metal. This is easily done with a wire brush or sanding disk in a drill motor, although it can be done just as effectively by hand with sandpaper. To complete the preparation for filling, score the surface of the bare metal with a screwdriver or the tang of a file or drill small holes in the affected area. This will provide a good grip for the filler material. To complete the repair, see the subsection on *filling and painting*.

Repair of rust holes or gashes

8   Remove all paint from the affected area and from an inch or so of the surrounding metal using a sanding disk or wire brush mounted in a drill motor. If these are not available, a few sheets of sandpaper will do the job just as effectively.

9   With the paint removed, you will be able to determine the severity of the corrosion and decide whether to replace the whole panel, if possible, or repair the affected area. New body panels are not as expensive as most people think and it is often quicker to install a new panel than to repair large areas of rust.

10   Remove all trim pieces from the affected area except those which will act as a guide to the original shape of the damaged body, such as headlight shells, etc. Using metal snips or a hacksaw blade, remove all loose metal and any other metal that is badly affected by rust. Hammer the edges of the hole on the inside to create a slight depression for the filler material.

11   Wire brush the affected area to remove the powdery rust from the surface of the metal. If the back of the rusted area is accessible, treat it with rust inhibiting paint.

12   Before filling is done, block the hole in some way. This can be done with sheet metal riveted or screwed into place, or by stuffing the hole with wire mesh.

13   Once the hole is blocked off, the affected area can be filled and painted. See the following subsection on *filling and painting*.

Filling and painting

14   Many types of body fillers are available, but generally speaking, body repair kits which contain filler paste and a tube of resin hardener are best for this type of repair work. A wide, flexible plastic or nylon applicator will be necessary for imparting a smooth and contoured finish to the surface of the filler material. Mix up a small amount of filler on a clean piece of wood or cardboard (use the hardener sparingly). Follow the manufacturer's instructions on the package, otherwise the filler will set incorrectly.

15   Using the applicator, apply the filler paste to the prepared area. Draw the applicator across the surface of the filler to achieve the desired contour and to level the filler surface. As soon as a contour that approximates the original one is achieved, stop working the paste. If you continue, the paste will begin to stick to the applicator. Continue to add thin layers of paste at 20-minute intervals until the level of the filler is just above the surrounding metal.

16   Once the filler has hardened, the excess can be removed with a body file. From then on, progressively finer grades of sandpaper should be used, starting with a 180-grit paper and finishing with 600-

grit wet-or-dry paper. Always wrap the sandpaper around a flat rubber or wooden block, otherwise the surface of the filler will not be completely flat. During the sanding of the filler surface, the wet-or-dry paper should be periodically rinsed in water. This will ensure that a very smooth finish is produced in the final stage.

17   At this point, the repair area should be surrounded by a ring of bare metal, which in turn should be encircled by the finely feathered edge of good paint. Rinse the repair area with clean water until all of the dust produced by the sanding operation is gone.

18   Spray the entire area with a light coat of primer. This will reveal any imperfections in the surface of the filler. Repair the imperfections with fresh filler paste or glaze filler and once more smooth the surface with sandpaper. Repeat this spray-and-repair procedure until you are satisfied that the surface of the filler and the feathered edge of the paint are perfect. Rinse the area with clean water and allow it to dry completely.

19   The repair area is now ready for painting. Spray painting must be carried out in a warm, dry, windless and dust free atmosphere. These conditions can be created if you have access to a large indoor work area, but if you are forced to work in the open, you will have to pick the day very carefully. If you are working indoors, dousing the floor in the work area with water will help settle the dust which would otherwise be in the air. If the repair area is confined to one body panel, mask off the surrounding panels. This will help minimize the effects of a slight mismatch in paint color. Trim pieces such as chrome strips, door handles, etc., will also need to be masked off or removed. Use masking tape and several thicknesses of newspaper for the masking operations.

20   Before spraying, shake the paint can thoroughly, then spray a test area until the spray painting technique is mastered. Cover the repair area with a thick coat of primer. The thickness should be built up using several thin layers of primer rather than one thick one. Using 600-grit wet-or-dry sandpaper, rub down the surface of the primer until it is very smooth. While doing this, the work area should be thoroughly rinsed with water and the wet-or-dry sandpaper periodically rinsed as well. Allow the primer to dry before spraying additional coats.

21   Spray on the top coat, again building up the thickness by using several thin layers of paint. Begin spraying in the center of the repair area and then, using a circular motion, work out until the whole repair area and about two inches of the surrounding original paint is covered. Remove all masking material 10 to 15 minutes after spraying on the final coat of paint. Allow the new paint at least two weeks to harden, then use a very fine rubbing compound to blend the edges of the new paint into the existing paint. Finally, apply a coat of wax.

6   Body repair - major damage

1   Major damage must be repaired by an auto body shop specifically equipped to perform unibody repairs. These shops have the specialized equipment required to do the job properly.

2   If the damage is extensive, the body must be checked for proper alignment or the vehicle's handling characteristics may be adversely affected and other components may wear at an accelerated rate.

3   Due to the fact that all of the major body components (hood, fenders, etc.) are separate and replaceable units, any seriously damaged components should be replaced rather than repaired. Sometimes the components can be found in a auto salvage or wrecking yard that specializes in used vehicle components, often at considerable savings over the cost of new parts.

7   Hinges and locks - maintenance

Once every 3000 miles, or every three months, the hinges and latch assemblies on the doors, hood and trunk should be given a few drops of light oil or lock lubricant. The door latch strikers should also be lubricated with a thin coat of grease to reduce wear and ensure free movement. Lubricate the door and trunk locks with spray-on graphite lubricant.

8   Windshield and fixed glass - replacement

Replacement of the windshield and fixed glass requires the use of special fast-setting adhesive/caulk materials and some specialized tools and techniques. These operations should be left to a dealer service department or a shop specializing in glass work.

9   Hood - removal, installation and adjustment

Refer to illustration 9.3
Note: *The hood is heavy and somewhat awkward to remove and install - at least two people should perform this procedure.*

Removal and installation

1   Use blankets or pads to cover the cowl area of the body and both fenders. This will protect the body and paint as the hood is lifted off.
2   Open the hood and support it on the prop rod.
3   Scribe alignment marks around the bolt heads to insure proper alignment during installation (a permanent-type felt-tip marker also will work for this) **(see illustration)**.
4   Disconnect any cables or electrical wire harnesses which will interfere with removal.
5   Have an assistant support the weight of the hood. Remove the hinge-to-hood bolts.
6   Lift off the hood.
7   Installation is the reverse of removal.

Adjustment

8   Fore-and-aft and side-to-side adjustment of the hood is done by moving the hood in relation to the hinge plate after loosening the bolts. The hood must be aligned so there is a 0.16-inch gap to the front fenders and flush with the top surface.
9   Scribe or trace a line around the entire hinge plate so you can judge the amount of movement.
10   Loosen the bolts and move the hood into correct alignment. Move it only a little at a time. Tighten the hinge bolts and carefully lower the hood to check the alignment.
11   Adjust the hood bumpers on the radiator support so the hood is flush with the fenders when closed.
12   The safety latch assembly can also be adjusted up-and-down and side-to-side after loosening the bolts.
13   The hood latch assembly, as well as the hinges, should be periodically lubricated with white lithium-base grease to prevent sticking and wear.

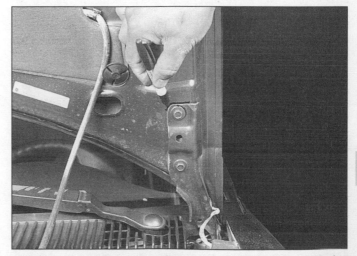

9.3 Use a marking pen to outline the hinge plate and bolt heads

11

These photos illustrate a method of repairing simple dents. They are intended to supplement *Body repair - minor damage* in this Chapter and should not be used as the sole instructions for body repair on these vehicles.

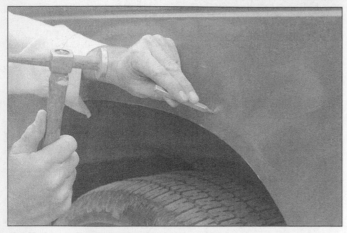

1 If you can't access the backside of the body panel to hammer out the dent, pull it out with a slide-hammer-type dent puller. In the deepest portion of the dent or along the crease line, drill or punch hole(s) at least one inch apart . . .

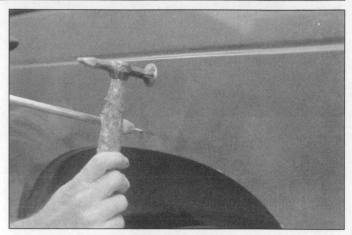

2 . . . then screw the slide-hammer into the hole and operate it. Tap with a hammer near the edge of the dent to help 'pop' the metal back to its original shape. When you're finished, the dent area should be close to its original contour and about 1/8-inch below the surface of the surrounding metal

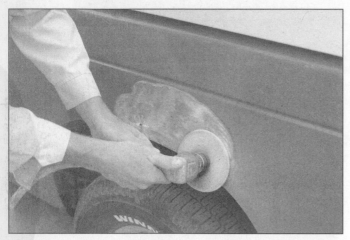

3 Using coarse-grit sandpaper, remove the paint down to the bare metal. Hand sanding works fine, but the disc sander shown here makes the job faster. Use finer (about 320-grit) sandpaper to feather-edge the paint at least one inch around the dent area

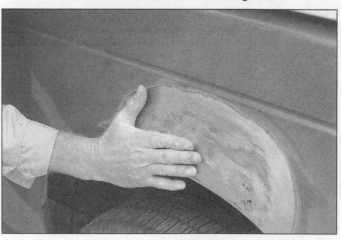

4 When the paint is removed, touch will probably be more helpful than sight for telling if the metal is straight. Hammer down the high spots or raise the low spots as necessary. Clean the repair area with wax/silicone remover

5 Following label instructions, mix up a batch of plastic filler and hardener. The ratio of filler to hardener is critical, and, if you mix it incorrectly, it will either not cure properly or cure too quickly (you won't have time to file and sand it into shape)

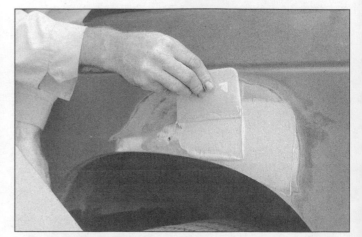

6 Working quickly so the filler doesn't harden, use a plastic applicator to press the body filler firmly into the metal, assuring it bonds completely. Work the filler until it matches the original contour and is slightly above the surrounding metal

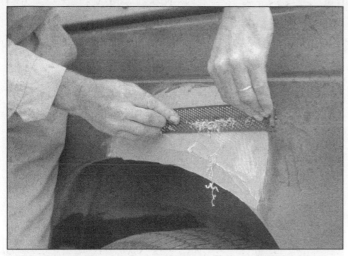

7   Let the filler harden until you can just dent it with your fingernail. Use a body file or Surform tool (shown here) to rough-shape the filler

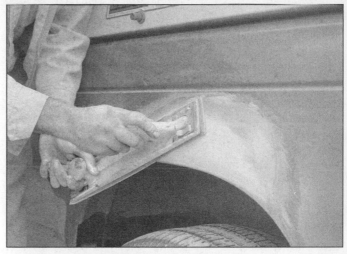

8   Use coarse-grit sandpaper and a sanding board or block to work the filler down until it's smooth and even. Work down to finer grits of sandpaper - always using a board or block - ending up with 360 or 400 grit

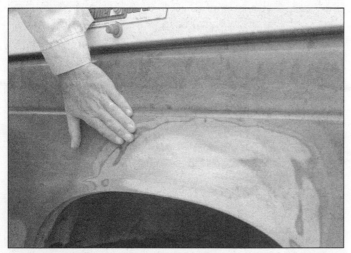

9   You shouldn't be able to feel any ridge at the transition from the filler to the bare metal or from the bare metal to the old paint. As soon as the repair is flat and uniform, remove the dust and mask off the adjacent panels or trim pieces

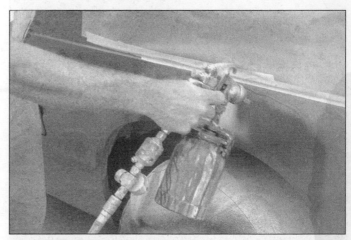

10   Apply several layers of primer to the area. Don't spray the primer on too heavy, so it sags or runs, and make sure each coat is dry before you spray on the next one. A professional-type spray gun is being used here, but aerosol spray primer is available inexpensively from auto parts stores

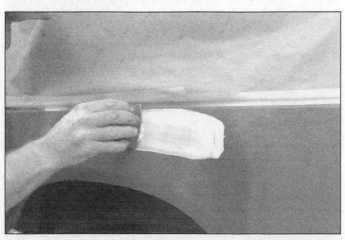

11   The primer will help reveal imperfections or scratches. Fill these with glazing compound. Follow the label instructions and sand it with 360 or 400-grit sandpaper until it's smooth. Repeat the glazing, sanding and respraying until the primer reveals a perfectly smooth surface

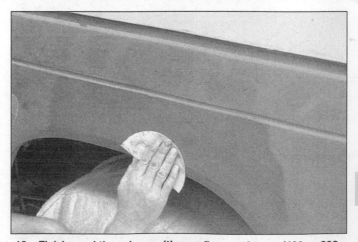

12   Finish sand the primer with very fine sandpaper (400 or 600-grit) to remove the primer overspray. Clean the area with water and allow it to dry. Use a tack rag to remove any dust, then apply the finish coat. Don't attempt to rub out or wax the repair area until the paint has dried completely (at least two weeks)

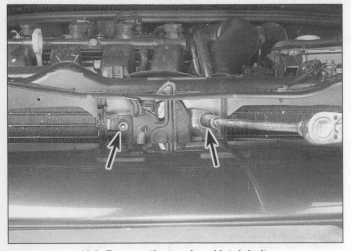

10.3 Remove the two hood latch bolts

10 Hood latch and cable - removal and installation

Warning: *These models have airbags. Always disconnect the negative battery cable and wait two minutes before working in the vicinity of the impact sensors, steering column or instrument panel to avoid the possibility of accidental deployment of the airbag, which could cause personal injury (see Chapter 12).*

Latch

Refer to illustration 10.3

1   Open the hood and support it on the prop rod.
2   Remove the radiator grille (see Section 11).
3   Remove the bolts and detach the latch assembly, then disconnect the release cable from the hood latch. **(see illustration)**.

Cable

Refer to illustrations 10.5a and 10.5b

4   Disconnect the release cable from the hood latch.
5   In the passenger compartment, remove the left front kick panel **(see illustration)**. Remove the screws securing the hood release handle and move the handle away from the cowl panel **(see illustration)**.
6   Under the dash, remove the cable grommet from the firewall.
7   Connect a piece of heavy string or flexible wire to the engine compartment end of the cable, then pull the release cable and wire through the firewall into the passenger compartment. Disconnect the string or wire from the old cable.

10.5a Carefully pry the kick panel free and remove it

8   Connect the string or wire to the new cable and pull it through the firewall into the engine compartment.
9   The remainder of the installation is the reverse of removal.

11 Radiator grille - removal and installation

Refer to illustration 11.2

Warning: *These models have airbags. Always disconnect the negative battery cable and wait two minutes before working in the vicinity of the impact sensors, steering column or instrument panel to avoid the possibility of accidental deployment of the airbag, which could cause personal injury (see Chapter 12).*

1   Open the hood and support it on the prop rod.
2   Remove the screws and detach the grille from the radiator closure and the park/turn signal assemblies **(see illustration)**. Remove the grille from the vehicle.
3   Installation is the reverse of removal.

12 Bumpers - removal and installation

Front bumper

Refer to illustrations 12.4a, 12.4b, 12.5 and 12.6

Warning: *These models have airbags. Always disconnect the negative battery cable and wait two minutes before working in the vicinity of the*

10.5b Remove the handle mounting screws (arrows)

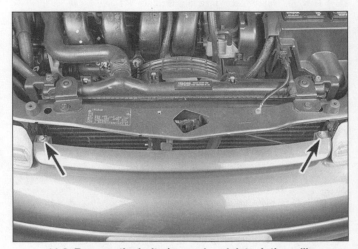

11.2 Remove the bolts (arrows) and detach the grille

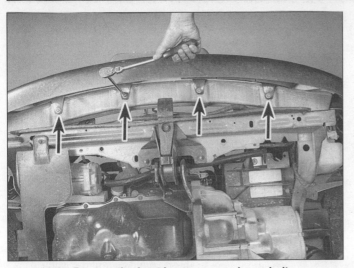

12.4a Remove the front bumper cover lower bolts . . .

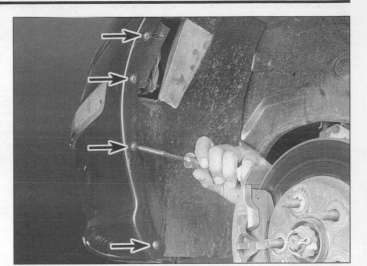

12.4b . . . then remove the screws on the sides, in the fenderwells

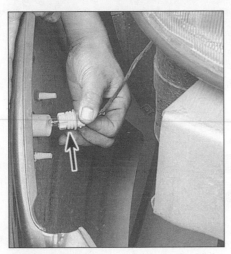

12.5 Pull the bumper away from the body, disconnect the side marker lights from each side, then remove the bumper

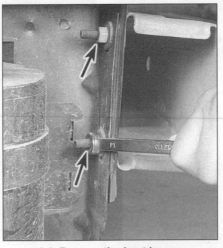

12.6 Remove the front bumper reinforcement nuts (arrows) on each side

12.12a Remove the lower push-in fasteners . . .

impact sensors, steering column or instrument panel to avoid the possibility of accidental deployment of the airbag, which could cause personal injury (see Chapter 12).

1   Remove the radiator grille (see Section 11).

2   Disconnect any wiring or other components that would interfere with front bumper cover removal.

3   Support the bumper with a jack or have an assistant support the bumper cover as the bolts and nuts are removed.

4   Remove the front bolts and side screws and partially remove the front bumper cover **(see illustrations).**

5   Disconnect the side marker lights from the bumper **(see illustration)** from each side, then remove the front bumper cover.

6   Remove the two nuts on each side and detach the front bumper reinforcement **(see illustration).** The bumper can now be removed.

7   Installation is the reverse of removal.

Rear bumper

Refer to illustrations 12.12a, 12.12b and 12.13

8   Open the trunk lid.

9   Disconnect any wiring or other components that would interfere with bumper cover removal.

10   Support the bumper with a jack or have an assistant support the bumper cover as the bolts and bolts are removed.

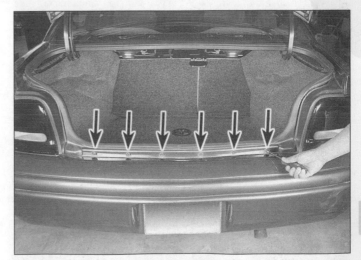

12.12b . . . and upper screws, then remove the rear bumper cover

11   Remove the rear license plate light assembly (see Chapter 12).

12   Remove the lower bolts and the top push-in fasteners and detach the rear bumper cover **(see illustrations).**

11

12.13 Remove the rear bumper reinforcement nuts and remove the unit

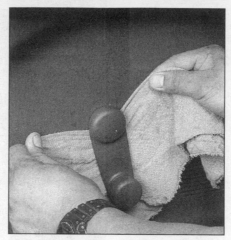

13.3 A shop cloth or thin towel will make window crank removal much easier

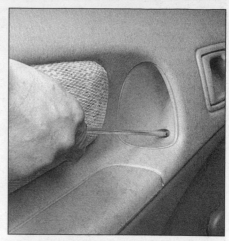

13.4 Remove the screws and remove the pull cup (four-door model shown)

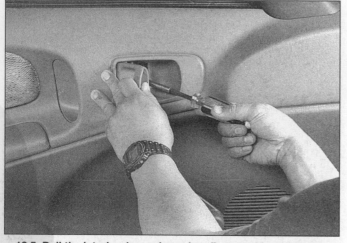

13.5 Pull the interior door release handle out and remove trim panel-to-door mounting screw

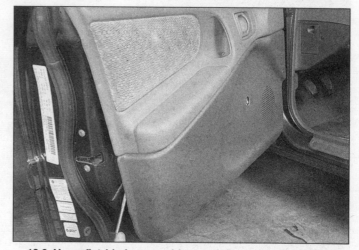

13.6 Use a flat-blade screwdriver and disengage the push-in fasteners around the perimeter of the trim panel , tilt the trim panel outward to clear the locator pins and detach the door trim panel

13   Remove the nuts and detach the rear bumper reinforcement **(see illustration)**.
14   Installation is the reverse of removal.

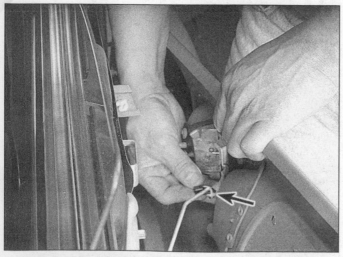

13.8 Partially move the trim panel away from the door and disengage the door handle latch linkage

13   Door trim panel - removal and installation

Refer to illustrations 13.3, 13.4, 13.5, 13.6 and 13.8
Note: *This procedure applies to both the front and rear doors on four-door models.*
1   Disconnect the negative cable from the battery.
2   Open door and completely lower window glass.
3   On manual window models, remove the window crank retaining clip by working a cloth back-and-forth behind the handle to dislodge the retainer **(see illustration)**.
4   Remove the screws and remove the pull cup **(see illustration)**.
5   Remove screw holding the trim panel to the door **(see illustration)**.
6   Disengage the push-in fasteners around the perimeter of the trim panel **(see illustration)**. Tilt the trim panel outward to clear the locator pins on backside of the trim panel.
7   Grasp the trim panel and pull up sharply to detach it from the retainer channel in the inner belt weatherstrip on top of the door.
8   Move the trim panel away from the door and disengage the clip holding the latch linkage from the backside of the door handle **(see illustration)**.
9   **Caution:** *Do not allow the trim panel to hang from the electrical wires.* On models so equipped, disconnect the electrical connectors from the power door lock switch, the mirror switch and power window switch and remove the trim panel.

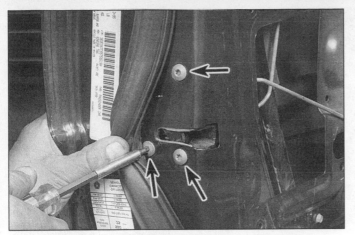

14.4 Use a Torx-head driver and remove the three screws (arrows)

14.5 Carefully detach the clips from the control rods, lower the rods, then remove the latch

10   Reconnect any electrical connectors and engage the latch linkage to the door handle clip.
11   Press trim panel down into place and seat all fasteners.
12   Install the door panel screw **(see illustration 13.5)**, the pull cup and window crank.

14 Door latch, lock cylinder and outside handle - removal and installation

Note: *This procedure applies to both the front and rear doors on four-door models.*
1   Close the window completely and remove the door trim panel (see Section 13).

Latch

Refer to illustrations 14.4 and 14.5
2   Disconnect the link rods from the latch.
3   On power door lock models, disconnect the electrical connector from door lock motor.
4   Remove the three mounting screws from the end of the door (it may be necessary to use an impact-type screwdriver to loosen them) **(see illustration)**.
5   Detach the clips from the control rods and detach the latch from the door **(see illustration)**.
6   Place the latch in position, install the screws and tighten them securely.
7   Connect the link rods to the latch.

Lock cylinder

8   Disconnect the link, use a screwdriver to push the key lock cylinder retainer off and withdraw the lock cylinder from the door handle assembly.
9   Installation is the reverse of removal.

Outside handle

10   Disconnect the links, remove the mounting nuts and detach the handle from the door.
11   Place the handle in position, attach the links and install the nut. Tighten the nut securely.

15 Door window glass - removal, installation and adjustment

Removal

Refer to illustrations 15.2, 15.3, 15.4, 15.5, 15.7 and 15.9
1   Remove the door trim panel (see Section 13).

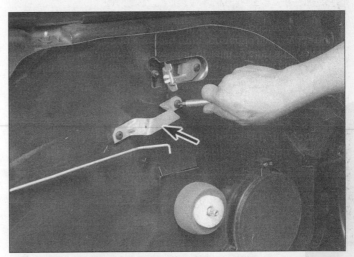

15.2 Remove the Torx screws and the mounting bracket (arrow)

15.3 Carefully pull the watershield free from the door

2   Remove the door speaker (if so equipped) and the door trim pull cup mounting bracket **(see illustration)**. Disengage the linkage clip from the lock button bell crank.
3   Remove the water shield **(see illustration)**.

11

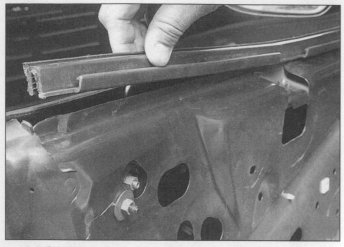

15.4 Carefully pull up and remove the inner belt weatherstrip

15.5 Loosen the inner belt stabilizer nut

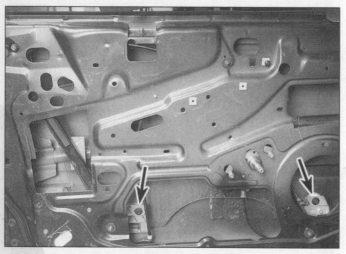

15.7 Lower the window glass to access the two nuts holding the regulator lift channel to door glass - carefully support to glass while removing these nuts

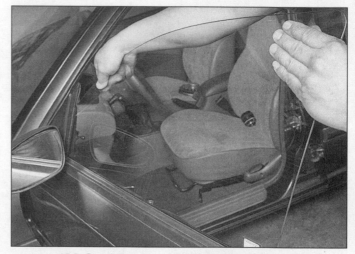

15.9 Carefully pull up and lift the door glass out

4   Carefully pull up and remove the inner belt weatherstrip **(see illustration)**.
5   Loosen the inner belt stabilizer nut **(see illustration)**.
6   If not already down, lower the window to gain access to the glass attachment fasteners.
7   Carefully support the glass, then remove the two nuts holding the regulator lift channel to door glass **(see illustration)**.
8   On four-door models, remove bolts holding the window regulator lift plates.
9   Carefully lift door glass up and out of opening at top of door **(see illustration)**.

Installation

10   Installation is the reverse of removal. Raise the window completely prior to tightening the inner belt stabilizer nut. Tighten all bolts and nuts securely. Make sure there is enough adhesive remaining on the water shield to seal properly, replace adhesive if necessary.

Adjustment

Refer to illustrations 15.11a, 15.11b and 15.14

Front door

11   If up-stops adjustment is necessary, loosen the up-stop nuts, close the door and raise the window completely. Adjust the up-stop to achieve proper glass height **(see illustrations)**. Adjustment is correct if a piece of paper can be pulled between the glass and weatherstrip with some tension. Tighten the nuts securely.

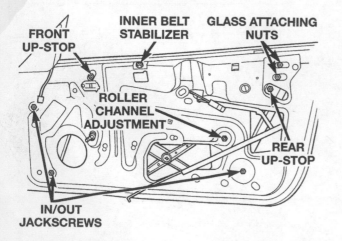

15.11a Loosen the front and rear up-stop nuts, close door and raise window completely. Adjust the glass height (two-door models)

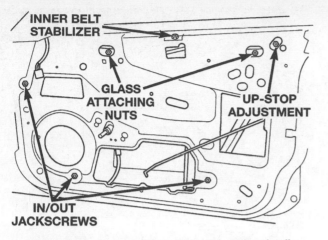

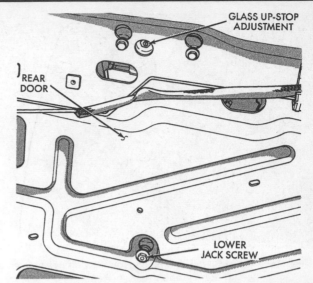

INNER BELT STABILIZER

GLASS ATTACHING NUTS

UP-STOP ADJUSTMENT

IN/OUT JACKSCREWS

15.11b Four-door model up-stop nut location details

GLASS UP-STOP ADJUSTMENT

REAR DOOR

LOWER JACK SCREW

15.14 Loosen the up-stop jamb nut, close the door and raise the window completely to adjust the glass height

12   If the top of the glass in-and-out adjustment is necessary, loosen the lower jack screw jamb nuts, close the door and raise the window completely. Using an Allen wrench, rotate the jack screws to achiever proper glass in-out position at the top edge of the glass (see illustrations 15.11a, 15.11b). Tighten the jamb nuts securely.

13   If the front-to-rear adjustment is necessary, lower the window completely. Loosen the three bolts holding the window regulator lift plates (see illustration 15.7). Close the door and raise the window completely. Adjust window glass to fit the B-pillar seal so there is a gap of 1/2-inch between the glass and the B-pillar appliqué. Tighten the two visible bolts, lower the window and tighten the remaining bolt securely.

Rear door

14   If the up-stop adjustment is necessary, loosen the up-stop jamb nut, close door and raise the window completely. Adjust the up-stop to achieve proper glass height (see illustration). Adjustment is correct if a piece of paper can be pulled between the glass and weatherstrip with some tension. Tighten the nut securely.

15   If the top of the glass in-and-out adjustment is necessary, loosen the lower jack screw jamb nut, close the door and raise the window completely. Using an Allen wrench, rotate the jack screws to achiever proper glass in-out position at the top edge of the glass (see illustration 15.14). Tighten the jamb nut securely.

16   Door window regulator - removal and installation

Note: *Door window regulator removal and installation procedures are identical for both manual and power operated windows.*

Two-door models (either door)

Refer to illustrations 16.3, 16.7, 16.9a and 16.9b
Warning: *On power window models, do not remove the motor from the regulator assembly without first clamping the sector gear to the mounting plate or serious injury may result.*

1   Remove the door trim panel (see Section 13).
2   On power window models, make sure the electrical connector is unplugged.
3   Remove the two nuts holding the regulator lift channel to the door glass (see illustration).
4   Raise the door glass and secure it in the up position.
5   Mark the position of the roller channel rear bolt to the inner door panel. This will make installation easier.
6   Remove the rear bolt securing the roller channel to the door panel.
7   Loosen the front bolt securing the roller channel to the door panel. Separate the roller channel from the door panel (see illustration).

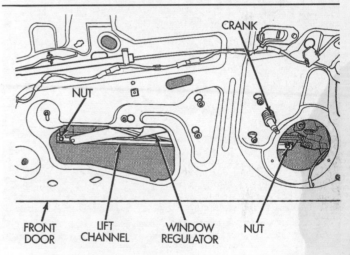

CRANK

NUT

FRONT DOOR   LIFT CHANNEL   WINDOW REGULATOR   NUT

16.3 Remove the two regulator lift channel-to-door glass mounting nuts

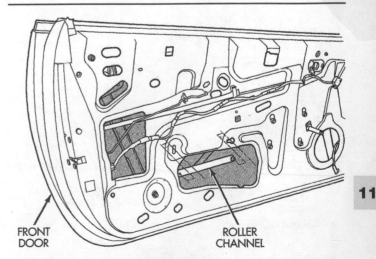

FRONT DOOR

ROLLER CHANNEL

16.7 Loosen the front roller channel-to-door panel bolts, then separate the roller channel from the door panel

11

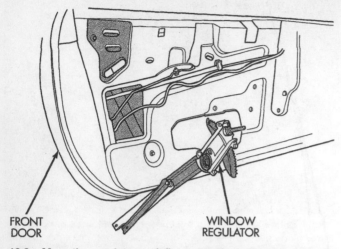

16.9a Move the regulator and disengage the bolt heads from the key slots, then lift the regulator rearward and out of the access hole (manual windows)

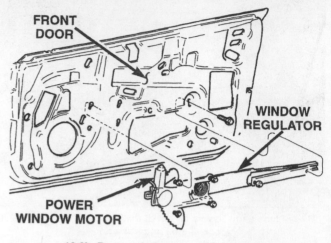

16.9b Power window removal details

16.14a Remove the three window regulator-to-inner door panel mounting bolts (manual windows)

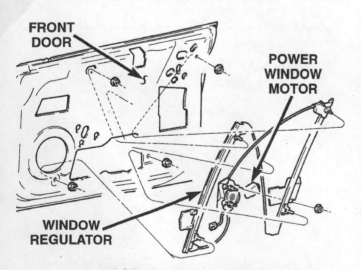

16.14b Power window removal details

8   Loosen the bolts holding the window regulator to the inner door panel.

9   Move the regulator and disengage the bolt heads from the key slots in the inner door panel. Remove the window regulator from the large access hole in the door **(see illustrations)**.

10   Installation is the reverse of removal. If necessary, adjust the door glass (see Section 15).

Four-door models

Front door

Refer to illustrations 16.14a and 16.14b

Warning: *On power window models, do not remove the motor from the regulator assembly without first clamping the sector gear to the mounting plate or serious injury may result.*

11   Remove the door trim panel (see Section 13).

12   Remove the door window glass (see Section 15).

13   On power window models, make sure the electrical connector is unplugged.

14   Remove the bolts holding the window regulator to the inner door panel **(see illustrations)**.

15   Loosen the bolts securing the roller window regulator to the door panel.

16   Move the regulator and disengage the bolt heads from the key slots in the inner door panel. Remove the window regulator from the large access hole in the door.

17   Installation is the reverse of removal. If necessary, adjust the door glass (see Section 15).

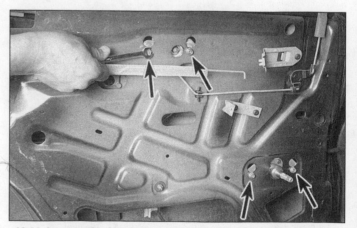

16.21 Loosen the four bolts holding the window regulator to the inner door panel

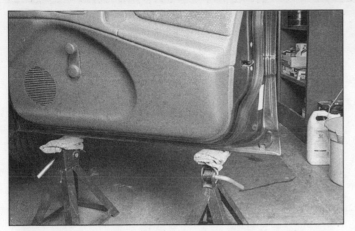

17.4 Place shop towels on top of the jack pad, then place the jack stands under the door

17.5 Remove the clip from the lower hinge pin, then remove the lower hinge pin. Do the same for the upper hinge pin, then lift off the door

Rear door

Refer to illustration 16.21

Warning: *On power window models, do not remove the motor from the regulator assembly without first clamping the sector gear to the mounting plate or serious injury may result.*

18   Remove the door trim panel (see Section 13).

19   Remove the door window glass (see Section 15).

20   On power window models, make sure the electrical connector is unplugged.

21   Loosen the four bolts holding the window regulator to the inner door panel **(see illustration).**

22   Move the regulator and disengage the bolt heads from the key slots in the inner door panel.

23   Loosen the bolts holding the window regulator lift bar to the inner door panel, then disengage the bolt heads from the key slots in the inner door panel. Remove the window regulator from the large access hole in the door.

24   Installation is the reverse of removal. If necessary, adjust the door glass (see Section 15).

17   Door - removal and installation

Refer to illustrations 17.4 and 17.5

1   Remove the door trim panel (see Section 13).

2   Disconnect any wire harness connectors and push them through the door opening so they won't interfere with door removal.

3   Remove the bolts and detach check strap from the door hinge.

4   Place a jack or jack stands under the door or have an assistant on hand to support it when the hinge pins are removed **(see illustration).**
Note: *If a jack is used, place a rag between it and the door to protect the door's painted surfaces.*

5   Remove the clip from the lower hinge pin, then remove the lower hinge pin **(see illustration).**

6   Remove clip from the upper hinge pin, make sure door is properly supported then remove upper hinge pin **(see illustration 17.5).** Remove the door.

7   Installation is the reverse of removal, making sure both hinge pin clips are properly secured in the hinge pins.

18   Quarter glass - replacement

Refer to illustrations 18.4 and 18.5

1   Remove the back seat (see Section 28).

2   Slide the lower seat belt anchor cover up the webbing. Remove the belt anchor bolt from the floor and separate the belt from floor.

3   Remove the coat hook.

4   Carefully disengage the quarter panel hidden clips, feed the upper belt trough the opening in the panel and remove the quarter trim panel **(see illustration).**

5   Remove the mounting nuts holding the quarter glass to the quarter panel opening **(see illustration).**

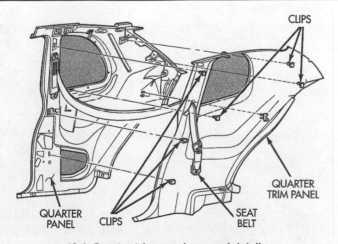

18.4 Quarter trim panel removal details

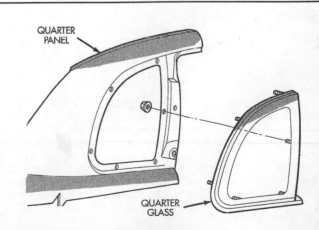

18.5 Remove the quarter glass mounting nuts and remove the glass

11

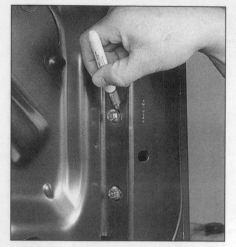

19.3 Use a marking pen to outline the hinge plate and bolt heads

19.4 Remove the hinge bolts and lift the trunk lid off

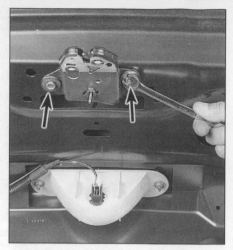

19.9 Remove the latch bolts, lower the latch and detach the remote cable

6   Remove the B-pillar appliqué.

7   Have an assistant hold onto the quarter glass on the outside. Working on the inside of the vehicle, using a sharp knife, push outward on the glass while cutting the butyl tape adhesive around the perimeter of the glass. Remove the quarter glass.

8   Clean the old butyl tape adhesive from the quarter panel glass opening. If the original glass is going to be reinstalled, clean all old tape residue from the glass panel. **Note:** *Be sure to remove all tape residue to ensure a good water-tight seal when the glass is installed.*

9   Prime the perimeter of the quarter panel glass fence opening and the perimeter of the quarter glass with black-out primer.

10   Apply a 5/16-inch bead of round butyl tape around the perimeter of the quarter glass.

11   Install the quarter glass into the opening and secure it with the nuts. Tighten the nuts securely in a crisscross pattern.

12   Install the B-pillar appliqué.

13   Install the quarter trim panel and tighten the seat belt bolts securely.

19   Trunk lid and latch- removal, installation and adjustment

Trunk lid

Refer to illustrations 19.3 and 19.4

1   Open the trunk lid and cover the edges of the trunk compartment with pads or cloths to protect the painted surfaces when the lid is removed.

2   Disconnect any cables or electrical connectors attached to the trunk lid that would interfere with removal.

3   Use a marking pen to make alignment marks around the hinge bolt heads **(see illustration)**.

4   While an assistant supports it's weight, remove the hinge bolts from both sides and lift the trunk lid off **(see illustration)**.

5   Installation is the reverse of removal. **Note:** *When reinstalling the trunk lid, align the hinge bolt heads with the marks made during removal.*

6   After installation, close the lid and see if it's in proper alignment with the surrounding panels. Fore-and-aft and side-to-side adjustments of the lid are controlled by the position of the hinge bolts in the holes. To adjust it, loosen the hinge bolts, reposition the lid and retighten the bolts.

7   The height of the lid in relation to the surrounding body panels when closed can be adjusted by loosening the lock striker bolts, repositioning the striker and retightening the bolts.

Latch

Refer to illustration 19.9

8   Open the trunk.

9   Remove the latch bolts and lower the latch from the trunk **(see illustration)**.

10   Detach the remote cable and disconnect the trunk ajar electrical connector from the latch and remove it. The lock cylinder link will stay attached to the trunk.

11   Installation is the reverse of removal, making sure the lock cylinder link meshes properly with the latch assembly.

20   Instrument panel top cover - removal and installation

Refer to illustrations 20.2 and 20.3

Warning: *These models have airbags. Always disconnect the negative battery cable and wait two minutes before working in the vicinity of the impact sensors, steering column or instrument panel to avoid the possibility of accidental deployment of the airbag, which could cause personal injury (see Chapter 12).* **Caution:** *This cover can be easily scratched, take care in removing the top cover to avoid damage.*

1   Disconnect the negative cable from the battery.

2   Carefully pry up and lift up the bottom outer areas of the top cover and along the rearward edge of the panel top cover and disengage the mounting clips **(see illustration)**.

20.2 Using a flat-blade screwdriver, carefully pry up and lift the bottom outer areas of the top cover and along the rearward edge of the panel top cover to disengage the mounting clips

20.3 Using both hands, pull the assembly toward the rear until the forward pins disengage, then remove the cover panel

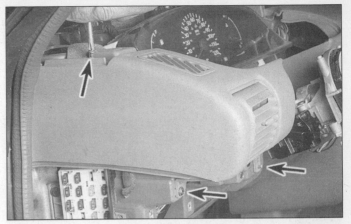

21.3 After removing the mounting screws, detach the left trim panel

3   Pull the panel top cover assembly toward the rear until the forward pins disengage from the instrument panel **(see illustration)**.
4   Installation is the reverse of removal. Position the spring clips on the panel top cover and push them on until correctly seated.

21 Dashboard trim panels - removal and installation

Warning: *These models have airbags. Always disconnect the negative battery cable and wait two minutes before working in the vicinity of the impact sensors, steering column or instrument panel to avoid the possibility of accidental deployment of the airbag, which could cause personal injury (see Chapter 12).* **Caution:** *The following trim covers can be easily scratched, take care in removing them to avoid damage.*

Left trim panel

Refer to illustration 21.3
1   Remove the instrument panel top cover (see Section 20).
2   Remove the steering column covers (see Section 24).
3   Remove the two bottom and one top attachment screws, pull toward the rear and detach the left trim panel **(see illustration)**.
4   Installation is the reverse of removal.

Right trim panel

Refer to illustrations 21.7 and 21.8
5   Remove the instrument panel top cover (see Section 20).
6   Reach under the panel and unplug the rear window defogger and/or fog lamp switch wiring connector(s).
7   Remove the six forward portion attachment screws, pull the

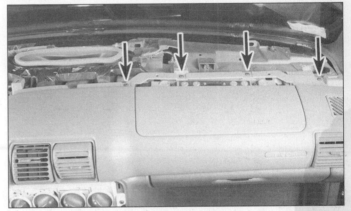

21.7 Remove the attachment screws (arrows), then pull the flange forward to disengage the three locator pins

flange forward to disengage the three locator pins **(see illustration)**.
8   Pull the panel toward the rear until the clips along the bottom disengage and remove the assembly **(see illustration)**.
9   Installation is the reverse of removal.

Center bezel

Refer to illustrations 21.12 and 21.14
10   Remove the steering column covers (see Section 24).
11   Remove the radio (see Chapter 12).
12   Remove the ash receiver **(see illustration)**.

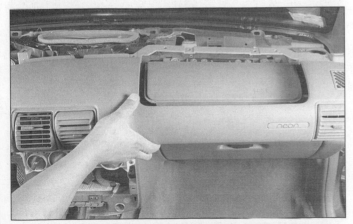

21.8 Pull the panel toward the rear, releasing the clips and remove the assembly

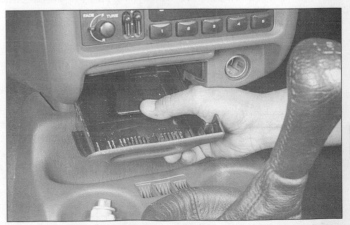

21.12 Pull out and remove the ashtray, remove the two ashtray bracket screws and remove the bracket

21.14 Using both hands, pull the bezel toward the rear and remove it

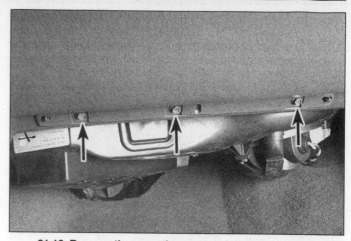

21.16 Remove the mounting screws (arrows) and open the glovebox

13   Remove the two ash receiver receptacle attachment screws and remove receiver.

14   Grasp the bezel on each side, pull it toward the rear and remove it **(see illustration)**.

15   Installation is the reverse of removal.

Glovebox

Refer to illustrations 21.16 and 21.17

16   Remove the screws along the bottom edge and open the glovebox **(see illustration)**.

17   Squeeze the sidewalls in and remove the glovebox from the dashboard assembly **(see illustration)**.

18   Installation is the reverse of removal.

22   Passenger airbag - removal and installation

Refer to illustrations 22.5, 22.6, 22.7a and 22.7b

Warning: *Always disconnect the negative battery cable and wait two minutes before working in the vicinity of the impact sensors, steering column or instrument panel to avoid the possibility of accidental deployment of the airbag, which could cause personal injury (see Chapter 12).*

1   Disconnect the negative cable from the battery.

2   Remove the instrument panel top cover (see Section 20).

3   Remove the instrument right trim panel (see Section 21).

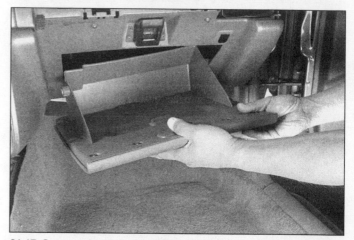

21.17 Squeeze in on the glovebox sidewall and remove it from the instrument panel

4   Open the glovebox, squeeze the sidewalls in and hinge the glovebox all the way down.

5   Remove the four screws securing the airbag to the top of the instrument panel **(see illustration)**.

6   Remove the two nuts securing the airbag to the support structure **(see illustration)**.

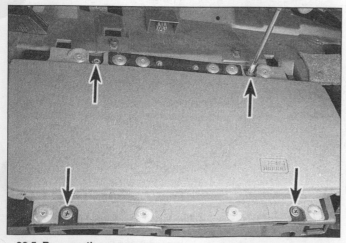

22.5 Remove the passenger air bag mounting screws (arrows)

22.6 Under the instrument panel, remove the two mounting nuts (arrow) - left nut not visible in this photo

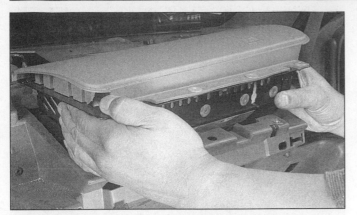

22.7a Lift the airbag module up and out of the instrument panel

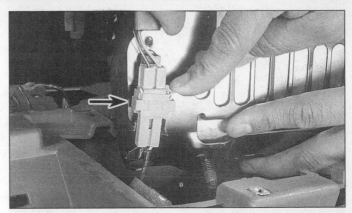

22.7b Unplug the four-pin electrical connector (arrow) and remove the airbag module. Refer to Warning in text regarding how to safely carry the airbag assembly

7   Lift the airbag module up **(see illustration)**, squeeze the red locking tab, compress the lock and unplug the 4-pin module electrical connector **(see illustration)** and remove the airbag module. **Warning:** *Carry the airbag with the trim cover side FACING AWAY from your body to minimize injury if the airbag module accidentally deploys. Set the airbag module aside in a safe, isolated location and set it down with the trim cover side facing up.*

8   **Warning:** *Do not reconnect the airbag module electrical connector yourself. Take the vehicle to a dealer's service department and have the airbag system checked prior to reconnecting the connector.* Installation is the reverse of removal. Ensure that the red locking tab is in the locked position after attaching the connector **(see illustration 22.7b)**. Tighten the screws and nuts securely.

9   From the *driver's side* of the vehicle, turn the ignition switch to the Off position, then turn it to the On position. Check that the instrument cluster AIRBAG lamp illuminates for six to eight seconds and then goes out indicating the airbag system is functioning properly. If the lamp fails to light, blinks on and off or stays on, there is a malfunction in the airbag system. If any of these conditions exist, the vehicle should be diagnosed by a dealer service department.

23   Instrument panel - removal and installation

Refer to illustrations 23.13, 23.14, 23.15, 23.17, 23.18a, 23.18b, 23.19, 23.20a, 23.20b, 23.21, 23.22, 23.23, 23.24a, 23.24b and 23.25
Warning: *These models have airbags. Always disconnect the negative battery cable and wait two minutes before working in the vicinity of the*

impact sensors, steering column or instrument panel to avoid the possibility of accidental deployment of the airbag, which could cause personal injury (see Chapter 12). **Caution:** *These panels can be easily scratched, take care in removing the panels to avoid damage.*
Note: *It is not necessary, but it is suggested to remove both front seats to allow additional working space and lessen the chance of damage to the seat during this procedure.*

1   Disconnect the negative cable from the battery.
2   Remove the steering wheel (see Chapter 10).
3   Remove the passenger airbag assembly (see Section 22).
4   Remove the center console (see Section 25).
5   Remove the right and left trim panels (see Section 21).
6   Remove the center bezel and glovebox (see Section 21).
7   Remove the steering column cover and liner (see Section 24).
8   Remove the instrument panel top cover (see Section 20).
9   Remove the instrument cluster (see Chapter 12).
10   Remove the center vent duct, defroster duct and inner defroster duct.
11   Remove the radio (see Chapter 12).
12   Remove the heater/air conditioning control assembly (see Chapter 3).
13   Remove the right side air duct **(see illustration)**.
14   Disconnect the windshield wiper motor electrical connector from the resistor and pull the wire harness through the firewall grommet **(see illustration)**.
15   Remove the fuse panel mounting screws and move the panel out of the way **(see illustration)**.

23.13 Pull back and remove the right side air duct

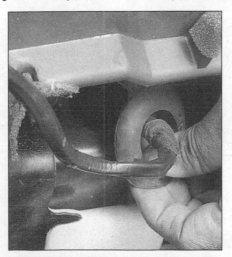

23.14 Pull the wire harness through the firewall grommet

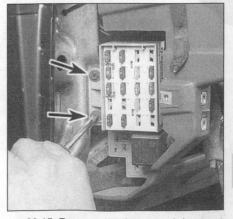

23.15 Remove the fuse panel door, remove the fuse panel mounting screws (arrows) and move the panel out of the way. It is not necessary to disconnect the fuse panel electrical connectors

11

23.17 Remove the pin from the steering shaft joint

23.18a Remove the steering column front mounting
nuts (arrows) . . .

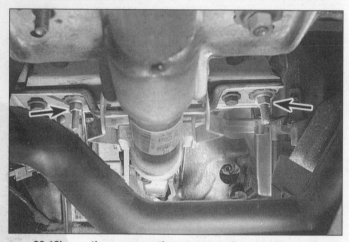

23.18b . . . then remove the rear mounting nuts (arrows)

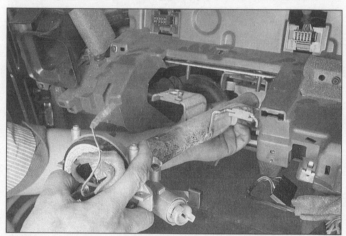

23.19 Pull the steering column straight out and remove it from the
instrument panel

16   Disconnect all electrical connectors interfering with removal.

17   Mark the relationship of the universal joint to the steering gear input shaft, then remove the pin from the steering shaft joint (see illustration).

18   Remove nuts attaching the steering column to the instrument panel (see illustrations).

19   Remove the steering column (see illustration).

20   Remove the center floor pan bracket bolts on each side (see illustrations).

21   Remove the four nuts securing the instrument panel at the base of the windshield (see illustration).

22   Remove the powertrain diagnostic connector mounting screw and move the connector out of the way (see illustration).

23   Remove the lower side bracket mounting bolt on each side

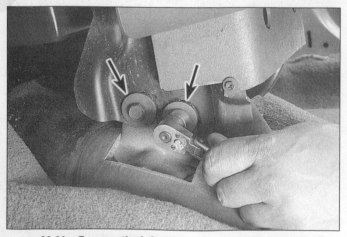

23.20a Remove the left side center floor pan bracket
bolts (arrows) . . .

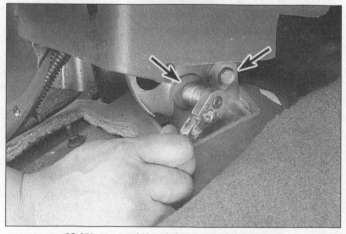

23.20b . . . and the right side bolts (arrows)

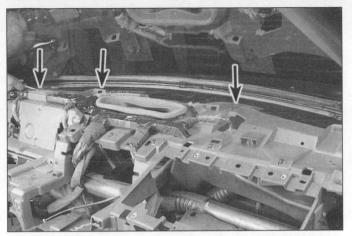

23.21 At the base of the windshield, remove the four instrument panel mounting nuts (arrows) (only three are shown)

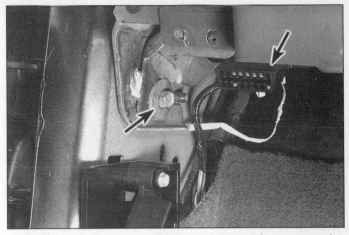

23.22 Remove the diagnostic connector mounting screw and move the connector (right arrow) out of the way. Remove the lower left side bracket mounting bolt (left arrow)

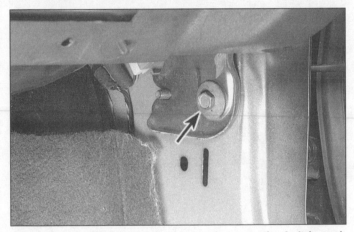

23.23 Remove the lower right side bracket mounting bolt (arrow)

23.24a Remove the upper left side mounting bolt (arrow) . . .

(see illustration).

24   Remove the upper mounting bolt on each side (see illustrations).

25   Carefully pull the instrument panel assembly away from the windshield and the dash/plenum and then remove the assembly out through the door opening (see illustration).

26   Installation is the reverse of removal.

24   Steering column covers - removal and installation

Refer to illustrations 24.2, 24.4a, 24.4b and 24.5

Warning: These models have airbags. Always disconnect the negative battery cable and wait two minutes before working in the vicinity of the

23.24b . . . then remove the upper right side mounting bolt (arrow)

23.25 Using both hands, pull the instrument panel assembly down and toward the rear, then remove the assembly out through either door opening

11

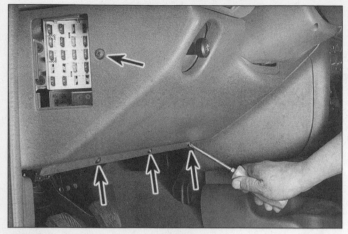

24.2 Remove the three screws (arrows) along the bottom and the one screw (arrow) on the left side.

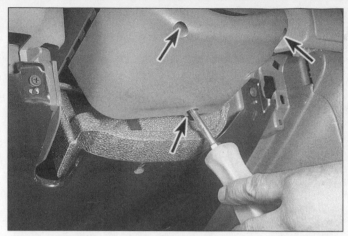

24.4a Remove the three steering column cover screws (arrows) . . .

24.4b . . . then separate the lower and upper covers and remove them

24.5 Remove the three screws (arrows) (one screw not visible) and remove the steering column cover liner

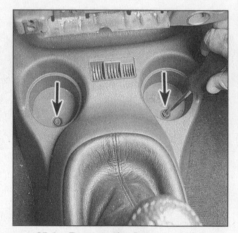

25.4a Remove the front retaining screws (arrows) . . .

impact sensors, steering column or instrument panel to avoid the possibility of accidental deployment of the airbag, which could cause personal injury (see Chapter 12). **Caution:** *This cover can be easily scratched, take care in removing the column cover to avoid damage.*

1   Disconnect the negative cable from the battery.

2   Remove the three attachment screws along the bottom and the one screw on the left side of the steering column cover **(see illustration)**.

3   Grasp the cover and pull toward the rear to disengage the retaining clips, remove the cover.

4   Remove the three steering column shroud attachment screws and remove the lower and upper shrouds **(see illustrations)**.

5   Remove the two attachment screws at the upper area and the one screw on the lower left corner of the steering column cover liner **(see illustration)**.

6   Grasp the cover and pull toward the rear to disengage the retaining clips, remove the cover liner.

7   Installation is the reverse of removal.

25   Center console - removal and installation

Refer to illustrations 25.4a, 25.5b and 25.6

Warning: *These models have airbags. Always disconnect the negative battery cable and wait two minutes before working in the vicinity of the impact sensors, steering column or instrument panel to avoid the possibility of accidental deployment of the airbag, which could cause per-*

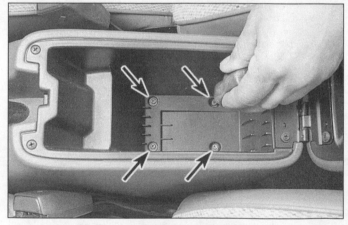

25.4b . . . and the rear screws (arrows)

sonal injury (see Chapter 12). **Caution:** *The center console can be easily scratched, take care in removing the assembly to avoid damage.*

1   Disconnect the negative cable from the battery.

2   Completely raise the parking brake lever.

3   On 1997 models, remove the rear side trim plates and remove the retaining screws on each side.

4   Remove the front and rear plugs and center console retaining screws **(see illustrations)**.

25.6 Lift the rear portion up and over the shift lever and parking brake handle and remove it from the vehicle

26.1a The interior mirror fits over a button bonded to the windshield and is held in place by a Phillips head set screw - loosen this screw . . .

26.1b . . . and slide the mirror up off the button

26.4a Unsnap and partially remove the inner cover . . .

5   On manual transaxle models, remove the shift lever knob.
6   Lift the rear portion of the center console up and over the shift lever and parking brake handle and remove from vehicle **(see illustration)**.
7   Installation is the reverse of removal.

26 Mirrors - removal and installation

Interior

Refer to illustrations 26.1a and 26.1b
1   Use a Phillips head screwdriver to remove the set screw, then slide the mirror up off the button on the windshield **(see illustrations)**.
2   Installation is the reverse of removal.

Exterior

Refer to illustrations 26.4a, 26.4b and 26.6
3   Remove the door trim panel (see Section 13).
4   Unsnap and partially remove the inner cover **(see illustration)**. Remove the Allen screw mounting the adjustment cable assembly, then remove the cover **(see illustration)**.

11

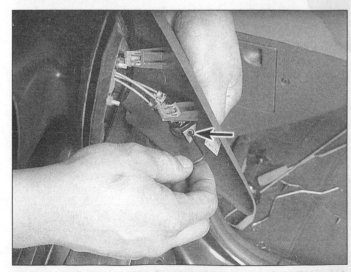

26.4b . . . remove the Allen screw and disconnect the adjustment cable assembly from the cover

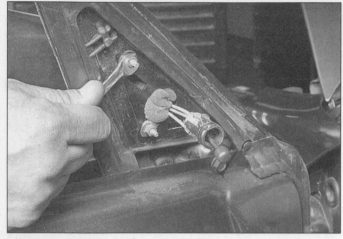

26.6 Remove the mounting nuts and detach the mirror from the mirror stanchion

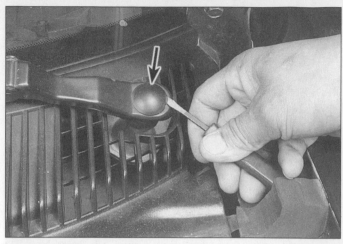

27.1a Pry off the plastic trim cap (arrow) . . .

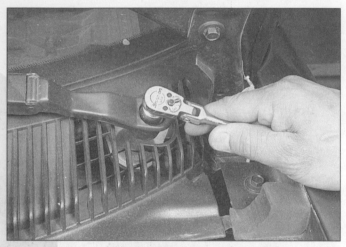

27.1b . . . remove the wiper arm retaining nuts . . .

27.1c . . . and remove both wiper arms

5   On power mirrors, remove the watershield (see Section 13), then unplug the electrical connector.
6   Remove the nuts and detach the mirror from the mirror stanchion on the door **(see illustration)**.
7   Installation is the reverse of removal.

27 Cowl cover - removal and installation

Refer to illustrations 27.1a, 27.1b, 27.1c, 27.2 and 27.3
1   Pry off the plastic trim cap on the windshield wiper arms, then detach the wiper arm retaining nuts and remove the wiper arms **(see illustrations)**.

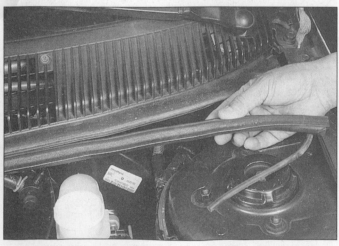

27.2 Carefully remove the rubber hood sealing strip from the front edge of the cowl cover

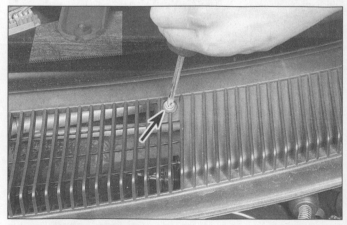

27.3 Remove the retaining screw (arrow) on each side and remove the cowl cover

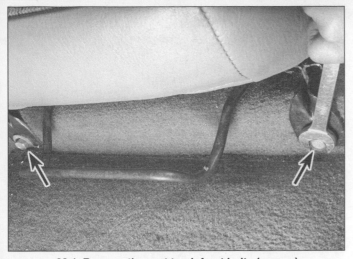

28.1 Remove the seat track front bolts (arrows)

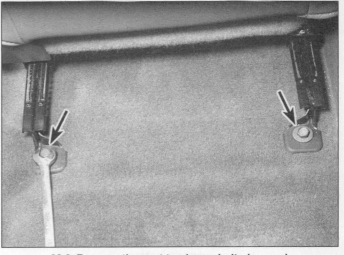

28.2 Remove the seat track rear bolts (arrows)

2   Carefully remove the rubber hood sealing strip **(see illustration)**.
3   Remove the retaining screw on each side securing the cowl cover and remove it **(see illustration)**.
4   Installation is the reverse of removal.

28 Seats - removal and installation

Front

Refer to illustrations 28.1 and 28.2

1   Move the seat rearward and remove the seat track front bolts **(see illustration)**.
2   Move the seat forward and remove the seat track rear bolts **(see illustration)**.

3   Unplug any electrical connectors attached to the seat and lift the seat from the vehicle.
4   Installation is the reverse of removal.

Rear

Refer to illustrations 28.7a and 28.7b

5   Remove the seat cushion by grasping the front edge securely, then pulling up sharply to detach the cushion.
6   On child restraint seat models, open the child seat and remove the lining. Remove the two retaining bolts within the lining area.
7   Remove the seat back and seat and seat belt retaining bolts **(see illustration)**, lift up at the rear to disengage the hooks from the slots and remove the seat back out of the vehicle **(see illustration)**.
8   Installation is the reverse of removal.

28.7a Remove the seat back and seat belt retaining bolts (arrows) . . .

28.7b . . . lift up at the rear to disengage the hooks from the slots (arrows) and remove the seat back

11

Notes

Chapter 12
Chassis electrical system

Contents

Specifications

Light bulb types

Front
Fog light	GE881
Headlight	9007
Park/turn signal	3157NA
Side marker (front)	168
Underhood light	105

Interior
Ash tray	161
Cigar lighter bulb	203
Climate control bulb	203
Console gear selector (ATX)	194
Dome light bulb	578
Glove box bulb	194
Ignition key bulb	161
Instrument pane and cluster light bulb	PC194
Rear cargo	912

Rear
Backup light	3157
Brake/turn signal/taillight	3157
Center high-mounted brake light	921
License plate light	168
Side marker (rear)	916

1 General information

The electrical system is a 12-volt, negative ground type. Power for the lights and all electrical accessories is supplied by a lead/acid-type battery which is charged by the alternator.

This Chapter covers repair and service procedures for the various electrical components not associated with the engine. Information on the battery, alternator, distributor and starter motor can be found in Chapter 5. **Warning:** *When working on the electrical system, disconnect the negative battery cable from the battery to prevent electrical shorts and/or fires.*

2 Electrical troubleshooting

A typical electrical circuit consists of an electrical component, any switches, relays, motors, fuses, fusible links or circuit breakers related to the component and the wiring and connectors that link the component to both the battery and the chassis. To help pinpoint an electrical circuit problem, wiring diagrams are included at the end of this Chapter.

Before tackling any troublesome electrical circuit, first study the appropriate wiring diagrams to get a complete understanding of what makes up that individual circuit. Trouble spots, for instance, can often be narrowed down by noting if other components related to the circuit are operating properly. If several components or circuits fail at one time, chances are the problem is in a fuse or ground connection, because several circuits are often routed through the same fuse and ground connections.

Electrical problems usually stem from simple causes, such as loose or corroded connections, a blown fuse, a melted fusible link or a bad relay. Visually inspect the condition of all fuses, wires and connections in a problem circuit before troubleshooting it.

If testing instruments are going to be utilized, plan ahead of time where to make the necessary connections to accurately pinpoint the trouble spot.

The basic tools needed for electrical troubleshooting include a circuit tester or voltmeter (a 12-volt bulb with a set of test leads can also be used), a continuity tester (which includes a bulb, battery and set of test leads) and a jumper wire, preferably with a fuse or circuit breaker incorporated, which can be used to bypass electrical components. Before attempting to locate a problem with test instruments, use the wiring diagram(s) to decide where to make the connections.

Voltage checks

Voltage checks should be performed if a circuit isn't functioning properly. Connect one lead of a circuit tester to either the negative battery terminal or a known good ground. Connect the other lead to a connector in the circuit being tested, preferably nearest to the battery or fuse. If the bulb of the tester lights, voltage is present, which means the part of the circuit between the connector and the battery is problem free. Continue checking the rest of the circuit in the same fashion. When you reach a point where no voltage is present, the problem lies between that point and the last test point with voltage. Most of the time the problem can be traced to a loose connection. **Note:** *Keep in mind that some circuits receive voltage only when the ignition key is in the Accessory or Run position.*

Finding a short

One method of finding a short in a circuit is to remove the fuse and connect a test light or voltmeter in its place to the fuse terminals. There should be no voltage present in the circuit. Move the wiring harness from side-to-side while watching the test light. If the bulb lights, there's a short to ground somewhere in that area, probably where the insulation has rubbed through. The same test can be performed on each component in the circuit, even a switch.

"Short finders" are also commonly available. These reasonably priced tools connect in place of a fuse and pulse voltage through the

circuit. An inductive meter (included with the kit) is then run along the wiring for the circuit. When the needle on the meter stops moving, you've found the point of the short.

Ground check

Perform a ground test to check whether a component is properly grounded. Disconnect the battery and connect one lead of a self-powered test light, known as a continuity tester, to a known good ground. Connect the other lead to the wire or ground connection being tested. If the bulb lights, the ground is good. If the bulb doesn't light, the ground is no good.

Continuity check

A continuity check is done to determine if there are breaks in a circuit - if it's capable of passing electricity properly. With the circuit off (no power in the circuit), a self-powered continuity tester can be used to check it. Connect the test leads to both ends of the circuit (or to the "power" end and a good ground) - if the test light comes on the circuit is passing current properly. If the light doesn't come on, there's a break (open) somewhere in the circuit. The same procedure can be used to test a switch by connecting the continuity tester to the switch terminals. With the switch on, the test light should come on.

Finding an open circuit

When diagnosing for possible open circuits, it's often difficult to locate them by sight because oxidation or terminal misalignment are hidden by the connectors. Merely wiggling a connector on a sensor or in the wiring harness may correct the open circuit condition. Remember this when an open is indicated when troubleshooting a circuit. Intermittent problems may also be caused by oxidized or loose connections. Electrical troubleshooting is simple if you keep in mind that all electrical circuits are basically electricity running from the battery, through the wires, switches, relays, fuses and fusible links to each electrical component (light bulb, motor, etc.) and to ground, where it's passed back to the battery. Any electrical problem is an interruption in the flow of electricity to and from the battery.

3 Fuses - general information

Refer to illustrations 3.1a, 3.1b, 3.2a, 3.2b and 3.3

The electrical circuits of the vehicle are protected by a combination of fuses, circuit breakers and fusible links. The fuse block is located in the left side of the instrument panel kick panel under a cover, easily accessible by opening the driver's door **(see illustration)**.

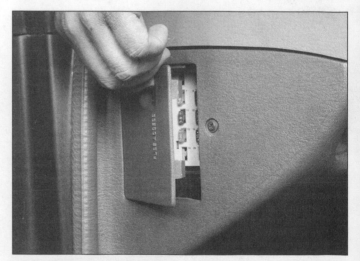

3.1a The fuse block is located at the left end of the instrument panel on these models - open the driver's door and unclip the cover for easy access

3.1b The power distribution center is located in the engine compartment and contains both fuses and relays

3.2a Each of the fuses is designed to protect a specific circuit, and the various circuits are identified on the fuse panel . . .

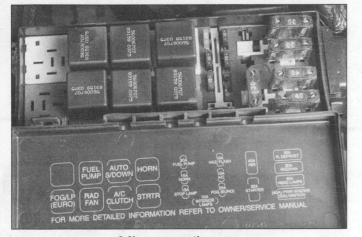

3.2b . . . or on the cover

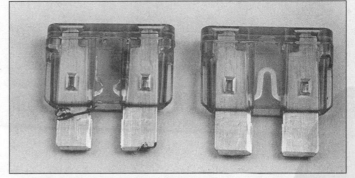

3.3 The fuses used on these models can be checked visually to determine if they are blown (good fuse on right, blown fuse on left)

A fuse and relay block, called the Power Distribution Center (PDC) is located on the left side of the engine compartment (see illustration).

Each of the fuses is designed to protect a specific circuit, and the various circuits are identified on the fuse panel or on the cover (see illustrations).

Miniaturized fuses are employed in the fuse block. These compact fuses, with blade terminal design, allow fingertip removal and replacement. If an electrical component fails, always check the fuse first. A blown fuse is easily identified through the clear plastic body. Visually inspect the element for evidence of damage (see illustration). If a continuity check is called for, the blade terminal tips are exposed in the fuse body.

Be sure to replace blown fuses with the correct type and rating. Fuses of different ratings are physically interchangeable, but only fuses of the proper rating should be used. Replacing a fuse with one of a higher or lower value than specified is not recommended. Each electrical circuit needs a specific amount of protection. The amperage value of each fuse is molded into the fuse body.

If the replacement fuse immediately fails, don't replace it again until the cause of the problem is isolated and corrected. In most cases, the cause will be a short circuit in the wiring caused by a broken or deteriorated wire.

4   Fusible links - general information

The circuit from the output terminal of the alternator to the starter motor terminal is protected by a fusible link. Links are used in circuits which are not ordinarily fused, such as the starting or ignition circuit(s).

Although the fusible links appear to be a heavier gauge than the wires they're protecting, the appearance is due to the thick insulation. All fusible links are four wire gauges smaller than the wire they're designed to protect. Fusible links can't be repaired, but a new link of the same size wire can be installed. The procedure is as follows:

a) Disconnect the negative cable from the battery.
b) Disconnect the fusible link's eyelet from the starter motor and from the wiring harness.
c) Cut the damaged fusible link out of the wire just behind the connector.
d) Strip the insulation back approximately 1-inch.
e) Spread the strands of the exposed wire apart, push them together and twist them in place.
f) Use rosin core and solder the wires together to obtain a good connection.
g) Use plenty of electrical tape around the soldered joint. No wires should be exposed.
h) Reconnect the eyelet to the starter motor and tighten the screw securely.
i) Connect the negative battery cable. Test the circuit for proper operation.

5   Circuit Breakers/Positive Temperature Coefficient (PTC) devices - general information

Circuit breakers and positive temperature coefficient (PTC) devices protect components such as power windows, power door locks, the headlights and various engine solenoids. Some circuit

12

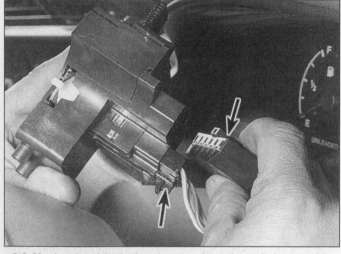

8.3 Unplug the electrical connectors from the switch assembly

breakers and positive temperature coefficient devices are located in or behind the fuse block. The headlight circuit breaker is an integral part of the headlight switch. The PTC acts like a solid state fuse. On some models the circuit breaker resets itself automatically, so an electrical overload in the circuit will cause it to fail momentarily, then come back on. If the circuit doesn't come back on, check it immediately. Once the condition is corrected, the circuit breaker will resume its normal function. Some circuit breakers must be reset manually.

6   Relays - general information

Several electrical accessories in the vehicle utilize relays to transmit current to the component. If the relay is defective, the component won't operate properly. The fuse block and power distribution center, located in the engine compartment contain several relays **(see illustrations 3.2a and 3.2b)**.

If a faulty relay is suspected, it can be removed and tested by a dealer service department or a repair shop. Defective relays must be replaced as a unit.

7   Turn signal/hazard flasher - check and replacement

Warning: *These models have airbags. Always disconnect the negative battery cable and wait two minutes before working in the vicinity of the impact sensors, steering column or instrument panel to avoid the possibility of accidental deployment of the airbag, which could cause personal injury (see Section 29).*

1   The turn signal/hazard flasher is a small unit located in the fuse block located in the driver's side of the instrument panel kick panel under a cover **(see illustration 3.2b)**.

2   When the flasher unit is functioning properly, an audible click can be heard during its operation. If the turn signals fail on one side or the other and the flasher unit doesn't make its characteristic clicking sound, a faulty turn signal bulb is indicated.

3   If both turn signals fail to blink, the problem may be due to a blown fuse, a faulty flasher unit, a broken switch or a loose or open connection. If a quick check of the fuse box indicates the turn signal fuse has blown, check the wiring for a short before installing a new fuse.

4   To replace the flasher, simply detach it from the fuse block receptacle and plug in the new one.

5   Make sure the replacement flasher unit is identical to the original. Compare the old one to the new one before installing it.

6   Installation is the reverse of removal.

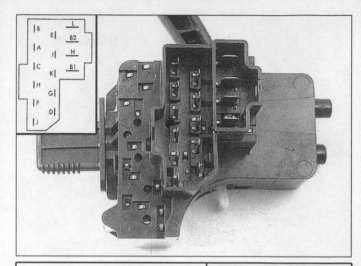

SWITCH POSITION		CONTINUITY BETWEEN TERMINALS
Turn Signal	**Hazard Warning**	
Neutral	Off	F and H F and K A and E
Left	Off	F and H C and K C and I A and E
Right	Off	F and K C and H C and J A and E
Neutral	On	B and E C and H C and K C and I C and J
SWITCH POSITION		**CONTINUITY BETWEEN TERMINALS**
Low beam		B2 and L
High beam		B2 and H
Optical horn		B1 and H

8.4 On the multi-function switch, follow the chart and check for continuity between the indicated switch terminals with the switch in each position

8   Multi-function switch - check and replacement

Refer to illustration 8.3

Warning: *These models have airbags. Always disconnect the negative battery cable and wait two minutes before working in the vicinity of the impact sensors, steering column or instrument panel to avoid the pos-*

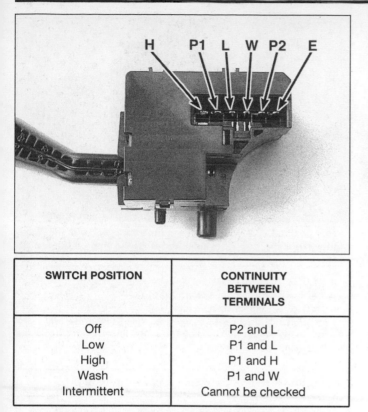

SWITCH POSITION	CONTINUITY BETWEEN TERMINALS
Off	P2 and L
Low	P1 and L
High	P1 and H
Wash	P1 and W
Intermittent	Cannot be checked

9.4 Follow the chart and check for continuity between the indicated wiper/washer switch terminals with the switch in each position

sibility of accidental deployment of the airbag, which could cause personal injury (see Section 29).
1   The multi-function switch is located on the left side of the steering column. It incorporates the turn signal, hazard warning, headlight dimmer and optical horn functions into one switch.
2   Remove the steering column cover (see Chapter 11).
3   Unplug the electrical connectors (see illustration).

Check

Refer to illustration 8.4
Note: *It may be easier to remove the switch for testing (see Step 5).*
4   Use an ohmmeter or self-powered test light and the accompanying chart to check for continuity between the switch terminals with the switch in each position (see illustration). If any portion of the switch is faulty, the entire switch assembly must be replaced.

Replacement

5   Remove the mounting screw(s), then detach the switch from the steering column.
6   Installation is the reverse of removal.

9   Wiper/washer switch - check and replacement

Warning: *These models have airbags. Always disconnect the negative battery cable and wait two minutes before working in the vicinity of the impact sensors, steering column or instrument panel to avoid the possibility of accidental deployment of the airbag, which could cause personal injury (see Section 29).*
1   The wiper/washer switch is located on the right side of the steering column. It incorporates the windshield wiper and washer functions into one switch.

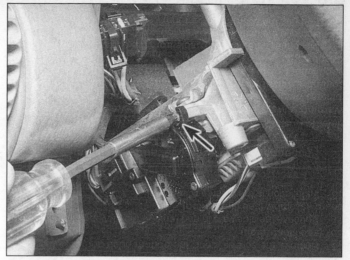

10.5 On the left side, remove the No. 10 Torx screws securing the ignition switch

2   Remove the steering column cover (see Chapter 11).
3   Unplug the electrical connectors.

Check

Refer to illustration 9.4
4   Use an ohmmeter or self-powered test light and the accompanying chart to check for continuity between the switch terminals with the switch in each position (see illustration). If any portion of the switch is faulty, the entire switch assembly must be replaced.

Replacement

5   Remove the mounting screws, then detach the switch from the steering column.
6   Installation is the reverse of removal.

10   Ignition switch - replacement

Warning: *These models have airbags. Always disconnect the negative battery cable and wait two minutes before working in the vicinity of the impact sensors, steering column or instrument panel to avoid the possibility of accidental deployment of the airbag, which could cause personal injury (see Section 29).*

General information

The ignition switch in the RUN position connects power from the Power Distribution Center (PDC) to the 30 amp fuse in the fuse block and back to the bus bar in the PDC. The bus bar, through various fuses, then energizes circuits for the Powertrain Control Module (PCM), the evaporation control system duty cycle purge solenoid, the EGR solenoid and the ABS system. The bus bar in the PDC feeds the various relays (radiator fan, air conditioner compressor clutch, fuel pump). It also energizes the Airbag Control Module (ACM).

Replacement

Refer to illustrations 10.5 and 10.6
1   The ignition switch is located on the left side of the steering column and is activated by, and attached to, the key lock cylinder.
2   Disconnect the negative cable from the battery.
3   Remove the key cylinder (see Section 11).
4   Remove the steering column covers (see Chapter 11).
5   On the left side, remove the No. 10 Torx screws (see illustration).
6   Depress the retaining tabs, then detach the switch and lower it

12

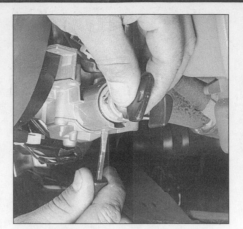

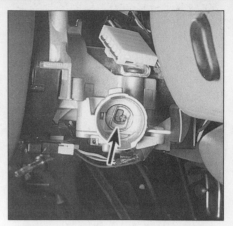

10.6 Depress the retaining tabs, then detach the ignition switch and lower it from the steering column

11.5 With the key in the Run position, depress the release button and pull the lock cylinder out

11.6 Insert the lock cylinder in the Run position, and align the shaft at the end of the lock with the socket in the end of the housing (arrow)

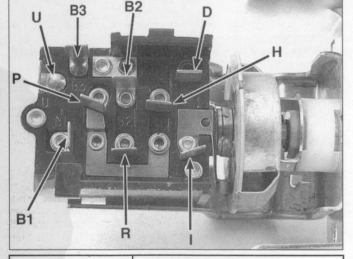

SWITCH POSITION	CONTINUITY BETWEEN TERMINALS
Off	B1 and P optical horn
Park (middle position)	B1 and P optical horn B2 and R parking lamps B3 and U headlamps on warning circuit
On	B1 and P optical horn B2 and R parking lamps B1 and H headlamps B3 and U headlamps on warning circuit
On	B2 and I dimmer switch for instrument cluster illumination lamps
Turn switch full right then full left	1-7 ohms

12.4 Headlight switch terminal locations and continuity chart - the switch must be in the indicated position for each check

from the steering column **(see illustration)**.
7   Unplug the electrical connector.
8   Installation is the reverse of removal. Insert the switch and index the tabs on the switch with the notches in the lock cylinder, install the Torx screws and tighten securely.

11   Ignition key lock cylinder - replacement

Refer to illustrations 11.5 and 11.6
Warning: *These models have airbags. Always disconnect the negative battery cable and wait two minutes before working in the vicinity of the impact sensors, steering column or instrument panel to avoid the possibility of accidental deployment of the airbag, which could cause personal injury (see Section 29).*
1   The ignition key lock cylinder is located on the right side of the steering column.
2   Disconnect the negative cable from the battery.
3   Remove the steering column cover (see Chapter 11).
4   Insert the key and turn the switch to the RUN position.
5   Depress the retaining tab with a small screwdriver and unseat the lock cylinder, then remove the lock cylinder from the ignition switch **(see illustration)**.
6   Insert the lock cylinder in the Run position, and align the shaft at the end of the lock with the socket in the end of the housing **(see illustration)**.

12   Headlight switch - check and replacement

Warning: *These models have airbags. Always disconnect the negative battery cable and wait two minutes before working in the vicinity of the impact sensors, steering column or instrument panel to avoid the possibility of accidental deployment of the airbag, which could cause personal injury (see Section 29).*
1   The headlight switch is located on the lower left side of the instrument panel.
It controls the headlights, all exterior lights and adjusts the brightness of the instrument cluster lighting.
2   Remove the headlight switch (see Steps 7 through 11).
3   Unplug the electrical connector.

Check

Refer to illustration 12.4
4   Use an ohmmeter or self-powered test light and the accompanying chart to check for continuity between the switch terminals with the switch in each position **(see illustration)**. If any portion of the switch is faulty, the entire switch assembly must be replaced.

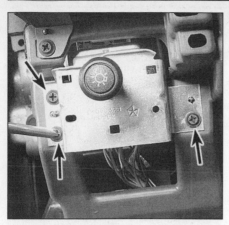

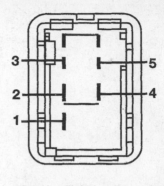

12.6 Headlight switch mounting screw locations

12.7 Release the clip and detach the electrical connector (arrow)

13.4 Headlight leveling switch check details

Replacement

Refer to illustrations 12.6 and 12.7

5   Remove the steering column cover and liner (see Chapter 11).
6   Remove the three mounting screws, then detach the mounting plate and switch from the instrument panel opening **(see illustration)**.
7   Pull the switch assembly part way out, release the clip and detach the electrical connector and ground wire **(see illustration)**.
8   Depress the release button on the bottom of the switch, then pull out and remove the switch knob.
9   Remove the switch mounting nut and detach the switch from the mounting plate.
10   Installation is the reverse of removal.

13   Headlight leveling switch - check and replacement

Warning: *These models have airbags. Always disconnect the negative battery cable and wait two minutes before working in the vicinity of the impact sensors, steering column or instrument panel to avoid the possibility of accidental deployment of the airbag, which could cause personal injury (see Section 29).*
1   Remove the headlight leveling switch (see Steps 8 through 11).
2   Unplug the electrical connector.

Check

Refer to illustration 13.4
Note: *If the LED is not illuminated, perform the following check procedure.*
3   Turn the headlight switch ON and in the low beam position. Ensure the instrument panel dimmer switch is in the daytime light driving position. Leave the switch in this position for Steps 4 through 6.
4   Connect the positive voltmeter lead to Pin No. 4 and the negative lead to Pin No. 3 of the wiring harness connector **(see illustration)**. If voltage is present, replace the switch. If there is no voltage, connect the ground lead to a good ground, if voltage is present; repair the ground circuit. If there is still no voltage, refer to the wiring diagrams and test the circuit back to the headlight switch.
5   Connect the positive voltmeter lead to Pin No. 2 and the negative lead to Pin No. 3 of the wiring harness connector. If voltage is present, replace the switch. If there is no voltage, go to Step 6, if there is voltage, go to Step 7.
6   Connect the ground lead to a good ground. If there is no voltage, refer to the wiring diagrams and test circuit back to the headlight switch. If voltage is present; repair the Pin No. 3 ground circuit.
7   Turn the headlights OFF. Connect the electrical connector to the switch. Turn the headlights ON and in the low beam position. Check voltage at Pin No. 5, while rotating the headlight leveling knob through the four positions. The voltage readings should change during knob rotation to each position. If voltage does no vary, replace the switch. If

the voltage varies, the problem is in the leveling motors and/or circuit to the motors.

Replacement

8   Remove the instrument panel top cover and cluster bezel (see Chapter 11).
9   Disengage the bezel from leveling switch, then pull the switch and bezel backwards from the opening in the panel.
10   Detach the electrical connector and ground wire.
11   Installation is the reverse of removal.

14   Headlight bulb - replacement

Refer to illustrations 14.3, 14.4 and 14.5
Warning: *Halogen bulbs are gas-filled and under pressure and may shatter if the surface is scratched or the bulb is dropped. Wear eye protection and handle the bulbs carefully, grasping only the base whenever possible. Don't touch the surface of the bulb with your fingers because the oil from your skin could cause it to overheat and fail prematurely. If you do touch the bulb surface, clean it with rubbing alcohol.*
Note: *This procedure is shown with the headlight lens assembly partially removed and pulled forward for clarity only. It is not necessary to perform this for bulb replacement.*
1   Open the hood.
2   Disconnect the negative cable from the battery.
3   Remove the retaining ring **(see illustration)**.

14.3 Remove the retaining ring

12

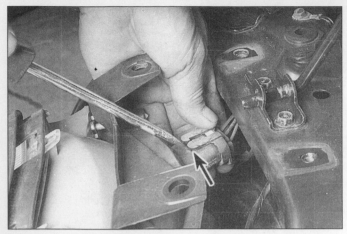

14.4 Disengage the clip (arrow) and disconnect the electrical connector

14.5 Detach the bulb and holder and remove the bulb from the holder

15.3 Remove the upper retaining bolts

15.4 Remove the inner retaining bolts within the grille area (arrows)

16.1a Turn the vertical spring-loaded adjustment screw . . .

4   Disengage the clip and disconnect the electrical connector **(see illustration)**.
5   Grasp the bulb base and unplug it from the holder **(see illustration)**.
6   Insert the new bulb into the holder.
7   Install the bulb holder in the headlight assembly and plug in the connector.

15 Headlight housing - removal and installation

Refer to illustrations 15.3 and 15.4
Warning: *Halogen bulbs are gas-filled and under pressure and may shatter if the surface is scratched or the bulb is dropped. Wear eye protection and handle the bulbs carefully, grasping only the base whenever possible. Don't touch the surface of the bulb with your fingers because the oil from your skin could cause it to overheat and fail prematurely. If you do touch the bulb surface, clean it with rubbing alcohol.*
1   Open the hood.
2   Disconnect the negative cable from the battery.
3   Remove the upper retaining bolts **(see illustration)**.
4   Working within the grille area, remove the inner retaining bolts **(see illustration)**.
5   Working under the bumper facia, remove the outboard retaining bolt.

6   Unplug the electrical connector **(see illustration 14.4)**, and remove the housing.
7   Installation is the reverse of removal. After you're done, check the headlight adjustment (see Section 16).

16 Headlights - adjustment

Refer to illustrations 16.1a and 16.1b
Warning: *The headlights must be aimed correctly. If adjusted incorrectly, they could temporarily blind the driver on an oncoming vehicle and cause an accident or seriously reduce your ability to see the road. The headlights should be checked for proper aim every 12 months and any time a new headlight is installed or front end body work is performed. The following procedure is only an interim step to provide temporary adjustment until the headlights can be adjusted by a properly equipped shop.*
1   The headlight assemblies have two spring loaded adjust screws, one to control the up-and-down movement and the other one to control left-hand right movement **(see illustrations)**.
2   Adjustment should be made with the vehicle sitting level, a full gas tank and a normal load in the vehicle.
3   This procedure requires a flat blank wall 25 feet in front of the vehicle.
4   Position a masking tape line vertically on the wall in reference to the centerline of the vehicle and the headlights. **Note:** *It may be easier*

16.1b ... or the horizontal spring-loaded adjustment screw in either direction until the headlight is properly adjusted

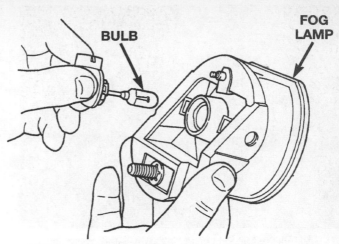

17.2 Remove the two mounting nuts and pull the fog light housing out - then replace the bulb

to position the tape on the wall with the vehicle parked only a few inches away, then move the vehicle directly backwards away from the wall.

5   Rock the vehicle side-to-side three times, then push down on the front bumper to jounce the front suspension up-and-down three times. This will allow the suspension to stabilize prior to adjustment.

6   Measure the distance up from the floor to the centerline of the headlight lens. Transfer this dimension to the flat wall and place another masking tape line horizontally at this measurement.

7   Measure the distance from the centerline of the headlight lens to the center of the vehicle. Transfer this dimension to the flat wall on each side of the vertical centerline tape line and place a masking tape line vertical at this measurement on each side.

8   Starting with the low beam adjustment, position the high intensity zone so it's 2 inches above or below the horizontal line and two inches to the right or left of the vertical lines. Adjustment is made by turning the adjust screws in either direction to achieve the correct alignment. The high beam pattern should be correct after proper alignment of the low beam.

9   Have the headlights adjusted by a dealer service department or service station at the earliest opportunity.

17 Bulb replacement

Fog light
Refer to illustration 17.2
Warning: *Halogen bulbs are gas-filled and under pressure and may*

shatter if the surface is scratched or the bulb is dropped. Wear eye protection and handle the bulbs carefully, grasping only the base whenever possible. Don't touch the surface of the bulb with your fingers because the oil from your skin could cause it to overheat and fail prematurely. If you do touch the bulb surface, clean it with rubbing alcohol.

1   Remove the retaining bolt and lower the housing from the radiator enclosure panel for access to the bulb holder.
2   Pull the bulb and holder straight out from the housing **(see illustration)**.
3   Installation is the reverse of removal.

Front park and turn signal light
Refer to illustrations 17.5, 17.6 and 17.7
4   Open the hood.
5   Remove the retaining screws and remove the housing from the headlight module for access to the bulb holder **(see illustration)**.
6   Pull the bulb and holder straight out from the housing **(see illustration)**.
7   Release the clip and pull the bulb straight out of the holder **(see illustration)**.
8   Installation is the reverse of removal.

Front side marker light
Refer to illustration 17.10
9   Reach behind the bumper facia in front of the front wheel.

17.5 Remove the retaining screws and remove the housing

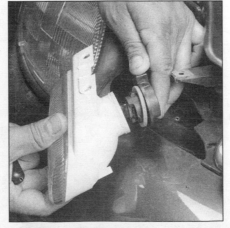

17.6 Pull the bulb and holder straight out from the housing

17.7 Release the clip and pull the bulb straight out of the holder

12

17.10 Pull the bulb and holder straight out from the housing

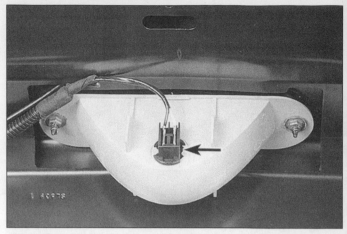

17.13 Squeeze the tabs and pull the bulb and holder (arrow) out of the high-mounted brake light housing

17.17 Rotate the bulb holder counterclockwise to remove it

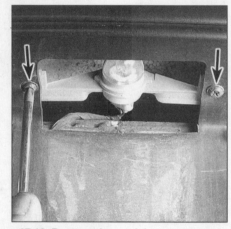

17.19 Remove the retaining screws and remove the housing from the rear bumper

17.20 Pull the bulb and holder straight out from the housing and remove the bulb

10   Pull the bulb and holder straight out from the housing, then pull the bulb straight out of the holder **(see illustration)**.

11   Installation is the reverse of removal.

Center high-mounted brake light

Refer to illustration 17.13

12   Open the trunk.

13   Pull the bulb and holder straight out from the housing, then pull the bulb straight out of the holder **(see illustration)**.

14   Installation is the reverse of removal.

Tail, stop, back-up and turn signal light

Refer to illustration 17.17

15   Open the trunk.

16   Separate the trunk lining from the rear closure panel.

17   Rotate the bulb holder, then pull it straight out from the housing, then pull the bulb straight out of the holder **(see illustration)**.

18   Installation is the reverse of removal.

License plate light

Refer to illustrations 17.19 and 17.20

19   Remove the retaining screws and remove the housing from the rear bumper for access to the bulb holder **(see illustration)**.

20   Pull the bulb and holder straight out from the housing, then pull the bulb straight out of the holder **(see illustration)**.

21   Installation is the reverse of removal.

Underhood lamp

22   Disconnect the wiring harness from the lamp assembly.

23   Rotate the bulb counterclockwise, then remove it.

24   Installation is the reverse of removal.

Dome lamp

Refer to illustrations 17.25 and 17.26

25   Carefully insert a trim stick (plastic or wood) between the head-liner and dome lamp lens **(see illustration)**. Carefully pry downward on all four corners of the lens and remove it.

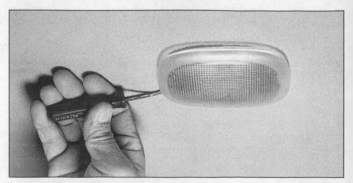

17.25 Carefully insert a broad-bladed screwdriver between the headliner and dome lamp lens and carefully pry downward on all four corners of the lens to remove it

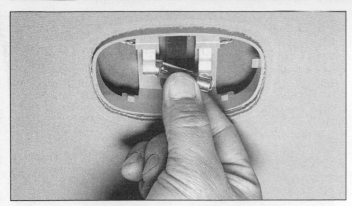

17.26 Remove the bulb from the socket

26   Grasp the bulb and remove it from the socket **(see illustration)**.
27   Installation is the reverse of removal.

Visor vanity lamp

28   Lower the visor.
29   Carefully insert a trim stick (plastic or wood) between the visor and vanity lamp lens. Carefully pry outward and remove it.
30   Grasp the bulb and remove it from the socket.
31   Installation is the reverse of removal.

Rear cargo lamp

32   Open the trunk.
33   Carefully insert a trim stick (plastic or wood) between the rear self reinforcement panel and cargo lamp lens. Carefully pry downward and remove it.
34   Grasp the bulb and remove it from the socket.
35   Installation is the reverse of removal.

---

18 Radio and speakers - removal and installation

Warning: *These models have airbags. Always disconnect the negative battery cable and wait two minutes before working in the vicinity of the impact sensors, steering column or instrument panel to avoid the possibility of accidental deployment of the airbag, which could cause personal injury (see Section 29).*

Radio

Refer to illustrations 18.3, 18.4 and 18.5

1   Disconnect the negative battery cable from the battery.
2   Remove the dashboard lower center bezel (Chapter 11).
3   Remove the mounting screws **(see illustration)**.

18.5 Pull straight out and disconnect the antenna lead

18.3 Remove the radio mounting screws

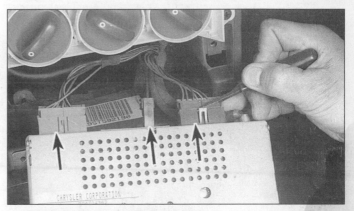

18.4 Pull the radio partially out of the instrument panel, then release the clips and disconnect the electrical connectors and the ground wire (arrows)

4   Pull the radio out of the instrument panel. Release the clips and disconnect the electrical connectors and the ground wire **(see illustration)**.
5   Carefully disconnect the antenna lead **(see illustration)**, then remove it from the vehicle.
6   Installation is the reverse of removal.

Speakers

Door

Refer to illustrations 18.8a and 18.8b

7   Remove door inner trim panel (see Chapter 11).
8   Remove the screws and detach the speaker **(see illustration)**.

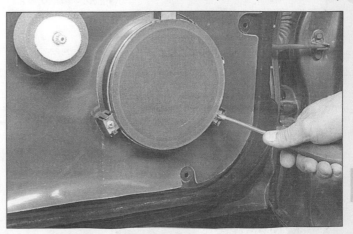

18.8a Remove the three Phillips head screws . . .

12

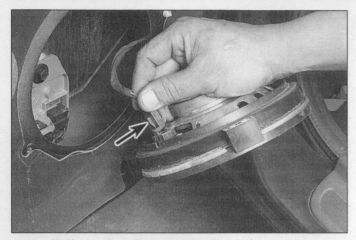

18.8b . . . then disconnect the electrical connector

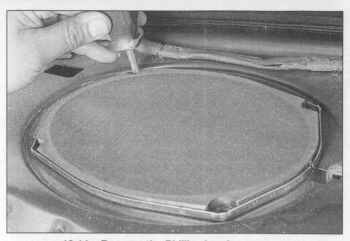

18.14a Remove the Phillips head screws . . .

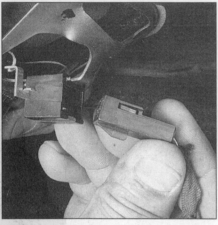

18.14b . . . then disconnect the electrical
connector and remove the speaker

19.2 Unscrew the antenna nut with a
small wrench

19.5a Remove the screws from in
the fenderwell . . .

Pull the speaker out of the door, unplug the electrical connector and remove the speaker from the vehicle **(see illustration)**.

Instrument panel

9   Remove the instrument panel top cover (see Chapter 11).
10   Remove the screws, pull the speaker up, then unplug the electrical connector and remove the speaker from the vehicle.

Rear shelf

Refer to illustrations 18.14a and 18.14b
11   Remove the entire rear seat assembly (see Chapter 11).
12   Pry out the rear portion of the seat belt trim bezel.
13   Partially remove the rear parcel shelf trim panel, slide it down and out of the way.
14   Remove the screws and detach the speaker **(see illustrations)**.
15   Installation is the reverse of removal, making sure that the wire connectors face toward the center of the vehicle.

19 Antenna - removal and installation

Refer to illustrations 19.2, 19.5a, 19.5b and 19.6
Warning: *These models have airbags. Always disconnect the negative battery cable and wait two minutes before working in the vicinity of the impact sensors, steering column or instrument panel to avoid the possibility of accidental deployment of the airbag, which could cause personal injury (see Section 29).*
1   Detach the cable from the negative battery terminal.

2   Use a small open end wrench and unscrew the antenna mast **(see illustration)**.
3   Working in the right side interior kick panel area under the instrument panel, disconnect the antenna cable from the cable lead.
4   Raise the vehicle and place it securely on jackstands. Remove the front right wheel and the inner fender splash shield.
5   Remove the right fender well inner panels sufficiently to gain access to the antenna base **(see illustrations)**.

19.5b . . . then pry out the plastic fasteners on the fenderwell
inner panel to gain access to the antenna base

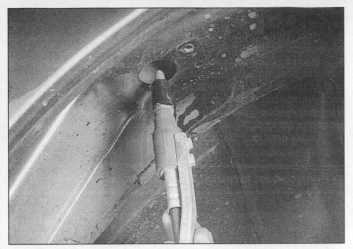

19.6 After removing the antenna lead and grommet from the fender panel access hole, remove the antenna mounting screw and remove the antenna assembly from the fender

20.3 Remove the four cluster mounting screws (arrows) and remove it from the instrument panel

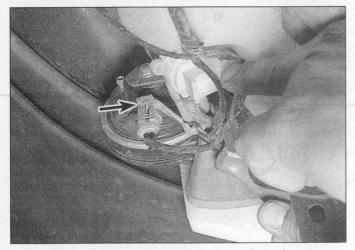

21.2a Unplug the electrical connector (arrow) . . .

21.2b . . . connect one lead of a voltmeter to a ground and the other to the positive terminal and check for voltage

6   Working in the right fender well, carefully pull the antenna lead and grommet from the fender panel access hole. Remove the antenna mounting screw and remove the antenna assembly from the fender (see illustration). Don't lose the antenna adapter in the top of fender opening.

7   Installation is the reverse of removal. If removed, align the antenna adapter tongue with the fender hole and push into place.

20   Instrument cluster - removal and installation

Refer to illustration 20.3
Warning: These models have airbags. Always disconnect the negative battery cable and wait two minutes before working in the vicinity of the impact sensors, steering column or instrument panel to avoid the possibility of accidental deployment of the airbag, which could cause personal injury (see Section 29).

1   Detach the cable from the negative battery terminal.
2   Remove instrument top cover and cluster bezel (see Chapter 11).
3   Remove the four screws and detach the cluster from the cluster housing (see illustration).
4   Unplug the electrical wiring harness connector and withdraw the cluster from the dash.
5   Installation is the reverse of removal.

21   Horn - check and replacement

Warning: These models have airbags. Always disconnect the negative battery cable and wait two minutes before working in the vicinity of the impact sensors, steering column or instrument panel to avoid the possibility of accidental deployment of the airbag, which could cause personal injury (see Section 29).

Check

Refer to illustrations 21.2a, 21.2b and 21.3

1   If the horn doesn't sound, check the horn fuse in the power distribution center located in the engine compartment. If the fuse is blown, replace it and retest. If it blows again, there is a short circuit in the horn or wiring between the horn and fuse block.

2   To test the horn, unplug the electrical connector (see illustration). Connect one lead of a voltmeter to ground and the other to the positive terminal (see illustration). If no voltage is present, there is a fault in the wiring. If there is voltage, use an ohmmeter to check for continuity to ground. If there is continuity and the horn still doesn't sound, it is faulty.

3   If the fuse and horn are good, in the engine compartment, remove the horn relay and use an ohmmeter to check for continuity between

12

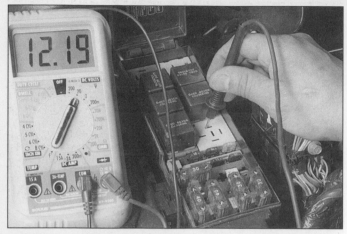

21.3 Remove the horn relay and check for continuity between ground and terminal 65 of the power distribution center

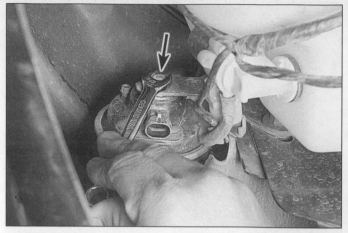

21.5 Unplug the electrical connector and remove the horn mounting nut

22.9 Unplug the electrical connector from the wiper motor

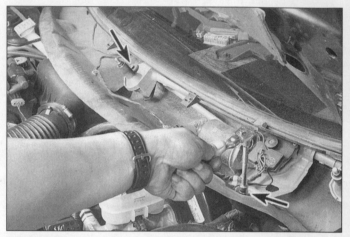

22.10 Remove the mounting screw and the wiper housing module

ground and terminal 65 of the power distribution center **(see illustration)**. There should be continuity only when the horn button is depressed. If this isn't the case there is a problem with the horn switch or wiring.

4   Connect a jumper wire between terminals 63 and 66 of the power distribution center. If the horn sounds, the relay is faulty. Replace it.

Replacement

Refer to illustration 21.5

5   Unplug the electrical connector and remove the mounting nut **(see illustration)**.

6   Installation is the reverse of removal.

22   Windshield wiper motor - check and replacement

Check

1   If the wiper motor does not run at all, first check the fuse block for a blown fuse and the power distribution center for a blown fuse or faulty relay (see Section 3).

2   Check the wiper switch (see Section 9).

3   Turn the ignition switch and wiper switch on.

4   Connect a jumper wire between the wiper motor and ground, then retest. If the motor works now, repair the ground connection.

5   If the wipers still don't work, turn on the wipers and check for voltage at the motor connector. If there's voltage, remove the motor and check it off the vehicle with fused jumper wires from the battery. If the

motor now works, check for binding linkage. If the motor still doesn't work, replace it.

6   If there's no voltage at the motor, the problem is in the switch or wiring.

Replacement

Refer to illustrations 22.9 and 22.10

7   Disconnect the negative cable from the battery.

8   Remove both wiper arms and the cowl cover (see Chapter 11).

9   Unplug the wiper motor electrical connector **(see illustration)**.

10   Remove the wiper housing module mounting screws **(see illustration)**. Remove the module.

11   To remove the linkage from the motor crank, insert a screwdriver between the crank and the linkage, then twist the screwdriver and lift straight up on the linkage.

12   Remove the motor retaining screws and lift the motor out of the linkage housing.

13   Installation is the reverse of removal.

23   Rear window defogger switch - check and replacement

Warning: *These models are equipped with airbags. The airbag is armed and can deploy (inflate) anytime the battery is connected. To prevent accidental deployment (and possible injury), disconnect the negative battery cable whenever working near airbag components. After the battery is disconnected, wait at least 2 minutes before begin-*

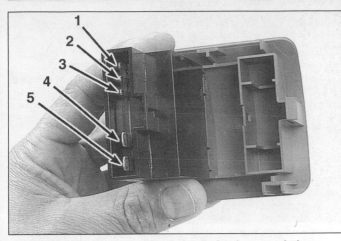

23.3 Battery voltage check details for the rear window defogger switch

23.8 Carefully pry the rear window defogger switch assembly away and remove it - wrap the tip of the screwdriver with tape to prevent scratching

9   Disconnect the electrical connector and remove the switch **(see illustration)**.
10   Installation is the reverse of removal.

24   Rear window defogger - check and repair

1   The rear window defogger consists of a number of horizontal elements baked onto the inner surface of the rear window glass.
2   Small breaks in the element can be repaired without removing the rear window.

Check

3   Turn the ignition switch and defogger system switches to the ON position.
4   Working within the back seat area, ground the negative lead of a voltmeter to terminal A (lower corner passengers side) and the positive lead to terminal B (lower corner drivers side) of the defogger grid.
5   The voltmeter should read between 10 and 15 volts. If the reading is lower, there is a poor ground connection.
6   Contact the negative lead to a good body ground. The reading should stay the same.
7   Connect the negative lead to terminal A, then touch each grid line at the mid-point with the positive lead.
8   The reading should be approximately six volts. If the reading is 0, there is a break between mid-point C and terminal B.
9   A 10 to 14 volt reading is an indication of a break between terminal A and mid-point C. Move the lead toward the break; the voltage will change when the break is crossed.

Repair

10   Repair the break in the line using repair kit recommended specifically for this purpose, such as Mopar Repair Kit No. 4267922 (or equivalent). Included in this kit is plastic conductive epoxy.
11   Prior to repairing a break, turn off the system and allow it to de-energize for a few minutes.
12   Lightly buff the element area with fine steel wool, then clean it thoroughly with rubbing alcohol.
13   Use masking tape to mask off the area of repair.
14   Mix the epoxy thoroughly, according to the instructions on the package. **Warning:** *Read the warning instructions included with the kit relating to the chemical component makeup of the kit (epoxy resin and amine type hardener) and protect yourself accordingly.*
15   Follow the instructions in the kit and apply the conductive epoxy material to the slit in the masking tape, overlapping the undamaged area about 3/4-inch on either end.
16   Allow the repair to cure for 24 hours (at room temperature) before removing the tape and using the system.

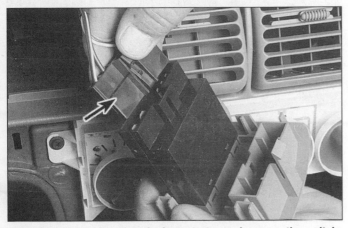

23.9 Disconnect the electrical connector and remove the switch

ning work (the system has a back-up capacitor that must fully discharge). For more information see Section 29.

Check

Refer to illustration 23.3
1   Remove the switch (see Steps 6 through 10), but do not disconnect the electrical connector from the switch.
2   Turn the ignition switch ON.
3   Use a voltmeter and backprobe the electrical connector as follows, check for battery voltage at Pin No. 3 and Pin No. 4 **(see illustration)**. There should be voltage. If okay, go to Step 4. If not okay, check the No. 8 fuse in the fuse block and the 30 amp maxi fuse in the Power Distribution Center. If fuses are okay, check the wiring circuit.
4   Check for voltage at Pin No. 5 with the switch in the ON position, there should be battery voltage. Turn the switch to the OFF position, there should be no voltage. If okay, go to Step 5. If not, replace the switch assembly.
5   Press the switch to the ON position. The indicator lamp should come on and remain on for approximately 10 minutes then go out. If the indicator lamp fails to come on and voltage is present, replace the switch assembly.

Replacement

Refer to illustrations 23.8 and 23.9
6   Detach the cable from the negative battery terminal.
7   Remove instrument top cover and cluster bezel (see Chapter 11).
8   Reach in behind the switch and disengage the left side bezel latch and carefully pry the assembly away from the instrument panel **(see illustration)**.

12

25   Cruise control system - description and check

1   The cruise control system maintains vehicle speed with a vacuum-actuated servo motor located in the engine compartment, which is connected to the throttle linkage by a cable. The system consists of the electronic Powertrain Control Module (PCM), brake switch, control switches, a relay, the vehicle speed sensor and associated wiring. Listed below are some general procedures that may be used to locate common cruise control problems.

2   Locate and check the fuse (see Section 3). Also check the vacuum hose to the cruise control servo to make sure it's not plugged, cracked or soft (which will cause it to collapse in operation. With the engine off, check the servo by applying vacuum (with a hand vacuum pump) to the vacuum fitting on the servo - the servo should move the throttle linkage if it's working properly.

3   Have an assistant operate the brake lights while you check their operation (voltage from the brake light switch deactivates the cruise control).

4   If the brake lights don't come on or don't shut off the cruise control, correct the problem and retest the cruise control.

5   Inspect the cable linkage between the cruise control servo and the throttle linkage. The cruise control servo is located on the left (driver's) side of the vehicle.

6   Visually inspect the wires connected to the cruise control servo and check for damage and broken wires.

7   Cruise controls use a variety of speed sensing devices. On these models the speed sensor pickup is located in the transaxle. Refer to Chapter 6 for information on checking this sensor.

8   Test drive the vehicle to determine if the cruise control is now working. If it isn't, take it to a dealer service department or an automotive electrical specialist for further diagnosis and repair.

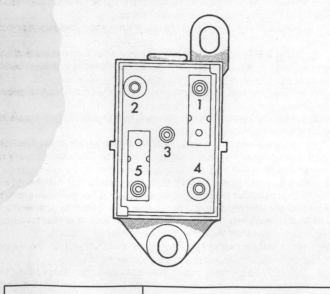

Switch position	Continuity between terminals
Off	Pin 1 and 4 Pin 2 and 5
Unlock	Pin 3 and 5 Pin 1 and 4
Lock	Pin 1 and 3 Pin 2 and 5

27.5 Power door lock switch terminal details

26   Electric rear view mirrors - description and check

1   Electric rear view mirrors use two motors to move the glass; one for up-and-down adjustments and one for left-to-right adjustments.

2   The control switch, located in the driver's door panel, has a selector portion which sends voltage to the left or right side mirror. With the ignition ON but the engine OFF, roll down the windows and operate the mirror control switch through all functions (left-right and up-down) for both the left and right side mirrors.

3   Listen carefully for the sound of the electric motors running in the mirrors.

4   If the motors can be heard but the mirror glass doesn't move, there's probably a problem with the drive mechanism inside the mirror. Remove and disassemble the mirror to locate the problem.

5   If the mirrors don't operate and no sound comes from the mirrors, check the 10 amp fuse for interior lights located in the Power Distribution Center (see Section 3).

6   If the fuse is OK, remove the mirror control switch from its mounting without disconnecting the wires attached to it. Turn the ignition ON and check for voltage at the switch. There should be voltage at one terminal. If there's no voltage at the switch, check for an open or short in the wiring between the fuse panel and the switch.

7   If the mirror still doesn't work, remove the cover and check the wires at the mirror for voltage with a test light. Check with ignition ON and the mirror selector switch on the appropriate side. Operate the mirror switch in all its positions. There should be voltage at one of the switch-to-mirror wires in each switch position (except the neutral "off" position).

8   If there's not voltage in each switch position, check the wiring between the mirror and control switch for opens and shorts.

9   If there's voltage, remove the mirror and test it off the vehicle with jumper wires. Replace the mirror if it fails this test (see Chapter 11).

27   Power door lock system - description and check

Refer to illustration 27.5

1   Power door lock systems are operated by bi-directional solenoids located in the doors. The lock switches have two operating positions: Lock and Unlock. These switches activate a relay which in turn connects voltage to the door lock solenoids. Depending on which way the relay is activated, it reverses polarity, allowing the two sides of the circuit to be used alternately as the feed (positive) and ground side.

2   Always check the circuit protection first. These vehicles use a combination of circuit breakers and fuses.

3   Operate the door lock switches in both directions (Lock and Unlock) with the engine off. Listen for the faint click of the relay operating.

4   If there's no click, check for voltage at the switches. If no voltage is present, check the wiring between the fuse panel and the switches for shorts and opens.

5   If voltage is present but no click is heard, use an ohmmeter or self-powered test light and the accompanying chart to check for continuity between the switch terminals with the switch in each position **(see illustration)**. Replace the switch if there's no continuity in either position.

6   If the switch has continuity but the relay doesn't click, check the wiring between the switch and relay for continuity. Repair the wiring if there's no continuity.

7   If the relay is receiving voltage from the switch but is not sending voltage to the solenoids, check for a bad ground at the relay case. If the relay case is grounding properly, replace the relay.

8   If all but one lock solenoid operates, remove the trim panel from the affected door (see Chapter 11) and check for voltage at the solenoid while the lock switch is operated. One of the wires should have voltage in the Lock position; the other should have voltage in the unlock position.

9   If the inoperative solenoid is receiving voltage, replace the solenoid.

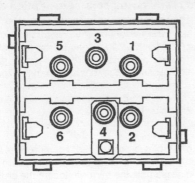

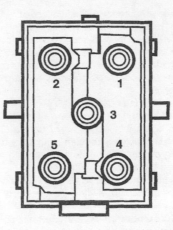

28.8b Passenger's side power window switch terminal details (use continuity chart in illustration 28.8a)

Driver's side window switch

Switch position	Continuity between terminals
Off	Pin 1 and 2
	Pin 1 and 4
	Pin 1 and 5
	Pin 1 and 6
	Pin 2 and 4
	Pin 2 and 5
	Pin 2 and 6
	Pin 4 and 5
	Pin 4 and 6
	Pin 5 and 6
Drivers side up	Pin 1 and 3
	Pin 2 and 4
Drivers side down	Pin 1 and 4
	Pin 2 and 3
Passenger side up	Pin 3 and 5
	Pin 4 and 6
Passenger side down	Pin 3 and 6
	Pin 4 and 5

Passenger's side window switch

Switch position	Continuity between terminals
Off	Pin 2 and 5
	Pin 1 and 4
Up	Pin 1 and 4
	Pin 3 and 5
Down	Pin 1 and 3
	Pin 2 and 5

28.8a Power window switch terminal details and continuity chart

10   If the inoperative solenoid isn't receiving voltage, check for an open or short in the wire between the lock solenoid and the relay. **Note:** *It's common for wires to break in the portion of the harness between the body and door (opening and closing the door fatigues and eventually breaks the wires).*

28 Power window system - description and check

Refer to illustrations 28.8a and 28.8b

1   The power window system consists of the control switches, the motors, glass mechanisms (regulators), and associated wiring.

2   Power windows are wired so they can be lowered and raised from the master control switch by the driver or by remote switches located at the individual windows. Each window has a separate motor which is reversible. The position of the control switch determines the polarity and therefore the direction of operation. The system is equipped with a relay that controls current flow to the motors.

3   The power window system operates only when the ignition switch is ON.

4   These procedures are general in nature, so if you can't find the problem using them, take the vehicle to a dealer service department or other qualified repair shop.

5   If the power windows don't work at all, check the fuse or circuit breaker.

6   Check the wiring between the switches and fuse panel for continuity. Repair the wiring, if necessary.

7   If only one window is inoperative from the master control switch, try the other control switch at the window. **Note:** *This doesn't apply to the driver's door window.*

8   If the same window works from one switch, but not the other, check the switch for continuity. Use an ohmmeter or self-powered test light and the accompanying chart to check for continuity between the switch terminals with the switch in each position **(see illustrations)**. Replace the switch if there's no continuity in either position.

9   If the switch tests OK, check for a short or open in the wiring between the affected switch and the window motor.

10   If one window is inoperative from both switches, remove the trim panel from the affected door (see Chapter 11) and check for voltage at the motor while the switch is operated.

11   If voltage is reaching the motor, disconnect the glass from the regulator (see Chapter 11). Move the window up and down by hand while checking for binding and damage. Also check for binding and damage to the regulator. If the regulator is not damaged and the window moves up and down smoothly, replace the motor (see Chapter 11). If there's binding or damage, lubricate, repair or replace parts, as necessary.

12   If voltage isn't reaching the motor, check the wiring in the circuit for continuity between the switches and motors. Check that the relay is grounded properly and receiving voltage from the switches. Also check that the relay sends voltage to the motor when the switch is turned on. If it doesn't, replace the relay.

13   Test the windows after you are done to confirm proper repairs.

12

29.1a Driver's air bag within the steering wheel . . .

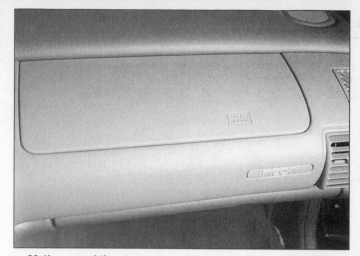

29.1b . . . and the passengers air bag in the instrument panel

29 Airbag system - general information

Refer to illustrations 29.1a, 29.1b, 29.3 and 29.4

These models are equipped with a Supplemental Restraint System (SRS), more commonly called an airbag system. This system is designed to protect the driver and front seat passenger from serious injury in the event of head-on or frontal collision. It consists of airbag modules in the center of the steering wheel and the right side top surface of the dashboard **(see illustrations)**, two crash sensors mounted at the front of the vehicle and an Airbag Control Module (ACM), mounted in the passenger compartment, which contains a safing sensor.

Airbag module

Each airbag module contains a housing incorporating the cushion (airbag) and inflator unit. The inflator assembly is mounted on the back of the housing over a hole through which gas is expelled, inflating the bag almost instantaneously when an electrical signal is sent from the system. The specially wound wire that carries this signal to the module is called a clockspring. The clockspring is a flat, ribbon-like electrically conductive tape which is wound so it can transmit an electrical signal regardless of steering wheel position.

Sensors

The system has three sensors: two crash sensors at the front of the vehicle behind the bumper and a safing sensor in the Airbag Control Module (ACM) located on the tunnel/floor pan between the shift lever and the parking brake lever under the center console **(see illustration)**.

The front crash sensors, located on the right and left side of the radiator closure panel under the hood, are basically pressure sensitive switches that complete an electrical circuit during an impact of sufficient G force **(see illustration)**. The electrical signal from the crash sensors is sent to the safing sensor in the ACM, which then completes the circuit and inflates the airbags.

Airbag Control Module (ACM)

The ACM contains the safing sensor, a capacitor that maintains electrical system power if the battery is damaged and an on-board microprocessor which monitors the operation of the system. It checks this system every time the vehicle is started, causing the AIRBAG light to go on, then off, if the system is operating properly. If there is a fault in the system, the light will go on and stay on, or the light will fail to go on, and the ACM will store fault codes indicating the nature of the fault. If the AIRBAG light does go on and stay on, the vehicle should be taken to your dealer immediately for service.

29.3 The location of the Airbag Control Module (ACM) under the center console

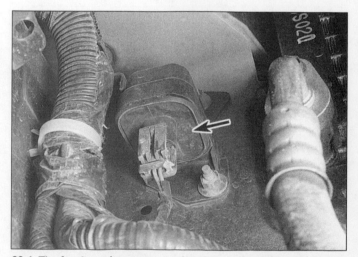

29.4 The front crash sensors are located on the right and left side of the radiator closure panel under the hood

30 Wiring diagrams

Since it isn't possible to include all wiring diagrams for every year covered by this manual, the following diagrams are those that are typical and most commonly needed.

Prior to troubleshooting any circuits, check the fuse and circuit breakers (if equipped) to make sure they're in good condition. Make sure the battery is properly charged and check the cable connections (see Chapter 1).

When checking a circuit, make sure that all connectors are clean, with no broken or loose terminals. When unplugging a connector, do not pull on the wires. Pull only on the connector housings themselves.

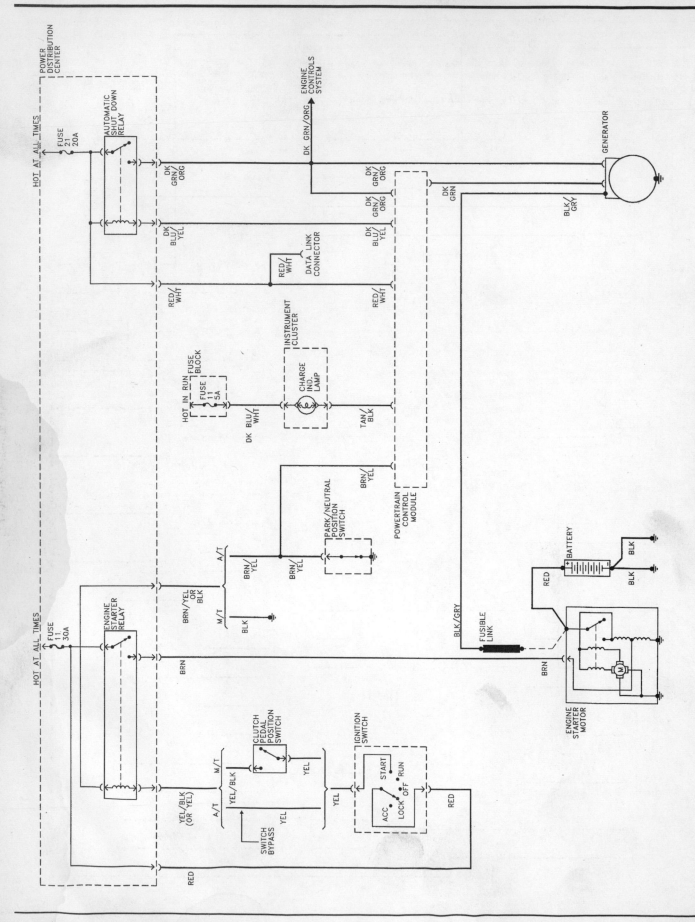

Typical starting and charging systems

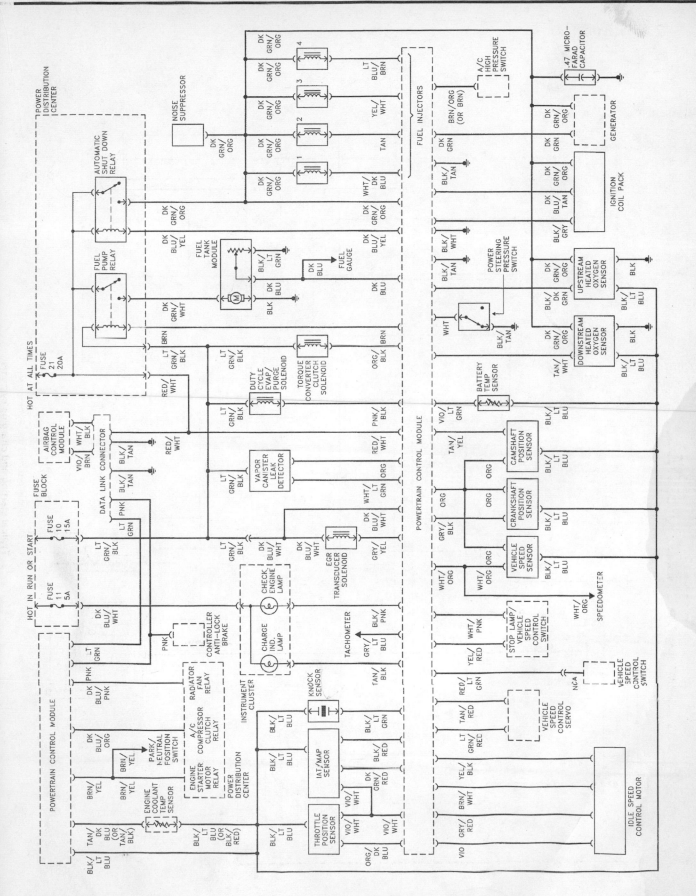

Typical engine control system

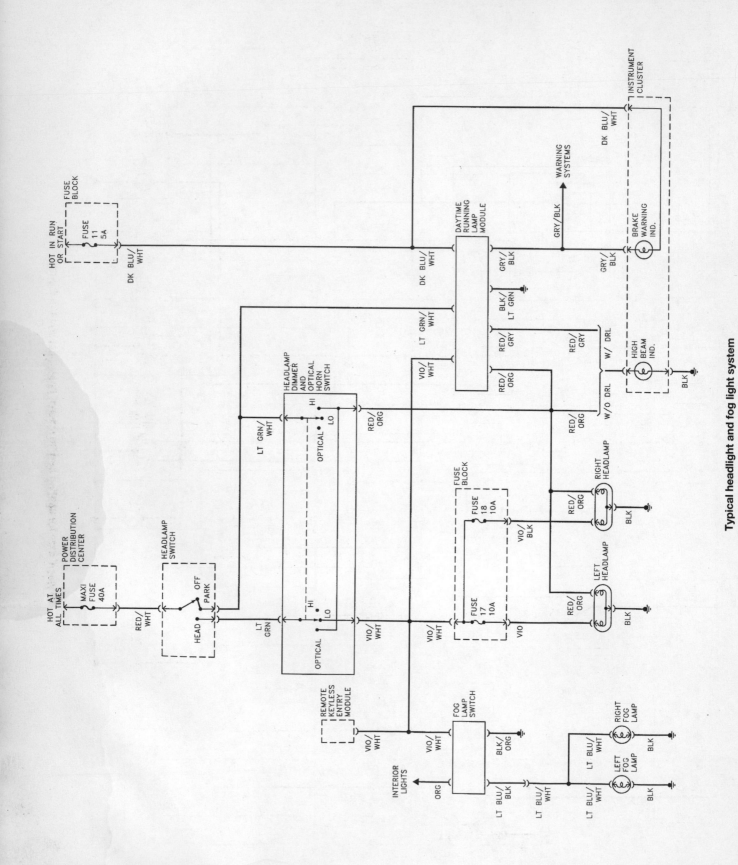

Typical headlight and fog light system

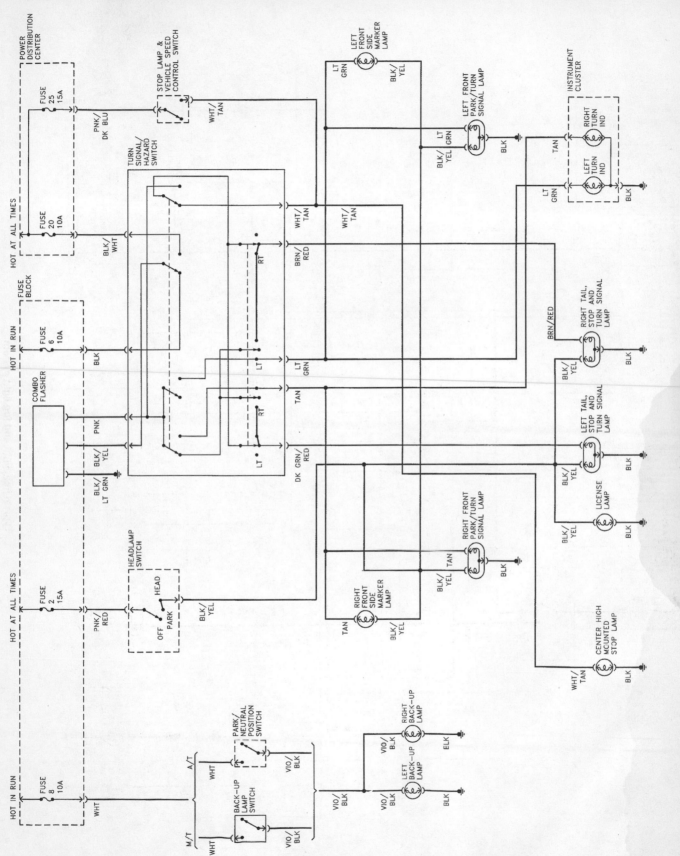

Typical exterior lighting system (except headlights and fog lights)

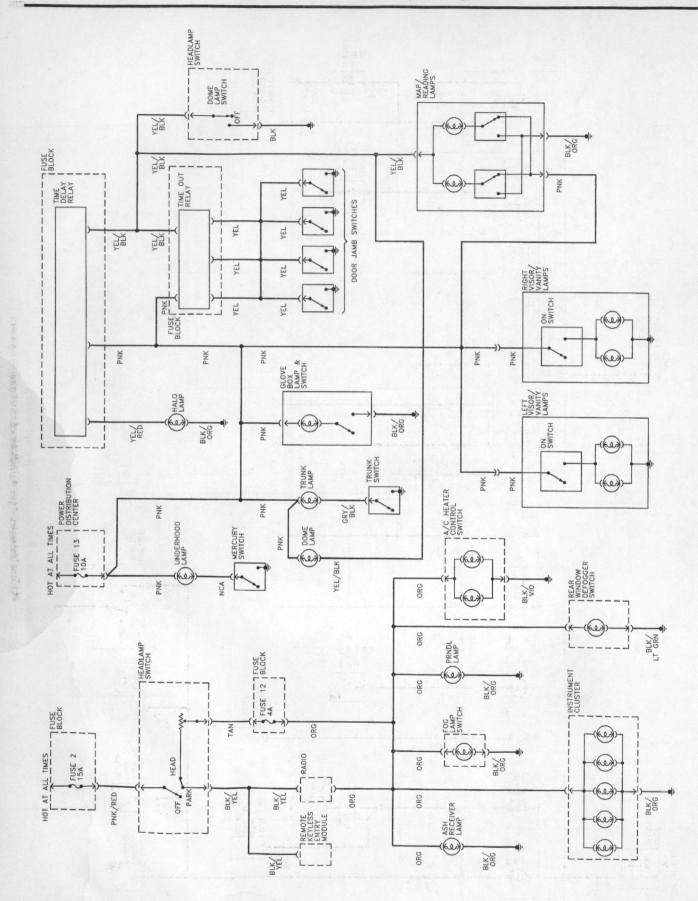

Typical interior lighting system

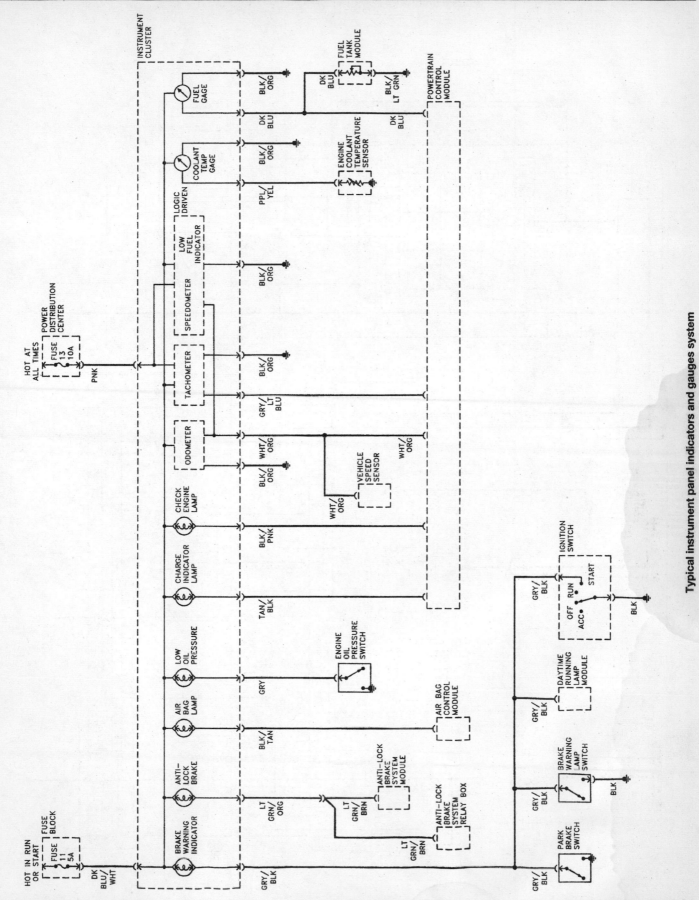

Typical instrument panel indicators and gauges system

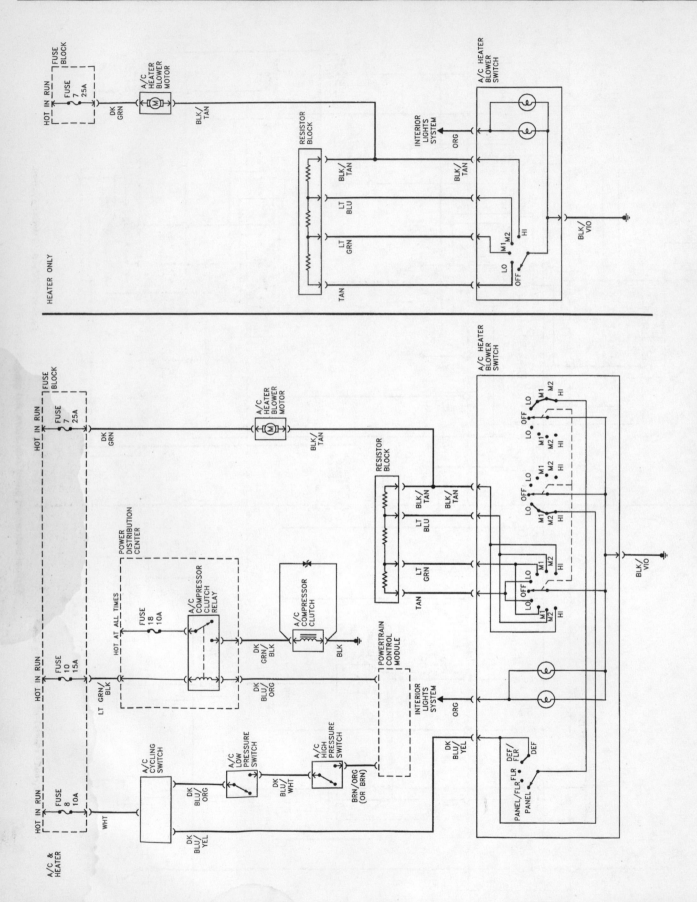

Typical heating/air conditioning system

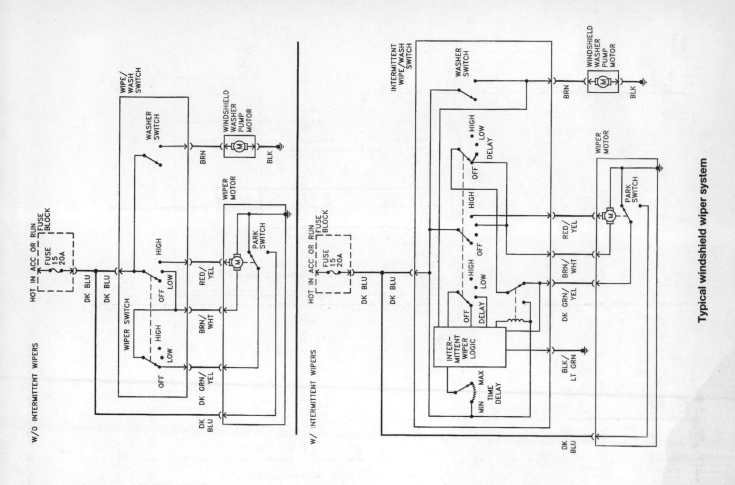

Typical windshield wiper system

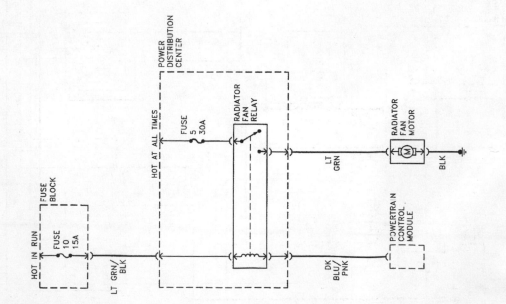

Typical radiator cooling fan system

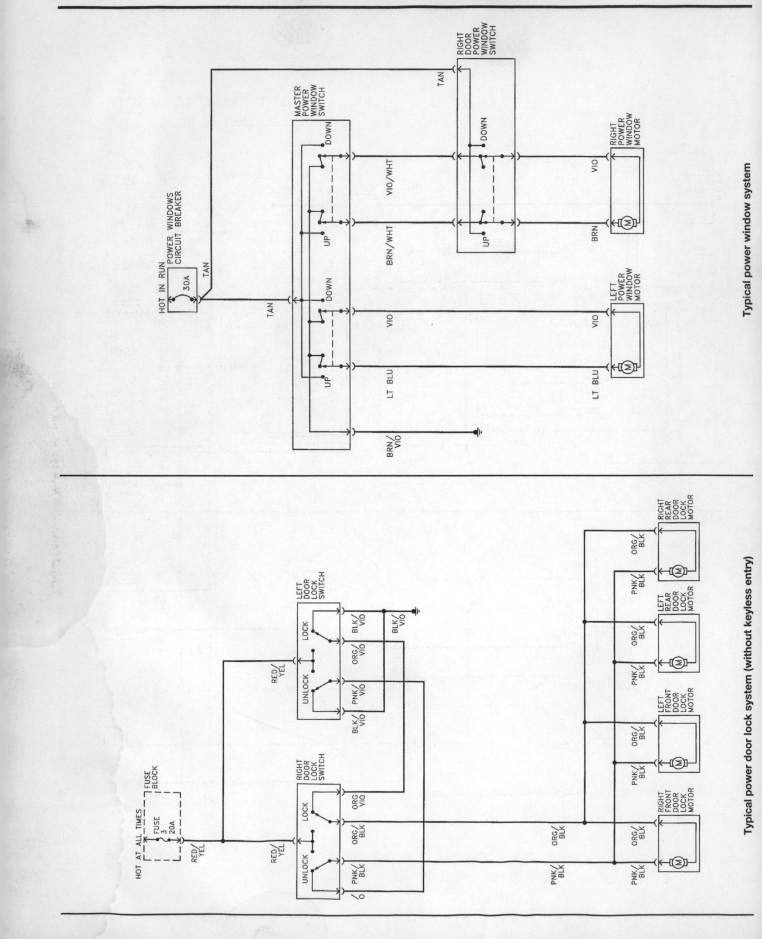

Typical power window system

Typical power door lock system (without keyless entry)

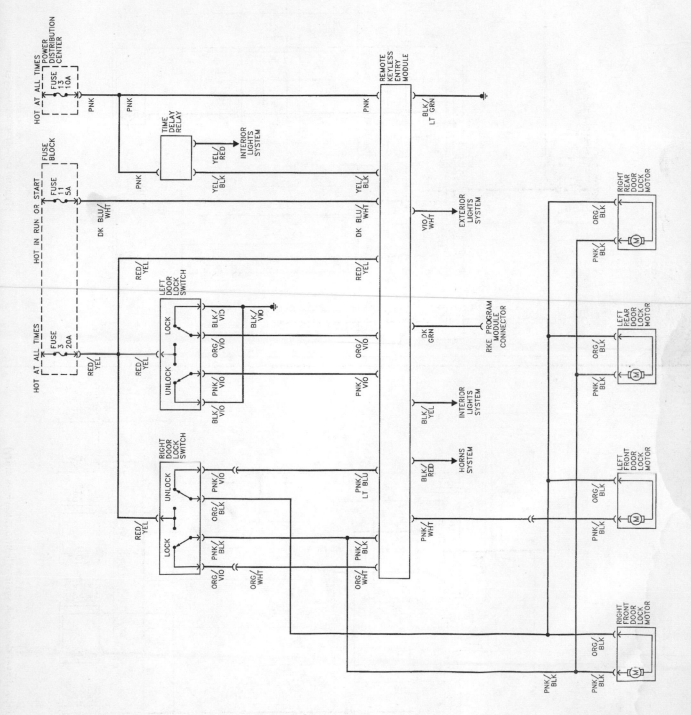

Typical power door lock system (with keyless entry)

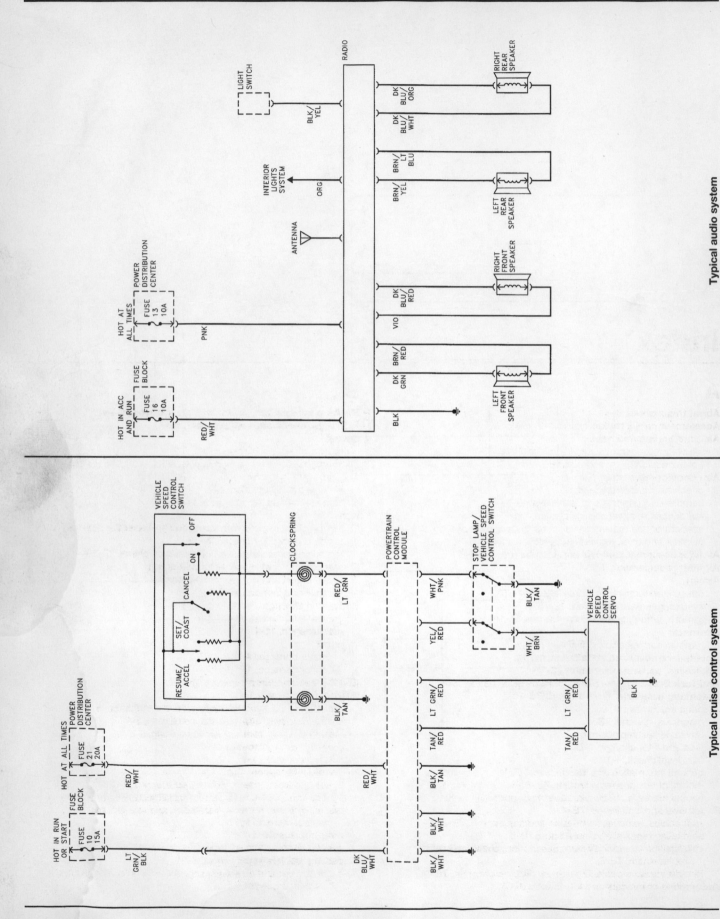

Typical audio system

Typical cruise control system

Index

Haynes Automotive Manuals

Haynes®

NOTE: New manuals are added to this list on a periodic basis. If you do not see a listing for your vehicle, consult your local Haynes dealer for the latest product information.

ACURA
*12020 Integra '86 thru '89 & Legend '86 thru '90

AMC
Jeep CJ - see JEEP (50020)
14020 Mid-size models, Concord, Hornet, Gremlin & Spirit '70 thru '83
14025 (Renault) Alliance & Encore '83 thru '87

AUDI
15020 4000 all models '80 thru '87
15025 5000 all models '77 thru '83
15026 5000 all models '84 thru '88

AUSTIN-HEALEY
Sprite - see MG Midget (66015)

BMW
*18020 3/5 Series not including diesel or all-wheel drive models '82 thru '92
*18021 3 Series except 325iX models '92 thru '97
18025 320i all 4 cyl models '75 thru '83
18035 528i & 530i all models '75 thru '80
18050 1500 thru 2002 except Turbo '59 thru '77

BUICK
Century (front wheel drive) - see GM (829)
*19020 Buick, Oldsmobile & Pontiac Full-size (Front wheel drive) all models '85 thru '98
Buick Electra, LeSabre and Park Avenue; Oldsmobile Delta 88 Royale, Ninety Eight and Regency; Pontiac Bonneville
19025 Buick Oldsmobile & Pontiac Full-size (Rear wheel drive)
Buick Estate '70 thru '90, Electra'70 thru '84, LeSabre '70 thru '85, Limited '74 thru '79
Oldsmobile Custom Cruiser '70 thru '90, Delta 88 '70 thru '85,Ninety-eight '70 thru '84
Pontiac Bonneville '70 thru '81, Catalina '70 thru '81, Grandville '70 thru '75, Parisienne '83 thru '86
19030 Mid-size Regal & Century all rear-drive models with V6, V8 and Turbo '74 thru '87
Regal - see GENERAL MOTORS (38010)
Riviera - see GENERAL MOTORS (38030)
Roadmaster - see CHEVROLET (24046)
Skyhawk - see GENERAL MOTORS (38015)
Skylark '80 thru '85 - see GM (38020)
Skylark '86 on - see GM (38025)
Somerset - see GENERAL MOTORS (38025)

CADILLAC
*21030 Cadillac Rear Wheel Drive all gasoline models '70 thru '93
Cimarron - see GENERAL MOTORS (38015)
Eldorado - see GENERAL MOTORS (38030)
Seville '80 thru '85 - see GM (38030)

CHEVROLET
*24010 Astro & GMC Safari Mini-vans '85 thru '93
24015 Camaro V8 all models '70 thru '81
24016 Camaro all models '82 thru '92
Cavalier - see GENERAL MOTORS (38015)
Celebrity - see GENERAL MOTORS (38005)
24017 Camaro & Firebird '93 thru '97
24020 Chevelle, Malibu & El Camino '69 thru '87
24024 Chevette & Pontiac T1000 '76 thru '87
Citation - see GENERAL MOTORS (38020)
*24032 Corsica/Beretta all models '87 thru '96
24040 Corvette all V8 models '68 thru '82
*24041 Corvette all models '84 thru '96
10305 Chevrolet Engine Overhaul Manual
24045 Full-size Sedans Caprice, Impala, Biscayne, Bel Air & Wagons '69 thru '90
24046 Impala SS & Caprice and Buick Roadmaster '91 thru '96
Lumina - see GENERAL MOTORS (38010)

24048 Lumina & Monte Carlo '95 thru '98
Lumina APV - see GM (38035)
24050 Luv Pick-up all 2WD & 4WD '72 thru '82
*24055 Monte Carlo all models '70 thru '88
Monte Carlo '95 thru '98 - see LUMINA (24048)
24059 Nova all V8 models '69 thru '79
*24060 Nova and Geo Prizm '85 thru '92
24064 Pick-ups '67 thru '87 - Chevrolet & GMC, all V8 & in-line 6 cyl, 2WD & 4WD '67 thru '87; Suburbans, Blazers & Jimmys '67 thru '91
*24065 Pick-ups '88 thru '98 - Chevrolet & GMC, all full-size pick-ups, '88 thru '98; Blazer & Jimmy '92 thru '94; Suburban '92 thru '98; Tahoe & Yukon '98
24070 S-10 & S-15 Pick-ups '82 thru '93, Blazer & Jimmy '83 thru '94,
*24071 S-10 & S-15 Pick-ups '94 thru '96 Blazer & Jimmy '95 thru '96
*24075 Sprint & Geo Metro '85 thru '94
*24080 Vans - Chevrolet & GMC, V8 & in-line 6 cylinder models '68 thru '96

CHRYSLER
25015 Chrysler Cirrus, Dodge Stratus, Plymouth Breeze '95 thru '98
25025 Chrysler Concorde, New Yorker & LHS, Dodge Intrepid, Eagle Vision, '93 thru '97
10310 Chrysler Engine Overhaul Manual
*25020 Full-size Front-Wheel Drive '88 thru '93
K-Cars - see DODGE Aries (30008)
Laser - see DODGE Daytona (30030)
*25030 Chrysler & Plymouth Mid-size front wheel drive '82 thru '95
Rear-wheel Drive - see Dodge (30050)

DATSUN
28005 200SX all models '80 thru '83
28007 B-210 all models '73 thru '78
28009 210 all models '79 thru '82
28012 240Z, 260Z & 280Z Coupe '70 thru '78
28014 280ZX Coupe & 2+2 '79 thru '83
300ZX - see NISSAN (72010)
28016 310 all models '78 thru '82
28018 510 & PL521 Pick-up '68 thru '73
28020 510 all models '78 thru '81
28022 620 Series Pick-up all models '73 thru '79
720 Series Pick-up - see NISSAN (72030)
28025 810/Maxima all gasoline models, '77 thru '84

DODGE
400 & 600 - see CHRYSLER (25030)
*30008 Aries & Plymouth Reliant '81 thru '89
30010 Caravan & Plymouth Voyager Mini-Vans all models '84 thru '95
*30011 Caravan & Plymouth Voyager Mini-Vans all models '96 thru '98
30012 Challenger/Plymouth Saporro '78 thru '83
30016 Colt & Plymouth Champ (front wheel drive) all models '78 thru '87
*30020 Dakota Pick-ups all models '87 thru '96
30025 Dart, Demon, Plymouth Barracuda, Duster & Valiant 6 cyl models '67 thru '76
*30030 Daytona & Chrysler Laser '84 thru '89
Intrepid - see CHRYSLER (25025)
*30034 Neon all models '95 thru '97
*30035 Omni & Plymouth Horizon '78 thru '90
*30040 Pick-ups all full-size models '74 thru '93
*30041 Pick-ups all full-size models '94 thru '96
*30045 Ram 50/D50 Pick-ups & Raider and Plymouth Arrow Pick-ups '79 thru '93
30050 Dodge/Plymouth/Chrysler rear wheel drive '71 thru '89
*30055 Shadow & Plymouth Sundance '87 thru '94
*30060 Spirit & Plymouth Acclaim '89 thru '95
*30065 Vans - Dodge & Plymouth '71 thru '96

EAGLE
Talon - see Mitsubishi Eclipse (68030)
Vision - see CHRYSLER (25025)

FIAT
34010 124 Sport Coupe & Spider '68 thru '78
34025 X1/9 all models '74 thru '80

FORD
10355 Ford Automatic Transmission Overhaul
*36004 Aerostar Mini-vans all models '86 thru '96
*36006 Contour & Mercury Mystique '95 thru '98
36008 Courier Pick-up all models '72 thru '82
36012 Crown Victoria & Mercury Grand Marquis '88 thru '96
10320 Ford Engine Overhaul Manual
36016 Escort/Mercury Lynx all models '81 thru '90
*36020 Escort/Mercury Tracer '91 thru '96
*36024 Explorer & Mazda Navajo '91 thru '95
36028 Fairmont & Mercury Zephyr '78 thru '83
36030 Festiva & Aspire '88 thru '97
36032 Fiesta all models '77 thru '80
36036 Ford & Mercury Full-size, Ford LTD & Mercury Marquis ('75 thru '82); Ford Custom 500,Country Squire, Crown Victoria & Mercury Colony Park ('75 thru '87); Ford LTD Crown Victoria & Mercury Gran Marquis ('83 thru '87)
36040 Granada & Mercury Monarch '75 thru '80
36044 Ford & Mercury Mid-size, Ford Thunderbird & Mercury Cougar ('75 thru '82); Ford LTD & Mercury Marquis ('83 thru '86); Ford Torino,Gran Torino, Elite, Ranchero pick-up, LTD II, Mercury Montego, Comet, XR-7 & Lincoln Versailles ('75 thru '86)
36048 Mustang V8 all models '64-1/2 thru '73
36049 Mustang II 4 cyl, V6 & V8 models '74 thru '78
36050 Mustang & Mercury Capri all models Mustang, '79 thru '93; Capri, '79 thru '86
*36051 Mustang all models '94 thru '97
36054 Pick-ups & Bronco '73 thru '79
36058 Pick-ups & Bronco '80 thru '96
36059 Pick-ups, Expedition & Mercury Navigator '97 thru '98
36062 Pinto & Mercury Bobcat '75 thru '80
36066 Probe all models '89 thru '92
36070 Ranger/Bronco II gasoline models '83 thru '92
*36071 Ranger '93 thru '97 & Mazda Pick-ups '94 thru '97
36074 Taurus & Mercury Sable '86 thru '95
*36075 Taurus & Mercury Sable '96 thru '98
*36078 Tempo & Mercury Topaz '84 thru '94
36082 Thunderbird/Mercury Cougar '83 thru '88
36086 Thunderbird/Mercury Cougar '89 and '97
36090 Vans all V8 Econoline models '69 thru '91
*36094 Vans full size '92-'95
*36097 Windstar Mini-van '95-'98

GENERAL MOTORS
*10360 GM Automatic Transmission Overhaul
*38005 Buick Century, Chevrolet Celebrity, Oldsmobile Cutlass Ciera & Pontiac 6000 all models '82 thru '96
*38010 Buick Regal, Chevrolet Lumina, Oldsmobile Cutlass Supreme & Pontiac Grand Prix front-wheel drive models '88 thru '95
*38015 Buick Skyhawk, Cadillac Cimarron, Chevrolet Cavalier, Oldsmobile Firenza & Pontiac J-2000 & Sunbird '82 thru '94
*38016 Chevrolet Cavalier & Pontiac Sunfire '95 thru '98
38020 Buick Skylark, Chevrolet Citation, Olds Omega, Pontiac Phoenix '80 thru '85
38025 Buick Skylark & Somerset, Oldsmobile Achieva & Calais and Pontiac Grand Am all models '85 thru '95
38030 Cadillac Eldorado '71 thru '85, Seville '80 thru '85, Oldsmobile Toronado '71 thru '85 & Buick Riviera '79 thru '85
*38035 Chevrolet Lumina APV, Olds Silhouette & Pontiac Trans Sport all models '90 thru '95
General Motors Full-size Rear-wheel Drive - see BUICK (19025)

(Continued on other side)

* Listings shown with an asterisk (*) indicate model coverage as of this printing. These titles will be periodically updated to include later model years - consult your Haynes dealer for more information.

Haynes North America, Inc., 861 Lawrence Drive, Newbury Park, CA 91320-1514 • (805) 498-6703

Haynes Automotive Manuals (continued)

NOTE: New manuals are added to this list on a periodic basis. If you do not see a listing for your vehicle, consult your local Haynes dealer for the latest product information.

GEO
Metro - see CHEVROLET Sprint (24075)
Prizm - '85 thru '92 see CHEVY (24060),
'93 thru '96 see TOYOTA Corolla (92036)
*40030 Storm all models '90 thru '93
Tracker - see SUZUKI Samurai (90010)

GMC
Safari - see CHEVROLET ASTRO (24010)
Vans & Pick-ups - see CHEVROLET

HONDA
42010 Accord CVCC all models '76 thru '83
42011 Accord all models '84 thru '89
42012 Accord all models '90 thru '93
42013 Accord all models '94 thru '95
42020 Civic 1200 all models '73 thru '79
42021 Civic 1300 & 1500 CVCC '80 thru '83
42022 Civic 1500 CVCC all models '75 thru '79
42023 Civic all models '84 thru '91
*42024 Civic & del Sol '92 thru '95
*42040 Prelude CVCC all models '79 thru '89

HYUNDAI
*43015 Excel all models '86 thru '94

ISUZU
Hombre - see CHEVROLET S-10 (24071)
*47017 Rodeo '91 thru '97; Amigo '89 thru '94;
Honda Passport '95 thru '97
*47020 Trooper & Pick-up, all gasoline models
Pick-up, '81 thru '93; Trooper, '84 thru '91

JAGUAR
*49010 XJ6 all 6 cyl models '68 thru '86
*49011 XJ6 all models '88 thru '94
*49015 XJ12 & XJS all 12 cyl models '72 thru '85

JEEP
*50010 Cherokee, Comanche & Wagoneer Limited
all models '84 thru '96
50020 CJ all models '49 thru '86
*50025 Grand Cherokee all models '93 thru '98
50029 Grand Wagoneer & Pick-up '72 thru '91
Grand Wagoneer '84 thru '91, Cherokee &
Wagoneer '72 thru '83, Pick-up '72 thru '88
*50030 Wrangler all models '87 thru '95

LINCOLN
Navigator - see FORD Pick-up (36059)
59010 Rear Wheel Drive all models '70 thru '96

MAZDA
61010 GLC Hatchback (rear wheel drive) '77 thru '83
61011 GLC (front wheel drive) '81 thru '85
*61015 323 & Protogé '90 thru '97
*61016 MX-5 Miata '90 thru '97
*61020 MPV all models '89 thru '94
Navajo - see Ford Explorer (36024)
61030 Pick-ups '72 thru '93
Pick-ups '94 thru '96 - see Ford Ranger (36071)
61035 RX-7 all models '79 thru '85
*61036 RX-7 all models '86 thru '91
61040 626 (rear wheel drive) all models '79 thru '82
*61041 626/MX-6 (front wheel drive) '83 thru '91

MERCEDES-BENZ
63012 123 Series Diesel '76 thru '85
*63015 190 Series four-cyl gas models, '84 thru '88
63020 230/250/280 6 cyl sohc models '68 thru '72
63025 280 123 Series gasoline models '77 thru '81
63030 350 & 450 all models '71 thru '80

MERCURY
See FORD Listing.

MG
66010 MGB Roadster & GT Coupe '62 thru '80
66015 MG Midget, Austin Healey Sprite '58 thru '80

MITSUBISHI
*68020 Cordia, Tredia, Galant, Precis &
Mirage '83 thru '93
*68030 Eclipse, Eagle Talon & Ply. Laser '90 thru '94
*68040 Pick-up '83 thru '96 & Montero '83 thru '93

NISSAN
72010 300ZX all models including Turbo '84 thru '89
*72015 Altima all models '93 thru '97
*72020 Maxima all models '85 thru '91
*72030 Pick-ups '80 thru '96 Pathfinder '87 thru '95
72040 Pulsar all models '83 thru '86
*72050 Sentra all models '82 thru '94
*72051 Sentra & 200SX all models '95 thru '98
*72060 Stanza all models '82 thru '90

OLDSMOBILE
*73015 Cutlass V6 & V8 gas models '74 thru '88
For other OLDSMOBILE titles, see BUICK,
CHEVROLET or GENERAL MOTORS listing.

PLYMOUTH
For PLYMOUTH titles, see DODGE listing.

PONTIAC
79008 Fiero all models '84 thru '88
79018 Firebird V8 models except Turbo '70 thru '81
79019 Firebird all models '82 thru '92
For other PONTIAC titles, see BUICK,
CHEVROLET or GENERAL MOTORS listing.

PORSCHE
*80020 911 except Turbo & Carrera 4 '65 thru '89
80025 914 all 4 cyl models '69 thru '76
80030 924 all models including Turbo '76 thru '82
*80035 944 all models including Turbo '83 thru '89

RENAULT
Alliance & Encore - see AMC (14020)

SAAB
*84010 900 all models including Turbo '79 thru '88

SATURN
87010 Saturn all models '91 thru '96

SUBARU
89002 1100, 1300, 1400 & 1600 '71 thru '79
*89003 1600 & 1800 2WD & 4WD '80 thru '94

SUZUKI
*90010 Samurai/Sidekick & Geo Tracker '86 thru '96

TOYOTA
92005 Camry all models '83 thru '91
92006 Camry all models '92 thru '96
92015 Celica Rear Wheel Drive '71 thru '85
*92020 Celica Front Wheel Drive '86 thru '93
92025 Celica Supra all models '79 thru '92
92030 Corolla all models '75 thru '79
92032 Corolla all rear wheel drive models '80 thru '87
92035 Corolla all front wheel drive models '84 thru '92
*92036 Corolla & Geo Prizm '93 thru '97
92040 Corolla Tercel all models '80 thru '82
92045 Corona all models '74 thru '82
92050 Cressida all models '78 thru '82
92055 Land Cruiser FJ40, 43, 45, 55 '68 thru '82
92056 Land Cruiser FJ60, 62, 80, FZJ80 '80 thru '96
*92065 MR2 all models '85 thru '87
92070 Pick-up all models '69 thru '78
*92075 Pick-up all models '79 thru '95
*92076 Tacoma '95 thru '98, 4Runner '96 thru '98,
& T100 '93 thru '98
*92080 Previa all models '91 thru '95
92085 Tercel all models '87 thru '94

TRIUMPH
94007 Spitfire all models '62 thru '81
94010 TR7 all models '75 thru '81

VW
96008 Beetle & Karmann Ghia '54 thru '79
96012 Dasher all gasoline models '74 thru '81
*96016 Rabbit, Jetta, Scirocco, & Pick-up gas
models '74 thru '91 & Convertible '80 thru '92
96017 Golf & Jetta all models '93 thru '97
96020 Rabbit, Jetta & Pick-up diesel '77 thru '84
96030 Transporter 1600 all models '68 thru '79
96035 Transporter 1700, 1800 & 2000 '72 thru '79
96040 Type 3 1500 & 1600 all models '63 thru '73
96045 Vanagon all air-cooled models '80 thru '83

VOLVO
97010 120, 130 Series & 1800 Sports '61 thru '73
97015 140 Series all models '66 thru '74
*97020 240 Series all models '76 thru '93
97025 260 Series all models '75 thru '82
*97040 740 & 760 Series all models '82 thru '88

TECHBOOK MANUALS
10205 Automotive Computer Codes
10210 Automotive Emissions Control Manual
10215 Fuel Injection Manual, 1978 thru 1985
10220 Fuel Injection Manual, 1986 thru 1996
10225 Holley Carburetor Manual
10230 Rochester Carburetor Manual
10240 Weber/Zenith/Stromberg/SU Carburetors
10305 Chevrolet Engine Overhaul Manual
10310 Chrysler Engine Overhaul Manual
10320 Ford Engine Overhaul Manual
10330 GM and Ford Diesel Engine Repair Manual
10340 Small Engine Repair Manual
10345 Suspension, Steering & Driveline Manual
10355 Ford Automatic Transmission Overhaul
10360 GM Automatic Transmission Overhaul
10405 Automotive Body Repair & Painting
10410 Automotive Brake Manual
10415 Automotive Detailing Manual
10420 Automotive Eelectrical Manual
10425 Automotive Heating & Air Conditioning
10430 Automotive Reference Manual & Dictionary
10435 Automotive Tools Manual
10440 Used Car Buying Guide
10445 Welding Manual
10450 ATV Basics

SPANISH MANUALS
98903 Reparación de Carrocería & Pintura
98905 Códigos Automotrices de la Computadora
98910 Frenos Automotriz
98915 Inyección de Combustible 1986 al 1994
99040 Chevrolet & GMC Camionetas '67 al '87
Incluye Suburban, Blazer & Jimmy '67 al '91
99041 Chevrolet & GMC Camionetas '88 al '95
Incluye Suburban '92 al '95, Blazer &
Jimmy '92 al '94, Tahoe y Yukon '95
99042 Chevrolet & GMC Camionetas Cerradas
'68 al '95
99055 Dodge Caravan & Plymouth Voyager '84 al '95
99075 Ford Camionetas y Bronco '80 al '94
99077 Ford Camionetas Cerradas '69 al '91
99083 Ford Modelos de Tamaño Grande '75 al '87
99088 Ford Modelos de Tamaño Mediano '75 al '86
99091 Ford Taurus & Mercury Sable '86 al '95
99095 GM Modelos de Tamaño Grande '70 al '90
99100 GM Modelos de Tamaño Mediano '70 al '88
99110 Nissan Camionetas '80 al '96,
Pathfinder '87 al '95
99118 Nissan Sentra '82 al '94
99125 Toyota Camionetas y 4Runner '79 al '95

* Listings shown with an asterisk (*) indicate model coverage as of this printing. These titles will be periodically updated to include later model years - consult your Haynes dealer for more information.

Over 100 Haynes motorcycle manuals also available

5-98

Haynes North America, Inc., 861 Lawrence Drive, Newbury Park, CA 91320-1514 • (805) 498-6703